# FAULT LINES

# FAULT LINES

## JOURNEYS INTO THE
## NEW SOUTH AFRICA

**DAVID GOODMAN**

PHOTOGRAPHS BY
PAUL WEINBERG

UNIVERSITY OF CALIFORNIA PRESS

BERKELEY    LOS ANGELES    LONDON

University of California Press
Berkeley and Los Angeles, California

University of California Press, Ltd.
London, England

Library of Congress Cataloging-in-Publication Data
Goodman, David, 1959-
    Fault lines : journeys into the new South
Africa / David Goodman ; photographs by
Paul Weinberg.
        p.   cm.
    Includes bibliographical references (p.   )
and index.
    ISBN 0-520-21736-5 (alk. paper)
    1. South Africa—Politics and government—
1994-   2. Goodman, David, 1959—
Journeys—South Africa.   I. Weinberg,
Paul.   II. Title.
DT1974.G66   1999
968-06'5—dc21                        98-43038
                                          CIP

Printed in the United States of America
9  8  7  6  5  4  3  2  1

The paper used in this publication is both acid-
free and totally chlorine-free (TCF). It meets
the minimum requirements of American
Standard for Information Sciences—Permanence of Paper for Printed Library Materials,
ANSI Z39.48-1984.

TO SUE,
WHO HAS SHARED
THE JOURNEY

# CONTENTS

## ACKNOWLEDGMENTS

The story that I tell in the following pages is about people. Real people, without whose indulgence there would be no book. I am glad finally to have the opportunity to thank them.

The eight characters at the heart of this book had to put up with my invading their lives. Little could each person suspect when I first contacted them that their entire life story was about to become fair game for me. They were left having to explain to their families who this American visitor was that kept calling, showing up at inconvenient times, asking all manner of annoying questions, then reappearing yet again. My sincere thanks goes to Kagiso and Rev. Frank Chikane; Paul Erasmus; Elize and Professor Wilhelm Verwoerd; Wilhelm and Melanie Verwoerd; Adelaide, Douglas, Moses, and Eric Buso; Tumi Modise; Lieb and Nanette Niemand; and Matthew Mpshe and Andrew Pooe. It was an honor for me to be allowed briefly into their lives and to be permitted to tell my version of their stories.

Ever since meeting photographer Paul Weinberg at Khotso House in Johannesburg in 1984, I have admired both his artistry and his commitment to the democratic struggle in South Africa. Paul is one of South Africa's finest documentary photographers, as well as being a dedicated activist and a friend. It has been a privilege and a pleasure to work and travel with him over the years, and to learn from him.

I owe a debt to a number of people who helped make this book possible. While in South Africa in 1996 and 1997, I was a Visiting Researcher in the Western Cape Oral History Project in the Department of History at the University of Cape Town. My thanks goes to Professor Bill Nasson, who was chair of the Department of History at UCT, and Clive Glazer, former director of the Western Cape Oral History Project, for sharing their resources and their thoughts on the project. Carin Favero was my ace transcriber. Vanessa Watson, Roger Behrens, Peter Wilkinson, and Kathy

Forbes of the Urban Problems Research Unit at UCT, where my wife, Sue Minter, was a Visiting Associate, were generous with their resources and their insights. They were also good friends and tea-mates.

In the course of this journey, numerous South Africans have extended themselves to me and my family. Whether it was a bed and meal, opinions, or camaraderie on the journey, these people made a foreign land feel like home, and shared their insights about their country. Thanks to Andre and Caroline van Halderan and family, Jeff Jawitz, Wadeedah Jaffer, Peter Mayson, Leigh Whitesman, June and Gert Bam, Anusuya Chinsamy, Yunis Turin, Greg and Di Maris, Johan and Christina Olivier, Herman and Suzie Mills, Pippa Green, and Hennie du Plessis and family. In the United States, my thanks goes to Mary Tiseo, Henry Murad, the late Bill Johnston, Tom Hertz, and Sonia Bock.

A special thanks to Father Michael Lapsley, Themba Vilakazi, and the late Anton Lubowski, who was killed by apartheid assassins in 1989 on the eve of Namibian independence, which he championed. Each of them has alternately challenged me and acted as patient guide through the often confusing terrain of the apartheid conflict over the years. Their commitment to the freedom struggle in southern Africa has been an enduring source of inspiration to me.

I am grateful to a number of people who read all or part of the manuscript and offered invaluable guidance at various stages of my writing and research: Adam Hochschild, Bill Finnegan, Tom Karis, Betty Medsger, Patrick Bond, and Francis Wilson. My agent, Anne Borchardt, offered helpful advice throughout the project. Monica McCormick, my editor at University of California Press, has been both an insightful and enthusiastic shepherd of this book. In addition, thanks go to copy editor Steve Gilmartin for his perceptive contributions, and to UC Press editor Juliane Brand.

My parents, Dorothy and George Goodman, and sister, Amy Goodman, have been faithful readers. They prodded me when I missed the mark, and reassured me that I was clever. Even when I wasn't.

My daughter, Ariel Goodman, who was four years old when she arrived in South Africa, regularly opened my eyes and made cross-cultural connections in ways I never could have done were she not there. Lastly, my deepest gratitude goes to my wife, Sue Minter. She has been with me on this journey from the beginning. I could not have reached the end without her.

# INTRODUCTION: FAULT LINES

*August 1984*
*Crossing Zimbabwe and Botswana*
*Zimbabwe Railways*

The train rolls slowly across the African veld. Outside my window, the dry, brown earth of southern Africa stretches for miles. The barren landscape is occasionally interrupted by green oases that teem with life. When the train stops at dusty railside villages, children with broad smiles run up alongside my steel carriage, screaming gaily and asking anyone who will make eye contact with them for candy or money. Hawkers shouldering a load of cooked mealie (corn) or bags of potato chips walk the length of the train shouting their menu of offerings. The locomotive abruptly lurches forward and signs of humanity vanish into the afternoon light—until the next stop, when this ritual is repeated all over again. In the most desolate stretches of the journey, I am amazed that this landscape can even support life. Harshness and vitality—it is the first paradox that I encounter here on the southern tip of Africa.

I am wedged into a small compartment of an old Zimbabwe Railways coach with five other travelers. The trappings of a vanquished colonial past surround us. The wood-paneled train compartment is ornately inscribed "RR"—Rhodesia Railways. This old railroad began as a gleam in the eye of Cecil Rhodes, Africa's consummate colonialist. It was to be a vital link in his audacious dream of establishing the reign of the British Empire from Cape to Cairo. But things didn't turn out quite the way he had planned back in 1890. In the first case, Rhodes's rail line only got as far as Tanganyika (now Tanzania) before another colonial power—Germany—blocked his passage.

Rhodes's fantasy started to unravel in more dramatic fashion in the 1960s. Blacks were chafing under the rule of the white minority in both

South Africa and Rhodesia. Tremors of resistance rumbled in both countries. Orderly opposition had exploded into open warfare in Rhodesia by the late sixties, where the population of one hundred thousand whites—a mere 1 percent of the population—suddenly found itself in the crossfire of angry guerrillas. By 1980, the numerical mismatch in this anachronistic outpost of empire resulted in an inevitable victory for the black majority. At midnight on April 17, 1980, as Bob Marley enthralled tens of thousands of citizens and dignitaries in Salisbury's Rufaro Stadium, Zimbabwe was born.[1] Black South Africans celebrated the victory in the townships, assuming that their northern neighbor's triumph signaled the imminent demise of white minority rule throughout southern Africa. Little could these South Africans know that it would take fourteen more tortuous years before this hope was realized.

Night falls on my bustling compartment as the train crosses the border from Zimbabwe into Botswana, heading south toward its final destination in Johannesburg, some thirty hours away. Tiny particles of coal belch forth from the old locomotive, coating everything and everyone. The sooty taste lingers on my tongue. For the four African men facing me, South Africa is a place that is at once a land of promise and anguish. They go there because they must: South Africa is the richest country on the continent. They come to make money there, send it home to their families, and then leave, hopefully with their bodies and souls intact.

For me, the journey into South Africa is for less certain reasons. My interest in South Africa began with a chance encounter: on my first day as a college student in 1978, a protester greeted me as I was en route to the customary freshman "tea" with Harvard University President Derek Bok.

"Do you know that Harvard supports apartheid?" the shaggy young man asked me, pressing a leaflet into my hands. I did not, I replied, but I was sufficiently curious (and brazen) to raise the question with Bok. Certainly an institution such as Harvard that was dedicated to fostering enlightened moral values would not go around with as unseemly an ally as South Africa.

When I asked Bok whether it was true that Harvard had some $350 million in stocks invested in companies that did business with South Africa, his polite smile grew taut on his jowl. He replied that institutions such as Harvard needed to remain "engaged," maintain "dialogue," and bring pressure on South Africa from the inside.

I was unimpressed. Two years after the Soweto riots, the white regime that I read about appeared to be utterly unmoved by polite "pressure" and the occasional diplomatic scolding. The simple reality was that the college president, like so many western leaders, could not bring himself to part with such profitable investments. My anti-apartheid activism began that day.

Why care about a rogue nation ten thousand miles away? In the pedantic world of university life, apartheid leapt out at me as an unambiguous moral affront. It was, in some sense, a relief to come upon a political system for which I could not fathom any credible defense. Undoubtedly it was also easier to deal with distant racial conflicts rather than those in my backyard. My school's complicity in supporting South Africa had transformed apartheid into a local issue for me. I became deeply involved in the college divestment movement; after university, I was active in a variety of local and national campaigns to isolate and pressure South Africa.

Six years after my exchange with Bok, I decided to see for myself what the apartheid of my protest chants was all about. Working as a fledgling freelance journalist, I was joined by my girlfriend (now wife) and fellow activist, Sue Minter, on a journey to the southern tip of Africa.

The men in my compartment are a convivial bunch. I am riding third class, the no-frills conveyance once reserved exclusively for blacks, now still segregated de facto by the logic of economics. Within hours of our meeting, we are involved in a rip-roaring game of poker, and libations flow freely. Among the group is Philip, a Zimbabwean schoolteacher who regales us into the night with stories from the *chimurenga,* the Zimbabwean liberation war.

"Now we ah *free!*" he declares proudly, his sweat-glazed face breaking into a broad grin. "Zimbabwe today, South Africa tomorrow!" he shouts, lubricated by the bottle of *chibuku* (homemade Zimbabwean beer) that is circulating among us. The other men in the compartment, an assortment of Zimbabweans and Botswanans, roar their approval.

The triumphant slogan has a nice ring to it. It seems so sensible, even too obvious to be revolutionary. How much longer can the apartheid regime hold out against the inevitable outcome that sheer numbers (whites constitute one-eighth of the population), to say nothing of justice, would dictate?

Hours later, conductors scurrying along the narrow corridors of the train awaken us from a fitful slumber. "Passports! Border control!" they bark. As the train slows down, the upbeat mood of my compartment ebbs away. Philip gazes blankly out the window, wondering what to expect in the South Africa he has heard so much about. I too stare and wonder. Our silent musings are answered abruptly as the train stops.

The tricolor flag of South Africa hangs limply from a pole standing forlornly in the still veld. The Ramatlhabama border post separating Botswana from South Africa demarcates a line in the sand. There is a loud rap on the compartment door. It slides open to reveal a tall, trim white man neatly packaged in a steel blue uniform. A thin leather strap arcs across his chest, ending at his revolver. His presentation is crowned by a crisp policeman's hat. The cop is momentarily nonplussed as he surveys the multicolored gaggle of passengers before him. "Off the train, passports out," he finally snaps.

We step outside and are immediately separated by a swarm of other officers. The Africans are herded over to a long queue behind a high barbed wire fence. Sue and I are politely directed to the other side of a fence and to a window with no lines. The sign over our window declares SLEGS BLANKES—EUROPEANS ONLY. After checking to make sure our names are not on a "prohibited entrants" list, our passports are stamped and we turn to get back on the train. A conductor blocks our entrance to the third-class compartment where we had been riding.

"You'll be riding in first class now," he insists. I knew this was coming, but I resent it nonetheless. I protest that I would rather sit with my friends. He places his arm squarely across the train door. "In South Africa, you must ride first class," he informs me brusquely. Then his voice softens, "It's much nicer up there anyway—you'll like it."

Arguing is pointless. Sue and I are nervous enough about whether we will encounter trouble at the border—who knows what the omniscient South African security police know about us? Just minutes inside the country, we are already in the thrall of police-state paranoia. We have traveled far to see apartheid firsthand; our introduction does not disappoint. We hustle up to a sterile compartment with fresh bedding and our own private sink. The rich wood trim, royal blue carpet, and pressed linen lend our new accommodations a faintly imperial air.

Outside the window, we can see Philip and our other companions still jostling for attention in the large penned-in area. The black men are milling around a white man who is processing their papers to be migrant workers in the gold mines. Philip steals a tense glance in our direction. My sullen, guilty gaze from the comfort of my spotless cabin is broken by a man dressed in a neatly pressed white uniform who knocks on our train compartment.

"Would you like tea, sir?" he queries politely.

*February 1997*
*Trans Karoo*
*South African Railways*

The train rolls along the steel spine of South Africa midway through the twenty-seven-hour journey from Johannesburg to Cape Town. Puffy cumulus clouds glow pink in the afternoon light. Cattle occasionally interrupt the otherwise desolate expanse of the Karoo, the barren desert center of the country. The land glows a warm gold in the waning hours of the day. The vista I peer out on somehow seems friendlier, softer than it did on my first journey here thirteen years earlier. Perhaps it is just that I no longer feel the fear and loathing that were undercurrents on all my previous travels.

It has been three years since black majority rule came to South Africa. On a stunning May day in 1994, Nelson R. Mandela stood framed by the Roman columns of the Union Buildings in Pretoria and took the oath of office as South Africa's first democratically elected president. The moving event was witnessed by forty-five heads of state and was capped by a fly-over from the South African Air Force—once a hated symbol of apartheid's global reach—trailing the colors of the new South African flag.

South Africa after apartheid feels like it has breathed a collective sigh of relief. Gone is the reflexively defensive posture of whites and the head-hanging glumness of blacks. Blacks are finally free to enjoy the mundane privileges of normal life: going about daily tasks unmolested, sitting where they like, and for the lucky few, acquiring a bit of wealth.

My train ride presents a microcosm of these changes. The second- and first-class carriages are integrated, but individual compartments are not. This unofficial segregation is courtesy of the white civil servants who remain in their jobs on the railways. The new South Africa is still run by the old white bureaucracy; it is one of the contradictions that appear everywhere in the country. South African Railways was notorious as an employment agency for poor Afrikaners. These workers, like other white civil servants, were guaranteed their jobs—it was a sop thrown to the National Party in the pre-election negotiations. When I asked the ticket salesman about seating in third class, he appeared pained. "Look," he said with circumspection, "there is a lot of drinking there. You'll be more comfortable in second class." He rang up a second-class ticket without further discussion.

I head to the dining car for dinner. The chief steward, Pieter Jordaan, greets me at my table. The Afrikaner has spent twenty-seven years working on the trains. He is dressed smartly in a white dinner jacket, roving the aisles of the old train, and checking on each diner. An obsequious smile is pasted on his face. I hail him down to chat. After some banter about food and wine, I get to my point. "Have the trains changed much since 1994?" I ask.

He continues beaming his saccharine smile. "In the past, other Africans didn't ride with us," he replies. "Now, with bus prices too high, they are coming back to us." I feign ignorance and ask him if the trains were once segregated. His head cocks to the side, as if he is shocked by my question.

"In the past, anyone could ride first class," he insists. "If you got the money, why not?" He is still smiling as he spins this yarn about the utter normalcy of South Africa. But I know that he is lying.

Back in my train compartment, I strike up a conversation with the assistant train manager, an older African man named Alfred (he declines to tell me his surname out of fear of "getting in trouble"). I ask him whether trains were segregated. He looks surprised by the naiveté of the query.

"Of course," he replies, adding that blacks were only allowed to ride first class in 1993. I tell him how the chief steward insisted to me that there was no segregation. He cracks a bitter half-smile and shakes his head in disbelief.

"I've worked on the trains for thirty-four years. But I couldn't check tickets or deal with white passengers on the mainline [intercity] trains."

"Racism," Alfred assures me, "is alive and well in the new South Africa."

In the years since the end of white minority rule in South Africa, everything has changed, and nothing has changed. South Africa remains one of the world's most schizophrenic places. It is a land of wrenching contrast: the make-believe manicured world of white South Africans continues to prosper alongside the gritty poverty of the black majority. And so Pieter Jordaan assures me cheerily that all is well in South Africa and always has been, while his black colleague Albert speaks of dignity denied—still.

The great divide that was a hallmark of apartheid South Africa remains firmly in place. It's just more confusing now, as disparate images crowd onto the same screen. Symbols of enormous change—embodied by an all-forgiving prisoner-cum-president—exist alongside signs of no change, evidenced by the oceans of impoverished squatter communities. The juxtaposition can be utterly disorienting. As I traveled throughout South Africa in 1996 and 1997, I would career alternately from feeling that South Africa had been miraculously saved, to fearing that it was on the brink of disaster.

South Africa is in the throes of reinventing itself. Out of a society based on division, greed, and bigotry, a new "rainbow nation" is struggling to be born. But years of apartheid have left the architects of this nonracial society-to-be bereft of navigational aids. The tension between an old order that refuses to die and a new order that has not yet taken root is excruciating. It is a transitional period that is at once baffling, frightening, exhilarating, and depressing.

"Why have you come to South Africa?" whites would routinely ask me during the year that I lived there. The question was posed with a tone of embarrassment, as if I'd disembarked from the plane here by accident, or had unsuspectingly stumbled upon a nation of naked people. My answer always astonished them: "Because you live in the most exciting country in the world."

That has always been my feeling about South Africa. Compared with the granitic political stability of the United States, South Africa is an incredibly dynamic landscape. Even in the darkest days of apartheid, I drew inspiration from those who insisted that they would defeat the seemingly overwhelming forces of the state and create a new democratic society. It was an outlandish pipe dream that I privately thought was unattainable. And then it came true.

What has repeatedly drawn me back to South Africa is an intensity that is unmatched by any other place that I have traveled, from Asia to Africa to North America. The conflicts, dramas, and resolutions seem larger than life. Everything about the place is cast in extreme hues: the warmth of the welcome, the driving beat of the *kwela* music, the stubbornness of the Afrikaner farmers, the commitment of township youths, the depth of emotions about the land. The intensity is both exhilarating and exhausting.

South Africa continues to act out its dramas in bold strokes even though world attention has shifted to other hot spots. Throughout 1995 and 1996, the entire country participated in a yearlong effort to write a new constitution. The result is a 180-page document that includes South Africa's first bill of rights and is hailed as one of the most inclusive, democratic bodies of law in the world.[2] It was published in eleven languages and proudly distributed throughout the country in March 1997. On a local level, whole bureaucracies are being wiped away and new ones put in place. In the Cape Town metropolitan area, home to three million people, the thirty-nine former municipalities (including separate town councils for each racial group) were collapsed into one new metropolitan council and six local councils in 1996. It is a time when everything seems up for grabs.

There is also a downside to this upheaval. Criminals are among the opportunists who have taken advantage of the changes. South Africa now has the dubious distinction of being the most murderous society on earth.[3] Violent crime is not new to South Africa—black townships have always been plagued by it—but it is relatively new to white South Africans. Despite the fact that blacks are twenty times more likely to be murdered than whites, the crime wave (which officials say has been declining since 1997) has left whites utterly demoralized and paranoid.[4] For their part, criminals have been emboldened by the new social freedoms. Car-jacking—assaulting drivers and stealing their vehicles—is now so commonplace that drivers in Johannesburg refuse to stop at red lights out of fear of attack. Ironically, some of the crime is attributed to the former township activists known as "comrades" who are now unemployed, angry, and disillusioned. They have been dubbed *comtsotsis* in the new parlance—a hybrid of "comrade" and *tsotsi* (thug). As for solving the crime problem, it doesn't help that South Africa's vaunted police force, so ruthless when it came to wiping out dissent, has proven to be inept at basic policing.

Such is the topsy-turvy nature of a society that has been turned on its head. The tumult prompted one South African journalist to reply glumly to my praise of his country's dynamism, "But I don't want to live in an *exciting* country. I want to live in a nice *boring* country like yours."

I had not intended to come to South Africa in 1984. The apartheid state was taboo, especially among foreigners active in anti-apartheid politics. I planned instead to visit Zimbabwe. My girlfriend Sue and I hoped to see what a "post-revolutionary" country looked and felt like, not a country locked in a time warp of racist oppression. I mentioned my travel plans to Themba Vilakazi, a friend who was then director of the Boston-based Fund for a Free South Africa and a longtime member of the African National Congress (ANC). An exiled South African, Themba was an impassioned public speaker who inspired me and many others to action; his good-humored counsel in the face of adversity kept us going.

"You should go to South Africa if you can get in," Themba insisted, to my surprise. "See for yourself what is really happening. But," he added, "when you come back, you will have a responsibility to tell people about it."

My decision to go to South Africa was ultimately catalyzed by what I didn't see when I reached Zimbabwe. I had planned to spend time in Zimbabwe experiencing "the revolution" that had culminated in independence in 1980. The problem was that the Zimbabwe that I saw was hardly revolutionary. The white oligarchy remained comfortably in control of the economy, President Robert Mugabe was outlawing opposition parties, government troops were rumored to be slaughtering black opponents in the southern part of the country, and the hope for niceties such as land reform was becoming increasingly remote. My rose-colored glasses were rudely yanked from my face.

After the Zimbabwean revolution that wasn't, South Africa offered the more promising prospect of a democratic revolution that might be. Sue and I reached Johannesburg and were quickly immersed in a crash course in South African politics. Each day we would troop to Khotso House, the headquarters of the South African Council of Churches and a variety of other social action groups. We would then join various field workers as they made their rounds in the townships, pass courts, community meetings, and rural areas.

It was ultimately our journey hitchhiking across the country in 1984 that gave us the most intimate view of the geography of apartheid. South Africa enjoyed a reputation among European travelers as one of the easiest places in Africa to hitchhike. Motivated by equal parts curiosity, innocence, and lack of funds, we set out on backroads through the black "homelands," through small rural farm towns, and into the major cities. Occasionally we would be picked up by black truckers and brought into the townships, where we were invariably ushered into the homes of community leaders and activists. In spite of the deep racial antagonisms in the country, black South Africans were remarkably warm and welcoming to us. We hung out in township *shebeens,* the informal (and illegal) bars in people's homes, and opened our eyes and ears to the world of black South Africans. They were eager to tell us their stories.

Late 1984 was a time of the most significant political agitation since the 1976 Soweto riots. I was astonished and humbled by the remarkable commitment and courage of the people we met. Bringing down the apartheid system seemed an utterly quixotic task. Yet for better or worse, numerous people threw themselves at the challenge with all their might, and sometimes with their lives. There was the township student who fought against police and armored troop vehicles with rocks, the only weapon available to him. There were the women of the squatter camps who battled regularly with police to save their shacks—the one place their families could be together. There were young whites being thrown into jail for refusing to serve in the South African Defense Force.

There was also the dark side of resistance politics. Suspected political "traitors" were tried in kangaroo courts and brutally killed on dubious evidence. And crime was rampant in the townships, with crooks often hiding their criminality behind the guise of "the struggle."

I set about chronicling the nuances of the grassroots opposition for a variety of publications in the United States and the United Kingdom. As I spoke with activists, I couldn't help putting myself in their shoes: Which one of these people would *I* be if I lived here? Would I devote myself to the struggle? Or would I hide behind middle-class comforts and turn a blind eye to the evil being perpetrated in my name? These were discomforting questions to which I had no answer.

From the comfort of foreign shores, it was easy to demonize those responsible for the hardship I witnessed. But as I traveled from black world to white, stereotypes of crude, greedy whites fell away. Time and again after being picked up by white travelers, this haggard pair of wanderers with strange accents would be offered accommodations, meals, rides, and referrals in the next town. Simply put, white South Africans were the most hospitable people I had met anywhere in the world. Perhaps it was a result of being citizens of an outcast nation that they extended such generosity to a rare pair of foreign (white) visitors. The genuine warmth of our reception was always disarming and quite welcome at the end of a long day. These intimate encounters added a complexity and depth to my picture of South Africa that I had not anticipated.

The generosity we received was all the more jarring when juxtaposed with the racism that our hosts would invariably express. The lectures about how "our blacks are different than your American blacks" was depressingly inevitable and sounded like it had all been read from the same script. Bigotry was always dressed up as something more sophisticated, of course. The language of apartheid was positively Orwellian: blacks were not victims of forced removals, they were beneficiaries of "separate development"; whites were not racists, they were simply "pro-white." And so an entire white population could view its racist policies not as forms of greed and injustice, but as helping the childlike blacks grow up. Viewed through this cheery and charitable lens, it became more understandable how good people could be doing such bad things. Such was the banal, smiling, Christian face of evil.

What could explain this bizarre duality of white South Africans? The answer lay partly in how successful apartheid was in separating people. What seemed to be an impossible task of physics—namely, hiding 87 percent of the population from view of the white minority—was in fact done remarkably well. As I shuttled back and forth between white and black worlds, I was surprised by how intimately familiar blacks were with white life, a result of providing the servant labor that made white middle-class life so comfortable. I was similarly struck by how comically naive whites were about black reality. As a foreigner who had spent only a few months crisscrossing their country, I could safely say that I had seen more of black life and culture than nearly any white South African I met.

Apartheid had long since become an exercise in self-delusion by the 1980s. Whites had created an elaborate fantasy world in which blacks featured only as maids and laborers. Whites then mistook this fantasy for reality. In the absence of any substantive interracial contact, whites conjured up ethnological theories about how blacks thought and felt, flights of fancy that they would unashamedly share with me. Separation and isolation were crucial elements in enabling whites to view blacks as subhuman at worst, childlike at best. Today in the post-apartheid era, many whites seem shocked to learn not only that blacks felt badly about the indignities heaped upon them, but that blacks felt anything at all.

A steady undercurrent of fear marked my travels in South Africa and war-torn Namibia in the mid-1980s. Paranoia is the elixir of police-state life. If you did anything that trampled the divide between the races, you had reason to be nervous. As a white American, I bore relatively few risks besides being *uitgeskop* ("out kicked") from the country. Nevertheless, I was apprehensive about getting caught in black areas by the police, of being exposed as a journalist while traveling under the pretext of being a tourist, and of being caught with a variety of "banned" literature. Fear was life in apartheid South Africa; if you wanted to see what was really happening, you just lived with it.

When I finally rode the train out of South Africa and crossed the border back into Zimbabwe in 1984, it was as if a weight had been lifted from my head. I went on to travel in the West African nation of Gabon and was stunned by the *joie de vivre* that was a part of daily life for blacks there. The Gabonese had a gaiety, lightness of step, and healthy indifference for the color of my skin that was in refreshing contrast to the dejected spirit of so many black South Africans. It was among the proud and cheerful people of "black Africa" that I recognized the depth of the tragedy that "white Africa" had perpetrated.

In June 1990, I was one of millions of Americans who attended mass gatherings to welcome the newly freed Nelson Mandela on his triumphant tour of the United States. As I stood shoulder to shoulder with tens of thousands of other people on the winding shores of the Charles River in Boston, I was deeply moved as the tall African gentleman with a fringe of silver hair ascended the stage to the strains of Hugh Masakela's trumpet. He spoke of reconciliation and freedom, and promised that South Africa's long nightmare would soon be over. His presence left the racially divided city where I lived with an all too brief afterglow of interracial harmony.

I returned to South Africa one month later to see for myself what life beyond apartheid might look like and to document the changing political landscape for several magazines. The South Africa of 1990 was a country still pinching itself to make sure it was not dreaming. The African National Congress and South African Communist Party were now legal. Many of the petty indignities of apartheid, such as the ubiquitous EURO-PEANS ONLY signs, had vanished. I was astonished to enter the Braamfontein Bookstore in Johannesburg and find racks of previously banned "subversive" texts, including tracts by Marx, Mandela, Lenin, Joe Slovo, Frantz Fanon, and Ché Guevara. Johannesburg's irreverent new independent Radio 702 brought the moribund airways to life with provocative talk shows that featured appearances by recently exiled and jailed liberation leaders. Freedom seemed so close . . .

And then disaster struck. On July 13, 1990—days after I had arrived in the country—a heavily armed gang of men opened fire on black commuters on the Soweto-Johannesburg train line. It was the beginning of a sustained period of politically organized bloodletting. The results were tragic. A Sunday in September 1990 that I spent in the black township of Kagiso, on the outskirts of Johannesburg, was all too typical. A long tide of people, chanting and gyrating the *toyi-toyi* protest dance, moved slowly down the rutted main thoroughfare. Dust swirled around us, coating me in a fine red film. Bobbing in the current of this human river were nineteen colorful boxes. Each box was draped in the black, green, and gold colors of the newly unbanned African National Congress. Inside each box was a body.

At the soccer stadium, the caskets were lined up and opened in an orderly row. This was the backdrop for yet another mass funeral. These funerals had become a weekly ritual as the toll from the township carnage mounted. The families filed by slowly to pay their last respects. I still remember their faces. The old mama whose soft visage twisted in grief at the sight of her dead son. The teenage boy who after catching a final glimpse of his lifeless brother collapsed in a heap next to me.

"This is the saddest thing I have ever seen in my life," I scribbled in my notebook, as I tried to compose myself to record the event.

As recently freed ANC stalwart Walter Sisulu rose to address the assembled crowd, a disturbance broke out. Residents began pointing and surging toward two white men who were holding a TV camera and appeared to be journalists. I asked another reporter if he recognized the men; he did not. But the local people did: they identified them as plainclothes security policemen. "Dogs!" the people began screaming. "Murderers!"

The two men began backing up toward an opening in the stadium fence. I followed the crowd as it advanced on the men. Suddenly, the two "journalists" pulled out guns and took aim. People began screaming and scattering. A primal fear surged through me and I instinctively sprinted away with the crowd. A panicked but courageous church minister stepped between the armed men and the crowd, pleading with the mob to back off peacefully. The anxious cops continued to flaunt their weapons, arcing them side to side. Finally, an armored police vehicle pulled up to the opening in the fence and whisked the men away. For once, this township funeral would not be a prelude to another one.

The story that Kagiso residents told me that day is one I heard in numerous other townships I visited during that bloody period: police came earlier in the week to disarm the men in the hostels. The next day, a group of vigilantes from Inkatha, the Zulu political organization that had degenerated into a right-wing paramilitary force, came and attacked. When township residents tried to come to the aid of the hostel dwellers, white policemen appeared and drove back the rescuers, allowing the massacre to continue unabated. The attack was then dutifully reported in the press as a chilling example of "black on black" violence.

I asked a family member of one of the Kagiso victims about the roots of the violence. "This violence is not tribal," she insisted emphatically. "It is factored, well-fabricated violence to destabilize us and distract us from our main goal: getting to the constitutional [negotiating] table." She was right, of course.

The "free" South Africa I had come to see was not quite ready to be born. For nearly four years, South Africa teetered precariously on the brink of civil war. Fourteen thousand people died under the reign of President F. W. de Klerk—co-recipient, with Nelson Mandela, of the 1993 Nobel Peace Prize—double the total of political deaths that occurred in the previous forty years.[5] It was an excruciating contradiction: Mandela was free, yet the suffering of black South Africans had only deepened. It was a sobering harbinger of things to come.

And then, finally, the moment South Africans had dared to long for: from April 26 to 29, 1994, South Africa held the first democratic elections in its history. The much-feared all-out war promised by the white right wing never materialized. And the bloody black backlash that white South Africans spent their lives fearing stayed firmly in the realm of fantasy, where it always belonged. As Nelson Mandela ascended the steps of the Union Buildings in Pretoria on a brisk autumn day in May 1994 to become South Africa's first black president, a miracle happened. Or so the world wanted to believe.

What happened to South Africa? What became of apartheid? These were the questions that lured me back to South Africa in 1996. I came with my wife and daughter to spend a year exploring a historic transformation.

Nelson Mandela, already a twentieth-century political icon, was president, and a nation was struggling to re-create itself as something it had never been: a nonracial democracy. It was a chance to witness history as it was made. And maybe it was a chance to resolve the obsession with a distant country that had begun nearly two decades earlier for an impressionable college student.

I found much that was both confounding and inspiring in "the new South Africa" as I settled with my family in Cape Town. The poignant symbols of change were the first thing that grabbed me. Even white right-wingers I met were moved by Mandela's emergence from prison to forgive his tormentors. His magnanimity was at once politically shrewd and emotionally breathtaking.

Then there has been the image of South Africa's triumphant return to the world stage after years of isolation. Mandela has been widely acclaimed as the world's most popular statesman, a reputation that is confirmed by the glowing receptions he has received in the world's capitals. South Africa was welcomed back into the United Nations and the Commonwealth of Nations, and international sanctions were lifted. Queen Elizabeth paid a historic visit to the former British colony.

For South Africa's sports-mad whites, by far the greatest post-apartheid benefit has been the end of the boycott that grounded their beloved sports teams for decades. South Africa's athletes have even risen to the occasion: the nation came to a standstill when the national rugby team, the Springboks, upset New Zealand to claim the 1995 World Cup title. (Mandela outraged many black activists by appearing on the field dressed in a team jersey and celebrating the triumph of the Springboks, once a hated symbol of white culture. It was a brilliant political gesture, as his appearance instantly deflated the sails of the white right.) This was followed closely by the national soccer team, Bafana Bafana, winning the Africa Nations Cup, and the 1996 Olympic gold medals for miner-cum-marathoner Josia Thugwane and swimmer Penny Heyns.

Throughout 1996 and 1997, I was touched by numerous other scenes of a nation rebuilding and recovering. I watched the women of the Victoria Mxenge housing project outside Cape Town hefting cinder blocks and erecting new homes alongside their squatter shacks, brick by brick. There were the squatters of Marconi Beam who were finally moving into their first permanent homes in the development they named Joe Slovo

Park, after the late ANC leader and housing minister. There were the long-suffering mothers of the Guguletu Seven—young men who were killed by police in 1986—who sang and danced after hearings of the Truth and Reconciliation Commission in which they finally learned the truth about what happened to their slain sons, and heard policemen apologize. And I watched as ministers of the Dutch Reformed Church appeared before the TRC to express contrition for their complicity in apartheid, and embrace their former nemesis Archbishop Desmond Tutu in heartfelt hugs.

But the miraculous images tell only part of the story. The greatest legacy of apartheid is the enduring poverty. And the vexing reality that lies just beyond view is this: apartheid lives on in South Africa. It endures in the profound contradictions between white wealth and black poverty. It continues in the chance encounter of a former activist and the man who tortured her—a cop on the "new" South African police force. It lives on in the squatter camps that swell like the sea, lapping ever closer to the heart of the cosmopolitan cities.

Apartheid disparities remain not by chance but by design. As negotiators hammered out the high-stakes deals that led to the historic 1994 elections, a central theme emerged. Whites would give up political power in exchange for preserving their economic privilege. And so the ANC made commitments that a new government would not engage in any major redistribution of resources. Land that may have been taken illegally or by force by the apartheid regime could only be restored to its rightful owners on a willing-buyer willing-seller basis. The bloated white civil service, a key power base of the then-ruling National Party, would remain largely intact. The apartheid debt burden—sapping twenty cents of every rand the new government spent—would be paid. The stage was set for old inequities to remain as if frozen in time from the heyday of apartheid.

South Africa has had a revolution without change. There has been a profound political transformation, with blacks assuming top leadership roles in government and some businesses. But these same new leaders have been reluctant to bring about any equivalent economic revolution that would most directly affect those on the ground.

The economic and social legacy of the apartheid era is dire. South Africa is the second most economically polarized country in the world (only Brazil has greater income inequality). About half of South Africans are poor (earning less than $75 per month). The ranks of the poor are disproportionately filled by nonwhites: 61 percent of "Africans" and 38 percent of "coloreds" are poor, while just 1 percent of whites are impoverished.* Only 21 percent of South Africans have piped water, 28 percent have sanitation facilities, and less than half of the populace has electricity. Twelve percent of adult South Africans—mostly poor blacks—have AIDS in 1998; this figure is expected to double in a few years. And three children in five live in destitute households. In striking contrast, the average household income of whites is nearly five times that of Africans, and the wealthiest 6 percent of South Africans consume over 40 percent of the nation's goods and services.[6]

The income and consumption gap will remain entrenched because of South Africa's biggest problem: the lack of jobs. By 1998, national unemployment was officially 34 percent, but the figure rises to over 80 percent in many black townships.[7] President Mandela declared in February 1998 that a planned "jobs summit" was "the most important event since our first democratic elections." But as University of Cape Town economist Francis Wilson told me, "The paradox is that Mandela comes to power when he is least able to use economic power to change society." And so the economic chasm separating South Africans remains vast.

The result of South Africa's unfinished revolution is a society in a state of tremendous flux and tension. Some people have experienced dramatic reversals of fortune, for better or worse. Others have found themselves on the threshold of unprecedented opportunities. But the majority of South Africans have been left with raised but unrequited hopes.

Just as the struggle to liberate South Africa touched on moral issues that transcended the embattled African nation, so too does its transformation resonate with universal themes. What can be done with the memory of past evils? What hope do the poorest people have of breaking out of poverty? Is reconciliation between past antagonists possible? Who profits from the new dispensation? Has apartheid been eradicated, or has it just assumed new forms? What will it take to unmake apartheid?

* In the apartheid lexicon, "Indian" referred to people descended from India, "colored" referred to people of mixed race, and "African" referred to Bantu-language speakers. In the 1970s, activists began referring to nonwhite South Africans as "black" in an effort to promote a pan-racial identity of all oppressed people. To maintain consistency with quotes, references, and realities from South Africa, these terms are used here.

These were some of the questions that I sought to answer as I set out across the new South Africa. I wanted to look beyond the poignant symbols and the easy talk of "miracles" to understand the experience of South Africa's transformation at the grass roots. Over the course of nearly a year, I went in search of pairs of people who captured the sharp-edged extremes of a society in transition. My travels took me from the Atlantic coast of Cape Town to the verdant valleys of the "dragon mountains," from the gritty streets of Soweto, to the expansive farms of the *platteland.*

My journey followed the fault lines of the new South Africa. Faults, be they geologic upheavals or a confession of human failings, embody great tension, simultaneously holding the potential for destruction and regeneration. The characters I ultimately chose to profile straddle the great divides of South African society. There is rich and poor, famous and obscure, powerful and weak, white and black. Each pairing of people represents opposite poles of a major challenge confronting South Africa. They dramatize the conflicts and contradictions that are woven into the fabric of the young democracy. All but two of the people (Adelaide Buso and Tumi Modise) have some relationship with their counterparts.

The first part of the book deals with a victim and a perpetrator of apartheid violence. Reconciliation has been the preeminent focus of South Africa's first democratically elected president. The story of activist Reverend Frank Chikane and his would-be police assassin Paul Erasmus explores the sharply differing worlds in which each man grew up, and how their early experiences influenced their later actions. Their story is about how ordinary people were drawn to do extraordinary deeds, and the difficulties of reconciling today.

The second part looks at the odyssey of the Verwoerd family. Former Prime Minister Hendrik Frensch Verwoerd is known as the "architect of apartheid." His son Wilhelm Verwoerd Sr. still cherishes and defends his father's grand scheme. But the grandson of H. F. Verwoerd has left the protection of the fabled Afrikaner laager: Wilhelm Verwoerd Jr. is a member of the ANC and worked for the Truth and Reconciliation Commission documenting the fallout from his grandfather's policies. His wife, Melanie, is a member of parliament for the ANC. The story of the Verwoerds offers a window into the rise and fall of Afrikaner nationalism through the changing fortunes of one family. The tale of alienation between father and son also touches on the elusive nature of reconciliation, and of the uncertain future confronting Afrikaners.

In part 3 I look at the divergent experiences of a poor woman and a rich woman in the new South Africa. Adelaide Buso is a squatter, domestic worker, trade unionist, and a new city councilor in the wealthy community where she cleans houses. She is a walking contradiction: she has political power but no economic clout. Buso represents one of South Africa's most burning problems, the challenge of uprooting poverty. Tumi Modise is part of the emerging class of black nouveau riche. She has come up from the ghetto, but she offers unsentimental and politically unfashionable assessments of black poverty, the labor movement, and what it takes to break out.

In the fourth part I travel to the *platteland*. The land—South Africa's most emotive issue—remains a source of tension and conflict. In a country where whites make up 13 percent of the population but own 87 percent of the land, the question of economic justice looms large. Lieb and Nanette Niemand are successful farmers in the conservative town of Ventersdorp. Part of Lieb's past includes having been involved in the forced removal of a small black farming community called Mogopa. The farmers of Mogopa, exemplified by Matthew Mpshe, have returned to start over. This is the saga of the tense peace in the *platteland*, of how these neighbors struggle to move forward despite their onerous baggage.

In the conclusion I reflect on how South Africa has fared with "unmaking apartheid." By taking the measure of the new South Africa through these eight lives, I try to capture where South Africa has come from, where it is now, and the direction that it is heading.

These characters tell one part of South Africa's story; by no means have I covered every facet of this complex country. I try to let my characters speak for themselves. They are eloquent storytellers, and it was a privilege for me to have the opportunity to hear their tales. With the exception of Chikane and the Verwoerds, these individuals are not famous. This is deliberate: I strove to find faces in the crowd who could give voice to the struggles of ordinary South Africans.

Throughout the book, I digress to include vignettes of experiences I have had over the years that dramatize some aspect of South African life and politics. This, after all, is the story of a journey—my own, these individuals', and South Africa's.

PART ONE | **VICTIM AND PERPETRATOR**

# VICTORIOUS VICTIM

REVEREND FRANK CHIKANE:
ACTIVIST, THEOLOGIAN, GOVERNMENT LEADER

Rev. Frank Chikane
makes his point as
a member of the
Independent Electoral
Commission, 1994.

Rev. Frank Chikane
in the Naledi AFM
Church, Soweto, 1997.

Rev. Frank Chikane
speaking at a United
Democratic Front
rally, Johannesburg,
mid-1980s.

**REVEREND FRANK CHIKANE,** a twenty-six-year-old pastor, was standing naked on the fourth floor of the Krugersdorp police station. His head hung down limply; dried blood was caked in dark brown clumps in his hair and on his face. He had been standing continuously for over forty hours in a room furnished only with steel chairs and a table, his hands chained to a heating pipe behind him.[1]

Ten brawny white policemen surrounded the cleric, each taking turns savaging him. It was sport to them. One kicked him hard in the testicles, roaring with laughter as the slight young man shrieked in pain. Another slammed him in the ribs with a cricket bat. Occasionally the policemen knocked him to the ground and all piled on. Smashing. Crushing. Breaking. Cutting. There was blood everywhere. During a break in the assault, Chikane looked up and recognized the man supervising his torture: he was a deacon in the white branch of his church, a fellow born-again Christian.

Chikane (pronounced chi-KAH-nee) was new in town. He had been sent by his church, the Apostolic Faith Mission, to minister to a congregation in Kagiso, the black township outside Krugersdorp, on the outskirts of Johannesburg. One week after he took up his new post in June 1976, the Soweto uprising began. Protests spread like a veld fire through every township in Johannesburg. Within days, every government building, liquor store, bar, and shop in Kagiso had been burned to the ground. The protests were an angry catharsis for local residents, an explosion of pent-up rage against apartheid.

The police clamped down on the township and many community leaders suddenly vanished. The families turned to their new minister to intervene with the authorities. Rev. Chikane suddenly found himself in a war situation. He retained lawyers to confront the police, demanding to know the whereabouts of people who had presumably been detained.

Within a year, the police had had enough of this cheeky minister. Local police had free rein to detain and harass activists of their choosing. Now it was Chikane's turn to "disappear."

In the middle of the night on June 6, 1977, Chikane heard the dreaded banging on his front door. Flashlights shone into his bedroom and armored police vehicles surrounded the church manse where he lived. Several policemen dragged him half-dressed out of his house and threw him in the back of a pale yellow pickup truck, the "squad car" of the South African Police. The assault began with slaps and punches. That was just a warm-up.

Back at the Krugersdorp police station, a team of interrogators set to work on Chikane in earnest. They were strapping Afrikaner men from the *platteland*. Most of them were junior security policemen trying to impress their bosses, and each other. But they had never encountered a prisoner quite like Chikane. They responded to his intransigence with unchecked brutality.

"Where do you get your orders from?" demanded one of the men as he yanked Chikane's head back by his hair.

"I follow the word of God," replied the pastor. He cried out as another policeman slammed him in the ribs with a wooden broomstick.

"Tell us where the communists are hiding!" bellowed another cop.

"I don't know any communists. People are protesting against apartheid—they don't need communists to tell them they are being oppressed." Nothing the police tried seemed to work. They hung him upside down and beat him back and forth like a punching bag until Chikane lost consciousness. They forced him to hold contorted positions with his feet chained together, burned him with cigarettes, and suffocated him under water until he nearly passed out. They offered him money to inform for them. The young cleric gave them nothing.

After six weeks of torture, Chikane could barely walk. The Krugersdorp cops decided to subject him to a final all-out torture to break him. Maybe he would survive it, maybe not.

Chikane was dragged out of his cell and dumped in a room full of police. The white church deacon yanked the pastor to his feet by his ears and ordered him to stand. For the next fifty hours blows rained down on him. Teams of interrogators came and went in eight-hour shifts, beating him twenty-four hours a day. They had abandoned all restraint and were just venting their fury against this insolent kaffir.* Every time he would crumble they would yank him back to his feet. Pieces of his hair, skin, and teeth lay around him on the floor.

After forty-eight hours, a large mustachioed policeman who was particularly sadistic said nonchalantly to the prisoner, "You can tell us who your communist friends are Chikane, or you can die here slowly but surely." Peering up through his swollen eyes, Chikane somehow mustered the wherewithal to reply.

"If I die now, I will be with the Lord. This is gain for me and for the Kingdom." The young clergyman spoke haltingly; every word was a struggle. "But if you let me live I will still live for Christ, and I will continue to challenge your evil apartheid system."

"So you are choosing to die?" bellowed the agitated interrogator, the muscles in his neck straining with anger.

"No, *you* must choose whether to kill me or let me live. And if you kill me, you must face the Lord on the Day of Judgment."

The cop flew at him in a rage. For over two days, they had failed to break him. He punched Chikane and slammed his knee into his ribs. The young pastor could only whimper; he was numb to all but the most severe pain by now. Secretly, Chikane thought to himself that if he were going to die, the faster the better.

After fifty hours of nonstop torture, his interrogators gave up. They drove him to a prison in nearby Rustenburg, dumped his limp body in a cell, and forgot about him. Chikane could barely move. His jailers laughed at him, saying he had "danced" to some "good music."

A few days after he'd arrived in the jail, Chikane asked a guard for a Bible. The request was denied. *"Dit maak jou 'n terroris,"* the jailer replied, slamming the steel bars on the wounded cleric. "It makes you a terrorist."

After six months of solitary confinement, Chikane was released. No charges were ever filed.

The silver spoon makes a delicate tingling sound as Frank Chikane stirs his tea. He slowly brings the gold-rimmed teacup to his lips and takes a

---

* The term *kaffir* comes from Arabic meaning "nonbeliever." South Africans use it pejoratively to refer to blacks—the equivalent of "nigger."

sip. His lips pucker from the hot drink, and he places the teacup down with a soft clink of china on china. Then he resumes telling me about his torture, some twenty years earlier.

We are sitting in Chikane's office in Tuynhuys, the Office of the President in Cape Town. To find Chikane, I pass through the bleached white Roman columns outside the building and am ushered into a large foyer with a long deep brown wooden table polished to a mirror finish. A guard directs me to a sitting room filled with gray stuffed chairs and all manner of pomp, where I sit and exchange stares with South Africa's former leaders. Strijdom, Verwoerd, Vorster—their portraits are all here, peering down solemnly on the interlopers now inhabiting this sanctum.

Finally, a young Afrikaner woman dressed in a tight skirt and blazer retrieves me. "Please excuse the mess," says Natassia sheepishly over her shoulder as she strides briskly up the grand staircase. "It's our first day back in three months." I am mystified by her apology—the place is immaculate.

I peer down a long white hall lined by blonde wood doors as I wait for Chikane. I recognize President Mandela's aides scurrying about. This is a sterile place that resonates power and patrimony but not warmth. Chikane's office is decorated in the nondescript shades of authority. The muted green walls are bare save for a large South African flag hanging opposite his desk.

Chikane smiles broadly and extends his hand as I enter. He is a short, trim man and a dapper dresser. He is meticulously attired in an avocado Christian Dior shirt, pleated black trousers, and polished black leather shoes. He has an easygoing formality about him, exuding at once the poise of power and the warmth of an old friend. When he smiles, which is often, it is with his whole face; he puts guests and even adversaries at ease. One could mistake his friendly manner for a man who enjoys hanging out and spinning yarns of the struggle. But Frank Chikane is consumed by his calling, and he clearly thrives on giving his all to the demands of the moment. He is a man with no time, as he abruptly informs me.

After a brief "hi-how-are-you" Chikane makes clear that I am imposing on him. "I really shouldn't be doing this," he says, darting about his office and handing documents to Natassia. She sprints in and out of his space, guarding his time, screening his calls, reminding him of appointments. "Every minute I take with you is a minute the deputy president must take to do things I have not attended to," says Chikane. His cherubic face is stretched into a smile even as he is gently scolding me for my persistence. His cellular phone chirps to emphasize his point; he hands it to Natassia to answer.

Tuynhuys is the seat of power in South Africa, and few people are surprised that Chikane is now one of its occupants. Starting with the detentions that forever politicized him, Chikane has earned a reputation as a persuasive leader, an independent thinker, and an activist with deep roots in the community. Two decades of high-profile activism have led him to his current post as director-general of the office of Deputy President Thabo Mbeki, Nelson Mandela's heir apparent.

An aura of sainthood frequently infuses descriptions of Chikane. "Frank gets his strength from God," muses Irene Meadows, the secretary at the South African Council of Churches who worked under both Archbishop Desmond Tutu and Chikane when each headed the organization. She witnessed Chikane at work on the front lines. "You as a human being don't have that strength. It's divine."

The high esteem in which Chikane is held is evident in stories like the one about a black security policeman who refused to lock the door of Chikane's prison cell. When the guard was reprimanded, he punched his white superior and was swiftly fired. Other black guards have smuggled newspapers and letters into his cell.[2]

But I am skeptical of such deification. It obscures the tough pragmatism and bald ambition that are the hallmark of political leaders, and makes the intrigue of high office appear nobler than it is. Chikane has always been a consummate political operator. His theological credentials have perhaps confused people into thinking that politics is a mere sideline for him. It is not. Chikane has been a loyal soldier in the South African wars. He has coveted authority and usually been duly rewarded. The struggle for power—for his people, his country, and himself—has been a central theme in his political and spiritual life.

Chikane is a far more complex man than legend conveys. He wrestles with forgiving apartheid perpetrators, which President Mandela has put forth as a civic duty. And the economic policies that he is advocating have impressed the World Bank but infuriated many former progressive colleagues who accuse the government of reneging on its commitment to the poor. Chikane wonders privately whether the policies he is advancing will even make a difference to his own brother, who is trying, against the odds, to succeed in business.

Suffice it to say that Chikane has endured far more hardship than most mortals can conceive of. Since 1977 he has survived six rounds of detention, countless hours and unspeakable methods of torture, a year of hiding during the 1986 state of emergency, and, finally, a 1989 assassination attempt which very nearly succeeded. Over the years, such abuse has left him at various times paranoid, confused, unable to walk, sleep, or speak. Yet every blow and epithet only seemed to fuel his determination to fight back with his whole being. The apartheid enforcers failed to break him, but it was not for lack of trying.

Chikane is the first to decline the mantle of godliness. "I am no saint," he insisted in his 1988 autobiography, *No Life of My Own,* written at the tender age of thirty-seven. He and his wife, Kagiso, now the parents of three sons who range in age from six to sixteen, have "normal human concerns about the family, my safety, and the type of life we are living."

"If I was asked whether I would have liked to live the type of life I am living now, I would most certainly have said 'no!' . . . I would have chosen to live a normal life like other people," he began his book. "It seems that as long as the apartheid system exists we shall not be able to live a normal life as a family."

Suffering is an essential part of the Chikane worldview. It was a given that blacks suffered under apartheid. For Chikane, the challenge was to make his suffering meaningful or "redemptive." He chortles as he recalls the thinking of many blacks during the seventies and eighties. "You get detained even if you don't do anything, so you rather better do something to be able to justify your detention!" The goal became to "do as much damage to the system as you can before they catch up with you."

But Chikane's commitment went a step further: he was willing to die for what he believed. He often spoke of dying for his convictions as if it were inevitable. And he seemed at times to mock death, to dare his torturers to make a martyr of him.

"Dying in a just cause is not a vain death," he told a reporter in 1987. "Christ offered his life for us. We can do no more than he did. We black South Africans have nothing else to give. We offer our lives."[3]

Wasn't he being a bit cavalier about death? He answers matter-of-factly as we talk over tea in Tuynhuys. He sits back confidently as he speaks, steepling his hands under his chin. "What motivated me was commitment to the Lord—if I have to use theological, spiritual language—which meant that you should be prepared to die for the particular beliefs you hold. And if your Lord was crucified for that, then you should be willing to make that sacrifice too."

Paradoxically, Chikane probably owes his life to the fact that he was willing to die. His audacity flummoxed his torturers, and he recalls how they were "captured in the belief that you were superhuman." They were amazed when he would break down and cry under the strain of interrogation. Chikane says such breakdowns were a strength. "That just shows our humanity."

For Chikane, only religion can explain such suffering, and so religion provides him the faith and courage needed to challenge it. God sides with the oppressed, the underdog. Apartheid is a sin against God; removing that injustice will hasten the Kingdom of God on earth, a just place where all people will be free. Chikane writes and speaks often about the Kingdom, and bringing it about remains his mission in life. As one journalist who profiled him observed, Chikane "sees no difference between God's purposes and his own political objectives."[4]

These words could of course be used to describe any religious fanatic. Such single-minded zeal is chilling. History is fraught with examples of how such fervor has as often been the rationale for oppression as it has been for liberation. What redeems this force in Chikane's case is simply his humanity. He is a warm, compassionate man, quick to smile and laugh. He has few pretenses, and so he can move easily between his poor congregation in Soweto, conservative Boers preparing to vote in the farm town of Klerksdorp, and the halls of power in Pretoria.

Chikane believes that all revolutionaries are motivated by deep spiritual faith. He recalls one evening when Joe Slovo came to dinner at his house after returning from exile. Slovo, the most prominent white member of the ANC high command, was born to Lithuanian Jewish parents but declared himself an atheist in later life. He was head of the South African Communist Party and chief of staff of the armed wing of the ANC—making him a hero to blacks and Satan incarnate to most whites. After the 1994 election, Slovo became Mandela's first minister of housing, but he died of cancer in January 1995. Chikane recalls how the conversation that evening turned to their respective faiths—or in Slovo's case, the seeming lack of faith.

Slovo conceded that he had been willing to die for what he believed in.

Chikane insisted to the jocular guerrilla, "The fact that you can also go and die for that cause, it sounds like religion for me. It's a question of what type of religion really."

Chikane concluded, "I don't believe there's a person without faith. There's something that motivates people to do things that they do. In my case, I'm saying it's on the basis of my faith."

Frank Chikane was born in 1951, the second of eight children of James and Erenia Chikane. His father worked for a sanding company in Johannesburg, while his mother raised her family in the rural town of Bushbuckridge on the Mozambique border. In the late fifties the children moved to their father's house in Soweto, the vast black township that lies outside Johannesburg, to attend school; their mother moved in with them in 1962. The Chikane children cooked their own food and washed and pressed their own clothes by the age of nine. Frank recalls that his black school pants were covered with burn marks from his inattentiveness while ironing.

Soweto, an acronym for South West Township, was itself an apartheid creation. It was built in the fifties as a dumping ground for blacks who were forcibly removed from surrounding communities such as Sophiatown, a storied, racially mixed working-class ghetto. Today Soweto has a population of three to four million people.[5]

Like all parents, James and Erenia Chikane tried hard to shelter their children from the harsher aspects of life under apartheid. They made sure their children attended school, didn't let them shirk their homework, and encouraged them to strive for professional careers. Despite their best efforts, reality always found a way to intrude.

One day when Frank was thirteen, his mother's youngest sister came to stay. His aunt was about to give birth to her seventh child, and she had come to Soweto from her rural home so that she could be close to the hospital. All her previous children had been delivered by cesarean section, and her family was concerned about her health. She arrived in the afternoon and planned to go to the hospital the following day.

But the police quickly noticed the newcomer on the block. Without warning, a group of policemen swooped down at 2 A.M. and demanded to see a pass, or *dompas,* for the visitor. All black people were required to carry a *dompas,* which stated where they were permitted to live. Blacks were only allowed to stay in Soweto if they were born there or worked in the area. Barring that, you needed permission to be in the city, which Frank's aunt did not have.

The Chikane children awoke to witness their pregnant aunt being dragged out of the house in her nightclothes. At the police station she was thrown on a cement floor to wait in the bare cell until the following morning, when a senior officer would decide what to do with her. For young Frank, it was a rude awakening to the reality that blacks were considered less than human by white society. It wasn't long before Frank experienced this firsthand.

Frank Chikane was not quite sixteen. It was a warm summer day and he was strolling down the street to visit a friend. Roads in Soweto were rutted dirt thoroughfares shared by pedestrians, farm animals, trucks, cars, and horse-drawn carts. Around him lay the Soweto landscape of mile upon mile of identical four-room "matchbox" houses. Often the only distinguishing feature between houses was the number that the authorities had crudely painted on each door.

Frank was sauntering absentmindedly and didn't notice the white Ford sedan pull up alongside him. Inside were three white policemen. Frank had already grown accustomed to playing cat-and-mouse when he spotted the police. Blacks must begin carrying a *dompas* at age sixteen, and teenagers were routinely stopped to ascertain their age. If they didn't have a *dompas,* they would be arrested and held until their parents arrived with a birth certificate to prove they didn't need a pass.

"Good morning *meneer* [sir]," said the nervous boy, careful to look down as he spoke. The three white men in police uniforms emerged from the car and approached him menacingly.

"*Meneer?*" leered a strapping fellow with a bushy mustache. "Did you say *meneer?*" His neck muscles tightened as he stepped closer to the boy.

"Cheeky kaffir—you call me *baas!*" Chikane was not sufficiently practiced in dealing with whites to understand the fine points of slave parlance. He had been taught to address white adults as *meneer.* But that might imply you were equals. Whites insisted that blacks address them as *baas* (boss) in perpetual acknowledgment of their mastery.

The portly man suddenly buried his fist in Chikane's solar plexus. The slight boy was lifted up in the air by the blow. He felt a sharp pain as he landed on hard ground, and he could taste the dust as it hung limply around his head. He gasped for breath, straining for wind against the spasm in his abdomen. He thought he was suffocating. The policeman grabbed his white shirt and yanked him forward.

"Let's see your *dompas,* kaffir!" he snapped.

The young man was flustered. "Yes, *baas,*" he mumbled between gasps as he searched his pockets. "I have the papers . . . somewhere."

Chikane was still fumbling when the next blow slammed into his temple, followed by another in his jaw. He was crying now, shrieking helplessly between sobs. He was on the ground, scrambling away, trying desperately to avoid the men. But there were three of them, and they formed a circle around him. One of the other policemen kicked him in the groin, causing Chikane to let out a high-pitched scream.

"Please, *baas.* I have it somewhere, my *baas,*" he sputtered. Blood ran in deep crimson streaks from his nose and down his white school shirt. But they were on him again, picking him up and throwing him back down onto the hard dirt.

"I'll give you the papers, *baas,*" wailed the frightened teenager. He was too old to be a boy, too young to be a man. He lay crumpled on the ground, praying that they would spare him.

James Chikane encouraged his second son to be a lawyer from a young age. But the young Chikane excelled at math and instead considered a career as a physicist or mathematician. Frank's math talents were unusual, as "Bantu education" typically offered little to students of the sciences.

Chikane enrolled in 1972 at the University of the North in Turfloop (near Pietersburg), one of South Africa's "bush universities" that were designated exclusively for "nonwhites" starting in 1959.[6] Like all "bush" schools, it was located far from the "white" cities. Among his classmates and friends at university were Cyril Ramaphosa, who went on to head the National Union of Mineworkers and led the ANC in the pre-election negotiations with the National Party in the early 1990s. Most of the student leaders, including Chikane, were members of the South African Students Organization (Saso), an organization led by black-consciousness leader Steve Biko. Biko was killed at the hands of security police in 1977, and Saso was subsequently banned.

Chikane's studies in math and physics were soon disrupted by politics. In September 1974, students at Turfloop staged a "Frelimo rally" to celebrate the victory of the Mozambican liberation movement against Portuguese rule. The school was not far from Mozambique, and many black South Africans identified strongly with the anti-colonial guerrilla movements in the neighboring African states. The celebratory rally was abruptly dispersed when police attacked with dogs, *sjamboks* (leather whips), and tear gas. Many students were badly injured. Chikane observed that a simultaneous anti-Frelimo protest by students of Portuguese descent went off without incident.

The Frelimo rally was followed by a six-day sit-in during which many student leaders were arrested. Chikane was elected a trustee of a student legal defense fund, which assumed the responsibilities of the student representative council, most of whose members were in detention. Chikane was suddenly thrust into the leadership limelight. He testified against the police and the university at a subsequent commission of inquiry into the unrest.

When Chikane attempted to take his exams later that year, the strain of all that was happening was too much for him. He had a nervous breakdown and was admitted to a hospital. The university administration refused to let him retake his exams. When he returned to school to resume his studies the following January, a sympathetic professor informed him that he would be victimized, and suggested he not return. At the age of twenty-three, Chikane's hopes for a university degree and a career as a scientist were dashed.

The Chikane family was deeply religious. They were members of the black branch of the Apostolic Faith Mission (AFM), an evangelical Pentecostal church whose services are richly participatory. Like many charismatic churches, AFM congregations are composed largely of the poor. Throughout the services the faithful shout out the name of the Lord, speak in tongues, lay on hands, and dance, stamp, and sing their devotion to God. Frank describes African spirituality as "holistic," in which the spiritual and social worlds are intimately intertwined and God is involved in all aspects of life.

James Chikane led church services in the family's Soweto home, but the size of the congregation soon outgrew the living room. A church was eventually built in Naledi, a poor community on the far western side of Soweto. James became a pastor in 1975 and officially took over the congregation.

Frank Chikane was involved in the church from an early age. He delivered his first sermon at the age of eight, and was secretary of his father's congregation by the time he was eighteen. But by the time Frank reached high school, he began questioning the role and relevance of the churches in the society around him. While he continued to be a devoted member of his father's congregation, he saw that the church as a whole was doing nothing to challenge the oppression that weighed on black congregants. Politicized youth in his Soweto high school were eager to point out how whites had historically given blacks the Bible while stealing their land; they seized upon the Marxist slogan that "religion was the opiate of the people." Frank observed, "To be a Christian to them therefore was to help the minority white racist regime to continue to oppress the people. It was an act of collaboration and cooperation with the enemy."

Chikane was deeply troubled by this schism between his spiritual and political lives. This conflict boiled over in 1971 when students at Chikane's high school got into a violent confrontation with a group of devout Christians. A mass meeting was called, and the young Chikane was asked to speak. He was forced to reevaluate his own spirituality. He declared at the meeting that the Bible had indeed been used to dispossess blacks, but that this was a grave misuse. He asserted that blacks had to reclaim the Bible, and he coined the slogan, "Re-read the Bible and re-interpret it in the light of truth, and turn it against the oppressor." This was a step that ultimately led Chikane to be in direct conflict with his church.

Chikane's experience at Turfloop solidified his political outlook. He was deeply impressed by Steve Biko's philosophy of "black consciousness." Biko spoke of the need for both physical and psychological liberation for blacks. Slogans of South Africa's black consciousness movement—such as "black power" and "black is beautiful"—echoed the Black Power movement of the late sixties in the United States. Elements of the black consciousness movement later split with the ANC, with the former advocating all-black leadership in a new South Africa while the latter called for nonracialism. Chikane always held that black consciousness and nonracialism were compatible, that psychological liberation was a key component of black freedom.

When Chikane left Turfloop in 1974 in the wake of student unrest, he was uncertain about his future career. He finally decided to heed an old calling and become a pastor in his church. This decision was fraught with contradictions: the Apostolic Faith Mission was cautious by reputation and led by conservative Afrikaners (like most churches in South Africa, the AFM had separate divisions for whites, blacks, coloreds, and Indians). But, Chikane insisted to his critical friends, "This is the church in which I was brought up."

Chikane's posting as a pastor in Kagiso the week before the Soweto riots was fateful. In the aftermath of the uprising, he instituted a variety of self-help schemes aimed at addressing the pressing problems of poverty. His church became a center for job assistance, literacy programs, and health care advocacy. His social action ministry quickly earned him the loyalty of his congregation and the wrath of the authorities.

Frank Chikane was taken from the Rustenburg jail in January 1978. His savage six weeks of beatings had left him unable to walk for some time, and it took weeks before he could think clearly following his release after six months of solitary confinement.

Chikane's treatment was not particularly unusual. While he was not well known outside the township at that time, he was a visible and effective local leader. Local police had sweeping authority in the black townships, and they routinely harassed, brutalized, and even killed activists at will. Chikane's experience at the hands of local cops was standard treatment for blacks in countless South African towns.

Chikane was hauled before an austere looking magistrate with six other men, most of whom he had never met. The black-robed white magistrate surveyed the bedraggled looking septet. "You are charged with public violence," intoned the official. Chikane was surprised. During his entire detention and torture, no one had asked him about or accused him of "public violence," nor had he been involved in such a thing. The magistrate was uninterested in Chikane's comments. He set bail at R 200 ($175 in 1978) and told the men to return in six days.*

---

* The rand / dollar exchange rate has varied widely over the years. In general, the dollar value of the rand has dropped steadily since the 1970s, and plummeted in the 1990s. In January 1980, R 1 equaled $1.20, but had dropped to $.50 by 1985, and was only worth $.39 by 1990. As of September 1998, R 1 equaled $.15. Throughout the book, I convert rand values here at the exchange rate of the date in question. (Source: U.S. Federal Reserve Board, historical data.)

Chikane was overjoyed to return to his congregation. Community people greeted him warmly, mustering their scarce resources to throw him a small party. But on the day he was to return to court, a loud banging on the door of the church manse at 2 A.M. awoke him. He knew who it was.

Police stormed in and were greeted by Chief Deacon Isaac Genu, who tried to stop them. They forced the older man back into his room at gunpoint. They found Chikane in his bedroom, and immediately began assaulting him. Punches, whips, and wooden batons tore into his skin. They dragged him out of the house in his pajamas. Taunts—"Kaffir!" "Terrorist!"—punctuated the morning stillness.

The assault continued in earnest in the back of the police vehicle. They began pulling out the pastor's hair and punching him in the face. "Why are you doing this?" shrieked Chikane. Blind rage was their only reply.

When he arrived at the Krugersdorp police station, Chikane was pushed to the ground and ordered to pick up all his hair, which lay on the floor in bloody clumps. The police drove him, hours away, to his court appointment, assaulting him the whole time. They eventually arrived at the wrong court and then had to backtrack all the way to Krugersdorp.

When Chikane finally stepped into the serene white courtroom, he was a mess. His head hung down limply, his eyes were swollen shut. Blood was still oozing from where his hair had been pulled out. His pajamas protruded from beneath his pants. He looked like a vagrant who'd fallen asleep in the road and been run over by a truck.

The courtroom was packed with members of Chikane's congregation. They gasped in horror at sight of their pastor. "Shame!" they cried out. "Killers!" Guards advanced on them threateningly, intimidating them into silence. But the congregants' rage boiled over onto the streets outside after the magistrate spoke.

*"Daar is nie 'n saak teen die man nie,"* the magistrate said flatly as he flipped through the police report with a look of disinterest. "There is no case against this man."

Chikane could not sleep for months after his second arrest. He jumped at loud sounds or abrupt movements. Friends counseled him to leave the country, as they feared his life was in danger. He refused. "If we all left, no one would be there to minister to the people who had no option but to face the pain and misery of living under an oppressive, white minority racist regime," he told them.

Chikane was detained a third time in November 1980. He had just married his wife, Kagiso, when he was rounded up. The occasion for this latest arrest was the awarding of the Freedom of Krugersdorp Medal to Prime Minister P. W. Botha.[7] To celebrate that freedom, police swooped down on the township and rounded up scores of people. This was to be Kagiso's first experience of life with her new husband. As she stood among concerned people in her house, "it was as if life had come to a standstill for me," she said.

The leadership of the AFM Church was unhappy with the radical pastor's activities. During his second detention, the local AFM leadership removed Chikane from his congregation. They cited the fact that he was a "terrorist," by virtue of the fact that he was detained under the Terrorism Act. His congregation refused to agree to the order, and Chikane returned to preach there after each release from jail.

The AFM relented and ordained Chikane in 1980 with the warning that he "not engage in politics." But the church soon charged him with doing just that. Chikane protested in a letter to church leaders that "politics" had different meanings. "When it involves whites in South Africa it is party politics, which is not sin. When one is black and supports the South African Government . . . one is not involved in politics. But if one sees some wrong in the Government of South Africa, however genuine he may be or Biblically justifiable, he is taken as being actually involved in politics."

Chikane went on to insist that "the church in Southern Africa is in a conflict or war situation . . . Many lives are going to be lost as is already the case today." He challenged the church "to be the conscience of the State, to undertake the ministry of reconciliation, peace maker, demand justice, reprimand, demand love and that man live righteously."

Chikane's challenge fell on deaf ears. In October 1981, the AFM suspended him for a period of one year until he "repented." The church leadership again charged that he was "involved in politics" because he "appeared in the newspapers."

Chikane was deeply wounded by his church's action. But he was jailed again in November 1981 and held for nine months, so there was little he could do to clear his name. The most painful episode of that year was the treatment that his wife, Kagiso, received. The church ordered Chikane and his family to vacate the church manse where they lived, but Frank was detained before they could find alternative accommodations. The church didn't care. On the eviction date, a six-man AFM delegation arrived at Chikane's house to evict Kagiso and her sixteen-month-old son Obakeng. They dismissed her pleas for help, saying, "When your husband did what he did, he must have been aware of the consequences."

Chikane wrote later, "My wife was never as hurt by the church and by Christians as she was then. It is a miracle that she remained a Christian."

Upon his release from his fourth round of detention in July 1982, Chikane attempted unsuccessfully to be reinstated by his church. Friends encouraged him to start a new church or join another denomination. But Chikane was adamant that he would remain in the church where he was born, even though the AFM leadership continued to view him as a heretic and an opportunistic troublemaker. His congregants from both Kagiso and Naledi fought the suspension for years. But the church hierarchy was to spurn Chikane for the rest of the decade.

"For us to win against the system we need *power!*" The staccato cadence, the knife-like emphasis, the thrusting of the fist—Rev. Frank Chikane was on fire. His impassioned oratory had been honed by years of preaching from ramshackle township pulpits. Now he was galvanizing the crowd from the steps of Khotso House in downtown Johannesburg. It was a blustery winter day in August 1983, and Chikane was addressing a demonstration in his new capacity as national vice president of the newly formed United Democratic Front (UDF). The swelling throngs responded with cheers, slogans, and promises of their undying commitment to the struggle. "*Viva UDF, VEEE-VA!*" came the response.

"No powerful oppressor has ever gone out of office without being removed . . . We need people's *power* to bring change in South Africa . . . *Now is the time* for all the organizations in South Africa to work for a joint action to break *the system!*"

Frank Chikane had finally burst onto the national political stage. His concurrent battles with the police and his church had thrust him into the limelight as one of the most eloquent and effective community leaders around Johannesburg. Most important, he had credibility among a broad range of political groups. So when the UDF coalesced in 1983, Chikane was a natural choice to lead its largest branch. He also became deputy president of the Soweto Civic Association in 1984, an influential and militant community organization.

Chikane's suspension as a pastor paradoxically freed him to engage in politics, with a vengeance. He was initially reluctant to take a high-profile position in the UDF, fearing it would confirm his church's accusations against him. But his fellow activists complained that the churches had monopolized the best activists, thereby depriving the anti-apartheid movement of leadership.

In the end, Chikane threw in his lot with the activists to join them "in their hour of need." He had increasingly identified with Third World liberation theologians who actively campaigned on behalf of oppressed people. He attacked the hypocritical way in which the church was "strong on moralizing and prescribing methods to be used in striving for change. But the church never tries these methods itself." The time had come for Chikane to unequivocally take sides.

The UDF was an alliance of over six hundred organizations representing an estimated three million students, women, trade unions, civic organizations, and religious groups.[8] It was launched at a rally outside Cape Town on August 20, 1983, where Chikane delivered the opening address. The launch is best remembered for "three little words" uttered to thunderous applause by Rev. Allan Boesak: *all, here,* and *now.* "We want *all* our rights, we want them *here,* and we want them *now.*"[9]

Under the slogan "UDF Unites, Apartheid Divides," the UDF was catalyzed by Prime Minister P. W. Botha's so-called apartheid reforms. In 1982, Botha announced a series of changes that were part of his "Total Strategy" to combat the "total onslaught" of communism and the ANC. Total Strategy had a two-pronged approach. It aimed to create a small, conservative African middle class as a way of countering unrest in the black townships. Total Strategy also attempted to win the "hearts and minds" of township dwellers. To that end, a variety of social programs were undertaken, such as paving streets and providing basic services to poor communities.

The second component of Total Strategy was aimed at eliminating the military threat of the liberation movements. In the early eighties, Botha authorized a series of cross-border raids to attack ANC bases in the neighboring black-ruled countries. These attacks succeeded in hampering the ANC's ability to stage guerrilla actions.

A key part of the Total Strategy on the home front was the creation of a new constitution that would pave the way for Indian and colored participation in national government. Africans would only get locally elected municipal councils, a veiled attempt to neutralize the influence of the militant civic organizations that were springing up in townships.

White South Africans now had to accept that their all-white parliament would be supplemented by a House of Representatives for coloreds and a House of Delegates for Indians. For the first time since the fifties, some nonwhite voters could vote in national elections for a tricameral parliament to be held in August 1984. The fundamental flaw in the Total Strategy—quite intentional—was that it once again excluded the African majority, who made up three-fourths of the population.

Botha's strategy was a classic case of "one step forward, two steps back." The white populace was the only group that viewed the advent of the tricameral parliament as a reform. The changes represented a tactical and psychological shift for the National Party (NP). It was being forced to acknowledge that nonwhites would somehow have to be brought into the governing process, although NP strategists couldn't quite figure out how. Right-wing whites were sufficiently offended by any notion of sharing power with nonwhites that they broke from the NP. In 1983, during negotiations for the new constitution, Transvaal NP leader Andries Treurnicht split with his party and formed the Conservative Party.

But the right-wingers could only object to appearances. In reality, the Indian and colored parliamentarians would have little power. Any contentious legislation would be decided by the President's Council, which was dominated by white politicians.

Under the guise of reform, the tricameral parliament actually strengthened apartheid. With separate voters' rolls for Indians and coloreds and no vote for Africans, it was merely another version of the old apartheid strategy of divide and rule. The so-called reform put an end to the hope of black moderates that apartheid could be dismantled through elected political structures. The only outlet for the black majority now would be through grassroots militance.

I first arrived in South Africa just as the elections for the tricameral parliament were taking place in August 1984. Colorful UDF posters declaring "Boycott the Vote" were everywhere, far outpacing the government's ability to sanitize the event. I traveled the townships around Johannesburg to gauge sentiment toward the elections. It was easy to distinguish who lived where: the standard of living in a township was directly related to the fairness of skin of its residents. Thus the Indian community of Lenasia consisted of well-kept working-class cottages painted in pleasant pastoral colors. The colored township of Eldorado Park was more densely packed and run down, with multifamily dwellings dominating the landscape. Soweto featured miles of cinder-block houses that were interspersed with squatter shacks.

One sentiment ran consistently through these balkanized communities in 1984: I was hard-pressed to find anyone who supported the sham "reforms." The election results were to bear out my impressions. Of the people who registered to vote, only 30 percent of coloreds and 20 percent of Indians cast ballots on election day. It was a stunning show of strength by the anti-apartheid movement.[10]

The UDF brought together the largest collection of political groups in South Africa in thirty years. It was essentially a legal front organization for the banned ANC. But unlike the ANC, a key feature of the UDF was that the organization resembled a hydra: the alliance could not be easily suppressed by the arrest of one person or by being banned. I was in Khotso House when police raided the UDF offices there in 1984, arresting many top leaders. By the next day, new leaders had already stepped forward to replace them. But this grassroots structure had a downside. The organization was so decentralized that it often found itself leading from behind, responding to the actions of angry township youths who were taking initiatives on their own.

Anger and activism came to a head on September 3, 1984. In Cape Town, the new constitution that once again codified the disenfranchisement of blacks came into effect in a ceremony in parliament full of pomp and circumstance. Botha, who shed the title of prime minister and was anointed state president, celebrated the event alongside the newly elected colored and Indian legislators, who were decked in the eccentric costumes of Afrikaner pageantry, which included homburgs and morning coats.

Nine hundred miles north, in the squalid townships south of Johannesburg known as the Vaal Triangle, a different display of power was going on. Local residents were angered by the actions of black municipal councilors, who had gained their titles in elections that were widely boycotted, thanks to the UDF. The councilors were viewed as apartheid stooges; resentment was exacerbated when the councilors announced a rent increase. Trade unions called a work stayaway for September 3, and young activists were enforcing the decree by erecting picket lines and barricades to prevent buses from entering the townships. The townships were paralyzed for a week. Angry activists killed several black councilors and police engaged residents in running street battles; thirty-one people died in the disturbances that week.[11]

The revolt spread quickly throughout the country. On September 23, seven thousand soldiers were called in to suppress the Vaal uprising. I recall vividly how the Johannesburg region suddenly looked as if it were embroiled in a full-scale war. Armored troop carriers and heavy weaponry took over the highways that were normally clogged with commuters; the noise of army helicopters overhead added to the sense of a siege. It was the first time in a quarter-century that South African troops had been used to put down domestic unrest. As historian Tom Lodge observed, "The longest and most widespread period of sustained black protest against white rule in South Africa's history had begun."[12]

> Dear Kagiso,
> We are here in a big cell together with most of the people's leaders and those who will be part and parcel of the future leadership of a just and peaceful society of South Africa . . . Reading about history is an exciting and enjoyable game . . . But making the history is not a nice thing at all . . . It involves enormous sacrifices in terms of family, friends, etc. I really miss you . . ."[13]

It was February 1985, and the state had finally reacted to the gauntlet thrown down by the UDF. Rev. Frank Chikane was arrested along with fifteen others and charged with high treason. He was in jail with the leading lights of the UDF, including veteran anti-apartheid activists Albertina Sisulu, Archie Gumede, and others. This arrest was different than previous ones: the accused leaders now faced the death penalty.

Chikane was released on bail three months later. His joy at being out of jail was short-lived. Two days after he was released, he awoke at 3 A.M. to the sound of a loud blast in his Soweto home. Three petrol bombs had been thrown into his house, nearly consuming his eight-month-old son Otlile in flames. He scooped up Otlile while Kagiso grabbed five-year-old Obakeng and ran outside. Neighbors helped dowse the flames.

Chikane's ensuing trial consumed much of his energies that year. In December all fifteen treason defendants were acquitted. Throughout the trial, Chikane and his colleagues were accused of supporting communism and trying to overthrow the state. The accusation caused Chikane to reflect wryly, "Most of the things that are supposedly done by communists were done to me. My concrete knowledge of an evil satanic system therefore is the racist system of South Africa."[14]

In July 1985, President Botha responded to the wave of protests sweeping the country by imposing a state of emergency—the first time such harsh measures had been decreed since the aftermath of the Sharpeville massacre in 1960. The police and army had nearly unfettered powers during the eight-month siege, a fact borne out by the casualty figures: between September 1984 and January 1986, 955 people died in incidents related to the unrest, two-thirds of them killed by "state bodies."[15]

The repression did little to stem the tide of popular protest. A second state of emergency was imposed in June 1986, just before the tenth anniversary observance of the Soweto uprising. A week before the anniversary, the government panicked and swept across the country detaining hundreds of political leaders. Chikane knew he was "at the top of the list for arrest" and was forced into hiding. He lived underground for nearly a year, barely staying one step ahead of the police who were stalking him. He saw his family in carefully arranged covert meeting places and was often sheltered by people who didn't ask or know who he was. He finally slipped out of the country and fled to Europe.

But Chikane agonized about the people left behind. In March 1987, he decided to return to South Africa. Writing to friends on the eve of his return, he acknowledged those who said his reentry into South Africa was "suicidal," and conceded the real risk that he "could be tortured even unto death" or assassinated.

"I can not explain in reasonable terms the decision I have made," he wrote. He was inexorably drawn by "the cries of my people at home . . . the call of women, men and children in Soweto who believe that my presence . . . will make a difference. . . .

"I cannot therefore explain what I am doing except that I am going to be present with them, in life or in death." And, he admitted, he was "scared."[16]

Frank Chikane lived in two worlds throughout the struggle. When not detained, on the run, or leading rallies, he worked as general secretary of the

Institute for Contextual Theology (ICT), a think tank within the South African Council of Churches (SACC) that viewed theology in its social and political context. The SACC—derided as "the African National Congress at prayer" by its critics—was the leading anti-apartheid religious organization. ICT was the moving force behind the issuing of the seminal Kairos Document in late 1985. Kairos (a Greek word meaning "opportunity") was drafted by 151 clerics from sixteen church groups. It called upon Christians to "participate in the struggle for liberation and for a just society," and to support and encourage consumer boycotts, strikes, and civil disobedience.[17] It advocated what Chikane had been urging for nearly a decade: a nonviolent holy war against apartheid.

In July 1987, Chikane's stature as a maverick theologian was rewarded. Dr. Beyers Naude, the general secretary of the SACC who had himself endured years of banning and abuse for his anti-apartheid views, was insistent that his post should go to a black theologian. The top position had previously been held by Archbishop Desmond Tutu.

"Whom do you have in mind?" Naude was asked by his SACC colleagues. He answered without hesitation: Frank Chikane. "He has the trust of the grass roots, the political acumen—there is nobody who could do the job like him," the renegade Afrikaner cleric recounted to me.

Chikane learned of Naude's endorsement with chagrin. "You are sending me to the gallows by asking me to do this job," Chikane complained to Naude.

"We need you more than ever," came Naude's reply. "And even if you do go to the gallows, it will be like the sacrifice of Christ."

Chikane's nomination to lead the SACC was controversial. Even Archbishop Tutu initially opposed it, fearing, like many, that Chikane might be too political to lead the church organization. In the end, Chikane assured his critics that "he was not the kind of activist who simply wanted to demolish and destroy."[18]

I asked Naude whether he had really thought Chikane would be risking his life to take over the reigns of the SACC. The old Boer churchman, whom President Mandela had just honored that week in March 1997 with South Africa's highest civilian honor, stared me squarely in the eye, as he is accustomed to doing. His intense gaze is softened by his gentle smile. He replied emphatically, raising his open hand like a preacher on the pulpit. "We knew how *brutal* the system was. And we knew they wouldn't hesitate to eliminate him, especially because he's black." He concluded solemnly, "I felt it could be the price he'd have to pay."

"So Frank, *were* you a member of the ANC?"

It is a perfect summer day in 1997 as I am driving across Soweto with Frank and Kagiso Chikane. We are in a hurry—Frank Chikane is *always* in a hurry—on our way to church. Kagiso falls silent; her husband will have to field this one by himself.

This has always been a loaded question for Chikane. In the past, everyone from the security police to prying journalists wanted to know the answer. Reply—or even suggest—in the affirmative, go directly to jail and be shunned by church groups. Say anything that implies criticism of the liberation movement, and be rejected by township activists.

So Chikane coyly danced around the question during the eighties. He often defended the armed attacks of the ANC, but publicly called for nonviolence. When journalists would come to him seeking condemnation of a militant action by the "young lions" of the township, he would instead offer explanations and justifications for why apartheid had forced them to take such drastic measures.

Chikane chortles and breaks into a broad grin. "That's a question that has never been answered. I think lots of journalists wanted to know!" He then resorts, as he often does, to the royal "we" or "one" to speak about himself.

"One can say now that one has been involved fully with the ANC throughout . . . the liberation struggle. But that's not the thing one dramatizes."

"Were you actually a member during those years?" I press.

"Why would you carry a membership card so that it sends you to prison?" he replies. "It wasn't necessary. You became part of the ANC and did your work, underground and overboard, whichever way was strategic at that time . . . I mean anybody who would have taken a membership card during those times would be a fool actually."

Chikane recounted that he was twelve years old when Mandela went to prison, and thereafter the entire Mandela legacy was suppressed. "No one talked about it, no one reported about it—there was a total silence." Indeed, it was illegal for a newspaper to quote or publish photos of any banned people or political prisoners. The legacy and thinking of liberation leaders such as Mandela were thus relegated to folklore.

But Turfloop students discovered a loophole: records of court proceedings were still legally available. Students gained access to the Mandela trial records, and that was Chikane's first exposure to the ANC. He and his friends then began to seek out other items of banned literature, which inevitably connected them to the underground movement. By the late seventies, he "really got involved on the ground" with the ANC, working in grassroots community organizations.

Chikane's ANC membership is still a sensitive subject for him as a church leader. In 1990, Archbishop Tutu declared that Anglican clergymen (which Chikane is not) must choose between party politics and the church—they could not be leaders in both. The edict was hotly debated, highlighting the tension that existed between church and state.

"My membership with the ANC is not what I want to elevate," Chikane insists, despite having been elected to the National Executive Committee of the ANC in December 1997. "Because everybody knows that: the police know that, de Klerk knows that. So it's not an issue for me. But if you just raise that for the sake of it, strategically it doesn't benefit you anything really."

On a March morning in 1988, there was a loud knock on Frank Chikane's door in SACC headquarters in Khotso House. Without waiting for an answer, Warrant Officer Paul Erasmus of the security police flung open the door and barged into the spacious office. The churchman in the smart black suit greeted the cop in the black leather jacket cordially. "Good morning, good morning," offered Chikane. There was a surprising air of civility to this unwanted meeting. This was, after all, a regular get-together, occurring about once a month.

Erasmus swept in with four other security policemen and parked himself in the chair opposite Chikane. Chikane nodded his acknowledgment, then proceeded to ignore him. Erasmus reached over and took Chikane's diary and began copying information from it. The policeman then helped himself to a raft of stationery and a few books.

Erasmus proceeded to the anteroom where Chikane's secretary sat. Irene Meadows had been through this drill countless times, first with Tutu, then with Naude, now with Chikane. She admired the way Chikane never lost his cool, and she emulated him.

"Good morning sir," said the soft-spoken secretary. "If you need more time, we can leave the office open after hours," she added wryly.

Any levity about the security police raids ended on August 31, 1988. Chikane received a call in the early hours of the morning telling him to come quickly to Khotso House; there had been an explosion. As he navigated the darkened Johannesburg streets near his office, all he could see were the lights of the fire brigade, and smoke billowing from the tan six-story building. He felt a painful lump well up in his throat. It was like viewing the corpse of a friend: the entire front of the building was blown off. Twisted metal hung from shattered windows. Interior walls and stairwells ended abruptly in an abyss. Twenty-one people lay injured.

Throughout the night, church leaders, journalists, and activists appeared to console one another. This was an emotional frontal attack on the anti-apartheid movement. Khotso House was one of the few places where activists could gather and find like-minded company. It was a veritable nerve center of resistance activity.

As Chikane milled about, a familiar face suddenly emerged from the darkness to question him: it was the security cop who led Chikane's first, and most brutal, torture session in 1977. Chikane glared at the policeman, deeply suspicious that he or his police colleagues were behind the attack. The police later issued a statement saying that the blast was caused by explosives stored in the basement of Khotso House, making it seem as if the church headquarters was a munitions stash. Later, the police claimed that a well-known white activist was responsible for the blast.

Chikane angrily denied the charges, retorting that he doubted the police's intentions to fully investigate the attack. A month later, Khanya House, the Pretoria headquarters of the South African Catholic Bishops' Conference, was destroyed by fire. Soon after that, the building housing the Congress of South African Trade Unions (COSATU) in Johannesburg was blown up. Always circulating on the fringes of these event were Paul Erasmus and his security police colleagues. Chikane assumed they had a role in the attacks, but he couldn't prove it.

Somehow, Chikane didn't think they would go this far. He and his SACC colleagues were people of the cloth. With its international stature and faith as its shields, the SACC had enjoyed a faint bit of immunity from violent assault. But the state was upping the ante; the shield had just been ripped away.

Chikane knew this was a signal that the struggle was intensifying. The church, once considered relatively inviolable, was now a target. And Frank Chikane was the bull's eye.

Life for Rev. Frank Chikane had been frantic. As SACC general secretary and a gifted orator, he was in constant demand by business leaders, visiting political delegations, church groups, and community organizations. He often went weeks without seeing his family.

His 1989 trip to Namibia was typical of his high-flying mission. The South African administration of Namibia had previously banned him from the occupied nation. But with the advent of UN rule in Namibia in April 1989, Chikane figured he was free to enter. On April 23, 1989, he led an SACC delegation to assess the situation in conflict-plagued northern Namibia as the nation prepared for its March 1990 independence elections. Chikane entered the country without incident. The next morning, he donned new clothes from his luggage and joined his group for the long drive north to where the war between South Africa and the South West African People's Organization (SWAPO) had raged only months before.

About twenty-five miles from his destination, Chikane began to feel dizzy and vomited. Soon he felt his chest begin to tighten, as if someone was squeezing all the air out of his lungs. "This is not right," he sputtered to his colleagues in the car. Weakened and disoriented, he got out for some air, but things only got worse. His vision blurred, and his body began shaking uncontrollably. His hosts sped up on the long straight road. The Namibians in the group directed the driver toward Ondangwa—ironically, a South African military garrison, where there was also a Lutheran mission hospital. The sandy landscape became a blur as the vehicle raced toward an outpost better known as a flashpoint of war. By the time they reached the hospital, the South African cleric was battling for his life.

Two German doctors rushed to his aid and worked feverishly for five hours to keep him alive. Meanwhile, an urgent call went out to SACC headquarters in Johannesburg to dispatch a plane and medical help to retrieve Chikane in northern Namibia. Within hours, a chartered plane with a South African nurse and life-support equipment touched down in Ondangwa, scooped up the fallen cleric, and jetted back to a Johannesburg clinic. In the clinic his condition miraculously improved, and he was discharged after four days. His SACC colleagues attributed the illness to stress and overwork. They were thankful that the episode passed without further incident.

Three weeks later, Chikane departed for an important trip to the United States. He was part of a high-profile church delegation that included Archbishop Desmond Tutu, Dr. Beyers Naude, and Rev. Allan Boesak, a UDF patron and president of the World Alliance of Reformed Churches. They were scheduled to meet with President George Bush and members of Congress to urge the Americans to increase pressure on Pretoria. But within twenty-four hours of arriving at his first stop in Madison (Kagiso was taking courses at the University of Wisconsin), Chikane fell desperately ill. Once again, he was felled by vomiting, blurred vision, and difficulty breathing. Doctors at the University of Wisconsin Hospital were baffled, especially when Chikane recovered soon after being admitted. He was discharged after a week.

Forty-eight hours later, Chikane was on the brink of death. He was rushed back to the hospital, where he stopped breathing. He lost consciousness and was placed on a ventilator. Again his condition improved rapidly in the hospital. After a thorough evaluation, his doctors noted that aside from these mysterious attacks, he was in excellent health. He was discharged a week later—and within forty-eight hours was back in the hospital in critical condition for a third time.

As doctors struggled to unravel the puzzle of Chikane's illness it finally dawned on them that he might have been poisoned. Tests of his clothing and luggage revealed high levels of an organophosphate anticholinesterase—a toxic pesticide. Chikane swore that he had not been anywhere near farms or military areas where he would have been exposed to such a compound. That left one explanation: as SACC president Rev. Manas Buthelezi charged, it was a "deliberate attempt to assassinate our General Secretary."[19]

The 1990s were a blur of historic milestones that took many, including Chikane, by surprise. Nelson Mandela was released from prison in February 1990 and the ANC was legalized. The unthinkable began happening in rapid succession. Negotiations between the ANC and the South African government of F. W. de Klerk got under way in May 1990. But just as quickly, the country's first taste of freedom began to sour. In late March, police opened fire in the Vaal townships near Johannesburg, killing dozens. In July, the first of an escalating series of massacres on commuter trains occurred in Johannesburg. The worst incident was a September attack on black commuters in which twenty-six people died and over one hundred were injured. An orgy of bloodletting within the black community commenced. While there was mounting evidence that violence flowed from the cynical strategy of the de Klerk regime to play off black political factions against one another, there was also the disheartening reality, conceded by Mandela, that the poor communities were steeped in a "culture of violence."

Chikane began shuttling to the violence-torn province of Natal in a futile attempt to mediate between groups loyal to the ANC and the Zulu-based Inkatha Freedom Party. He was a vocal critic of the de Klerk government, charging that it was behind a secret "third force" that was instigating the unprecedented violence. "The time has come to name the devil," he declared in 1992.

The rapid pace of politics left the church in a quandary. Throughout the eighties and early nineties, the churches had deferred to the liberation movements as the voice of the oppressed. But now the ANC was assuming a quasi-governmental role as it negotiated an end to apartheid. Chikane had originally argued that the church should have observer status at the negotiations, but he was rebuffed—to his relief. He was slowly becoming aware that roles were shifting and the church still had to maintain its commitment to speak for the voiceless. "The cause of labor, the unemployed, women and other groups, whose concerns can so easily be forgotten in any encounter between the main players, is where we need to look to discern the will of God. We must be in critical solidarity with those who the Bible calls 'the least,'" he declared.[20]

Another sign of the changing times came in 1990 from the church that banished him. The Apostolic Faith Mission apologized to Chikane and announced that it was reinstating him as a pastor. He was promptly elected head of the black section of the AFM Church, and is now vice president of the newly unified nonracial church. He was eager to once again be "grounded" as a pastor serving a congregation. He declined the church's offer to serve a wealthy congregation and instead took over as pastor in the church in which he had grown up, the congregation begun by his father in the poor Soweto neighborhood of Naledi.

Chikane remained on the sharp edge of the democratic transition when he was appointed as a commissioner on the Independent Electoral Commission in late 1993. The IEC oversaw the April 1994 elections. The commission, like the elections, was controversial. Chikane was praised as "one of the few who emerged unscathed" for his last-minute success in organizing elections in the former homeland of Bophuthatswana.[21]

In July 1994, two months after Nelson Mandela became president, Chikane surprised his church colleagues when he announced that he was stepping down as head of the SACC. His seven years as its leader had been the most tumultuous in the history of the South African church. He had led the SACC with a rare combination of ferocity and humility that earned him the wrath—and eventually the respect—of his adversaries.

The South African Navy warship steams slowly toward its berth eight miles from Cape Town. The sailors are all in crisp dress whites, scurrying to and fro with stiff military precision. But their job on this February 1997 day is to act as waiters rather than soldiers: the ship has been transformed into a VIP clubhouse and they are serving the assembled guests hors d'oeuvres and drinks. The sailors are clearly uncomfortable with the assignment, as one of them struggles valiantly to keep a tray of fresh-squeezed orange juices from pitching into the ocean as the ship lists. On the stern, navy frogmen with all manner of knives strapped to their extremities peer into the deep blue yonder of the Atlantic Ocean in search of enemies.

Just a few years earlier these sailors would have found a ripe picking of foes among the guests milling on deck noshing warm croissants. But this is the new South Africa, and the erstwhile enemies are now the civilian bosses of this floating arsenal. South African Deputy President Thabo Mbeki is hosting U.S. Vice President Al Gore on a tour of Robben Island, the former prison colony where Nelson Mandela spent eighteen of his twenty-seven-and-a-half years in prison. Standing beside Mbeki, whose father, Govan Mbeki, occupied the cell next to Mandela, is Frank Chikane, the deputy president's right-hand man.

Despite the blazing hot summer sun, the dignitaries are dressed in the customary uniforms of power. Chikane is sporting a double-breasted navy blue suit and a red tie, and consequently the sweat is running off his forehead in steady rivulets. His air—glad-handing the Americans one moment, in a strategy huddle with Mbeki the next, and frequently hunched over his cell phone—is part celebrity, part diplomat.

Former Robben Island prisoner Ahmed Kathrada, now an aide to President Mandela, is regaling the guests with tales of prison life. The prison was dubbed the "University of Robben Island" by those who passed through it. It was a crucible of political debate and strategizing, a place where young activists first met the icons of the struggle, such as Mandela and former ANC internal leader Walter Sisulu. The last prisoners were moved from Robben Island in December 1996. The island is now open to the public and is being transformed into a "museum of the freedom struggle."

"We want Robben Island remembered as a place of suffering, but also as a triumph of the forces of justice over injustice, of the new South Africa over the old South Africa," Kathrada proclaims.

As I wait in front of Mandela's former cell for the dignitaries, a South African policeman ushers a contingent of Secret Service agents through. The Boer nods toward Mandela's cell and snips acerbically, "This is now a holy shrine."

Gore and Mbeki soon stroll down the narrow prison corridor to the accompaniment of flashing cameras. The names on the cells they pass read like a who's who of the South African government: President Mandela, provincial premiers Tokyo Sexwale (Gauteng), Ray Mhlaba (Eastern Cape), and Walter Sisulu. Mbeki then leads Gore into Mandela's six-by-nine-foot cell. Gore stares solemnly at the bare green walls, cement floor, steel bed, and lone barred window and is clearly taken aback by the Spartan conditions. "It's a very moving experience," he pronounces. Robben Island represents "a triumph of the human spirit. What they endured is unbelievable," he says, sounding canned in spite of himself.

The entourage then moves over to the rock quarry where Mandela and his colleagues spent years breaking large limestone rocks into smaller rocks. Finding Chikane among the bright white rocks, I ask him what it feels like to be on Robben Island. Although he was never imprisoned here, the place saddens him. "For me it's not something you could enjoy at all. But it remains a symbol of how people were able to survive this type of struggle. And it's been a miracle that we went through that experience and the country is free today."

What's the point of bringing Gore and other dignitaries here? Chikane is clear on this one. "So they will really be in touch with reality."

Reality. It has always been Chikane's strong suit. These days, when many old revolutionaries are getting drunk on the power of their new privilege,

Chikane is struggling to stay in touch with reality. So he has used his new-found wealth as a top government official to build himself a spacious home—not in the leafy enclaves of the formerly all-white Johannesburg suburbs, but in the gritty womb of Soweto. He and his family now occupy a new two-story home surrounded by ornately scrolled twelve-foot-high security gates in Diepkloof. It is a neighborhood that was once dubbed "Beirut" for the running street battles with police that used to take place there. From his bedroom he has a view overlooking the Diepkloof Hostels, the drab rows of human warehouses that were a flashpoint of ANC-Inkatha fighting in the early nineties.

Chikane's house has the unfinished feel of a place that he just passes through. It is his fate that his life will remain perpetually on the run. The living room walls are bare. The furniture is so new I feel like I am sitting in a showroom. Large plants sit in the window, eternally green, eternally fake. The main sign of life is the rock music that wafts in from the garage, where sixteen-year-old Obie Chikane is cranking the tunes from dad's new BMW.

Frank Chikane sits in one of the new stuffed chairs. He makes light of the fact that he hasn't had the time to set up the house much. "I've been too *busy*," he confesses sheepishly. The conversation inevitably migrates back to politics. "We never realized during this whole apartheid struggle—this whole moral fight—how it really worked. This house," he says motioning to the material kitsch that his neighbors can only fantasize about, "has no value." It is built in Soweto, a place where no one aspires to live. Deprived of an asset base, blacks have no way to obtain loans and thus no capital to invest in a business. It is the simple genius of apartheid, a system that carefully and methodically manufactured poverty.

"The majority of my [government] colleagues have moved out of Soweto," Chikane concedes. The flight of the black middle class is a source of bitter resentment among Sowetans. "We've decided we're going to stay with the people around here. The kids can manage—they can go to school in Yeoville," a multiracial Johannesburg neighborhood about thirty minutes away.

Reality is all around us as we set out driving across Soweto. In the car is the whole Chikane clan: Kagiso and three sons—Obakeng, thirteen-year-old Otlile, and six-year-old Rekgotsofetse. It is Sunday morning, and we are headed to church. Chikane takes leave from his relentless schedule of hosting foreign leaders and secret negotiations to minister in one of Soweto's poorest communities, near where he grew up. Naledi, he jokes, is Soweto's "Wild West."

Chikane wheels his spotless, steel blue BMW—a government perk—through the potholed streets. Around us are miles of small cinder-block homes. This vast black city is a jumbled amalgam of First and Third World customs. Cars mingle nonchalantly with the occasional horse-drawn cart on the road. Cows graze in the median strip. Look one way and you see a modern power plant. Look the other way and you glimpse a scene that could be carved from the formal black homeland of Transkei: women working in golden fields of mealie. Sowetans are survivors. They are nothing if not resourceful.

Chikane has described Naledi as "impoverished, violent and depressed," and explains "it is here that my ongoing struggle to make sense of the Christian faith is grounded. If what I believe and preach does not make sense [here among] 'the least' in society, then it is not the kind of theology which will ultimately matter too much in South Africa."[22] And so Chikane takes leave from the hallowed halls of power about twice a month to take a reality test in his childhood neighborhood.

This morning, Chikane has had to get up early to take care of two hours of urgent government business before going to church. As we drive, I ask him how he manages to go from feting world leaders one day to navigating dirt roads in Soweto the next. He laughs—he too is struck by the stark contrasts. "This is another world, but it's become part of me," he muses. As he often does, he explains his outlook in terms of his "integrated theology."

"For me, faith and religion . . . and all these other aspects of my involvement are about life. Therefore it's about how all these other activities contribute to the betterment of people's lives in a sense." His ability to move between worlds comes from his "spiritual perspective."

We finally arrive at the Apostolic Faith Mission of Naledi, an avocado green stucco structure that stands above the small low-slung houses of the community. Children are running around outside in a loosely organized Sunday school class, and many come up to greet their pastor, Rev. Chikane.

"Dumela," he greets them in Sotho, smiling broadly. Chikane points out with pride that the congregation built the church itself a few years ago.

After a bank refused to extend a loan to the church, Chikane implored the congregants to help themselves. They mustered scarce change, salvaged used bricks from a nearby demolition, and painted the building. "They owe no one," he declares like a proud father doting over his child.

The service has already begun by the time we enter. The small hall is filled with simple wooden pews that are overflowing with more than one hundred people. Tinted windows substitute for stained glass, and the beige walls are streaked with watermarks from the leaking roof. Soulful melodies ring out and people are swaying hypnotically to the music.

A baby sleeps in the center aisle, while his mother stomps the floor and sings next to him, her eyes closed, head back, arms open, and sweat running profusely from her brow. A man sitting next to me, bent over with age, has tears streaming down his cheeks as he sings. The thick smell of the township—anthracite coal smoke and diesel fumes—mixes with the scent of perfume and perspiration.

A quartet of young women moves to the front of the hall. A petite girl steps forward and begins to lead the congregation with a soaring gospel voice reminiscent of a young Mahalia Jackson. "I want to be able to walk in the footsteps of John to the city," she belts out. Just then, Chikane's cell phone chirps. He trots out of the church to field the call. Ten minutes later, he's back sitting in his pew, his flock hardly noticing the intrusion of his other world.

There is none of the formality and restraint of the mainstream Christian churches here. But then the AFM began with services held under trees; indeed, many of its rural branches still hold services outdoors or in people's homes.

Chikane strides over the worn red carpet to the pulpit. White lace and red ribbons are draped around the wooden lectern, and it is framed by plastic flowers. Behind him is a large rose-colored crucifix painted on the wall.

"Hallelujah!" exclaims Chikane, smiling warmly at the sight of his congregation.

"Hallelujah!" comes the excited choral response. Chikane is dressed smartly as always, sporting a trimly tailored designer shirt and a brightly colored tie promoting Cape Town's bid to host the 2004 Olympics.[23] As is customary, he begins by introducing his guests, photographer Paul Weinberg and myself—not that the two white faces in a sea of black had gone unnoticed. "You are welcome here!" he declares.

"*Yebo* [yes]—welcome!" comes the response from the floor.

Chikane then lowers his head and raises his hands. "We must say a special prayer for those victims of circumstance," he says. "In Lesotho, Angola, Zaire, Swaziland, where they gain nothing from the fighting. We call upon the Lord to find peace." Tears streak his face as he continues. "May God bless them."

The congregation breaks into song, and I immediately recognize the melody. It is a soulful version of "Nkosi Sikelel' iAfrika" (God Bless Africa), the plaintive African hymn that is now part of the new national anthem.

> God bless Africa,
> Let its horn be raised
> Listen to our prayers
> God bless, God bless
> Come spirit, come spirit
> Holy spirit
> God bless us.
> We, thy children.[24]

I have heard this tune sung defiantly with fists raised at protest rallies, sung drunkenly while waving the new South African flag at sports events, and sung blandly over an orchestral backdrop in the new parliament. The soaring melody, once banned as a potent symbol of black liberation, always moves me.

The heartfelt singing in the Naledi church is the most beautiful rendering of Nkosi that I have ever heard. My moist eyes blink involuntarily at this performance. It seems to well up from a place deep inside those assembled, and is expressed as an outpouring of their devotion to God, as the melody wafts out the open windows and over the township.

When the phone rang on June 28, 1995, Frank Chikane was expecting Paul Erasmus's call. Journalists from the South African progressive weekly newspaper *Mail and Guardian* had asked the cleric whether he would meet with Erasmus. He replied with a question of his own: Will Erasmus reveal who poisoned me? No, came the answer.

"I want the story," demanded Chikane. "He must say, 'I know who did it, and this is his name.' Then we can meet—*that* will be business." But

Chikane saw little harm in agreeing to speak with Erasmus on the phone. Despite his skepticism, he was intrigued to hear out his former tormentor.

"Why did you call me, Paul?" queried Chikane after some initial banter. Erasmus had already explained that he wanted to apologize, but he knew Chikane wouldn't settle for that explanation. Chikane's gentle, pastoral tone helped to disarm Erasmus.

The cop was frank: "I'd rather tell you the story than be sacrificed by some other guy at the top who tells you."

Chikane appreciated Erasmus's candor. The activist was not interested in the cop's sentimentalism and would not have believed it anyway. "He was very honest. I mean, he didn't say 'It's because I've repented,'" Chikane recounts. The churchman then asked Erasmus why he tried to kill him.

"We were taught that you were a communist terrorist who was going to destroy South Africa and take revenge on the whites," explained Erasmus. "We believed what we were told."

Chikane has surprising empathy for the foot soldiers of apartheid. "It was easy to understand," says Chikane of Erasmus's story. "You grow up in an Afrikaner family. You're made to believe all this stuff, and they take you at eighteen years. You become a policeman to deal with these guys who are causing the trouble and you do it with all your being and your heart, believing that you're doing the right thing."

At the same time, Chikane is dismissive of Erasmus, and doubts his version of the poisoning incident. Erasmus says that Chikane's clothes were poisoned at his residence, while the former victim has information that his luggage was opened and contaminated at Jan Smuts Airport in Johannesburg. "If he wasn't directly involved in the actual poisoning, he can only guess where it happened. But he is not telling me the real story," says Chikane.

The activist is also skeptical of how Erasmus has deflected blame to others. Throughout hearings of the Truth and Reconciliation Commission, everyone from government officials to township youths routinely pins blame for the worst acts on others while carefully maintaining their own innocence. They may simply be lying to save their own skin. Or perhaps it is a psychological technique that enables criminals to live with themselves. The worst crimes never had perpetrators, only spectators. The best example of this comes from former president de Klerk, who has audaciously and steadfastly maintained his ignorance of all apartheid crimes that occurred during his five-year presidency.

Perpetrators "have the tendency of telling the story around other people rather than themselves," muses Chikane. "Erasmus's whole story will always end up with somebody else killing, not himself. It is protection for themselves, really."

Yet there is something that compels Chikane and other victims to meet their tormentors. At worst, it reopens old wounds. At best, it permits closure on a painful past. "I'm still looking forward to meeting him one day," Chikane concludes, "but it will hurt if we meet and the story's not complete."

I ask him why the truth matters so much. Chikane explains, "Healing can't be complete until you know the truth. But if somebody could come up tomorrow and say, 'I did it and this is how we did it and that's it,' then it's over. You can forgive him and pass the matter."

Just tell the truth, and old wounds are miraculously healed. Does reconciliation come that cheaply? Chikane has already confided in me that he was recently hospitalized for a bad infection that doctors attribute to injuries that he sustained during his torture two decades ago. On a larger scale, the black community continues to struggle with a psychological inferiority complex that flows from years of subjugation. Then there are the scores of families condemned to poverty because a loved one was denied a job, or a home, or a life . . .

How does a nation deal with the memory of its brutal past? How can there be reconciliation without justice?

Nine thick-necked, burly white policemen walk single file into the packed tenth-floor hearing room at the Truth and Reconciliation Commission (TRC) headquarters in downtown Cape Town. The cops, many of whom currently hold senior positions in the madeover South African Police Service, take seats in the front row with their backs to the audience. They are here to testify about their role in the killing of the Guguletu Seven. On March 3, 1986, seven young men from the nearby black township of Guguletu were killed in an alleged shootout with these same policemen. The notorious incident became a cause célèbre. The authorities claimed that they had stopped a terrorist attack on that day. Eyewitnesses charged that many of the men had been captured and executed in cold blood by the police.

The hearing begins with a horrific police crime scene video, complete with close-ups of bullet-riddled heads and contorted corpses. Commissioners and other members of the audience let out involuntary gasps of revulsion. I am forced to divert my gaze; a white South African journalist sitting next to me throws her hands around her head in a reflexive act of self-defense.

As the video rolls, mothers and relatives of the dead youths sitting in the audience can take no more. A mother sitting next to me shrieks in grief, grabs her shoe, and throws it at the policemen sitting just ten feet away who had killed her son; several other mothers leap to their feet and break into high-pitched sobs. Pandemonium ensues: chairs tumble, I and other journalists duck, two of the cops bolt to the back, and TRC "briefers" take down the grief-stricken women in bear hugs and swiftly hustle them out of the room. The normally impassive truth commissioners are shaken; Commissioner Dumisa Ntsebeza, head of investigations, implores the audience "not to let this hearing degenerate into a farce."

In the mayhem, I crawl over to lead witness Superintendent William Rudolf Liebenberg, who is sitting near me. The blond, blue-eyed former head of the "terrorist tracking unit" of the Cape Town security police is dressed nattily in a pinstriped navy blue suit. He is startled when I appear alongside him; his large blue eyes are fixed on me like a doe caught in the headlights. I ask him how it made him feel to see the mothers here, upset as they were.

"It's terrible. We never would have done this—to show them these pictures of their children. It's really terrible." I am momentarily dumbstruck by his response. It is too bad he hadn't thought of this before he and his cronies opened up with shotguns and blew away the youths.

This is November 1996, and both the TRC audience and the commissioners are showing signs of battle fatigue. After seven months of hearing one-sided tales of police abuse, the commissioners, who had often sounded polite verging on timid, seem to have discovered their backbones. When Liebenberg strides to the stand moments later, a tenacious and impatient Commissioner Denzel Potgeiter confronts him.

"These people were led into an ambush and killed, weren't they?" charges Potgeiter. Liebenberg denies the accusation, but the commissioner is like a pit bull that won't let go of his prey. Potgeiter badgers, shouts, interrupts, contradicts, points, and stabs the air—after months of restraining himself, he has sprung to life. He says the TRC has new evidence that members of a security police death squad were involved in the operation and that weapons were planted on the youths. A decade after the incident, the commissioners explode the myth that this was merely a routine police maneuver and charge that this celebrated case was a calculated hit.

From a Truth Commission that seemed frightened by its own shadow when it started public hearings in April 1996, this hearing in November marks a turning point. Finally, the gloves have come off and a bit more truth is creeping into the grim puzzle of who did what during apartheid.

But there is still one nagging problem: these newly exposed cops, should they apply for amnesty, will most likely get away with murder.

When I first began attending hearings of the TRC in mid-1996, I was deeply skeptical of the process. South Africans had made a bargain with the devil, and its moral shortcomings were obvious: justice was traded for truth. Killers got freedom, while victims got nothing; whites ignored the hearings entirely. Tears were confined to the victims, just as they were in the past.

The South African Truth and Reconciliation Commission was the most lavishly endowed of the approximately twenty truth commissions that have been constituted around the world since 1974. Formed in late 1995, the TRC comprised seventeen commissioners and a staff of 250. It had a budget of $28 million. The commission was chaired by Nobel Peace Prize laureate Archbishop Desmond Tutu. Its purpose was "to bring about unity and reconciliation . . . based on the principle that reconciliation depends on forgiveness and that forgiveness can only take place if gross violations of human rights are fully disclosed." The commission's most controversial responsibility was the awarding of amnesty to killers. Amnesty would only be denied if an applicant failed to make a complete disclosure of his or her crimes, if the applicant's actions were not politically motivated, or if the deeds were disproportionate to the political goals.

I challenge Chikane to justify what some have decried as a miscarriage of justice. Surrounded by the accouterments of power in his elegantly appointed Tuynhuys office, Chikane does not look the part of haggard victim. But then he has never played that part, not even while he was suspended naked from the ceiling of the Krugersdorp police station during his savage 1977 interrogation. Chikane is a victor, always has been. But he surprises me by his refusal to be smug or vindictive.

Chikane is uncomfortable with the easy talk of reconciliation, and he is angered by the obstacles he encounters in trying to dismantle apartheid. His approach to reconciliation is guided not by saintliness, but by intense pragmatism.

"If I was the Biko family or Goniwe [family] I would say, like they are saying, 'I want these people to be brought to book.' Which is right—justice must be done. Amnesty International also says the same: bring these guys to book, don't give them amnesty." Chikane makes a fist and waves it for emphasis—this issue is dear to him. "My approach has been different, and I don't want everybody to follow that approach. It's a pragmatic approach. It is saying that if you didn't have amnesty and you didn't have the Truth Commission and you were waiting to get information to charge people, you wouldn't have the information, because they will not give you the information. The spectacular things we know [about apartheid crimes] are because of that amnesty. If you remove the amnesty, these guys would never come forward, and you'd depend on investigative capacity to find out [what they did]. And if all [perpetrators] agreed they were not going to give the story—it's *over*, you'll *never* know [the truth] until you *die*." The words roll off his tongue with the rhythmic staccato beat that is a hallmark of his political oratory.

The TRC was the child of compromise, he explains. In agreeing to grant amnesty to killers, the new government and indeed all apartheid victims "had to [balance] the risk of not knowing at all and continuing with life as if nothing has happened—that person who killed would be walking in your midst and could do it again—and the giving of amnesty and knowing and being able to monitor that person." His large round eyes are locked on me. "You know what I'm talking about . . . "

It is clear and unsentimental logic. It is nonetheless agonizing to make peace with. But for Chikane, this is just the hard-nosed calculus of *realpolitik*—something this veteran activist has practiced since he first dared his torturers to martyr him and face the wrath of an angry God.

What about his anger at the guy who poisoned him, I insist, the sadist who crushed his testicles and then roared with laughter?

"It's a pain. [But] I mean, I'm better off: others are dead," he says with a shrug. "You know, it's not just the guy who poisoned me. It's the fact that the top generals, the MPs, politicians, the lot are enjoying themselves. They have their pensions guaranteed, and are earning even double salaries for the death of our people.

"I sympathize with a lot of the policemen who had to do the dirty work," he continues. "For me, [Paul] Erasmus or [Eugene] de Kock [former head of a police death squad] are not the embodiment of evil. It's the guys who are enjoying themselves who are the embodiment of that evil. If you really wanted to do justice, it's not to lock up de Kock. It's to lock up the people who manipulated the madness in de Kock, because they needed half-mad people."

Chikane is not terribly interested in sending people to jail. The best revenge, in his view, is "to create a society that is humane. And you may have to make certain sacrifices to reach that particular goal.

"It's the humanity in you that so hates the thing that was done to you, that says to you, 'You can't do it to that person who did it to you because then you reduce yourself to the level of that person.' If you do that you are sunk—we are all animals [and] we may as well eat each other and that's the end of the world. You must go above that person. *That's* the only way you can save the world."

Reconciliation doesn't come cheaply for Chikane, but he is determined that it must come. "The healing for me is the knowledge. It's not the prosecution, it's not the imprisonment. It's that you've come to me and said 'I'm sorry, I did it.'" With that, this one victim has found a way to triumph over his past.

VICTOR VERSTER PRISON BIDS YOU WELCOME PRESIDENT MANDELA!

The large sign hanging over the heavily guarded entrance to the sprawling prison grounds evokes one of those new South Africa double takes. This is, after all, a prison, and Nelson Mandela its most famous prisoner. But this visit is quintessential Mandela, the high priest of reconciliation, South Africa's new civil religion.

It is November 1996, and Mandela has just been awarded the Freedom of Paarl award. Paarl is a picturesque town cradled in the beautiful Cape winelands. Like much of South Africa, Paarl has a schizophrenic history. It is home to the Taal Museum and Taal Monument, an enigmatic obelisk that is a mute tribute to the Afrikaans language. Paarl is a required stop on Afrikaner cultural pilgrimages.

I first visited Paarl for a very different reason: the TRC was holding three days of hearings on human rights abuses that had occurred there under apartheid. The hearings are being held in a heavily guarded local community hall. A TRC poster inside the door greets visitors: "Don't let our nightmares become our children's."

During the hearings, I hear wrenching testimony of how the nearby colored township Mbekweni was in a state of war for much of the eighties. Residents were under siege not only from the police, but also from a violent rivalry between political factions loyal to the Pan Africanist Congress (PAC) and those loyal to the ANC. In one moving exchange, a colored policeman finally reveals to a still-grieving father how his unarmed teenage son was randomly singled out and shot to death eleven years earlier by a white security policemen.

Mandela decided to pay a return visit to his old prison homestead while he was in town to receive the medal. Victor Verster Prison is a medium / maximum security jail on the rural outskirts of Paarl. Mandela spent the last two-and-a-half years of his twenty-seven-year confinement at this jail.

As soon as I pass the guardhouse at the entrance to the prison, I am immediately lost. I find myself in what appears to be a pleasant suburban community of pastel-colored homes. These are apparently for the staff.

I finally spot a few cars in the distance, and behind them, a pretty little house tucked behind some trees. A graceful archway fronts the house, now occupied by a prison colonel, and the lawn is neatly manicured. A rose bush gives the place a sweet scent. A local prison official on hand explains that this house was built specially for Mandela "as part of reintroducing him to civilized society." A small swimming pool sits in the backyard where Mandela swam daily. Over the back fence are spectacular views of steep rocky mountains and verdant winelands.

Mandela arrives dressed in a beautiful gold shirt (the colorful shirts have become known as Madiba Shirts and are popular items of political couture in South Africa. Madiba is Mandela's clan name.). He steps through the archway and a broad smile of recognition spreads across his face. His face is a rich yellow-brown, framed by a shock of short white hair. He has hearing aids in both ears now, and his gait is more a shuffle than a stride. His pace has been slowed lately due to chronic knee pain. He seems upbeat and happy to be here.

"Some of the best years of my life were spent here," he says, stopping in front of the house. It is an odd claim for an ex-prisoner to make, so he offers an explanation. "The negotiations with the government intensified here, and this was where I met many of the top ANC leaders for the first time." He stands amidst the small troupe of reporters and dignitaries and spins yarns of his time here. Did he ever consider escaping? "No, that would not have been consistent with what we were trying to accomplish," he insists.

Mandela's wry sense of humor is in evidence here. "The one temptation was that the people coming to visit me very much wanted to photograph me," he continues. Since it was illegal to publish photos of Mandela while he was imprisoned, the only extant pictures were ones from the mid-1960s, just after he went to jail. "One person offered me R 250, and I said no. Someone else offered R 500,000, and I said, 'Ohhhhhhhh, *that* is very interesting!' But it would go against the promise I had made [to the government], so I wouldn't allow it."

A touching moment comes when Mandela is reunited with the warder who lived with and cooked for him. Mandela wrote fondly of Warrant Officer James Swart in his autobiography, *Long Walk to Freedom,* detailing the close relationship that he had with both Swart and his family. As we crowd around him inside the house, Mandela asks what has become of Swart. One of his aides replies, "He's outside."

A tall, thin, mustachioed man with salt-and-pepper hair who is dressed in a jacket and tie then walks in. Mandela smiles and greets him warmly, holding Swart's hand as he speaks. "I'll never forget the kindness you and your wife showed me while I was here," he says, looking directly into his eyes. Swart is visibly nervous and at a loss for words. "Thank you very much," Swart mumbles quietly. I ask Swart what kind of prisoner Mandela was. "A real gentleman," he says in a barely audible voice.

Mandela finishes his visit by attending a function for the prison staff, who pack a small auditorium. The meeting begins with a performance by the prison choir, which is composed of inmates from the medium-security section. They sing "Oh What a Wonderful World." Swaying to a strumming guitar, the convicts croon, "I see every man as my brother, let's put away our differences and let's all be friends." I try to shut out the macabre thoughts that keep creeping into my mind about the crimes these men may have committed to earn a berth here. Instead, I concentrate on just taking in this surreal scene.

Mandela then speaks. He says that many people ask him how he has avoided being embittered by the time he spent in jail—more than a third of his life. "This place contributed to my own approach in this country," he says, explaining how most of the warders had treated him with dignity here. He tells the audience of both Afrikaner and colored guards, "Some Afrikaner guards were very crude and cruel. But when an Afrikaner changes, he changes 100 percent and becomes a real friend." The staff cheered him when he notes that he and his comrades had learned that warders were treated poorly by their superiors, and the activists exploited that to organize among the guards. Many of the guards are wearing T-shirts with the emblem of POPCRU, the progressive national police union.

The event ends with the euphoric prison staff passing their children up to Mandela to have their pictures taken with him. It is the old South Africa turned on its head: a former prisoner returning to thank people who collaborated in stealing his freedom. But by treating each other with dignity, jailer and prisoner alike learned to respect and even love one another.

It was while observing hearings of the Truth and Reconciliation Commission over the course of its first year that my skepticism about the amnesty-for-truth bargain began to fade. I even began to feel uneasy about facile criticisms being leveled at the commission—criticism that I had made myself. After attending numerous hearings and talking about the TRC daily with regular South Africans, I came to a surprising realization about this flawed, compromised national process of introspection and confession: it was working.

By the time the TRC finished most of its investigation in 1998, it had succeeded in exposing the truth behind nearly every major massacre and political assassination of the apartheid era. Among these were notorious cases—such as the assassinations of Steve Biko and the quartet of UDF activists known as the Cradock Four—that had remained shrouded in mystery despite numerous inquests. This track record is all the more impressive when one considers that as recently as 1994, an inquest into the deaths of the Cradock Four, whose burned bodies were discovered by a roadside in June 1985, ended inconclusively. Time and again the henchmen of apartheid proved their talent at keeping secrets. It seemed a grim truism that what the assassins didn't want to reveal would simply never be known. Maybe South Africa's new gumshoes would crack a few old mysteries, but without the TRC the truth behind most crimes would simply go to the grave with the killers.

Just as striking as the revelations were the benefits that many victims of apartheid violence told me they had gained from the TRC hearings. Many of the victim witnesses at the hearings said they felt a weight had been lifted from them by airing their story before their community. Echoing Chikane, victims told me that the hearings have enabled them to finally close the book on past tragedies.

Take Father Michael Lapsley, for example. When I first met him in Zimbabwe in 1984, he was a hip, young Anglican priest often seen buzzing around town on his motorbike. But he was an outspoken member of the ANC in exile, and that made him a marked man. In 1990, two months after Mandela's release from jail, Lapsley received a parcel bomb in Zimbabwe that blew off both his hands and an eye and left him fighting for his life. The TRC determined that it was the work of the Civil Cooperation Bureau, the death squad of South African military intelligence. An eloquent and moving speaker, Lapsley has told his story in forums around the world. In 1996, he told it to the TRC.

As we sat in his living room on a warm summer evening in Cape Town, "Father Mike" clutched a glass of beer in the steel hooks that he now has in place of hands. He reflected about his TRC testimony, "I felt that my own story was becoming a permanent part of the story of the people of South Africa. The fact that [the TRC] is an official commission set up by the state and the way in which the commission acknowledged the truth about what happened to me in a dignified way had a lot of importance for me."

Unfortunately, most white South Africans have pointedly ignored the testimonials of injustice, just as they did under apartheid. But it would be misleading to say that the attitudes of white South Africans have not also changed in important ways. Today, whites have been disabused of their ignorance about the past. The daily news reports about the TRC have worked like water on a stone: slowly but surely, a rough historical consensus has emerged about the injustices that were perpetrated under apartheid. Even right-wing whites grudgingly acknowledged to me that blacks were unjustly treated, and that there were widespread human rights abuses. This shift from denial to acknowledgment is crucial: there can be no reconciliation in the future without basic agreement about what happened in the past.

Of course, for some South Africans, truth is not enough. I asked the sister of one of the Guguletu Seven how she felt about giving amnesty to perpetrators. It was February 1997, and we had just emerged from a second round of TRC hearings on the fateful incident.

"I don't support amnesty," said the sister of Christopher Piet, her eyes still moist and swollen after seeing a photo of a smiling policeman standing next to her dead brother's body. "They should be punished. They don't look sorry for what they did. Now we have just opened the wounds again." Piet is not alone: Steve Biko's wife is the best known of those who would rather see her husband's killers go to jail than receive amnesty.

Yet what is surprising is how many South Africans *can* forgive what happened in the past. The majority of black South Africans with whom I spoke support the TRC process, including granting amnesty. They are tired of conflict and bloodshed. They want to move on and build their country. They say they are willing to forgive—but only if they know who to forgive.

What good is truth? The question nagged at me. Then I watched a report on South African TV about the Mothers of the Plaza de Mayo in Argentina. They are the mothers of people who disappeared in Argentina's "dirty war" against alleged leftists in the seventies. Each week since the late seventies the mothers have stood in grim silent witness in downtown Buenos Aires, bravely trying to ferret out the truth about what happened to their loved ones. They are a haunting symbol of what happens when a nation fails to reckon with its past.

The significance of this was driven home to me in March 1997, when mothers of victims of state violence marched again, this time in Guguletu, outside Cape Town. It was the eleventh anniversary of the killing of the Guguletu Seven. Cynthia Ngewu, mother of slain activist Christopher Piet, addressed the small crowd that gathered on the raw autumn day.

"I want to thank the Truth Commission because although it has opened up wounds, through that process we were able to know the truth," she said. "Now we know the perpetrators. I am asking God to forgive those people." A black man then shouted from the crowd, "Long live the TRC!"

That's when I understood the value of this confessional process to a nation struggling to deal with its brutal past. In South Africa, there will be no Mothers of the Plaza de Mayo. Because in place of most of apartheid's torturous secrets, there is now truth.

When Nelson Mandela took the reigns of power in May 1994, Rev. Frank Chikane had his pick of high offices. He was courted by top business and government leaders who were keen for his counsel and who lusted after the cachet of his impeccable struggle credentials. In typical Chikane style, he baffled his suitors by opting to leave behind the revelers at the party and strike out for far shores. His destination: Harvard University, the Mother Church of western capitalist thinking.

Chikane craved not just the trappings of power, but the tools. And he knew that fixing the economic damage wrought by apartheid was going to be the single greatest challenge facing the new government. Over the objections of Mandela and Deputy President Mbeki, Chikane left South Africa and pursued a master's degree in public administration at Harvard's Kennedy School of Government. He kept a low profile while there, but gradually his classmates learned who he was. Some of them questioned the logic of having him play the part of student when he knew more than the lecturers did. "I thought that myself at times," says Chikane with amusement, "especially when I had to sit through a course about negotiations and mediation."

In his final months at Harvard, he received a call from South Africa. A familiar gravelly voice crackled from the other end.

"We need you back home, Frank," implored Mandela. "*Now.*"

Chikane returned and was promptly drafted to be special advisor to Thabo Mbeki. The appointment was widely praised. Chikane enjoyed a reputation as an independent thinker who would offer Mbeki—who is praised for his intellect but criticized as aloof and uncharismatic—much needed counsel. Chikane also offered something that Mbeki lacked: a deep connection to the poor and the grass roots. "He's one of the last of the humanists," said a fellow activist of Chikane. It was a grounding that the heady new leaders sorely needed.

Chikane was quickly elevated to the post of director-general of Mbeki's office. By late 1996, Mbeki was already running the day-to-day affairs of government, freeing the seventy-eight-year-old Mandela to bask in the glow of revered elder statesman.

As top lieutenant to the president-in-waiting, Chikane is now ubiquitous at scenes of power. When U.S. Vice President Al Gore disembarks from his plane in South Africa, he is greeted by Chikane. When South Africa is secretly brokering talks between deposed Zairian dictator Mobutu Sese Seko and rebel leader (now Democratic Republic of Congo president) Laurent Kabila, it is Chikane making the deals and keeping the international media guessing.

I was with Chikane during the delicate Congo peace talks in early 1997. As we traveled around Soweto one morning, he reacted with a combination of amazement and disgust at the emerging media reports. "When you don't tell journalists what they want to hear, they simply make up stories and print them," he said, his voice rising in astonishment. He chuckled, "I would hate to be a historian relying on media accounts of these talks to write about what actually happened."

From his office in Pretoria, Frank Chikane has a commanding view over the urban sprawl to the broader South African landscape. Where he sits now, the dilemma of forgiving the excesses of brutal cops who wanted him dead suddenly doesn't loom so large. Reconciling the economy is proving far more bedeviling. Indeed, while some former liberation movement colleagues get drunk on the elixir of power, Chikane is sobered by the realities of his job.

"Since we came into government I've been introduced to the reality of the damage that apartheid has done, beyond one's imagination . . . During the struggle, we would not have realized how much these guys between the mid-eighties and the time of the negotiations actually escalated the debt of this country. They spent recklessly as they came close to ending power." He cites profligate spending by the National Party in the former black homelands that was intended to buy black votes, and enormous salary increases granted to white civil servants that "enriched them overnight."

Frank Chikane has now come face to face with the evil genius of apartheid. He recalls how his family was forcibly moved four times in his lifetime and how black entrepreneurs were forbidden to open shops in Soweto or enter into business partnerships. "It looked like just a stupid racist thing at the time," he says. "But in fact, it was a very clever, cruel structure to say 'exclude them completely so that the 13 percent [white minority] can enjoy themselves.' . . . You can see how this system was designed to impoverish and exclude you completely."

Soweto is an appropriate yardstick by which to measure progress in the new South Africa. To look around with an untrained eye, one sees 360 degrees of poverty. Corrugated metal shacks are shoehorned in behind brick houses. Open sewers run through the shantytowns. Every conceivable patch of earth is utilized in some way to support life.

The Chikane family has lived in Soweto for over forty years. They know firsthand all that is ugly and beautiful here. And they are eager to show me, a visitor, what has been accomplished by the new government.

Kagiso Chikane is a bright, soft-spoken mother of three who has been the rock of the family throughout her husband's tumultuous career. If there really is a saint in this family, Frank would readily bestow the title on her. She is a lecturer in literature at Soweto's Vista University. Kagiso is reserved and deferential around her husband, an unassuming presence next to her charismatic counterpart. But today she is animated. She is decked out in her Sunday finery, a bright floral dress topped by a straw hat. She is eager to speak her mind about her hometown.

"For me, a person staying in Soweto, when I hear people saying the new government hasn't done anything, there are no changes—they should ask *us*." Her face crinkles at the brow with frustration. We are stopped at a traffic light, surrounded by minibus taxis on one side, a horse-drawn cart on the other. The thick smell of diesel fumes hangs in the warm morning air.

Kagiso points to a road crew busy paving. "Look at this tarred road being constructed. Can you see?" she says, wagging her finger at the workers. "It's part of the RDP [Reconstruction and Development Program]. And here," she points to an intersection, "there used to be so many accidents. Now this new government has put up the traffic light. The old government didn't even *know* that this was a busy junction!"

We enter the community where Kagiso's mother-in-law lives. We pass rows of small houses and dusty plots of land. We slow down for another road crew. She recounts how she would invariably get a flat tire from driving these trash-strewn dirt roads in the past. Now the road is paved.

We stop at the home of Frank's mother, Erenia Chikane. Despite her son's new status and wealth, the Chikane matriarch has chosen to remain in the home her husband obtained in 1957. It is a modest brick house with a small dirt yard. The scrolled steel fence in front distinguishes her house from her neighbors. The elderly lady in thick glasses swaggers side to side as she ambles out to the car. She smiles broadly at me and shakes my hand as she climbs in.

Kagiso is on a roll—her pent-up aggravation with the carping is obvious. "My mother-in-law . . . used to pay lots of money to go to the clinic.

She is hypertensive. Now, she gets the medicine for free . . . To have free medical care for the elderly and children—that's a big thing.

"Who can tell us that nothing has changed? For an ordinary Sowetan who knows they can go to a clinic at any time and be attended to for free—then I don't know why people complain. That's a *major* change in people's lives."

She isn't finished. She points out some new homes under construction, but acknowledges that there is a large housing backlog. "People expect the government to change the apartheid era overnight. I mean how do you repair that damage that was done for so long? Suddenly people are saying houses have to be built, [when] houses were not built for years and years. People can't expect the government to build houses for all of us. I don't think there is any country where the government provides housing for everybody. It would just be bankrupt."

The problem of matching reality to expectations has dogged the new government. It is one of the paradoxes of the transformation process that people are voicing dissatisfaction at the slow pace of change. From one vantage point, the government has taken great leaps in providing housing, health care, and education to disadvantaged people. But measured against the enormous needs and the wild expectations of how life would change when apartheid fell, the government has done almost nothing.

Frank Chikane has spoken eloquently about his mission to serve "the least" in society. As we pass through the poor neighborhoods of his youth, I wonder out loud how long it will be before change trickles down to these, the poorest people.

Chikane replies by recounting his experience the previous week. He had to perform a funeral for a member of his congregation. The family lived in a squatter camp—or "informal settlement," in the new parlance—and it took three days for the family to clear a path through people's yards so that the hearse could get through. Even in that desperately poor area, a woman came up to him and expressed her gratitude.

"I was squatting there and [my shack was] being demolished by police every day," she told him. "Now I'm in a place where I can't be demolished."

The yardstick for change differs for each person, he insists. "For the child who went without a meal to school, now that there's one meal, you know, it's a dramatic change. It's like a doubling of whatever they had overnight. But for Frank Chikane one meal is not enough. I want shares on the stock market!

"I would say generally that there hasn't been a dramatic change in the country because you could never have it . . . you'd need a Marshall Plan with lots of resources from outside. We don't have that, so it wouldn't happen like that. [Change] is going to happen in small portions, which is painful, you know." He notes that his younger brother is struggling to make it as a businessman. But he can't qualify for any bank loans, which keeps his business from growing. "My brother may die before much change happens in his life.

"What *has* changed is that people can be human, can be themselves, can have their rights. But in economic terms, not much has changed."

How long will it take?

"The people at the bottom have more patience than the people at the top. You see, the people at the top have all sorts of possibilities and options. They know they can make another million tomorrow, but there is something that obstructs them. The people at the bottom don't even have the option to make the million. And so they understand the crisis better than the people at the top."

It is true that the poorest South Africans have so far been remarkably patient as the promised changes in their country remain frustratingly unfulfilled. But their desperation is being expressed in other ways: in South Africa's exploding crime rate, for example. Poor people may be patient, but when they are hungry some will do whatever it takes to eat.

I look forward to returning to the Naledi AFM Church. It is a place of raw spiritual power, where nothing mediates between the congregants and the spirits they are praying to.

An old man in a tattered black blazer limps up to the pulpit to receive communion. A spray of silver hair elegantly frames his black face. Rev. Chikane leans over and brings a chalice to his lips. "The blood of *Jeeee-zus* was spilled for me," the pastor sings along with the congregation.

A large woman clutching a gold staff steps forward. Kagiso Chikane leans over to explain to me that she is a "prophetess," a traditional healer. The church views these healers, known as *sangomas,* as anti-Christian witch doctors. This *sangoma* comes forward and Chikane and junior pastor Enoch Mbanta lay hands on her head. The entire congregation begins fervently speaking in tongues to purge the devil from its midst. The chanting crescendos. This is hotline religion, and it sends chills up my spine. People are shaking in the aisles. I turn and see tears streaking the faces of several women and men. Chikane stands with his eyes closed, hands raised, chanting feverishly, communing with God.

The chanting gives way to an octet that suddenly assembles in front of Chikane. As the choir sings, a tall thin young man steps forward, extends his long arms, and launches into a soaring alto solo. His head is thrust back and his eyes are closed.

"Help me Lord. Help me to walk this *fi-nal* mile. Ya know I've got this feelin' that everything is gonna be *alllll ra-ht,*" he sings.

"*Yebo!*" comes the fervent response from the congregation. "Everything gonna be all *right!*"

# THE VANQUISHED ASSASSIN

PAUL ERASMUS: WARRANT OFFICER,
SECURITY BRANCH, SOUTH AFRICAN POLICE

Paul Erasmus, 1997.

**THE THIRTY-SOMETHING MAN** in jeans and a leather jacket leaned against his car, his stylish blow-dried blond hair framing his bearded face. A cigarette hung limply from the corner of his mouth. Peering from behind dark Ray-Bans, he struck the pose of a cool street operator, gazing indifferently at everything and nothing at the same time.

But there was something unsettling about him. Maybe it was his Fu Manchu mustache that drooped in a permanent scowl. Or maybe it was that penetrating gaze, like the lazy stare of a predatory animal, that always made you feel like you were being sized up for the kill.

Across the street, a colorful assortment of people ranging from black township dwellers in their frayed overcoats to clergymen in collars and frocks entered and left a six-story tan building. The sign over its door said KHOTSO HOUSE—the name means "peace" in Xhosa. Inside was a beehive of activists: there was a group working for rural land rights; a photographic collective that was sending stark images of apartheid violence around the world; the Black Sash "advice office," which assisted people who were seeking help for pass law violations. At the center of this activity was the headquarters of the South African Council of Churches, headed by Rev. Frank Chikane. To the enforcers of apartheid, the occupants of this building were The Enemy.

Outside, the guy in the black leather jacket and jeans just waited. He reigned over his turf like a lion pacing his territory. His prominent gut bulged over his belt; when he turned around, a telltale bulge of a different sort sat snugly in the small of his back. I walked by him numerous times coming in and out of Khotso House in 1984, never suspecting who he was.

But to the activists inside Khotso House, the man struck the classic pose of a member of the dreaded Security Branch of the South African Police (SAP). Those who suspected his motives were justified in their paranoia.

His name was Paul Erasmus. His mission was simple: destroy The Enemy.

Paul Erasmus is hard to find these days. That's because Erasmus, once the hunter, is now himself a hunted man. After becoming disillusioned with police work in the early nineties, Erasmus began divulging the SAP's dirty secrets to the Goldstone Commission of Inquiry Regarding the Prevention of Public Violence and Intimidation in 1994. The Goldstone Commission (named for its chairman, Judge Richard Goldstone) was an independent body created in 1991 as part of a National Peace Accord. It was charged with investigating various acts of violence—including township massacres and so-called third force attacks backed by police—that were taking place with shocking regularity during the de Klerk rule. When Erasmus turned against the state, his former colleagues turned on him. Their brief: once again, destroy The Enemy—in this case, one of their own.

When I finally speak to Erasmus on the phone, he is apologetic about his delay in returning my call. "Sorry—I've been away," he says brusquely. His troubled tone makes me suspect there is more to his absence; I press him delicately for details.

"I've actually been in hospital. I'm suffering with post-traumatic stress syndrome—what you Americans would call 'Vietnam Syndrome.'" I reply sympathetically, but he dismisses my concern. "I guess you could say this is the spoils of the conflict."

I arrange to meet Erasmus in a picturesque seaside tourist town where he has been living of late. It is cloak-and-dagger stuff: he agrees to meet but refuses to let me near his house, and I must swear not to reveal to anyone where I am going. My instructions are to call him from a pay phone once I reach town. I do as told, wondering whether his paranoia is justified or if this is just his way of making himself appear more important than he really is.

We finally meet in the living room of a local bed-and-breakfast where I've arranged to stay. The ex-cop in his early forties shows up wearing his trademark black leather jacket, navy polyester pants, and a shirt open to mid-chest. A silver chain sparkles from amid a thick crop of black chest hair that protrudes from his shirt. I am surprised to spot a small earring hanging from his left ear—it is an incongruous sign of rebelliousness. His gut still bulges over his belt, and he sports a full beard that is now flecked with gray. A bit of his old swagger is evident, but he is too distracted to seem intimidating. His brow is deeply furrowed these days—his mind is always racing. He lights the first of a nonstop chain of Winfield cigarettes the moment he arrives.

So this is it, I think to myself: here before me sits one of apartheid's dreaded enforcers, one of the shock troops of repression—a schleppy overweight guy in polyester pants and gaudy necklaces. Sporting styles that are twenty years out of date, Erasmus reminds me more of a bad Elvis impersonation than the Rambo he once fancied himself.

He dispenses with small talk and cuts right to the point of our meeting. We settle into overstuffed chairs, surrounded by grandmotherly bed-and-breakfast kitsch. His pack of cigarettes and a mysterious attaché case at his side, Erasmus begins to tell me his story.

Paul Erasmus never dreamed he'd become a cop. As a young South African in high school, he shared a commonly held view of the South African Police as a haven for the dregs of Afrikaner society.[1] The main qualification needed to be a street cop, he thought, was brutishness and family connections—preferably both.

Erasmus lacked the traditional police pedigree. For starters, he was not a purebred Afrikaner. Erasmus was born on February 14, 1950, the youngest of three children of an Afrikaner father and an English-speaking mother. His ancestors trace their roots to South Africa's first white settlers: the first Erasmus came over as a cabin boy on Jan van Riebeeck's Dutch East India Company ship in 1652. His mother hails from the first large contingent of English settlers who arrived in South Africa in 1820. His grandparents fought on different sides during the Boer War. So Erasmus's family history is steeped in one of South Africa's most savage ethnic conflicts—the one that raged between the whites. I ask him which side of the family he identifies with.

"I've always valued the English side of my heritage," he says. "I must be very honest now: I actually look down on a lot of my Afrikaans counterparts. [My brother and sister and I] were brought up by my late mother and she instilled in us to never take on face value what you're told. Investigate, research it, get behind it. For example, I can remember as a very small child I was reading something in a newspaper and my mother saying, 'You know you cannot believe that.' I said to her, 'But that's impossible, it's in the newspaper.' She replied, 'That's the biggest mistake you can make.'"

His Afrikaner father provided the counterbalance to his liberal mother. The elder Erasmus was a loyal functionary in the Department of Native Affairs for four decades. A highlight of his career was working for then-Minister of Native Affairs H. F. Verwoerd, who later became prime minister. Oddly enough, Erasmus describes his father as a *kaffirboetie*—the pejorative Afrikaans equivalent of "nigger lover."

The Department of Native Affairs was universally despised by blacks. The department went through a comical series of name changes over the years, starting with Department of Native Affairs, then Department of Bantu Administration and Development, to Department of Plural Relations, to its final Orwellian incarnation as the Department of Cooperation and Development.[2] But the euphemisms could not disguise the fact that this was the ministry responsible for enforcing apartheid's most odious policies, such as forcibly removing black families from areas that were arbitrarily declared "white spots." Indeed, Erasmus's father was responsible for coordinating the logistics of forced removals. But his son insists that his father "never really agreed with [forced removals]." As proof, he claims his father would sometimes provide tents for communities whose homes had just been bulldozed, rather than leave the newly homeless standing in the barren veld amidst their belongings.

"My father looked at my going into the Security Branch with a pretty jaundiced eye," recounts Erasmus. "He definitely had a depth of feeling for the blacks which rubbed off on his other children. But definitely not on his youngest son."

It was the summer of 1975 and Paul Erasmus was walking home from school in Bedfordview, a pleasant white middle-class suburb of Johannesburg. Like many nineteen-year-old boys, he had only one thing on his mind: girls. He was dating Colleen, the love of his life, and his mind wandered mistily to thoughts of going to the dance that weekend.

When he arrived home, his mother handed him a tan envelope. He opened it with a sense of dread. Inside, a curt letter informed him that he was to report for call-up into the army's Fourteenth Field Regiment in the sultry farm town of Potchefstroom. He had known this was coming—conscription was mandatory for white men and his attempt to land a cushy posting in the navy had already been denied. But Potchefstroom? "That place is hell," he blurted out. Eighteen months in hell, to be exact.

Erasmus sulked for days. He was a gifted artist and hoped to pursue a career in the arts. How could he do that in the army? And what about Colleen? What about his long hair, bell-bottoms, and motorcycle? And his family, from whom he'd never been away?

The answer to his dilemma showed up on his door five days later. An old high school friend named Brian Attwell stopped by his house one evening. Paul was shocked to see him: his hair was shaved off, and he was wearing a crisply creased blue police uniform. "What the hell happened to you?" demanded Paul.

"I joined the police!" replied Attwell.

Paul could barely hide his disgust. "The police is for losers, man."

Brian cut him off. The new recruit recounted how he joined the police at first as a joke, but now was sold on its virtues. "Look here, man: don't go to the army—join the cops! You'll only be away from home for five months. You'll come back here to the police station just up the road. And you can see Colleen all you want."

Paul's brown eyes lit up. "That's *lekker* [excellent]," gushed Paul. Within two days, a police recruiting officer was in his living room showing him a movie about police life. There were wild car chases and gun battles with crooks—it was just like Hollywood. By the time his father flicked on the lights, Paul was wide-eyed and ready to sign.

June 16, 1976, dawned cold and clear in Johannesburg. Paul Erasmus had been on the job for six months at the slow-paced local police station in Bedfordview. His job consisted of the most mundane police work: driving his motorbike around town and delivering summonses. It was a bit boring and hardly the stuff of movies, but it sure beat sweating it out at an army base in the *platteland.*

Erasmus walked into the police station that Wednesday, hung up his pale blue police hat, and strolled into the charge office. He knew something was up when a grim-faced sergeant greeted him. "Erasmus," he barked, "park your motorbike and don't leave. The kaffirs are making *kak* [shit] in Soweto. We've been ordered to stand by."

The greenhorn police officer felt a mix of fear and excitement. He had never been in a black township before, and certainly never seen any police action to speak of. In fact, he didn't really know many blacks besides the domestic worker at his parents' house. This was his chance to "cross the line" and see how the blacks lived.

At midnight, he and the other officers were herded into a police truck and driven to another police station. Chaos reigned, with cops from all around the suburbs bumping into one another and jostling around a large box. Erasmus stepped forward and his eyes grew wide: each man was pulling out a South African–made R1 assault rifle and stuffing his pockets with .762-caliber ammunition. This was military hardware, not police gear. Erasmus obediently grabbed a rifle, slung it over his shoulder, and swaggered awkwardly to the side, as if he were an old combat veteran. In truth, he was terrified at the sight of all this firepower, none of which he'd ever touched before.

At 1 A.M., the heavily armed cops were herded back into trucks. This time, the vehicles rumbled to a stop in front of a tall fortress-like cement building in the heart of Johannesburg. This was John Vorster Square, the notorious police headquarters where many activists met an untimely end during interrogations. Some eight hundred policemen were standing around, and confusion again prevailed. Rumors flew through the uniformed ranks like wildfire crackling through the dry veld: blacks were attacking the city center . . . whites were being massacred . . . a communist revolution was under way.

Finally, a higher-ranking police officer addressed the men through a megaphone. "Communists are stirring up Soweto and encouraging people to riot," he declared. "Your job is to take all necessary measures to stop them."

An hour later, Erasmus was bouncing along in the back of an open-air troop transport lorry. A cold wind sliced through his inadequate polyester police uniform. He was tired, hungry, and scared—he lacked even a winter coat, and he hadn't eaten in over twelve hours. Soon the trucks slowed and heaved as they negotiated deep potholes and dirt roads. This must be Soweto, figured Erasmus. He and the other policemen peered glumly out the back. The black night was illuminated by fires burning everywhere. An acrid smog hung over the sea of small houses. The air had a pungent taste, a mix of coal and wood smoke. The truck came to a stop, and the policemen sat in the back, shivering. Erasmus desperately needed sleep, but he was too nervous and cold to doze.

At daybreak, the rifle-toting cops fanned out in a military-style phalanx. It was a surreal sight for the bright-eyed white teenagers from the suburbs. They suddenly found themselves in the urban equivalent of an African village. Women carried water buckets on their heads, children ran around barefoot, families huddled around wood fires to cook. Then there was the jarring juxtaposition of the urban landscape—row after row of dreary cinder-block hostels that housed the men who worked in the gold mines, and tens of thousands of four-room "matchbox" houses that are a Soweto trademark.

The enemy lay everywhere, and nowhere. Young black faces—were they kids at play or "terrorists"?—peered quizzically at the police show of force. Piles of rubbish burned on every corner, and barricades of smoldering tires blocked the roads. The black youngsters, flush with a taste of their newfound power, taunted the cops. Erasmus and his colleagues glared back, hurled insults, but held their fire. In the distance, they could hear the "pop-pop-pop" of gunfire. The sights and sounds kept him on edge, nervously fingering the trigger on his rifle.

The young schoolchildren were protesting against the inferior "Bantu education" that they were receiving. Students objected that their classes were being taught in Afrikaans, which they considered to be the language of their oppressor. They also resented the vast disparities in their education: the government spent ten times as much on a white pupil on average as on a black student.

But the overlords of apartheid were deaf to the complaints of black students. The purpose of Bantu education, explained former Prime Minister H. F. Verwoerd, was "to guide [blacks] to serve his own community . . . There is no place for him in the European community above the level of certain forms of labor."[3]

In short, black schools existed to train new generations of obedient black workers to take their place at the bottom of the socioeconomic heap. By this thinking, it only made sense to teach blacks in Afrikaans, the language of their future *baas*. When asked in May 1976 if this policy was creating resentment among blacks, the deputy minister of Bantu education, Andries Treurnicht, replied, "I'm not aware of any real problem."[4]

The Soweto uprising spread around the region like water that has burst from a dike. The next day, Erasmus and his men were called to patrol hostels near a white residential area. By Thursday night, he was moved into

Alexandra, the sprawling black settlement nestled alongside the wealthy suburb of Sandton. As his armored personnel carrier crawled through the dark, rutted alleyways of "Alex," someone spotted what they thought was a man throwing a petrol bomb. Two dozen policemen leaped to their feet, shouldered their weapons, and began blasting indiscriminately into the thick night. In a near panic, Erasmus pumped round after round in the direction of the man. A choking cloud of gunsmoke filled the air, muzzle flashes lit up the street. When the haze cleared, a spotlight shone on a prone corpse in the middle of the path, his body shot to pieces.

It was Paul Erasmus's first taste of battle.

Paul Erasmus's training at the police college in Pretoria lasted five months. Mixed in with training in police techniques were hefty doses of political indoctrination. Erasmus recalls his central textbook, *Criminology and Ethnology.* "If that didn't turn you into a racist then nothing on God's earth would have," he declares now. He chuckles in amazement as he recounts the "brainwashing" he endured.

"This was the whole National Party's perspective on race, culture, and creed of South Africa. It is all contained in that book. They would have chapters like, 'Why do black people steal?' And then they'd give you this little light classic: 'The black man who's a farmer has normally got a herd of shabby rundown cows. He gazes with envy over the wire at the healthy, thriving herd of the white man. And of course when it gets dark he cuts the wire and steals the cows. They steal because they have less culture. They murder more because they have less culture.'

"Somewhere in me I questioned some of it but it seemed like a logical argument about what was happening in the country. Nobody can dispute some of the facts mentioned. The crime rate is higher amongst blacks. What they didn't deal with for example is that if you suppress people for so long, obviously the crime in impoverished society is going to be more. Probably what happens with the American Negroes as well. I don't know. I wonder myself why I didn't think it was bloody rubbish at the time."

Soweto put a face on the enemy for the impressionable young Erasmus. But the face was not of grizzled revolutionaries, it was schoolchildren. I ask Erasmus if he knew that he was shooting at children. He peers from behind the cloud of cigarette smoke that lingers perpetually around his head. He answers matter-of-factly: "We all knew from press reports and from the radio that it was school kids at the vanguard of it. But your job as a policeman as defined by law was, 'It doesn't matter where it comes from, it's a riot situation and you suppress it. You stop it. You follow your orders without question—blindly.'"

Erasmus recalls a black colleague who refused to shoot in Soweto. "He was a popular guy, but after that he was absolutely hated . . . I thought [his refusal] was absolutely disgusting. Our training in the police force was 'Boy, you obey an order without hesitation.' And we did."

Three weeks after completing his police training, the uprising began and spread to townships around the country. The police responded in the way they had been taught: with overwhelming firepower. In the ten weeks following the start of the protests, police fired 16,433 rounds of ammunition. The death toll of the Soweto riots was around one thousand, many of them children. Up to twenty thousand people were arrested or detained.[5]

Soweto 1976 was a watershed event for South Africa. And it was to change Paul Erasmus's life forever. "For five days we were in townships and it was just carnage, destruction, and bodies. It was the first time I'd ever shot at somebody," he muses. "I went to the mortuary [and] I got sick [there]. It was horrific. That whole experience affected me. I can tell you I was a very happy-go-lucky type of guy—I never worried about anything in my life. [After Soweto] I suddenly took cognizance of the fact that there's a world out there and there's people dying out there."

The riots forced Erasmus to search for answers. "With all the propaganda telling us that the riots were caused by the communists—I wanted to find out more and I started to read. I'm a voracious reader at the best of times and within six months I'd pretty much formulated the ideas that these riots were the work of communists or socialist agitators operating amongst these innocent blacks." Erasmus decided that the revolution had to be stopped. And he was just the man for the job.

The five security policemen sit sullenly in the second row of the Pretoria City Council chambers on a morning in February 1997. A variety of their victims sit behind them in the gallery, straining to get a glimpse of their faces. These men—Brigadier Jack Cronjé, the former chief of the Security Branch, and Colonel Roelf Venter, Captain Wouter Mentz, Captain Jacques Hechter, and Warrant Officer Paul van Vuuren—were all security policemen in the rural northern Transvaal. They are applying to the Truth and Reconciliation Commission for amnesty for over sixty murders that they confessed to committing during the 1980s. Among their most notorious deeds was the killing of the Nietverdient Ten. In that case, the police lured ten youths to a meeting on the pretext that they would get information about joining the ANC. The young men were drugged and then blown up in a joint operation of the security police and army Special Forces.

These former policemen are trying to bargain with their enemies: in exchange for telling all about what they did, they hope to walk free. There is remarkable politeness between the five truth commissioners (only two of whom are white) and the ex-policemen—a civility that the policemen had probably never shown to people of color. In the topsy-turvy realities of the new South Africa, the lives of these former hit men suddenly depend on being nice and telling the truth to their onetime foes.

The ex-cops have been spilling forth a grim litany of horrors for several days already. On this day, the lawyers for the policemen are trying to draw a picture of the way security policemen in South Africa were indoctrinated to hate blacks. These cops are victims, too, they argue. They open their case by showing a police training video from the 1980s.

The video begins with menacing music and a picture of young white children sitting at a Wimpy fast food restaurant. A black man is then seen furtively setting a car bomb nearby. Then the screen explodes into an orgy of violence. The restaurant appears shattered into rubble by a massive explosion—shredded children's clothing hangs from the furniture, and blood-spattered bodies lie strewn in contorted positions. Adults, presumably parents, stand around weeping.

"MOORD" [murder] flashes on-screen. The film abruptly cuts to pastoral farm country. The camera pans a picturesque farmhouse, and then moves to a horrific scene inside: a white farmer's wife, her head jerked unnaturally sideways, hangs from the ceiling by an electrical cord.

The carnage continues. The screen runs red with footage of stabbings, dismembered bodies, blown-off limbs, and machine-gunned corpses. Black vigilantes are shown attacking a crowd in a squatter camp. Some of these attacks the Truth Commission has since learned were the work of police, but that matters little; the goal of this propaganda film was to cultivate fear, revulsion, and hatred among the new police recruits. It undoubtedly succeeded.

Gasps go up from the audience as the grisly footage rolls; one woman sobs quietly. Truth commissioners grimace, wagging their heads from side to side. I feel my jaw tightening as I watch, and am finally forced to divert my gaze as the camera pans on an amputated leg, still pulsing a last few spurts of blood from its torn arteries.

Juxtaposed with the mayhem is footage of political rallies and youths dancing the *toyi-toyi,* the rhythmic, foot-stomping protest that is a combination of dancing, singing, and marching. The film makes a crude attempt to trample the distinction that police might have made between peaceful protest and murder. The propaganda message is simple: blacks kill, so kill them first.

Following the film, Captain Jacques Hechter, a particularly prolific assassin, is asked how government propaganda and the experience of violence on the job affected him. Looking stiff and out of character in a navy blue blazer, striped shirt, and gray slacks, he reads from a prepared text: "I believed that what I did was in the interests of the Republic of South Africa, my religion, and my Christian convictions." He speaks in a monotone, like a nervous schoolboy. "Today I am uncertain where I stand. I am sorry about the loss of lives. I hope this will result in reconciliation in South Africa. I am also a committed citizen of the new South Africa."

The flat, emotionless delivery sounds hopelessly disingenuous, especially when his partner, Warrant Officer Paul van Vuuren, follows him and reads a nearly identical statement. TRC amnesty commissioner Judge Andrew Wilson abruptly cuts him off. "Isn't this word for word what the previous witness testified? Can't he just confirm it?" he bellows angrily from the dais.

A chastened police attorney pipes up, "As you wish, Mr. Chairman."

That afternoon, I stop Captain Hechter on his way out of the hearing. He is a trim, solidly built, youthful looking fellow with a steely visage— a South African version of the Marlboro Man. He waves me off contemptuously, directing me to his lawyer. I persist. "That apology you read didn't really sound like your words," I say as I follow him. "Do you really feel sorry for what you did?"

Hechter wheels around and glares at me. He walks with crutches now, the result of a car accident. But his metallic blue eyes and square jaw can still tighten in a menacing glower. "Okay, I'll tell you what I think. But put that thing away," he snaps, pointing to my tape recorder. It is as if it was ten years earlier and he is ordering a journalist around the townships where he reigned supreme. Only now he is a toothless tiger, one of the many vanquished killers of the former era. I indulge this little power play and listen intently.

"Ach, I'm not fuckin' sorry for what I did," he says defiantly, his mouth cocked in a macabre half-smile. He stares directly at me, as if his stare could freeze me in place. "Look—I fought for my country, I believed in what I did, and I did a good job. They were my enemy at the time. That oke over there was a terr," he says, motioning to a black activist who was waiting to testify. Hechter had tortured the man with electric shocks and beat him to the verge of death. "I gave him the hiding of his life that he'll never forget. I did my job well. And I'd do it again if the circumstances called for it."

"No, man," he reiterates with bored disdain, continuing to stare right through me, "I'm not really fuckin' sorry for what I did."

They were the James Bonds of the South African Police. To a street cop like Paul Erasmus, the Security Branch had cachet. They drove their own cars, wore their hair long, and sported stylish clothes. Wearing jeans and leather jackets, they looked deliberately like any white man on the street. They had an unsettling cocksure air, like lawmen from the Wild West who answered to no one. Their work, according to former Security Branch chief General Coetzee in 1982, was to disrupt, destroy, and demoralize "individuals and organizations, operating from within and without [South Africa], who practice or attempt subversion or revolution."[6]

Their methods were deadly and their reach was vast. The victims of the Branch ranged from the liberation movements to the churches—in a nutshell, anyone who spoke publicly against the government was likely to garner the attention of the security police. According to Security Branch general Smit, the Branch had "given attention to" 314,000 individuals and 9,500 organizations by 1990. The Human Rights Commission calculated that the security police were responsible for the detention without trial of some eighty thousand political activists, tortured scores of them, and caused the death in detention of at least seventy-three people.[7] Their operations had an especially crippling effect on the armed wing of the ANC: for every three guerrilla attacks (usually small-scale sabotage actions), the security forces on average killed or captured two ANC guerrillas, recovered seven hand grenades, three firearms, and two limpet mines.[8] Indeed, while the ANC's military effort had great propaganda value in the townships, the reality was that its guerrilla units often ended up as suicide squads.

Soweto simultaneously inspired and demoralized Erasmus. After months of eating, breathing, and reading conspiracy theories and propaganda about left-wing revolutions (he jokes proudly that he is one of the few people in South Africa to have read much of the work of Lenin: "I don't know anybody that can read that stuff, but I tried"), he decided to apply for a transfer to the Security Branch. If he failed, he was going to quit the police, whose mundane work he felt was beneath him. Maybe he'd return to his childhood dream of being an artist after all.

Erasmus snapped to attention when the Security Branch commander called him into his office. It was a drab place, a typical bureaucrat's warehouse of nondescript offices and windowless cubicles in John Vorster Square, police headquarters in Johannesburg. The Afrikaner commander skipped the pleasantries and got right down to business: "Why should we let you into the Security Branch, Erasmus?" They both knew the sticking point: the Branch was a closed club of Afrikaners with family connections. And here was an English-speaking street cop—which in itself was "as rare as hen's teeth," Erasmus chuckles—asking to be let in.

Erasmus had rehearsed his answer. He fidgeted nervously in his chair, and launched into his prepared explanation. "I have quite a deep interest in politics and I wish to further my career in the police force," he began stiffly in Afrikaans. He noted delicately that he had completed high school, an achievement that distinguished him from many other cops. The commander looked bored by it all, flipping through papers as he talked. Erasmus then offered his trump card: "I'm English speaking and I feel this will be a big advantage because, after all, the country's enemies are English speakers."

The commander was unimpressed. He lectured Erasmus sternly on how the Branch needed loyal, hardworking men who would back each other up like *broeders* (brothers). "The Branch is a family," said the commander, and made his point by noting how many fathers and sons worked there. Just as Erasmus was preparing to leave in defeat, the commander noticed the name of Erasmus's uncle on his application. The two had served together fighting in North Africa against Nazi general Erwin "Desert Fox"

Rommel, where Erasmus's uncle was later held as a prisoner of war. That led the commander to recall that he attended the wedding of Erasmus's parents. Suddenly the dour commander's demeanor changed. "Welcome to the Security Branch," he said warmly, reaching across his cluttered steel desk to shake the young recruit's hand.

Erasmus was thrilled. He had made the grade, become one of the elite. He drove home excitedly to tell his mother. He gave her a warm hug at the door of the modest home in which he grew up and announced proudly, "I'm going to be a security policeman, ma!"

The smile evaporated from his mother's face; she was crestfallen. "You know they've killed people," she shot back at him in a quivering voice. As a closet liberal, she knew all about the Suppression of Communism Act and the Riotous Assemblies Act and how they had been used to silence government critics. She begged him to consider another career. "Why not go back to school? You could be an artist like you always wanted to be," she pleaded.

Her son looked back at her glumly from beneath the stiff black brim of his police cap. "Ach ma, this is a big break for me. Besides," he offered half-heartedly, "the Security Branch doesn't do those illegal things anymore. I'll be a good cop."

Two weeks later, Paul Erasmus's mother dropped dead.

The paved road was safe, I was assured. South African soldiers had swept it for mines that morning. I nevertheless drove gingerly, fearing that the vaunted South African military machine might be more fallible than folklore let on. Around me was the landscape of war: the road was surrounded by a broad lifeless corridor that had been recently defoliated. The better to spot terrorists, I was told. Also dotting the countryside were small villages, or kraals, always demarcated by their wooden fences. Sometimes the fences were curiously absent or broken down, leaving the livestock to wander off. South African soldiers were trying to persuade these villagers to move out of the "operational area." When gentle coaxing failed, they had other methods: they would destroy the village water pump, severing the thin lifeline of the desert inhabitants.

This was Namibia in 1984. Namibia sits on South Africa's northwest border. It is twice the size of California and, with 1.6 million people, is among the world's most sparsely populated nations. A former German colony, Namibia was administered by South Africa under a League of Nations mandate after World War I. The mandate was to have been turned over to the UN in 1945 in preparation for decolonization and independence. But South Africa refused to relinquish its colony. Instead, it announced that it would annex the territory that it called South West Africa.

In response to South Africa's intransigence, the South West African People's Organization (SWAPO) was formed in 1960 with the aim of gaining independence for Namibia; it launched a quixotic armed struggle in 1966. The young apartheid regime, displaying its new "world-be-damned" attitude, flouted numerous UN and International Court of Justice decisions and intensified its armed occupation. By the 1980s, there were one hundred thousand South African troops in Namibia fighting to keep the vast, arid country under South Africa's influence. An estimated one-tenth of South Africa's government budget was going toward Namibian war expenditures.[9]

When I visited Namibia in the mid-eighties to report on this forgotten war, I was a bit baffled by South Africa's costly obsession. After all, Namibia's most expansive feature is the Kalahari Desert—an inhospitable ocean of sand and scrub inhabited by the San people, or Bushmen. There were two conventional explanations for why South Africa clung to this outpost. The first was money: Namibia was rich in natural resources, notably diamonds, copper, and uranium, and had a vast Atlantic coastline to fish. South African companies were busily plundering these riches throughout the occupation.

The other reason that South African *troepies* (troops) were prowling the bush was geopolitics. South African State President P. W. Botha and his securocrats were convinced that Namibia was a communist domino threatening to fall on South Africa's doorstep. This provided the excuse for South Africa's raids into Angola, the huge country on Namibia's northern border where the South African Defense Force was deeply involved in fighting a fifteen-year-long proxy war against the Marxist government.

The scale of the war that I witnessed begged for better explanations than these. Everywhere I traveled in Namibia, I would pass vast South African armored columns en route to the battlefront on the Angolan border. It was only when I returned to South Africa and witnessed the conflict brewing there that I gained a new insight: Namibia was merely a dry run for the civil war in South Africa. Paul Erasmus learned this firsthand—he fought in both wars.

A couple of months after signing on with the Security Branch, Warrant Officer Erasmus was offered the chance to serve with a special police unit in Namibia. He had heard a lot about "the border" from other security cops. Some South African security policemen served in a special counterinsurgency unit known as Koevoet, which means "crowbar," in honor of the way they pried information out of people. He jumped at the chance to go.

When I traveled around Namibia in the eighties, Koevoet also had another meaning: terror. Koevoet was notorious as the most brutal and sadistic fighting unit in the war. It was well known that Koevoet took no prisoners—it was a coldly efficient killing machine. Its founder was a man named Eugene de Kock, who was sentenced to 212 years in prison in October 1996 for his responsibility in the deaths of eleven people while running Vlakplaas, the death squad of the Security Branch. De Kock—nicknamed "Prime Evil" by his colleagues—has been implicated in more than sixty-five murders in South Africa alone. He was a legend in Namibia, reportedly surviving over 350 firefights.[10]

Erasmus was assigned to an intelligence gathering unit that worked alongside Koevoet in northern Namibia. His specialty was interrogations. One morning, Erasmus was lazing around the Koevoet base with his buddies in Oshakati, a small, dusty garrison town in northern Namibia. One of his superiors fetched him from the bar and told him he had "work to do"; he would find his subject in a small windowless cell behind the barracks. Inside was an elderly man with an easy smile. Erasmus was surprised—most of the prisoners were younger. A colleague explained that Koevoet suspected this man of being a medic for SWAPO guerrillas; Erasmus was to lead the interrogation.

Erasmus was hung over from the nightly ritual of nonstop drinking and was in no mood to take guff. But the old man decided to make Erasmus's job easy: he offered to take the soldiers to his kraal to show them where he lived. Erasmus and two others climbed into a Casspir, a large armored troop carrier, and set off across the sandy veld. They placed a bag over the man's head so he couldn't see, and then cracked open some Lion Lagers; it's never too early to start drinking in Koevoet. This elfish old-timer was a change from the routine and Erasmus sort of enjoyed him. He removed the bag from the man's head and offered him some beer. The old man laughed, drank eagerly, and thanked him.

The Casspir stopped at a small kraal. Goats and chickens milled about, as did the old man's curious grandchildren. A few grass huts stood clustered together, surrounded by a large stick fence that encircled them. Sand, the ground cover of Namibia, was everywhere. Erasmus's partner removed the handcuffs from the prisoner and let him climb out from the huge rumbling vehicle. The old man chatted with his grandkids, and Erasmus joked around with his colleagues. All of a sudden the old man began running. He skipped across the sand with his wiry old legs and bare feet like a limber young springbok. As he ran he made a noise like "Humba! Humba! Humba!"

Erasmus panicked. He suddenly thought he heard gunfire and he suspected an ambush. "Get down!" he yelled to his partners. Sand sprayed him in the face as his large torso hit the ground. Sweat ran profusely off his brow, and adrenaline coursed through his body. Animal instinct took over: the three men crawled forward in a line. Finally the trio emerged in a large clearing with a giant eight-foot-high anthill in the middle. They saw the old man cowering behind the hill. Suddenly the man bolted again. Erasmus raised his R1 assault rifle, lined up the hunched old-timer in his sights, and blasted furiously toward him. The lithe old man slammed forward into the dirt like he'd been run over by a truck. He lay there, motionless.

The men warily approached the prone body. Erasmus mentioned the gunshot he'd heard, but his partner scoffed. There was no gunshot, really no danger at all. Erasmus just panicked. Erasmus let out a nervous laugh. "Hey, we got one!" Erasmus called out, kicking the corpse. His buddies insisted they stop and pose for photos. Erasmus stood proudly with his left foot atop the man's lifeless body, his rifle held upright in his right hand. He grinned maniacally, like a trophy hunter gloating over his prize kill. He was flush with the excitement of the hunt.

The three men dragged the body to the Casspir and threw it in the back, leaving the man's half-shot-off arm to hang over the edge like an animal carcass. As he walked around to climb into the driver's seat, Erasmus suddenly encountered the old man's grandson. The boy just stared numbly at the crazed, bearded white man who'd just killed his grandfather. Erasmus flinched, recoiling as if the lad had hit him. But the boy just kept staring. No tears, no words. Just a flat stare that sliced through Erasmus like the bullets that felled the old man. Erasmus yanked himself away, freaked out by the chance encounter.

Meanwhile, the other soldier went into the old man's hut and came out with a bottle of Danish-made penicillin (it was well known that Scandinavia was a strong supporter of the southern African liberation movements). "That's good enough for me," said a fidgeting Erasmus. "It proves he must have been SWAPO."

That evening was festive on the Koevoet base. Tucked into their sandlot stronghold beneath the sparkling desert sky, the Koevoet boys celebrated Erasmus's coming of age. He had lost his virginity, and had the souvenir corpse to show for it. Afrikaner beer songs wafted into the night air, mixing with the smell of numerous small wood fires from the surrounding villages. The boys from South Africa punctuated their songfest by firing their R1 rifles into the air. Liquor flowed freely as always on the base. Alcohol was the lubricant for their madness.

That night, Paul Erasmus lay in his bed trying to sleep. But as he stared up at the metal roof of his barracks, all he could see were the eyes of the old man's grandson. No matter which way he tossed and turned, those haunting young eyes followed him. Then, from somewhere deep inside him, the killer began to cry uncontrollably.

As we sit in the bed-and-breakfast living room, Paul Erasmus takes me on a surreal journey into the mind of an apartheid killer. I ask him about the interrogation techniques he used in Namibia. Erasmus at first pretends to be reluctant to talk about it. He is aware that normal South Africans—the people he was fighting for—would be repulsed by the depravity of what he and his mates did. But he is also curiously eager, boasting at one point that "I have much better stuff than Dirk Coetzee," the former Vlakplaas chief who defected to the ANC and has confessed in graphic detail to killing anti-apartheid activists. Finally, his story begins to flow.

"There were things that were barred in South Africa because you knew you had an inspector of detainees and that every two weeks a doctor would visit that detainee in a cell. But up there [in Namibia] there was nothing. If you killed, it didn't matter. And they died like flies. To sum it up in one sentence, David: we beat and shocked with electrical shocks the hell out of people, like you cannot believe. I watched human beings bite their own tongues off. A friend of mine who is not normal to this day— he was an incredible guy—went off his head one night. He was beating a guy that had been dead already for a couple of hours. And he was still hitting him when they found him."

Church and human rights officials documented a variety of torture techniques that were commonly employed by Koevoet. South African Defense Force (SADF) and Koevoet soldiers often raped female villagers during raids. Another favored technique was to burn victims on the exhaust pipes of army vehicles. There are several documented cases of people being roasted alive during interrogation. Sixty-three-year-old Ndara Kapitango was roasted on a spit but survived for two weeks to tell what had happened to him. As punishment, his interrogators were eventually fined R 50 (about $50).[11]

Erasmus puffs steadily on his cigarettes as the words keep flowing. He lowers his voice and his chest tightens as he speaks. His nervous twitches are tacit concession of the repugnance of his war stories. His job, he explains, was to gather "grassroots intelligence," which often consisted of rounding up villagers and "suspected terrorists," keeping them in corrugated steel cages, and typically depriving them of food and water—itself a form of torture in the hot desert environment. "We had this endless succession of people in the cells that we took out every day to interrogate. We'd chuck them back in the cells and the following day they were interrogated again or you interrogated them until they dropped or died.

"You see, if that guy didn't talk, one of your fighting units could get it," he offers as justification. "He might have been part of a group of two hundred SWAPO infiltrators. You had to find out where the other guys were. And let me tell you it was a brutal war on both sides. It's one thing for me to sit here and say 'Ja, we were bad, and we did this and we did this.' But I saw what SWAPO did as well. I've got photos which I'll show you. Land mines hitting *bakkies* [pickup trucks] with innocent people, wife and kids on the back and all the grandmothers and mothers and everything like that—blown to little bloody pieces."

There were unquestionably human rights violations committed by all combatants. But it was a grotesquely unequal war, pitting a pastoral population against Africa's mightiest war machine. The SWAPO insurgency was highly ineffective; infiltrators were typically hunted down and killed within miles of crossing into Namibia. Some ten thousand Namibians died in the conflict—one-tenth of the population—as well as untold scores of South African soldiers.[12] Despite being thoroughly routed on the battlefield, SWAPO easily won the political side of the conflict. When UN-supervised elections were finally held in November 1989, SWAPO won with a landslide 57 percent of the vote.

Paul Erasmus and his buddies were sitting around the Koevoet base feeling groggy and somewhat irritable after a long night of partying. Colonel Meyer intruded on their morning hangover to bring them news: they had just received information about an arms smuggling network that was using Namibian truckers to ferry weapons to SWAPO "terrs" in Katatura, the black township outside Windhoek, the Namibian capital. Erasmus was instructed to pick up Rosavita, the wife of a man who had been arrested in Katatura.

Erasmus, his partner Buks, and their Ovambo interpreter Johannes climbed into a Casspir and set off. With their mine-deflection wings and huge tires the Casspirs resembled giant insects prowling the Namibian outback. They entered the woman's kraal in the usual fashion: they drove back and forth through her mealie fields, destroying the village's vital crops. Then they slammed through the wood stockade that embraces each kraal like a nest, a village's thin line of defense against predators.

Johannes jumped out and quickly identified Rosavita, whom the three men then dragged kicking and screaming into the Casspir. The men proceeded to scan the village for any other possible "terrs"; they hauled in a terrified young man for good measure. Another Casspir soon joined them, and they ransacked the village, emptying personal effects and foodstuffs into a large pile on the ground. Indiscriminately terrorizing the local populace was Koevoet's calling card. It taught the people who was *baas*.

Buks and Erasmus took Rosavita into the bush. They joked about "combining business with pleasure": lighting a *braai*—the traditional South African barbecue—drinking beers, and abusing their captive in any way they pleased. They began questioning Rosavita, but she wasn't giving them the answers they wanted. When did her husband last visit her kraal? Silence.

Erasmus felt the veins in his neck tighten at the insolence of this kaffir. He began cursing at her, punching and slapping her. The more Rosavita tried to defend herself, the angrier he became. He and Buks grabbed hold of her feet and began dragging her through the thorny bush. The sharp weeds cut into her skin and she began to bleed. Erasmus planted his steel-toed army boot in her ribs, and Buks slammed repeated blows into her head. As they continued dragging her face down through the veld, the top of her dress came off.

Rosavita was hysterical. Tears streamed down her face and she screamed out in her native Ovambo. Johannes came over to interpret. The discussion went slowly, annoying Erasmus no end. Johannes finally turned to Erasmus, pointed to the woman's swollen breasts, and informed him, "This woman has a baby. She wants food for the child."

Erasmus assumed this meant the woman was pregnant and he feared she would abort if they kept kicking her; he didn't want to deal with that. "Awright lads," he informed his pals, "let's use other methods." He started things off by pulling out his revolver and placing it next to her head. She begged him to spare her; she was a mother. Then he fired—deliberately missing her. The woman recoiled in fright and lay momentarily still, thinking she'd been hit. The men roared with laughter at the sight of her cowering and blubbering in the sand.

Erasmus and his buddies returned to his *braai*. Per their usual practice, the men had been drinking steadily. It helped loosen their inhibitions during interrogations. Erasmus came up with the idea that their barbecue forks might come in handy. He heated up a metal fork until it glowed red. Buks and Johannes then ran over and pinned Rosavita to the ground. Erasmus swaggered over and glared at the woman. This junior South African cop was God here in the Namibian outback. He reveled in his power. Erasmus stared down at his squirming prey, feeling flush and aroused by the control he had over her. Rosavita's brown eyes glowed large, and she vainly pulled against her captors' tight grip.

In a sudden and swift motion, Paul Erasmus thrust the hot brand into her face. She let out a blood-curdling shriek; her son's sobs could be heard in the distance. The sickening smell of burning flesh hung limply in the night air.[13]

Tony Weaver was a correspondent in Namibia for several South African daily newspapers from 1983 to 1985. He distinguished himself as one of the few reporters with the courage and conviction to tell the full story about what was going on in Namibia. The SADF kept a tight reign on journalists throughout the war. Weaver's exposés of SADF atrocities earned him the enmity of the South African military. When they couldn't silence him by revoking his press credentials, they tried to silence him by other means. After surviving several attempts on his life, Weaver was ultimately forced to leave Namibia in 1985.

A lanky, handsome battle veteran who was himself a member of SADF Special Forces in the mid-seventies, Weaver appeared before the Truth Commission in November 1996 to explain the role of the South African security police in Namibia. "Koevoet was set up as a training unit for the South African security police," he recounted to me afterward. "They were totally ruthless in their operations: they are credited with 85–90 percent of all deaths of guerrillas in Namibia. We're talking six hundred to one thousand deaths per year for a force of about two thousand men.

"There was a ritual of getting 'blooded' into Koevoet. You had to either kill someone in battle or execute a captured interrogated guerrilla. That meant taking their sidearms and blowing someone's brains out. The interrogation techniques they used were what became fairly standard for the South African security police: rubber hoods for strangling and choking someone, immersing someone in water until they nearly drowned, electric shock torture using hand-cranked or socket-powered generators . . . Women suspects were routinely raped as a means of interrogation, often in front of parents or husbands or lovers."

"They weren't terribly picky," Weaver continued. "In South Africa, if the Security Branch tortured somebody to death, it would be subject to a judicial inquiry. In Namibia, in Ovamboland and Kavango, there was such an air of lawlessness that if they tortured someone to death, they could just claim they were killed in battle."

In early 1985, one of Weaver's contacts in SADF military intelligence gave him some disturbing news. (The SADF and Koevoet hated one another as much as they hated the enemy. Koevoet felt the SADF conscripts couldn't be counted on to do the dirty work needed to win the war; the soldiers thought Koevoet was "barbaric.")

"The dogs are about to be set loose in South Africa," Weaver's military informant told him. Weaver understood his meaning: the security police were being called back to apply their expertise in South Africa's townships. The war at home was about to enter a new phase.

In the Oshakati canteen that night, Erasmus and Johannes resumed their beerfest. The Lion Lagers were flowing as they recounted their exploits to their comrades. In the course of the boasting Johannes pointed out that Rosavita wasn't pregnant, she was breast-feeding—her child was back in the village. This bit of information gave Erasmus an idea: he'd use her child to get her to talk.

The following morning, Erasmus released Rosavita from the sweltering cage in which she had been locked up. They drove her back to her village, and allowed her to nurse her son. She was grateful, but wary of this uncharacteristic display of civility. Her son stared up in fright at his mother's disfigured face and blood-caked body. Johannes collected the boy's clothes and put mother and child in the Casspir. Erasmus soon revealed his hand.

Erasmus ordered the Casspir to a halt and grabbed the boy from his mother's clutch. He stepped outside and held the baby up in the air. The young boy wailed in terror, reaching out futilely to his mother. Erasmus then shoved the barrel of his rifle in the boy's soft belly. Johannes had a nervous smile on his face; even this torture-hardened soldier was uneasy about what might transpire. Erasmus began barking questions, and Johannes obediently translated. Rosavita started to talk.

Her husband wasn't in SWAPO. She'd never seen the weapons they were describing, such as an AK-47. She had seen her husband earlier in the month, but he was alone.

Erasmus was not pleased—he wanted di erent answers. When they reached the Koevoet base in Oshakati, he asked Rosavita if she liked the radio. Yes, she nodded glumly, trying to look calm in front of her panicked child. Erasmus said they would introduce her to Radio Moscow.

Before she could respond, Johannes grabbed the boy away and threw the mother down on a steel bed frame. The room was empty save for the bed frame and a few metal chairs. He tied her hands and feet to the bed. Rosavita strained to escape the imminent assault, but Johannes and Erasmus easily overpowered her. Johannes tied her down while Erasmus clipped a wire to her mouth and her armpit. Erasmus then began cranking a small generator attached to the wires. Suddenly a searing hot flash of electricity ripped through Rosavita's body. She bit down so hard on her tongue that the end fell o . Blood spurted from her mouth. Erasmus roared with laughter.

He screamed at her. "You remember where SWAPO is hiding now, Rosavita?" and leered.

He grabbed the clips and refastened one on her nipple and another on her toes. He repeated the routine. Rosavita's back arched violently and the bed frame lurched sideways. She let out an animal-like scream. Erasmus increased the voltage and repeated the routine. He cackled as Rosavita's body crashed up and down. Blood oozed around her ankle and wrist restraints.

Still, she wasn't telling them what they wanted to hear. By 4 P.M., Erasmus retreated to the canteen with his mates again. The interrogator was furious. His savage reputation depended on delivering either the information or a body. "The bitch is lying," he bellowed over another round of beers. "Let's finish her off."

They returned to Rosavita, who was staring numbly at the ceiling, still tied to the bed frame. Then Johannes proposed an idea: "let's place an electrode in her vagina!" The men all looked at each other, then broke out laughing.

Erasmus was titillated and repulsed at the same time. He had never touched a black woman's genitals, nor had Buks. It was beneath them— Johannes should do the honors. Just as the Namibian was preparing to insert the electrode, Colonel Meyer stepped into the room. He glanced quickly at the scene, and was silent.

Then he turned to Erasmus. "We just got a call that they're coming from Windhoek to collect her and the baby. Make sure the boy is fed. Oh," he added as an afterthought, "you can stop this now."

"How could you do it?"

Paul Erasmus stares glumly at me, his furrowed brow and wrinkled face showing the strain of too many years of battle. He fumbles to light up another cigarette as he stalls for time. He sits across from me looking tough but vain with his well-kempt hairdo and his stylish leather jacket.

I try to imagine Erasmus as a sadistic interrogator. I can almost see it: the permanently scowling mouth, the deep-set eyes that lock on you like a gun sight, the furrowed brow. The squat body. The brawny fists.

Then I notice the cigarette shaking in his large hands. The scared look in his face as his eyes dart about with paranoia. I am staring at the shell of a man. He has been destroyed by the deeds that he has perpetrated.

The Namibian experience was a crucial link in the repressive machinery of apartheid. Bright-eyed South African white boys weren't born to hate and kill. They were normal kids with ordinary dreams. Namibia was the key to making monsters out of men. In the anonymity of a foreign desert, young men broke the taboos of civilized society. They murdered. Raped. Tortured. And then woke up and did it again. Erasmus spent only five months in Namibia, returning in late 1981. But by the time he and his Koevoet colleagues returned to South Africa, they were killing machines.

His first kill was a turning point for Erasmus. "I couldn't handle it. It just like, hit me. It took me a couple of days to even normalize as it were. I'd actually killed somebody. When you squeeze that trigger, you've got that power, you're going to take somebody's life. It's awesome responsibility." Erasmus is now reminded regularly of that fateful day: the infamous photo of him smiling with his foot on the corpse flashes across South Africa every Sunday night on a popular weekly TV show about the Truth Commission. "I've never really found answers to these things—why they happen, the morality of it. I suppose there is no morality in war. It's horrific.

"Every time you were exposed to something like that, just a little part of you either dies or hardens," says Erasmus. The jocular tone, the boastful war stories—they're gone now. It is just him left to deal with his memories and his conscience.

"When I came back I was pushing life to the limit. Not necessarily trying to kill myself, but being reckless—like driving my motorcycle fast. I just needed that adrenaline. I'd go to bars and look for fights. My whole values changed, my whole foundations changed. I got drunk one night, and I went to church with my rifle. I just like, sat there and stared at these people. I was slightly moggy." He chuckles nervously at the image, but then catches himself. "I was back a week [from Namibia] and I was the most unhappy person. And I've never been unhappy in my life.

"I think having killed somebody one crosses a certain line. It makes it easy to do it a second time 'round. After I came back, it wasn't a matter of throwing paint on people's walls—I started shot-gunning houses and cars. It was reckless abandonment."

Erasmus found that only by being a cop, and being around cops, could he keep his memories at bay. "I found solace in working hard. So I carried on with these illegal attacks on the left."

Erasmus's security police beat was to surveil and harass the leading lights of the Johannesburg white left. His superiors encouraged him and his colleagues in *drukking*—applying pressure. His boss, a Major J. H. L.

Jordaan, told him one evening, "You know Paul that the *jong manne* go out a lot at night and sometimes they make a bit of *kak*. I must warn you, though, that if you ever go with them, you must never get caught. You must realize what damage can be done to us if these *verdomde* [cursed] left-wingers ever find out that it's us. You must also be careful of the Uniform Branch [street cops] and the detectives who might try to make a name for themselves by nailing a security policeman."[14]

It was up to Erasmus's imagination and creativity to decide what form *drukking* should take. Helen Joseph was one of Erasmus's targets. Joseph was a close friend of Nelson Mandela's and a high-profile ANC member since the fifties. An elderly white lady who lived alone, she was a particularly vulnerable target. Erasmus discovered that her greatest joy was her gardening. So he had workmen come and cut down her trees and flowers. He also preyed on her by destroying her car, shooting her house, and harassing her night and day on the phone.

Erasmus takes credit too for personally firebombing St. Mary's Cathedral in Johannesburg and, with his colleagues, burning down the Alexandra Clinic, the lone medical center for thousands of township residents.

Rev. Beyers Naude, the distinguished anti-apartheid Afrikaner clergyman who headed the Christian Institute and later the South African Council of Churches, was also among his charges. Erasmus firebombed two of Naude's cars, threw bricks into his house, ordered unwanted supplies, and would regularly make harassing phone calls. The old churchman used to infuriate Erasmus because he would reply to all the telephoned epithets by saying simply, "God bless you."

The day began like most others at John Vorster Square. Erasmus and his colleagues in the Security Branch sat around the coffee table in a circle. Then they bowed their heads and a dominee (minister) from the local Dutch Reformed Church led them in prayer. "Oh God, protect us in this day. Help us to save our people from the onslaught of evil and communism that threatens us. May the Lord Jesus Christ bless us in our tasks and deliver us safely." With the almighty firmly on their side, the security police went about wreaking havoc and sowing fear.

The security police was compartmentalized in the same way as apartheid society: there was a division that investigated blacks, one for Indians, another for coloreds, and a fourth for whites. The units even had the same skewed prestige that apartheid conferred, with an elite white division and a low-status black unit. There was a role for blacks in the Security Branch as *askaris,* former guerrillas who had been "turned" to work for the police, often as hit men. Erasmus, by virtue of his English and his high school education, was assigned to cover the white left.

The common enemy of all units of the security police was communists. "You didn't learn to fight communism spiritually or just physically—you learned to hate them. And I mean *hate* them like unbelievable," he recounts.

"What is a communist?" I ask.

"Satanic," he fires back. "They were anti-Christian and therefore satanic."

Erasmus jokes that the "Security Branch had a very strong idiot factor," noting that few policemen actually knew what communism was. But precise definitions mattered little; anti-communism was simply the glue that held the apartheid laager (the circled wagons of Afrikaner pioneers) together. "If you weren't a Nationalist [National Party member] you were a communist," says Erasmus of the apartheid worldview. "The Catholics were communists, the Hare Krishna's were communists—everybody was a bloody communist if you didn't fall into the National Party values."

The South African Council of Churches was unquestionably "communist" in this view. Its Johannesburg headquarters at Khotso House was a home for a range of anti-apartheid activists. Under the leadership of Bishop Desmond Tutu (later Archbishop), the SACC vigorously opposed the apartheid regime. They did this in part by providing a home for a broad front of anti-apartheid groups.

For anyone interested in getting a glimpse of apartheid in action, all roads led to Khotso House. Within one day of arriving in South Africa in 1984, I found myself at Khotso House being handed over to a community worker who took me around Soweto. When I wanted to learn about the plight of rural black South Africans, I was directed to the Transvaal Rural Action Committee—in the basement of Khotso House. You want to see the impact of the pass laws? Just find the packed waiting room of the Black Sash advice office in Khotso House. When I needed to interview leaders of the United Democratic Front, I just stopped by their office on the top floor of Khotso House.

All of which made the SACC and Khotso House a prime target for Paul Erasmus. It was there that Erasmus first met a dynamic young activist named Rev. Frank Chikane. The two first met shortly after Chikane had become head of the SACC in 1987. As a black theologian, Chikane would not ordinarily have fallen under Erasmus's jurisdiction. But in the thinking of the security police, no black man was intelligent enough to lead a dynamic organization like the SACC. "We thought he was a figurehead," a black front man for white communists, explained Erasmus.

Erasmus and Chikane soon began crossing paths on a regular basis. In 1986, President Botha declared a state of emergency in response to escalating anti-apartheid actions. Police were granted sweeping powers of search and arrest as black South Africa was plunged into three years of virtual martial law. Khotso House raids were so frequent that they became boring. "We used to call them 'stationery raids' because we were eventually going there not with any specific purpose apart from to steal as much stationery as what we could," recalls Erasmus. "We'd go in there and mess the documents up and steal dictionaries and telephone books and checkbooks and whatever we could fit in our suitcases. It was that bizarre—it was just a way of using the vehicle of the state of emergency to harass and disorganize these people."

Warrant Officer Paul Erasmus arrived for the second time in the same week at Rev. Frank Chikane's office. Erasmus was in a bad mood— Chikane had spoken at several large rallies, and the police brass told him in no uncertain terms to keep Chikane on a tighter leash. Chikane barely acknowledged Erasmus as the security cop strode in with a phalanx of policemen. The SACC leader continued talking on the phone as the police swarmed around him, looking for nothing in particular. Erasmus then reached over and hung up the phone. For once, Chikane became angry, scolding the policeman for his disrespectful behavior.

Erasmus just glared at him. "We're coming for you next Chikane," he growled.

Later that week, Erasmus's boss, Colonel Roelf Venter, stepped into his office at John Vorster Square and closed the door. Erasmus knew something important was brewing—the boss wasn't one for histrionics. Venter was an older fellow who'd been in the Security Branch for years. He was no stranger to dirty tricks.

"Paul," he began, "you've been here a long time and know the communists well. If you now had the chance to select some of them for permanent removal from society, who would you choose?"

Erasmus wasn't sure what to make of the question. In fact, it worried him: why wasn't this discussed at the morning meeting around the coffee table? But in the world of spooks, it wasn't for Erasmus to ask the questions, just to provide answers.

"I reckon I'd put two names on that list, Colonel," said Erasmus, fidgeting with his service revolver that lay on the desk. "Gavin Evans and the Rev. Frank Chikane."

Evans was a well-known left-wing journalist who had confronted and embarrassed Erasmus during a protest in downtown Johannesburg. Erasmus had put him on the list merely out of spite. Chikane made the grade because he was a rising star in the anti-apartheid movement and was causing too much trouble, not only for the government but for Erasmus.

Not long after this conversation, Erasmus's police partner stopped in his office. Erasmus and his partner were close friends: they often socialized together when they weren't working. "I need your help tonight. We're going to pay Frank Chikane a visit," he said. Erasmus, as always, was a willing accomplice.

Erasmus and his colleague prowled slowly in their car through the Johannesburg suburbs toward Soweto. They were looking for St. Barnabus College, where Chikane was staying. His partner explained that he needed to test the security of the house. Erasmus didn't ask why, just offered his help. They spotted the residence, turned off the headlights, and got out.

His partner led the way with a dim flashlight. Tall grass crackled and waved as they crept through the brush. Erasmus repeatedly stumbled. He was a city boy, out of his element on rough terrain. Making matters worse, it was a cold winter night, and Erasmus had not dressed warmly enough. When Erasmus waded into a marshy area and sank up to his ankles in muck, he protested to his colleague that he'd had enough. His partner suggested that he just return to the car and wait. Erasmus was more than happy to oblige.

A few weeks later, an intelligence report was dropped on Erasmus's desk. He opened it up and read the top item: Frank Chikane was near death in a Wisconsin hospital. The cause? He had been mysteriously poisoned.

To hear Paul Erasmus tell it, he's been an innocent bystander while bad things have happened with amazing regularity around him. He put the names of two men on a list for "permanent removal from society" but claims he thought that meant they would just be locked up for a while. He was involved in scouting Chikane's house, but he knew nothing of the subsequent poisoning. He similarly scouted Khotso House, COSATU House, and Khanya House but had no idea that the three buildings would be reduced to rubble in huge bomb blasts and arson fires a short time later.

Paul Erasmus may be a liar. Or he may just be the Zelig of the South African security police. Zelig was the central character in a Woody Allen film of the same name who found himself an unwitting participant at great moments in history, through no credit of his own. Much like Erasmus—always close to notoriety, but miraculously adept at keeping his nose clean.

I challenge Erasmus on this point. How can he expect me—or the Truth Commission, for which he's just spent a month completing an amnesty application—to believe that he was never directly involved in the dirtiest tricks? Erasmus grows irritated with me, looking away and sputtering. He concedes that it's a hard line to swallow. But he replies exasperatedly, "Very rigidly applied in the Security Branch was the need to know. If you didn't need to know it, you didn't know it. You weren't told . . . It wasn't prudent to push someone and demand to know what he had been doing."

Erasmus's half-hearted confessions are typical of many former security operatives. They are at once eager to enhance their image by saying they were key players, but keen to distance themselves from the worst atrocities. They find themselves in a curious bind: their only cachet is their notoriety, which could form the basis of their post-apartheid careers. Erasmus has written an autobiography that he hopes to get published. But if he didn't do anything bad, no one (such as foreign journalists or publishers) is interested in him. If he did something too heinous and was denied amnesty by the Truth Commission, he could be liable for prosecution. So Erasmus has crafted an image of himself as a monster . . . with a conscience.

Erasmus soon saw his star rise in the Security Branch. In 1990, he joined Stratcomm—short for "strategic communications"—the intelligence gathering and dirty tricks arm of the State Security Council. The State Security Council was established in 1972 under then–Prime Minister John Vorster, but only rose to prominence under State President P. W. Botha.

The SSC consisted of cabinet ministers whose job it was to coordinate various aspects of the government's "total strategy" to combat communism and terrorism. F. W. de Klerk served on the SSC, first as a cabinet minister and later as state president.

Stratcomm is officially acknowledged to have been in existence from about 1990 until 1992. It was supposedly disbanded soon after its involvement in backing black vigilantes was exposed by journalists from the *Mail and Guardian* in 1991. However, Erasmus has documents indicating that Stratcomm was operating as early as 1984, and that some of its projects continued unofficially until 1995.

Erasmus's promotion to Stratcomm was recognition that he was more than just a cop—he was a cop with brains. He was soon involved in running overseas propaganda projects, and he reported directly to the SSC. After years of working in the trenches as a security cop, he reveled in carrying out high-level policy initiatives and being intimately involved in executing the political strategy underlying de Klerk's negotiations with the ANC.

In the Stratcomm course that Erasmus took in October 1990, he was provided with a new political mandate. He explained to me, "We were told by the high hierarchy of the security establishment in the South African Police that we had four years to achieve a goal: that was to reduce the ANC to just another political party. The means that you used to achieve that goal were entirely up to you. The money was available, lots of money, as much as what anybody would ever want, and every facility was to be afforded to make this possible."

An eager student of politics, Erasmus understood what this meant. "The National Party was negotiating with Mandela on the one hand and on the other hand they were stabbing him in the back."

De Klerk followed a two-pronged strategy to undermine the ANC. The first was to bolster the ANC's main adversary, the Zulu-based Inkatha Freedom Party led by Chief Mangosuthu Buthelezi. The IFP had a much smaller following than the ANC, with its power base limited primarily to rural Zulus in Natal province. But the IFP could, through violence, wield influence far out of proportion to its numbers. The Stratcomm strategy involved arming and training the IFP to enable it to carry out vigilante attacks against ANC targets. These shadowy, violent police-backed groups came to be known as the "third force." The conflict that resulted was the worst period of bloodletting in South Africa since the Anglo-Boer War at the turn of the century. In the four years between Mandela's release from prison and the April 1994 elections, fourteen thousand people died as a result of political violence, according to the Human Rights Commission.[15]

The second part of the National Party's strategy was to attack the ANC itself. "How did you attack the ANC? You attack the people in the ANC—character assassinations," says Erasmus. "For example, we found that we couldn't get any dirt on Mandela himself so Winnie became the prime target. That was my baby, was breaking her. I believe to this day I've played a big role in their divorce," he boasts. "But anyway, the president has denied it so I won't comment on it."

The smear campaign against Winnie Mandela included spreading rumors that she was having extramarital affairs, smoking marijuana, was an alcoholic, and was sponsoring a campaign of terror in the townships. Erasmus takes credit for rumors that ultimately found their way into feature articles in major American magazines that "exposed" Winnie's transgressions. His bosses were ecstatic.

How many of the smears were true? I ask him. Erasmus becomes cagey. Either he doesn't know himself, or he retains a vested interest in the misinformation. He repeatedly mentions his plans to write a book, and that he wants to keep some of his better secrets for his own material. He finally offers, "We worked with an old propaganda precept: 'Stick to the truth but embellish on the truth.' The formula was 70-30: 70 percent truth and 30 percent fiction. Sometimes they'd reverse it and you'd have something that was 30 percent truth and we'd embellish it up to 70 percent fiction."

I press him about a well-known rumor that Winnie had an affair in the mid-eighties with former bank executive Chris Ball. Ball was a liberal businessman who was cultivating contacts with the ANC; the rumor cost him his job at the bank. Were the rumors true?

Erasmus stares back at me coldly. "I don't know. I honestly don't know." Finally he adds, "I don't believe it."

And what about Peter Mokaba, the fiery ANC Youth League leader who was branded a police informer in an Erasmus smear campaign—was he a spy? "I don't know," repeats Erasmus.

The early nineties were heady times for the street cop-cum-political strategist. Suddenly Erasmus was dealing in the international arena, trying to wage a global smear campaign against the ANC. These were the best days of his career, and he is visibly more jocular as he sits back and holds forth about his heyday.

"I expanded operations that I began in October 1990 into 1991, and within a few months I had people that were feeding information to the White House, to John Major's government, to influential people in Britain, politicians and opinion makers across the board."

Among his questionable accomplishments were to bring Chief Buthelezi to the United States to address a Republican think tank, and bringing over an American academic (whom he declines to name) to take him on "guided tours in a police Casspir to see what damage the ANC had done in the townships." He had also forged an invitation to the ANC's seventieth anniversary party and sent it to leaders of the Irish Republican Army in 1992. When Erasmus then leaked the invitation to the press, the British government was in an uproar. These embarrassments were timed to undermine Nelson Mandela's fundraising trips abroad.

"We put our stuff in the South African papers, and I'm pretty sure American papers would pick it up—you know how the media circus works. I mean, it just goes from one to the next.

"The whole idea was to make the ANC realize that they didn't have the support of major powers that they thought they had. Obviously that was the first thing. The second thing would be to bring diplomatic pressure on them to get people like Winnie and Peter Mokaba and the rest of them out of the way. These people just couldn't be negotiated with. They had to be removed from the structures. And, of course, obviously [we tried] to weaken the ANC itself."

Erasmus is suddenly filled with the bluster of his faded glory as he recounts his exploits. But it is all pathetically naive. The South African regime had been isolated for so long that it mistook any sign of foreign interest for a major political breakthrough. When I press Erasmus about his foreign contacts, he reveals that his key conduit was the ex-president of the fanatical World Anti-Communist League. His overseas influence, it is safe to say, was marginal at best.

Erasmus was enjoying the life and notoriety of a top-level spook. But skeletons were starting to tumble out of his closet. In 1982, Dr. Neil Aggett, a well-known white physician and trade union activist, died in police detention. It was a screwup: Aggett had been tortured by being kept awake for several days of interrogation, a standard security police technique. After three days, Aggett was found hanging in his cell. The police claim it was suicide; Aggett's family insists he was murdered. In typical fashion, Erasmus asserts he was not part of the interrogation team, but his buddies were. He nevertheless shows me graphic photos that he shot of Aggett hanging in his cell. He insists that Aggett simply "cracked" and killed himself.

Faced with a national outcry, the police attempted to show that Aggett had a history of suicidal behavior. Erasmus broke into the home of Aggett's parents to look for damning psychiatric records just days after his death. This time, the dirty tricks veteran got caught by a neighbor. Erasmus's superiors assured him that he should take the rap for the "illegal search" charge and not worry about it. But Erasmus felt that the blemish on his record—he received a six-month suspended sentence and a small fine—was used to deny him promotions.

By the late 1980s, Erasmus was becoming disillusioned with security police work. A watershed moment came in 1988 when he received instructions from one of his superiors "to obtain samples of the AIDS virus to be spread amongst the anti-government community." Erasmus looked at him and replied, "You're playing with a monster."

"It was just bizarre," he tells me, "it was Lunatic Plots Volume 56. I didn't actually refuse it, I just laughed at it. It was too incredible."

Then there were Erasmus's personal problems. He had married his wife, Linda, in 1983, and had a daughter two years later. In 1987 a son was born with cerebral palsy. Suddenly the family needed a father. It was a role he had ignored—work always came first. By 1990, his son was in a special school in Johannesburg and was exhibiting behavioral problems. The school requested a meeting with both parents; only Linda showed up. Finally, school officials demanded to see Paul. The couple arrived for a meeting and were confronted by doctors and psychiatrists.

"Your son has problems that are aggravated by the fact that he hasn't got a father," began the head psychiatrist. Erasmus couldn't hide by burying himself in work any longer—he was part of the problem. It was time to make changes.

Erasmus had other reasons to change his ways. He was suffering from a variety of bizarre stress-related symptoms. The worst was that he couldn't sleep. It was a problem that he'd first experienced in Namibia—beginning the night after his first kill. By the late eighties, he'd often go several days without sleep until he was disoriented "like a zombie." Finally, Linda took him to a doctor, who referred him to a psychiatrist. The therapist took one look at the bleary-eyed policeman and declared, "You're going to the hospital right now and you're going to sleep for a week." So began the first of many rounds of sleep therapy, which he continues to receive periodically.

When Erasmus's boss was told that he had been sent to the hospital to sleep, he was outraged. He called Linda and ordered her to wake up her husband to deal with some routine Stratcomm business. It was clear to Paul that the police didn't want to hear about his problems.

But Erasmus knew too much for the police to let him just leave. And there was also the matter of maintaining an income and health insurance for his son. Paul and Linda dabbled in starting an export-import business on the side, but it failed. They needed Paul's job to survive.

By 1991, the strain of both his son's and his own illnesses had become too much. In spite of his professional successes, Erasmus requested a transfer out of Johannesburg for medical reasons. He was relocated to what he assumed would be a relatively quiet security police post in Mossel Bay, a picturesque beach town along South Africa's famous Garden Route. But as Erasmus quickly discovered, the paranoid, corrupt culture of the security police pervaded the entire institution, no matter how far-flung the *dorp* (town).

Arriving in Mossel Bay, Erasmus met the chief of the local security police, Colonel Rommel van der Merwe. The colonel was thrilled to have such an accomplished dirty tricks operator at his disposal. He promptly ordered Erasmus to establish a wide-ranging program of espionage, wiretaps, intelligence gathering, and sabotage.

"I refused," says Erasmus flatly. "It was all for his personal gain. He wanted to put pressure on his enemies in town, and he saw himself as a sort of 'beau geste'—you know, like he had this power second to God only. There was this whole little corrupt thing going on. Rommel owned Mossel Bay. He was in with the bank managers and senior people from Mossgass and Fidelity Guards [a private security firm]. He was having an affair with one of the policewomen and every morning sitting, praying, you know. It was this whole old sick thing that I had gone through before, all over again. I refused to do it, absolutely refused."

But refusing orders was not an option in the Security Branch. If Erasmus wouldn't play along, then van der Merwe would put the squeeze on him—*drukking*—just like Erasmus had done to his enemies. The easiest way to do this was to financially strangle the insubordinate cop.

Erasmus had bought himself "a dream house" on the ocean, drove a nice sports car, and had a large boat. Life was good for this warrant officer. But he was vulnerable. Suddenly his monthly salary dropped to R 350 ($125). Then he found out that his phone was tapped. Erasmus's health deteriorated. He began going in and out of the hospital for insomnia and depression. The doctors finally gave his condition a name: post-traumatic stress disorder (PTSD).

By 1993 Erasmus couldn't take the strain anymore. In his mid-thirties, he requested early retirement from the police on the grounds of PTSD. But van der Merwe wasn't through with him yet. Erasmus's pension payments were mysteriously delayed. Creditors came knocking and Erasmus's world collapsed in front of his eyes. He lost his house, car, and boat, and the bank was seizing everything else. In desperation, Erasmus wrote to the top brass of the police and the National Party in an effort to expose van der Merwe's corruption and to clear his own name. But that only exacerbated the problem: van der Merwe had rank and power, Erasmus did not. Finally, his lawyer suggested a way to fight back. "Go to the newspaper," he instructed him.

The media was the Achilles' heel of the apartheid machine. The government was curiously schizophrenic about its barbarism. National Party leaders were always keen to maintain appearances of democracy. Although apartheid was unjust on its face, it was nevertheless painstakingly—and often comically—supported by an elaborate body of law. And the press had the appearance of being free, despite being severely restricted. The legal establishment and the press often came back to haunt their masters.

"The media was the most feared people of all," explains Erasmus. "You didn't trust them. You didn't deal with them." But Erasmus was at rock bottom: his family didn't even have enough money to buy food.

"Stressed Ex-Cop To Sue Police Minister" blared the headline of South Africa's largest newspaper, the *Sunday Times,* in May 1993. One day later, the police found the money that they owed Erasmus and wired it to him. One week later, Erasmus received his first death threat.

"Look under your *bakkie* [pickup truck]," came the deep, gravelly voice on the phone before hanging up. Erasmus immediately recognized it as the voice of his former partner. His partner had worked closely with Vlakplaas, the Security Branch's death squad. While officially disbanded by 1993, former Vlakplaas operatives were still active in political assassinations. And the death squads were not shy about killing ex-cops who they thought might spill the darkest secrets of the security police.

Killers know how killers think. Erasmus knew better than anyone how the police dealt with their enemies. So he responded swiftly with a counterthreat that upped the ante. He began calling everyone—friends, ex-colleagues, politicians, anyone he could reach—to declare what the stakes were.

"This is the situation," he told each of them. "I have papers and documents which would expose [police commissioner] Johan van der Merwe and de Klerk and the whole lot of them. I've sent them out of the country with instructions that if I die an unnatural death or if Linda and the children are hurt, this stuff must be made available to the press." Erasmus had information linking these top leaders to political assassinations and dirty tricks. If he talked, political careers could end abruptly.

The threats stopped. But the damage had been done. Erasmus officially retired from the police force on May 31, 1993. It was Republic Day, a veritable holy day for the Afrikaner faithful, the thirty-second anniversary of H. F. Verwoerd's declaring the Union of South Africa a republic.

Once out of the force, Erasmus became the subject of a different type of attack: the police tried to destroy his reputation. "It was the same type of discreditations we used with Dirk Coetzee when he defected and went to the ANC. We would get the public up against the guy and alienate his friends—he was a drug dealer and, even worse, he was smuggling in rhino horns, you know, he was addicted to cough mixture, he was an alcoholic.

"The stories they put out about me was that I'd gone off my head, I was insane. [There was a rumor that] the system had bent over backwards to accommodate me by giving me this 'golden handshake' which was worth a million rand. That has the effect of alienating your colleagues. The whole thing is to isolate you so you cannot influence people, especially people in the force and people in similar roles. And that worked very well. I lost a tremendous amount of my friends."

Erasmus and his family tried to hide. They moved to Cape Town, lived in seclusion, and "tried to forget about all of this. I just wanted to live my life." They bought a sailboat and planned to live on the water. But Erasmus's past would not let him drift away so easily. Five months after arriving in Cape Town, he received a surprise call from his former Stratcomm boss. It was meant as a signal: they knew where he was. The Erasmuses hurriedly packed up their belongings and left town. This time they headed for Knysna, a secluded tourist enclave on the Indian Ocean about five hours east of Cape Town. They covered their tracks as best they could, registering the phone under Linda's maiden name and telling no one their whereabouts.

But other events were overtaking Erasmus. The Goldstone Commission, investigating the so-called third force, was starting to expose the involvement of police in a number of violent incidents, including train and township massacres. Erasmus now had two things to fear: being arrested and being hunted down by his ex-colleagues. His disillusionment with the system that he once served, defended, and killed for was now complete.

"When the system turned on me I turned on them," he says. But he didn't have the courage to take the next step. So his wife did it for him. One morning in March 1994, with her husband pacing anxiously in the background, Linda picked up the phone and called the Goldstone Commission. Within twenty-four hours, agents from the Ministry of Justice were at his door, hustling the Erasmus family into unmarked cars under cover of night. Several days later, they were secretly flown to Denmark to begin briefing the Goldstone investigators. The time had come for Paul Erasmus to tell the truth.

In the comfort of a Copenhagen hotel, Erasmus ripped open the belly of the apartheid beast. Just one month before the elections that brought Nelson Mandela to power, Goldstone investigators listened with rapt attention as Erasmus cataloged the inner workings of Stratcomm and the security establishment. Among the incidents that he shed light on were:

> the bombing of Khotso House and COSATU House in the late 1980s, which he claimed were done with the knowledge of Minister of Law and Order Adrian Vlok;

> the activities of the Vlakplaas death squad;

> how Inkatha members were armed and trained by the SAP and carried out massacres and assaults in the townships between 1990 and 1994;

Operation Romulus, a disinformation campaign against the ANC in the 1990s;

security police harassment and torture of activists;

the poisoning of Rev. Frank Chikane.


Something else happened for Erasmus during the five months that his family lived in Denmark. It was the first time that he emerged from the laager to see how the larger world lived—the world he and his colleagues tried desperately to keep at bay for so long.

"In Denmark I saw what a real democracy is all about, not this fool's paradise that we've been living in in this country," he observes. His voice is tinged with bitterness as he recounts the events that turned his world upside down. "You see it in the streets: there's no getting hyped up about politics and the country is ordinary and the people are happy and there's no poverty. They look after the poor. Battered women get looked after by the state. Drug addicts get looked after by the state. People with psychological problems get looked after by the state. I mean, it's paradise. Incredible country.

"I realized that we weren't living in a democracy. Sure they used to hold elections every couple of years here. But I mean, that wasn't democratic at all."

It is a phenomenon oft-repeated in South Africa today: the revolutionizing effect of peering over the laager walls and glimpsing the real world. The apartheid state was a painstakingly crafted fantasy world, a political theme park created by and for Afrikaner nationalists and the privileged white elite. Its strength lay in keeping people separated—from each other, and from the world. Every time the walls were breached—whites meeting blacks, blacks traveling in other African countries, whites seeing their world from the outside—South Africans were thunderstruck by what they saw. The bogeymen they were raised to fear suddenly didn't exist. There was a big world beyond the laager. A world beyond apartheid.

Paul Erasmus knew too much. He knew the dirty work the police had been involved in. He knew the politicians who had authorized assassinations. And worst of all, he knew how his former colleagues hunted their prey. So when the Goldstone Commission returned him and his family to live in a safe house near Durban in late 1994, he felt anything but safe.

Erasmus and his family were supposedly in a witness protection program. Their identities would be shielded, and their protection assured. But the job was bungled from the beginning. For starters, the house was registered under the name of the Goldstone Commission. So was the phone and the electricity account. As a veteran black-bag operator whose stock-in-trade was ferreting out people on the run, Erasmus knew that his old mates would find him. It was just a matter of time.

It was a pleasant autumn evening in March 1995. Paul and Linda had finished putting their kids to bed and were relaxing in front of the TV. The house was nice enough—the carpets were new, the lawn was mowed, and the paint was fresh—but it wasn't home. It had the sterile feel of a holiday rental, and the family felt no attachment to the place: the walls were bare and they were living on the few items they could fit in suitcases. The children played outside, but only under the watchful eye of one of their parents. The ten-foot-high walls with surveillance cameras that ringed the property limited their view of the world. The children were accustomed to the fact that their dad never went anywhere without his old 9-mm service pistol tucked discreetly into his belt.

One morning Paul looked out the front window to see both of his cars with large ugly gray splotches splashed across them. He instantly recognized this old security police trademark: paint remover had been thrown on the vehicles, extensively damaging both of them. This message was intended to strike fear in the prey. He knew that they knew where he was.

The signal worked. Erasmus became highly agitated. He paced the house, unable to concentrate on anything. He kept his kids inside, the shades drawn, and peered out the window for any other signs. He and Linda had a contingency plan for what to do if the house was attacked; he insisted they review it several times that day. That night they dozed fitfully. They were awakened by a loud crash at 4 A.M.

A brick came sailing through the front window in a hail of shattered glass. It was another old trick intended to flush out the prey. Erasmus knew this and refused to behave like a victim. This was a battle between old predators; Erasmus would fight until the end.

Linda leaped up and grabbed the children. She dragged her terrified daughter by the arm and her son by the collar down a long hallway. The bullets began flying as they scrambled. A deafening roar ensued as steel ripped through the house, shattering lights and blasting holes in the walls around them. Plaster rained down on them as she shoved the kids below the kitchen sink and threw herself over them. There was little thought involved. She had practiced this routine, and her terror-fueled maternal instincts did the rest. Her eight-year-old son shook and whimpered quietly as his mother clutched her children tightly in a bear hug. If anyone was going to die, let it be her, Linda thought to herself.

Paul lunged for the pistol and ammunition clips that lay beneath his bed. He was on autopilot, acting on reflexes honed fifteen years earlier as a soldier in Namibia. "Get down! Get down!" he barked to his family like a military commander. The first rule of combat flashed across his mind: get everybody to ground, and return fire immediately to let the enemy know you can fight.

He lunged toward a window, took cover beneath it, and coldly returned fire. The ink black sky lit up with muzzle flashes. The roar continued for what seemed like hours. Erasmus blasted off thirty furious rounds, stopping only long enough to reload his trusty service pistol. For seventeen years he had lovingly cleaned and caressed this weapon in anticipation of a gun battle with the enemy. Little had he suspected during that time that the battle, now finally upon him, would be with men he once called friends. He fired back at every flash he saw and kept blasting after their guns fell silent. This was war, only this time he was fighting to save his family, not the apartheid state.

The slam of car doors and the squeal of tires signaled the end of the battle. An acrid metallic cloud of gunpowder hung limply in the air. Linda slowly relaxed her grip on the children. The trio crept cautiously down the hall and found their father at the window, frozen in combat position. He lay on his large belly, his legs splayed, his arms forward, his gun perched on the sill. It took Paul several minutes to realize that the danger had passed. Then he began shaking uncontrollably.

The assassination attempt against Erasmus was the final blow. Ironically, it liberated him. Erasmus figured that the more the public knew, the safer he was—there would be little accomplished by silencing him. A month after the attack, Erasmus was outraged to learn that the year-old Goldstone Commission final report was being suppressed by the Mandela government. (The report was originally given to F. W. de Klerk just before the April 1994 elections. De Klerk did not act on the report, and the Mandela government kept the contents of the report secret, apparently out of fear of provoking a "police revolt.") So Erasmus went directly to the crusading journalists he once harassed and personally released parts of the report that he had in his possession.

In a sensational edition of the *Mail and Guardian* on July 7, 1995, South Africans read for themselves the litany of atrocities that were committed in their name and cataloged by Goldstone. Among the findings of the Goldstone Commission:

> [T]he Security Branch of the SAP (now renamed the Criminal Intelligence Service) has been involved for many years in the most serious criminal conduct including murder, fraud, blackmail and a huge operation of dishonest political disinformation.

> A large number of police officers currently holding high office, including the Commissioner of Police, were not only aware of some of the earlier criminal activities, but must have approved it . . . So too . . . the then Minister of Law and Order, Mr. A. Vlok.

> The whole illegal, criminal and oppressive system is still in place and its architects are in control of the SAP.

> It is a bleak prospect that this country enters its first democratic election with this security structure in place.[16]

The Goldstone report—for which Erasmus was cited as a key witness—had enormous implications: it recommended that the Mandela administration immediately fire the top leadership of the police. It also implicated a variety of top National Party political leaders in previous crimes. As a result of the report, General Johan van der Merwe, the commissioner of police who Erasmus claims tried to have him killed, resigned.

Erasmus was intensely sensitive to the charge that he was betraying his old colleagues. He justified his actions, telling the *Mail and Guardian,* "I don't regard myself as another Dirk Coetzee or a traitor. However, I believe that unless the evils of the past are exposed, they may be perpetuated in the future."[17]

Erasmus knew that his revelations were only one part of what he needed to do; making amends for his past deeds was the other. In the same week that Erasmus had gone to the press, Rev. Frank Chikane wrote a letter to

Minister of Safety and Security Sydney Mufamadi requesting that the government reopen the investigation into his poisoning and the Khotso House bombing. Chikane was forcing Erasmus's hand.

"As you know, I am one of those few South Africans who are prepared to forgive those who were responsible for these hideous acts, but this must go with the willingness to voluntarily disclose the said acts as well as an indication of remorse on the part of the perpetrators," Chikane wrote to Mufamadi. "Failure to do so should open [them] to prosecution and punishment."[18]

Erasmus decided he should speak to Chikane himself rather than let someone else turn him in. Journalists at the *Mail and Guardian* suggested they meet face to face, but Chikane declined: unless Erasmus was willing to come clean about who poisoned him, Chikane didn't want to meet. But he agreed to speak with Erasmus by telephone.

For two days, Erasmus paced nervously about, terrified to pick up the phone. He was afraid of Chikane, afraid of the anger and abuse that Chikane might heap on him for what he'd done. Finally, he dialed the number.

"Rev. Chikane, this is Paul Erasmus. I was a security policeman assigned to you some years back," Erasmus recounts. Chikane greeted the nervous cop warmly.

"How are your wife and children?" the cleric inquired. He told him that he had read with concern in the *Sunday Times* about the attack on his family and that he was praying for them. Erasmus was momentarily speechless. Then he assured Chikane they were holding up under the strain.

"I want to apologize for the things that I did to you," said Erasmus haltingly. He had a lump in his throat, and spoke slowly. "I'm not proud of what I did. And I also want to apologize for what happened to you when you were poisoned."

Chikane paid him a compliment. "It is important and takes courage to take this stand. And I forgive you for what you did." Then Chikane got down to more serious matters. Erasmus knew this was coming.

"Who poisoned me?" he asked pointedly.

Erasmus was pained by the question. His partner was among his closest friends, and he did not want to betray him. He answered, "I believe it was my partner, but I can't tell you his name. I want him to come forward on his own accord when he is ready."

Chikane assured him, "I can wait. I will forgive him as well if he tells me the truth about what happened." The call was brief and ended amiably.

Erasmus was thunderstruck. In one brief phone call, his whole demonology had been turned upside down. "My feelings about the man since then—it's just fantastic. That somebody can go through an experience like that and, and forgive . . . I can't see myself ever doing that and forgiving as easily as, as readily as what he did. He's a better person than me. This is a guy I hated so much and wanted to kill."

It's been a difficult month for Erasmus. I am meeting with him in December 1996, and he has spent all of the previous month writing his application for amnesty to the Truth and Reconciliation Commission. "I have to list every incident I was ever involved in, you know. There were so many that I can't remember them all." He estimates he has over one hundred incidents to account for.

Linda has dutifully typed everything. She knew little of her husband's work until around 1994. And she didn't learn of her husband's firsthand involvement with dirty tricks until she typed the manuscript of the book that he hopes to publish. "She cried when she read the book," he says. "But she understands why it happened."

Erasmus is extremely protective of his family now. He won't let me visit his house or meet his wife and kids. "They've been through hell. We've moved eleven times in the last three years. This whole thing of being on the witness protection program—it's started us and my children going through identity crises. We were overseas as the Barnard family and the Ford family and Badenhorst and—you name it. It's terrible when you have to go to your children and say to them, 'Today you're Candice Ford, you're not Candice Erasmus.'"

Erasmus takes a break from baring his soul and suddenly announces, like a proud kid with baseball cards, "I've got some photos I thought you'd like to see." He pops open his black attaché case and pulls out a disorganized jumble of pictures. He pulls a faded snapshot of a group of young men in fatigues holding beer cans aloft. "That's my unit in Namibia," he says.

"This guy," he says, pointing to a smiling man sporting sunglasses, "was my partner at the time. He killed himself."

"That guy," he points nonchalantly to another man in his twenties, "he's not normal anymore. He's left the force. I don't know where he ended up. And that guy," pointing to a bare-backed skinny kid, "went off his head completely."

He flips through the deck and comes to several grisly close-ups that he shot of Neil Aggett hanging from the bars of his police cell, dead. "Look at that. Fucking insane you know?" he says shaking his head. "I look at it now—it's like, horrific."

We're back in Namibia again. Pictures of blown-up pickup trucks— "SWAPO limpet mine," he tosses off. Another mangled corpse: "Alex bomb factory . . . And here's a letter bomb we sent a guy to wake him up a bit."

He dotes proudly on a picture of a group of Namibian children whom his unit adopted and fed. "They were like our 'black boys,' ya know? We treated them like our own. And they loved us.

"Oh yeah, there's a Polaroid of the guy that I shot." The smiling visage of a bald-headed old man peers out from a well-thumbed photo. It's the sweet and the sour of the war experience.

"Oh, there's another guy I worked with. Dead now. Suicide," he says flatly.

The Namibia "family photo album" provides a stunning glimpse of the toll that the apartheid security system took on its own henchmen. The ubiquitous booze—"if you weren't an alcoholic going in, you most definitely were by the time you came out"—and the catalog of mental illnesses that resulted from the war and police experience is an unspoken casualty of apartheid. In 1997 more than ninety police officers committed suicide, a one-year increase of 24 percent.[19] Erasmus says going into therapy "saved his life," although he is still dependent on a daily dose of antidepressants by morning and sleep medication at night.

Erasmus closes his briefcase and we wander outside. It is nearly midnight now. A warm summer breeze engulfs us as we stand around chatting. A streetlight illuminates his face with yellow streaks. Erasmus used to be in his element at night. It's where he did his best work as a cop. But now the night has turned on him.

A lone figure walks down the street toward us. A car drives slowly the other way. Erasmus stops talking. He cannot take his eyes off the vehicle. He stares at it as if his gaze could stop it in its tracks. He follows the car's taillights with his eyes, tracking it vigilantly, involuntarily.

"Do you get spooked?" I ask him. He chuckles nervously.

"Ja, I am waiting to see who that guy is. He looks rather ominous at the moment," he says, tipping his head toward a man who is walking toward us wearing a hooded sweatshirt. Paul's stocky shoulders are raised, his arms tense. The man passes by without so much as looking at us.

"Ja, like maybe I won't react now, but maybe I'll react after it happens. Then 'Blaahhh!'" he suddenly throws his hands up as if he were shot. He says this is called "exaggerated response syndrome," a symptom of PTSD. Just then we hear the pop of a firecracker. Paul is suddenly on alert again, unable to speak. He manages a frantic drag on his cigarette.

Paul Erasmus is a shattered man. He bitterly blames de Klerk for abandoning the enforcers of apartheid to their own devices. In the long hours that we talk, the only time he becomes visibly emotional is when the subject turns to de Klerk.

"These icons of apartheid are the people that have sold us—my colleagues and I, the foot soldiers—down the river. Where's de Klerk to this day? . . . If de Klerk had had the guts, the courage to tell President Mandela during the negotiation phase, 'Yes, there was a third force, yes, we were responsible, yes, I was responsible, yes the police force was involved in whatever' . . . Um, then maybe there wouldn't have been a need for the Truth Commission." Erasmus is suddenly staring at me, his face reddening in anger.

"Basically our leaders left us to carry the can. I think that makes it even more disgusting . . . I would be happy to go to the grave knowing that de Klerk becomes the first person in history to be relieved of the Nobel Prize, I really would . . . The man is a master deceiver, like so many of his colleagues."

Erasmus's former colleague, ex-Vlakplaas death squad commander Eugene de Kock, reacted similarly when the subject turned to taking responsibility for apartheid crimes. During his eighteen-month multiple murder trial, de Kock only lost his composure once: when he spoke of the betrayal of his former boss, F. W. de Klerk. De Klerk has emphatically and repeatedly denied responsibility for the police's dirty tricks during his reign, instead blaming them on "rogue elements" of the security forces. When the TRC confronted de Klerk in June 1997 with details of police abuses under his reign, he replied to an incredulous commission, "I was as surprised as you were."

De Kock—whom Erasmus admiringly describes as an "incredible leader, a guy who stood behind his men to the end"—lashed out at de Klerk for being like "a small scared dog lying on his back wetting himself."[20] He said he admired Nelson Mandela more than de Klerk because Mandela "stood by his people."

For Erasmus, being betrayed by his former masters is not just politically repugnant. It undermines all that he once believed. He had been a loyal soldier, following orders no matter how heinous, believing he was doing his job for the good of the state, for God, for the survival of the white Christian world. Now the state wants nothing to do with him or his kind. For he and many of his colleagues, their world has come crashing down around them.

The week after Erasmus's revelations broke in the press, Greg Deegan, a former security police colleague, wrote a letter to the *Mail and Guardian.* He noted that he was angry when he heard that Erasmus had confessed the police's dirty tricks. But then he listened to what Erasmus was saying, and finally spoke to him on the phone. In "Letter from an angry footsoldier," Deegan wrote:

> We, the white South Africans of the previous political era, were brought up to detest communism in all its forms. We were taught that our "blacks" were the spear point of the communist thrust into our society and that only through apartheid would we keep the communist threat from our doors.
>
> . . . We believed that our "cause" was just, and we believed in our leaders. We believed in our leaders when we were called upon to fight the "total onslaught." We believed in our leaders when they urged us to fight "fire with fire." We believed in our leaders when they ordered us, either directly or by suggestion, to rid them of their enemies, and provided us with the means to do so.
>
> . . . Until now, Paul Erasmus has not implicated the "footsoldiers." The names he has mentioned are those of senior officers and politicians. Paul hasn't "dropped" his friends. Paul has done what he has done because, unlike the rest of us, he has realized that the "cause" for which we fought has been abandoned by our leaders. That *we* have been abandoned by our leaders. That our leaders now enjoy either well-paid positions within the present administration or are relaxing on massive state pensions.
>
> Paul Erasmus has opened the way for all of us. Now is the time to decide whether it is fair that we stand alone, or whether the architects of our "cause" should be held accountable.[21]

Victims of Erasmus's wrath have been less generous with their assessment of him. Gavin Andersson was a trade unionist whom Erasmus harassed with middle-of-the-night visits, phone calls, and threats. Andersson wrote a letter to the newspaper accusing Erasmus of being "cowardly." He slammed Erasmus's refusal to name names of his police colleagues. "They are thus enabled to continue in the police force, where they will probably resist the change processes." He claimed Erasmus was merely an opportunist intent on "rais[ing] his own stature to the level of a reliable informant, to the disadvantage of his opponents."[22]

Gavin Evans was the muckraking journalist—and underground ANC member—whom Erasmus confessed to placing on a death list. Evans is a short, energetic, cheeky man who doesn't shy from authority. He enraged Erasmus for having the temerity to attempt a "citizen's arrest" of the bullying cop at a 1985 street demonstration. For that, Erasmus wanted him dead.

Two years later, when Evans was being interrogated at John Vorster Square, Erasmus charged into the room and punched Evans, saying he was "insolent." Evans wrote of the incident, "While hitting a detainee was at the bottom level of the security police's arsenal, what made me remember the occasion vividly was the look of hatred that preceded it, followed by the smirk of satisfaction afterwards. When I was released, he made a point of telling me that I should 'expect some surprises' and that 'accidents do happen,' or words to that effect. I now understand something of what he had in mind."

Evans told me that Erasmus had inflated his own status by claiming to have put him on a death list. The journalist has since learned that those orders came from high up in military intelligence. But he conceded that Erasmus's confession had some value. As he concluded in his published reply to Erasmus, "As I remember him, Paul Erasmus was a thoroughly objectionable human being: bitter, resentful and violent. But, it seems, even the worst of the past regime's functionaries are capable of some redemption. In spilling the beans on his nasty past, and revealing more about the National Party government's role in criminal violence against its opponents, he has done the country a service."[23]

At the height of apartheid, Archbishop Desmond Tutu would often rail against the apartheid enforcers. "One day you will have to answer to *God*," he would harangue them. I would roll my eyes when I heard it. As if these guys really cared what God thinks, I muttered to myself.

Tutu was right: that day of personal reckoning has come. Paul Erasmus's lowest moments are when he is left alone with his thoughts. Watching Erasmus—once a cocky soldier, now a haunted man—I realize that one of the greatest punishments former victims can mete out to their oppressors is to forgive them. The ex-tormentors are left to deal with their own thoughts. That is when *their* torture begins. For many of them were not monsters; they were regular people who did monstrous things. Left to their own devices, they must now reconcile themselves to the depraved acts they committed.

Erasmus was granted early retirement from the police force based on his medical disability. He says it was the first and only time the police have granted a disability leave based on post-traumatic stress disorder. He occasionally works odd jobs; he says he just helped build a swimming pool. But mostly he just tries to keep his life together. He has not had much success with that.

I call Paul Erasmus to make arrangements to meet him again in March 1997, four months after our first meeting. I ask him how he is doing.

"Things at home are not going well at all," he replies.

I press gingerly, "Is it your marriage?"

"Ja, my marriage has cracked up. Linda has left and taken the kids. The strain has just been too much."

I reply that it's strange that she would leave now, after the worst is over. Erasmus is quick to psychologize. "I can say it might be a post-traumatic reaction for my wife. It's almost post-traumatic stress to everything we've been through over the past five years."

When I visit with him shortly after, he is looking somber, dressed in a navy blue suit. He can't spend much time. He is darting back and forth to his lawyer's office and court on this day. He is desperately trying to obtain an emergency interdict from the court to get his son back from Linda, and possibly his daughter, too. He claims his wife is beating the boy because he wants to see his father. His marriage and his family life were one of the last threads to remain intact in his fragile world. Now that too has just snapped.

The new South Africa has made for many strange bedfellows. But few are more bizarre than the symbiotic relationship that formed between Paul Erasmus and his most famous victim. In late 1997, Erasmus was drawn into a curious public campaign to clear the name of Winnie Madikizela-

Mandela. The former wife of Nelson Mandela was scheduled to appear before the Truth Commission to testify about her role in the 1988 murder of fourteen-year-old activist Stompie Sepei, who was killed in her Soweto home. Mandela's bodyguards were convicted of the killing. Winnie Mandela was convicted in 1991 of kidnapping in relation to the Sepei case and sentenced to six years in jail. Her conviction was upheld on appeal in 1993, but her sentence was reduced to a fine.

The TRC wanted to know the truth behind Madikizela-Mandela's involvement with the notorious deed, along with her role in seventeen other crimes ranging from kidnapping, to assault and murder. A range of high-profile activists, including Rev. Frank Chikane, described to the TRC in November 1997 the reign of terror that Madikizela-Mandela unleashed on Soweto during the 1980s. She was accused by anti-apartheid Bishop Peter Storey of being a pathological liar, and fingered by other residents as having ordered the deaths of men, women, and children who crossed her. The hearings were a devastating indictment of the woman who was once known as "The Mother of the Nation."

Anticipating that her former comrades were going to provide damning evidence against her, Madikizela-Mandela turned to her old enemy to clear her name in advance of the hearings. On September 10, 1997, South Africans were treated to the spectacle of Paul Erasmus speaking at a highly publicized press conference called by Madikizela-Mandela. Erasmus was there to repeat his confession about how he had smeared the president's former wife.

"We spared no effort in alleging that Madikizela-Mandela was a child killer," said a stiff, uncomfortable looking Erasmus. "Mandela was further made out to be a hater of white people and, who, with her husband at her side, would exact a terrible revenge for the way that the white capitalists had treated her and her family."

Erasmus then added the all-important caveat. "At no stage did I ever receive information to the effect that Madikizela-Mandela had killed Stompie Sepei or for that matter ordered anyone's death. If I had received such information, I would have been able to use this with devastating effect in the Stratcomm sense." Erasmus repeated his comments on a segment about Madikizela-Mandela that aired on CBS's *60 Minutes* that November.

Such is the long, twisted road to redemption in the post-apartheid world. Old enemies suddenly need one another in order to move forward.

For Paul Erasmus, it is a fate reminiscent of Dante's *Inferno:* his only value in the new South Africa is to perpetually confess his past sins. Erasmus's destiny is to ensure that South Africa—and he—will never forget.

In June 1998, a light was shone behind the veil of secrecy that surrounded the assassination attempt on Rev. Frank Chikane nine years earlier. During a week that veteran journalist David Beresford described as equal parts tragedy and farce, the Truth and Reconciliation Commission heard how some of South Africa's finest scientific minds were put in the service of devising ever more devious ways to kill. "In pursuit of a warped scientific quest for a means to create innocence out of murder," wrote Beresford, the scientists of the government Roodeplaat Research Laboratories (RRL) concocted a smorgasbord of over five hundred lethal brews and weapons. There were bottles of cholera; poison-tipped umbrellas; anthrax laced into chocolate, cigarettes, and the gum of envelopes; a plan to spike Nelson Mandela's medication with the poison thallium to impair his brain function; screwdrivers with spring-loaded syringes that could inject lethal toxins; extensive research into how to reduce the fertility of African women.[24] In the course of this macabre recitation came the story of the botched attempt to kill Frank Chikane.

Senior officers of the South African Defense Force had inquired about a way to kill Chikane that would leave no trace. The RRL doctors and scientists came up with the answer. A highly toxic substance known as paraoxane was applied to five pairs of Chikane's underpants. The plan was to poison him while he was far from help; his trip to Namibia provided the perfect setting for the crime. But the killer doctors erred, as they often did. The toxic underwear did not deliver a high enough dose of the poison. Had the poison covered a larger part of the body—as it would have had it been placed on a shirt or trousers—Chikane would likely have succumbed.

Army officers were furious about the blunder. RRL codirector André Immelman reportedly declared after the botched murder, "Hell, it's a real mess." He swore they wouldn't fail next time.[25]

One nagging secret remained after the revelations: the identity of the man who actually applied the poison to Chikane's clothes. Was it Paul Erasmus? His partner? In an interview with the *Cape Argus* following the hearings, Chikane expressed a desire to meet his would-be assassin. It was not just his need to "close that chapter," said the deputy president's top aide. "My forgiving him is not the real issue. The real issue is the healing of that person. It is important for me to see that person freed from anxiety."[26]

There is more to Chikane's plea than magnanimity. Vestiges of the apartheid security apparatus continue to bedevil the new government. Chikane and his political colleagues fear that former hit men are still at work, sabotaging internal efforts at reform and operating domestically and internationally as guns for hire. Chikane is aware that the public exposure he seeks would deny a killer his most important weapon—his anonymity.

Chikane prefers to emphasize his concern for the personal price being paid by South Africa's former hit men. Lurking around South Africa was a man "who has not declared himself," asserted Chikane. The secret assassin "is living a life of fear and guilt, who remembers every time he sees my name."

Paul Erasmus and I linger under the stars for a final few moments. He has some last things on his mind.

"David, if I could only turn the clock back," he says, looking up at the jet black night sky. "You know [ANC politician] Dave Dalling said publicly, when he read my revelations, 'What a wasted life.' Those words stick in my mind. I mean, there were so many things that I could have done. How I got sucked into that system and believed in it so strongly is beyond me. I mean—I messed my life up, short and sweet.

"I don't know, I've got this"—he pauses, groping for the right word—"like determination to correct something. Like maybe I could just explain why, for the sake of not only me, but for my colleagues, why these things happened." The words pour out of him in a confession of sorts.

"I'm ashamed of what I was involved in. If I helped prolong apartheid, as I understand it now, for even one minute, then I deserve the full weight of justice in this country. If it was just for one minute that my role extended it . . . my God, it was a sick system, on everybody. There's nobody in this country that wasn't affected. Nobody in this country that wasn't a victim. We're all victimized. Afrikaners are victimized, possibly more than any other grouping."

The fallen strongman pauses wistfully. "Terrible, hey?" he says, shaking his head and peering up at the crescent moon. "Things could have been so different."

PART TWO | **THE ODYSSEY OF THE VERWOERDS**

# ARCHITECT OF APARTHEID

PRIME MINISTER H. F. VERWOERD AND
PROFESSOR WILHELM VERWOERD SR.

Wilhelm Verwoerd Sr.
at his home, beneath
a portrait of H. F.
Verwoerd, 1997.

Of the men who have ruled South Africa . . . no one has been the guiding mind behind so much negative and oppressive legislation [as H. F. Verwoerd]. If any one man is remembered as the author of our calamity, it will be he.

*Chief Albert Luthuli, ANC president and Nobel Peace Prize recipient*

**HE IS A CHARMING MAN,** if a bit stiff. I find Professor Wilhelm Verwo- erd Sr.* in his office at the Chamber of Mines Building, home of the ge- ology department at Stellenbosch University. The front door of the building is adorned with the inscription 100 YEARS OF GEOLOGY, 1895– 1995, to remind entrants of the hallowed history of this place and this university. Stellenbosch is the premier Afrikaans university and was the intellectual nursery of many of the foremost apartheid theorists and politicians. The campus resonates with this heritage. As I look for Prof. Verwoerd, I pass the B. J. Vorster Building and, of course, the H. F. Ver- woerd Building.

Verwoerd appears somewhat nervous. His hands shake, and he dis- charges some of his nervous energy by constantly twiddling his thumbs. He asks me to join him for tea and to explain why I've come to speak with him. On the phone, he informed me he would give me thirty minutes.

I tell him that I am profiling his son, young Wilhelm, and want to tell some of the story of his family. This is a sensitive subject, as his son is no- torious among unreconstructed Afrikaners. He is the traitor—even his fa- ther has called him that—the Verwoerd who joined the ANC in 1992 and is now a staff member for the Truth and Reconciliation Commission. Wil- helm Jr. has been virtually disowned by his father. They are no longer on speaking terms, despite the fact that they see one another regularly when the grandchildren come to visit. Young Wilhelm has warned me that his father will probably not speak to me, since he was inundated with inter-

---

* Professor Wilhelm Verwoerd is actually Wilhelm Verwoerd II; his son is Wilhelm Ver- woerd III. Afrikaners often do not distinguish between family members with the same name, or they use nicknames; suffixes are "too American," insists Professor Verwoerd. For the sake of clarity, and with all due respect to Afrikaans custom, I follow the standard English usage of "Sr." to refer to the elder Verwoerd, and "Jr." to refer to his son.

views before the 1994 election and feels that the "liberal media" has been unsympathetic to him.

I explain that I want to revisit the history of his father. Hendrik Frensch Verwoerd (pronounced fer-VOORT) was prime minister of South Africa from 1958 to 1966. He is best known as the "architect of apartheid," and the man who withdrew South Africa from the British Commonwealth. He was assassinated by a deranged parliamentary messenger while sitting in parliament in 1966. Prof. Verwoerd is eager to set the record straight about his father, and he agrees to talk.

Wilhelm Verwoerd Sr. is a retired geology professor. He followed in the early footsteps of his father, who began his career as a professor at Stellenbosch. Verwoerd's geology department office is stacked floor to ceiling with papers. Beneath his desk are boxes crammed with rocks and geologist's hammers; a side table is also strewn with colorful geodes and crystals. Verwoerd apologizes for the mess, explaining that he had a much larger office before he retired, but this is where they put him now that he is emeritus.

Verwoerd explains that H. F. Verwoerd's father originally moved here from Holland in 1902 just after the Anglo-Boer War. He set up shop selling Christian books in the town of Brandfort. "You know where that is?" he asks me. Yes, I nod, but I know of the place for a different reason: the small, conservative town in the Orange Free State was where Winnie Mandela and her daughters were banished in the 1970s in a futile attempt to remove them from public view. Brandfort was yanked from its pastoral anonymity and suddenly attained international notoriety as a symbol of South African racism.

Our conversation drifts to the thirties and forties, formative years for Afrikaner nationalism. Verwoerd speaks of Afrikaner politics during World War II as a difficult time when Afrikaners were sharply divided. South Africa, under the Afrikaner general Jan Smuts, fought on the side of the Allies, but many of the *volk* still despised the British and openly supported the Nazis. "I guess that is much like today," he says glumly of the divisions that have rent Afrikaners in the post-apartheid era.

Wilhelm Verwoerd Sr. concedes that "separate development"—the euphemism that his father coined for apartheid—was a failure. I am surprised by his candor and ask him to explain. "The main reason it failed is not so much a fault of the white South Africans, but the black South Africans were not able to take up that challenge. [There were] too few [black] people with integrity, too much misuse of funds, too little initiative, and that sort of thing." Had blacks been smart enough to comprehend the brilliance of the grand apartheid plan—where each ethnic group, including whites, would have its own autonomous homeland within South Africa—they would have embraced it. The professor remains unable to accept that blacks rejected and resisted apartheid because they understood precisely what it was: a policy that would disenfranchise the black majority and relegate it to permanent servitude in "white" South Africa.

After an hour and a half, Verwoerd suggests that we continue our conversation in a month at his home. I accept his invitation.

"You know," he concludes mistily as we stroll toward the exit, "many blacks say my father was the best minister they ever had."

White settlers first arrived in South Africa in 1652. The Dutch East India Company had sent Jan van Riebeeck from Holland to establish a station at the Cape of Good Hope to resupply Company ships with food and water as they plied the spice route. Van Riebeeck was a physician, but his mates consisted of a crew of Dutch rabble. They were, as Allister Sparks observes in *The Mind of South Africa,* "a mixture of day-laborers, vagrants and local unemployed . . . They were social and economic dropouts who . . . had failed to make it in the competitive society of seventeenth-century Holland."[1]

Van Riebeeck was under orders not to interact with Khoikhoi herdsmen (later dubbed "Hottentots" by the Dutch) apart from purchasing cattle from them. Upon his arrival at the Cape, van Riebeeck promptly cut himself off from his neighbors by surrounding his colony with a hedge of bitter almonds. The tangled, impenetrable bushes were intended to isolate the white inhabitants from the vast expanse of Africa that lay around them, preserving a slice of Europe half a world away. Part of the thorny hedge still stands today in the Kirstenbosch National Botanical Garden in Cape Town. The siege mentality that it symbolized has only recently begun to wither.

Ironically, the Dutch riffraff who disembarked at the Cape considered themselves the "chosen people." Their sense of racial and social superiority was rooted in their austere Calvinist religious dogma, which stipulated that they were the Elect of God.[2] So began what was to evolve into a violent paradox within Afrikaner culture: their deep Christian faith and their rabid racism. As Sparks explains, "Piety coexists with cruelty, prayerfulness with an aggressive militarism, a yearning to be understood and to be loved with a national bellicosity and an impulse to tell the rest of the world to go to hell."[3]

The Afrikaners, as the Dutch settlers came to be known, began migrating into the South African interior. They were a tough and uneducated band of pioneers who existed beyond the reach of outside influences or laws. They carried no books except their Bible, which few of them could read as literacy faded with the generations. Their only contact with the outside world was with the occasional trader who might pass their way. These self-reliant Boers became kings of their own realm. They were an intolerant bunch who responded to conflict by simply pulling up stakes and pressing deeper into the interior, ever farther from the clutch of civilization.

But competition for land and resources interfered with the Afrikaner's desire to remain alone. The farmland that the Boers expropriated had other claimants, namely, the African tribes who were already living there. The Africans began fighting back. In 1820, the Boers were confronted with yet more competition, as some four thousand English settlers, lured by the false promise of free and fertile farmland, arrived from London. The Boers were losing the battle for space.

The majority of whites lived in the Cape Colony, which became a British colony in 1814. Afrikaners were subjected to British law, which they resented. The last straw came in 1833 when Britain abolished slavery in its colonies. Some thirty-five thousand slaves went free in South Africa. Adding further insult, the British returned some annexed land to African tribes in the eastern Cape in 1836. Under British law, even black servants could haul their white masters into court and charge them with maltreatment. This was too much to bear for the Boers. Placing Africans "on an equal footing with Christians," wrote forty-six-year-old Voortrekker Anna Steenkamp in 1843, was "contrary to the laws of God."

The Boers in the Cape responded predictably to the increasing pressure and the meddling into their affairs: "we rather withdrew in order thus to preserve our doctrines in purity," wrote Steenkamp.[4] Between 1835 and 1840, six thousand Boers in caravans of ox-wagons—one-tenth of the white population of the Cape Colony—embarked on the Great Trek.[5] For several years the Voortrekkers ("pioneers") journeyed north, seizing large tracts of land and battling African tribes in a bloody conquest. They established the Boer Republics of the Orange Free State and the South African Republic, or Transvaal. By the twentieth century, the mythology of the Voortrekkers had become the single most emotive and powerful symbol of Afrikaner nationalist aspirations.

The Afrikaners resumed farming on their newly acquired lands, but conflict with the British settlers intensified. By the late 1800s, South Africa was divided into four colonies: Natal and the Cape Colony were under British rule, and the South African Republic and the Orange Free State were under Afrikaner rule. But British authorities were intent on imposing their will over all of South Africa—or at least those parts of the country with valuable resources. Shortly after the discovery of diamonds in the Transvaal in 1867, the British occupied part of the colony, then annexed the entire Boer colony in 1877. They relinquished the Transvaal in 1881, but tensions remained high. In 1886, gold was discovered near Johannesburg in the southern Transvaal. The lure of a gold strike was too much for the British Empire to resist.

In 1899, the Boer War broke out. It was a war driven by bald-faced greed: the British wanted control of the gold mines of Johannesburg, which were part of the South African Republic of President Paul Kruger. Citing flimsy evidence that British subjects—known as *uitlanders* (foreigners)—were being oppressed in the Boer republics, the British massed troops on the border of Kruger's colony and provoked the Boers to attack.

The poorly equipped Boer commandos under the leadership of Generals Louis Botha and Jan Smuts won surprising victories in the early days of battle, before British reinforcements arrived from England. The ragtag commandos were quickly outnumbered and outgunned by the British, and they were routed in 1900. But the war didn't end there: Boer fighters regrouped into guerrilla bands and launched periodic attacks against the British. In response, British commander Lord Kitchener embarked on a scorched earth policy, burning down Afrikaner farms, rounding up Afrikaner families, and placing them in the world's first concentration camps (the vast refugee camps were strategically concentrated near railway lines and sources of water—hence the name "concentration camp").

The Boers finally lost the war of attrition. The toll of the war was staggering. Twenty-eight thousand Boers and at least fourteen thousand

Africans died in the concentration camps; the war claimed the lives of twenty-two thousand British soldiers.[6] On May 31, 1902, a peace treaty was signed in which the Boer colonies became British crown colonies. Parts of the peace treaty were hotly disputed, but the whites were in agreement on one point: blacks would be denied the vote in the newly unified South Africa. It was a harbinger of the more draconian restrictions that followed.

As is often the case with distant colonial conquests, the British won on the battlefield but lost in the court of world opinion. European sentiment was decidedly pro-Boer. The Afrikaner "people's army" was viewed as an underdog fighting valiantly against an imperialist aggressor. There were also growing economic and political strains between the four colonies, as the gold-rich Transvaal threatened to pull out of a customs union with the other colonies.

The solution was to unify the colonies as provinces under one government: on May 31, 1910, the British Parliament established the Union of South Africa, with Gen. Louis Botha as its first president. The Union represented a remarkable victory for the vanquished Afrikaners, who regained a significant measure of self-determination—and self-respect—in the newly united country.

Wilhelm Johannes Verwoerd was a religious man who lived in Holland but dreamed of becoming a missionary among the battle weary Afrikaners. He had seen Paul Kruger in 1900 when the Boer president visited Amsterdam at the start of his exile. Like many Dutch, the elder Verwoerd sympathized intensely with the Afrikaner cause. In 1903, when his son Hendrik Frensch was just two years old, Verwoerd acted on his inspiration and brought the family from Holland to South Africa.

The Verwoerds settled in the predominantly English-speaking Cape Town suburb of Wynberg, where Wilhelm became a building contractor and did missionary work among the Cape colored community in his spare time. In 1910 Verwoerd qualified as a lay missionary, and was called to assist the Dutch Reformed Church congregation in Bulawayo, Rhodesia. A loyal British colony, Rhodesia was no easy home for an Afrikaner. Young Hendrik bristled at being forced to recite the British national anthem each day at Milton Boys' High in Bulawayo. When World War I broke out, the Verwoerds were viewed with suspicion since no one in their family was joining up to fight with the British. Fortunately, Hendrik's father was soon called back to the Orange Free State in South Africa by his church. When Hendrik informed his school headmaster that he would be leaving and could therefore not accept a scholarship that he had qualified for, the Rhodesian snapped, "You're going to a rebel country—good riddance!"

Hendrik Verwoerd thrived in the small town of Brandfort, where his father owned a small Christian bookstore. It was the first time the Verwoerds lived in an Afrikaans environment. Although Wilhelm Verwoerd was easily distinguished as a foreigner by his Dutch accent, the deeply religious family was accepted by their adoptive community. They identified closely with the Boers' sense of grievance at the outcome of the Boer War and later, at the outrage many Afrikaners felt when their top generals, Jan Smuts and Louis Botha, committed the Union of South Africa to fight in "Britain's War" (when South Africa declared war on Germany in September 1914, a group of former Boer War generals staged an unsuccessful revolt against Botha's rule).

In 1919, Hendrik Verwoerd passed his high school matriculation exam with the highest score in the Orange Free State. He went on to study theology at Stellenbosch University, which had already earned a reputation as a fount of Afrikaner nationalism. Student politics quickly caught his attention. He was elected chairman of the student representative council (SRC) in 1923, and became a skilled debater. It was at Stellenbosch that his nationalist sympathies began to solidify. As SRC chairman, he attempted unsuccessfully to have Afrikaans used at church services in Stellenbosch. His luck improved when he convinced the Cape Town Municipal Orchestra to stop playing "God Save the King" at the end of its Stellenbosch concerts.[7] When he was offered the prestigious Abe Bailey scholarship to study at Oxford, he declined, citing the unacceptable imperialist sympathies of the scholarship's namesake. He opted instead to take a less lucrative scholarship to study psychology in Germany, just as Nazism was beginning to take root. This principled obstinacy was to become a hallmark of H. F. Verwoerd's career.

Verwoerd abandoned his theology studies and obtained his doctorate in psychology in 1924. His doctoral thesis was titled "The Blunting of the Emotions."[8] In January 1927 he married Elizabeth Schoombee, a farmer's daughter whom he met at Stellenbosch. They wed in Hamburg, where he was studying (he attended the Universities of Leipzig, Hamburg, and

Berlin), and they spent their honeymoon traveling through Europe and the United States. While overseas he was offered the chair in "applied psychology and psychotechnics" at Stellenbosch, a position that he assumed in 1928 at the age of twenty-six.[9]

A defining social problem confronting Afrikaners at this time was the growing phenomenon of destitute whites. The "poor white problem" in South Africa received international attention when the Carnegie Corporation of New York investigated the subject in the 1930s. In their landmark five-volume report, the Carnegie Commission found that of the 1.8 million whites living in South Africa in 1931 (a million of whom were Afrikaners), three hundred thousand were "living as paupers."[10]

Verwoerd became obsessed with the problem of white poverty. He coaxed Stellenbosch University to create a department of sociology which would address contemporary social issues; Verwoerd became its first chairman in 1932. He was considered a gifted academic, but he was far too ambitious to be confined to the ivory tower. He was a prime organizer of a national Volkskongres (People's Congress) to address white poverty. The conference took place in 1934, and Verwoerd delivered its first paper. It was here that he first gained attention as a forceful ideologist for Afrikaner nationalism.

Verwoerd's solution to white poverty was an early form of affirmative action: strong state intervention that gave preference to Afrikaner workers. He stated unabashedly, "When some of the economic proposals contain a discrimination in favor of the white worker it must be realized that it was not only what was beneficial to our problem group—the white poor—that was considered, but to the country! Where, for instance, a certain privilege for the white poor causes a difficulty—but a removable one—for the non-whites, it was chosen without hesitation." As Verwoerd biographer Henry Kenney observed, it was an early display of his "ingenious sophistry" to posit that "what was good for the Afrikaner was good for South Africa. It was an approach which logically led to authoritarian solutions to the problems he faced."[11]

Verwoerd's unrelenting identification with the Afrikaners had its roots in a deep insecurity: Verwoerd was not, in fact, an Afrikaner by birth. Indeed, many nationalists privately referred to him dismissively as *Die Hollander*.[12] Kenney writes:

In the white-hot atmosphere of Afrikaner nationalism, with its frequent invocations of the glorious past of the Voortrekkers and of Paul Kruger, origins became important. It was at the very least reassuring to know that one's forefathers had participated, however modestly, in building the Afrikaner heritage. Verwoerd could make no such claim. Not one of his ancestors was an Afrikaner. In his chosen career he could not but be acutely aware of his liability. He took the way typical of a convert: he set himself to be an Afrikaner of Afrikaners . . . One of his associates of those days wrote: "He was nearly fanatical about Afrikaans institutions and delighted in proving his loyalty to them."[13]

Verwoerd's insecurity was not unlike what many Afrikaners felt, albeit for different reasons. Afrikaner culture is founded on a fragile pride and an enduring sense of threat. The Boers have always struggled with a deep-rooted inferiority complex. Their cultural and economic backwardness in relation to the British was a source of long-standing humiliation; their defeat in the Boer War intensified this mortification. A fiercely proud people, they have been quick to rally when told that their cultural survival is at stake. The bogeymen were first the British, occasionally shifting to Jews, and finally settling on blacks and so-called communists.

In reality these "threats" had little to do with political or cultural oppression and everything to do with economics. Whichever group constituted the biggest obstacle to Afrikaner economic advancement at a given moment was suddenly demonized. Afrikaner politicians and church leaders conducted their affairs with one finger always on the panic button, ready to raise the alarm whenever their interests might be compromised. This lies at the heart of the famous laager reflex, wherein Afrikaners respond to perceived dangers by circling their wagons and blasting away at the enemy— whomever that is at the moment. Afrikaner nationalist leaders have long relied on raising the specter of a threat to cultural survival to muster an enthusiastic and compliant following.

In 1936 Hendrik Verwoerd was asked to become the first editor of *Die Transvaler,* the organ of the National Party in the populous Transvaal. He was a rising star in academia, but he chafed in the confines of the insular world of Stellenbosch. Despite objections from his father and the fact that he had no journalistic experience, Verwoerd wasted no time in accepting the chance to leap into the political arena. After a short stint at *Die Burger,* the National Party paper in Cape Town where he learned the rudiments of newspapering, Verwoerd moved his family to Johannesburg in 1937 and began his political life in earnest.

Wilhelm Verwoerd Sr. was born in 1930, the first of Hendrik and Betsy Verwoerd's five sons and two daughters. He grew up in Johannesburg, a vibrant cultural melting pot. The Afrikaner presence was relatively small in the metropolis, but his parents remained determined to impart a strong cultural identity. He attended a small Afrikaner school that met in a private home.

As a young boy, Wilhelm was a member of the Voortrekkers, the Afrikaans equivalent of the Boy Scouts (which was considered "too foreign, too English," says Verwoerd). He recalls, "The Voortrekkers was not political at all—we went out into the veld and learned how to track and camp. It also taught you loyalty to your country, your nation, and your language . . . It wasn't the Hitler Youth or anything like that."

The thirties were a tumultuous time for Afrikaners. In 1938, Afrikaners observed the centennial commemoration of the Great Trek by reenacting the ox-wagon journey across South Africa. Thousands of Afrikaners donned traditional Voortrekker garb, men grew long "Paul Kruger beards," and politicians used the occasion to rally pride in Boer heritage. In towns around the country, streets were renamed in honor of Boer heroes. Afrikaners were swept up by a tide of nationalist fervor.

This surge of cultural consciousness left Wilhelm with another memory: conflict with the English. "The big thing in my youth was the English-Afrikaans antagonism, especially during the Second World War. Ugly things happened at that time." A catalyst for the Boer-English conflict was the fact that many Afrikaners, including Hendrik Verwoerd, were violently opposed to South Africa's decision to enter World War II on the side of the British. Wilhelm remembers seeing the ethnic tensions boil over. Africans, who were to loom so large in later nationalist dogma, merited little concern at the time.

"A year after [the Great Trek commemoration], when the war started, people still wore beards and some of them were challenged by the soldiers. Their beards were shaven off in the streets. Some fighting took place as well." He recalls that returning English-speaking South African soldiers tried to burn down the building that housed *Die Transvaler,* which under his father was editorializing stridently against "Britain's war." When Wil-

helm was sixteen, he attended a town hall meeting with his father and
D. F. Malan, the head of the National Party. A woman in the audience
leaped forward and tore off Hendrik Verwoerd's coat. When they went to
leave, Verwoerd's car was mobbed by angry protesters. Even the bookish
young Wilhelm was moved to throw a few punches in the mad rush to
escape.

Afrikaners were sharply divided by the war effort. A coalition government of rival Afrikaner politicians, Jan Smuts and Barry Hertzog, broke
up in acrimony, with Hertzog resigning over Smuts's decision to enter the
war. A strong pro-Nazi movement developed, led by the Ossewa Brandwag (Ox-wagon Guard), or OB. The OB tried to sabotage Allied war
efforts in South Africa by blowing up train stations, post offices, and
other government installations. A number of Afrikaner leaders, including
future prime minister B. J. Vorster, were arrested for supporting the OB.

In his editorials, Hendrik Verwoerd walked a fine line between criticizing the OB—which was posing a worrisome political threat to the National
Party—while sympathizing with Nazi ideals. Verwoerd launched the first
issue of *Die Transvaler* in October 1937 with a lead article, "The Jewish
Question from the Nationalist Point of View." Verwoerd, who frequently
slammed the "sham democracy of the British-Jewish system," argued
that Jewish domination of certain professions squeezed out deserving
Afrikaners. His solution was to advocate a quota system of jobs, naturally
preserving the bulk of work for Afrikaners. What seemed like crass discrimination was an expression of vintage Verwoerdian logic: he wasn't
"anti-Jew," he insisted, he was merely "pro-Afrikaner."

Verwoerd rejected Nazism for South Africa because, like English culture, he felt it was foreign to the Afrikaner way. "The National Socialist
system can have great value for Germany, but we cannot conceivably help
to transfer it, or any related system, to our country."[14] He noted that the
Nazis advocated dictatorship, whereas the Afrikaner political tradition
was a democratic one. He was not repulsed by Nazi ideology—to the contrary, its call for white supremacy appealed to him—he was just an ardent
proponent of homegrown politics.

This fine distinction between rejecting Nazism for South Africa and em-
bracing many Nazi ideals was lost on the Johannesburg *Star*. In an October 1941 editorial entitled "Speaking up for Hitler," *The Star* accused Verwoerd of falsifying news and spreading Nazi propaganda. In what he later

conceded was a rare error of judgment, Verwoerd sued *The Star* for defamation. In a scathing decision, Justice Philip Millin ruled against Verwoerd, writing, "He did support Nazi propaganda, he did make his paper a tool of the Nazis in South Africa, and he knew it."[15]

Was Hendrik Verwoerd a Nazi? Every chronicler of Verwoerd feels compelled to address this question.

Wilhelm Verwoerd Sr. bristles at the suggestion. The retired professor with a shock of white hair resembles a trim version of his father. The trademark turned-up nose and erect posture are all there. But Wilhelm is a soft-spoken intellectual who lacks his father's renowned charisma.

"That is a misnomer, a misconception," he asserts sharply. "There were Afrikaners that had a big admiration for Hitler. Nobody knew what was happening to the Jews and all that—that came to light afterwards. Especially before, there were lots of my schoolmates talking about the wonderful things Hitler was doing for Germany. It's often been said if Hitler had died in 1941 he would have been an honored leader. He did a lot for his people, but it turned out otherwise." I refrain from pointing out that Hitler's anti-Semitic crusade—including state-sanctioned pogroms, rounding up Jews, and liquidating their assets—were well under way in the early thirties, long before Hitler's "final solution" of extermination was implemented.

Wilhelm dismisses the Ossewa Brandwag as a "fascist organization" and insists that his father was their "dead enemy." He recalls that OB supporters attempted to assault his father. "He was driving home in the evening after working at the newspaper and he saw that the gates were closed at the house. He had to get out to open the gates and as he got out of the car he saw two people with sawed-off shotguns . . . He jumped back into the car quickly and drove through the gates without opening them and saw [the men] scattering." He muses that intra-Afrikaner fighting over Nazism "was a temporary madness that evaporated when Germany lost the war."

Hendrik Verwoerd was undoubtedly an anti-Semite. He wrote and spoke often of the "Jewish question." In 1936, he was one of five professors at Stellenbosch who protested publicly against Jewish immigrants who were coming to South Africa to escape from Nazi Germany.[16] His racism took the form of oblique utterances rather than vulgar name-calling, a tactic which was surprisingly effective in confusing his adversaries. He was no more averse to Jews than he was to English or Germans, he liked to say, it was just that he loved his own people the most. He viewed the law as a useful vehicle for separating people and promoting their narrow interests accordingly.

As for Nazism, it is perfectly consistent with his views that Verwoerd would have declined membership in a foreign political party. But that should not distract from the more salient point: Verwoerd was an eager fellow traveler of his white supremacist brethren in Europe. H. F. Verwoerd was not a Nazi in fact, but he was in spirit.

How did apartheid happen? The question has long intrigued me. When I began traveling in South Africa in the 1980s, what struck me was not the hostility of the Boers, but their hospitality and warmth to a white visitor. How then did an entire society fall under the thrall of such a vicious ideology?

It is important to note that white domination was not invented by the Boers. Since Jan van Riebeeck arrived in 1652, British and Dutch settlers had been enthusiastically passing laws which undermined the economic and political power of Africans. The Union of South Africa formalized this exploitation. The Union was founded in 1910 on the premise that Africans would be denied voting rights in all but the Cape Colony, where they could vote but were ineligible to sit in parliament. The Boers and English together then erected the so-called pillars of apartheid: the 1911 Mine and Works Act reserved skilled jobs for whites and relegated blacks to cheap labor, the 1913 Land Act confined blacks to 7 percent of the land, and the 1923 Natives Act banished urban blacks to live in segregated townships outside the "white" cities and forced them to carry passes.[17] But *apartheid*—literally, "separateness"—did not become the official centerpiece of government policy until the National Party came to power. Then it took a visionary such as H. F. Verwoerd to begin crafting and implementing laws that would bring about the long-held dream of Afrikaner supremacy.

"Today, South Africa belongs to us once more. For the first time since Union, South Africa is our own. May God grant that it will always remain so."

So declared the dour-faced seventy-four-year-old D. F. Malan on May

28, 1948, as he formed South Africa's first exclusively Afrikaner government. Malan's National Party (NP) had lost by 181,000 votes but won the election against Jan Smuts's United Party. This electoral fluke resulted from a turn-of-the-century rule which disproportionately weighted the votes of rural whites.* Two key factors in the campaign contributed to South Africa's most famous electoral upset: the appeal of exclusive Afrikaner nationalism, and the promise of a swift implementation of apartheid.[18] And so it was that a minority of the white minority prepared to literally change the face of modern South Africa.

The NP government moved swiftly to implement a variety of laws aimed at separating the races. Between 1948 and 1950, a raft of legislation was passed in rapid-fire succession. The Prohibition of Mixed Marriages Act banned interracial marriage, the Immorality Act barred interracial sex, the Population Registration Act required every South African to be classified by race, the Group Areas Act mandated strict residential segregation, and the Separate Amenities Act extended segregation to public places and transportation.

For Hendrik Verwoerd, selling apartheid to the masses was all in the presentation. Verwoerd was appointed minister of native affairs in 1950. The arrogant, uncompromising ideologue was a natural choice for the job. Not only did he have ideas for how to implement *baasskap* (white domination), he could give this crude racism an intellectual gloss that it previously lacked.

Apartheid was not about subjugating blacks and stripping them of their wealth, according to the new minister. It was about "separate development," where each race would have its own homeland. Apartheid, Verwoerd explained in 1950 to the Africans who sat on the Native Representative Council, proposed "the supremacy of the Bantu in his own sphere." He went on to explain the rationale for Bantu education, whereby black schools, including the liberal mission schools, would be removed from the Department of Education and placed under the Department of Native

---

* English and Afrikaner leaders agreed in 1909 that in the Union of South Africa, rural constituencies would need 15 percent fewer voters than the norm, while urban seats would require 15 percent more voters. This had the effect of giving conservative, rural Afrikaners a disproportionate number of political representatives, which ultimately ensured Afrikaner dominance in national elections (Saunders, 271).

Affairs. This was done because the educational needs of Africans were special, he noted. "What the Bantu needs more than anything else today is a vocational training in many directions. There is one very clear proviso and that is that when he is educated he may not use his education to slip out of the company of his fellow Bantu and try to go among the white man and use the knowledge there."[19] When members of the Native Representative Council, an advisory body on black affairs, objected, Verwoerd passed legislation the following year which simply wiped the Council out of existence. It was classic Verwoerdianism: the choice was to agree with him, or be crushed.

Verwoerd replaced the piecemeal British-style approach to separating the races with an ambitious scheme to balkanize South Africa into separate "homelands" for each ethnic group. South Africa, he declared, was "a white man's country . . . In the reserves we are prepared to allow the Natives to be the masters, we are not masters there. But within the European areas, we, the white people in South Africa, are and shall remain the masters."[20]

Doublespeak was a Verwoerd trademark. His Afrikaner audiences marveled at his ability to recast their crass racism to sound as if whites were merely reacting sensibly to grave threats; blacks, in turn, should be grateful for their oppression. "Indeed, it is not the Native whose future is being threatened, it is that of the Europeans; the European is really the person who should say: 'My rights must be protected.'"[21]

Verwoerd embarked upon social engineering on a grand scale. His "native policy" involved stripping blacks of their citizenship in "white" South Africa and granting them citizenship in eroded native reserves (also known as "homelands" or "Bantustans") which many of them had never seen before. Africans would only be allowed in the "white" cities if they were born there or could produce a pass which showed that they worked there. A number of existing urban black communities were dubbed "black spots" in white areas. One of the first to go was the polyglot community of Sophiatown, a Bohemian hub of nightclubs, gangs, and politics in Johannesburg. In 1954, the sixty thousand residents of Sophiatown were hustled out of their homes and forcibly removed to the new South West Township, or Soweto. Sophiatown was promptly bulldozed, and in its place arose a sterile suburb of boxy houses for white residents called Triomf—"triumph."

The human toll of Verwoerd's "triumphs" was staggering. Over the next three decades, some four million black people were forcibly removed from their homes and dumped in overcrowded reserves.

In 1958, Verwoerd was rewarded for his fanatic zeal in promoting white supremacy. The "architect of apartheid" was chosen by his party to be the next prime minister.

I am surprised to see amid the clutter of Professor Wilhelm Verwoerd's office a biography of Jan Smuts sitting on his desk, a man whom his father bitterly opposed. Verwoerd acknowledges, "I'm no admirer of Smuts, but someone from overseas has asked me to write a short article about him so I must brush up."

Professor Verwoerd has just returned from a visit to India, where he was invited to speak at a conference. He tells me with a hint of pride that he met there with a multiracial group of scientists. "If someone is equally well educated, if we are talking about people with university degrees, I have no problem associating with those people, talking about our scientific work," he asserts. "We can also talk socially on an equal basis."

We return to discussing his father. As the oldest son, Wilhelm is the keeper of the flame of H. F. Verwoerd's legacy. His mission in life is to preserve his father's good name, and he tries against the odds to ensure his father a honored place in history. Indeed, this is presumably the only reason he indulges my repeated visits and my prying questions.

Professor Verwoerd does not have an easy task. His father's name has come to be a synonym for evil these days, and he is frequently spoken of as South Africa's Hitler. The comparison doesn't work that neatly. Verwoerd was certainly no match for Hitler when it came to murdering people. Their methods differed in other ways, too: Verwoerd rallied support by being a consoling father figure, not a fiery demagogue. But one can validly compare the ways that both leaders tore apart their respective societies in order to advance their racial interests.

Wilhelm Verwoerd Sr. is reflexively defensive, at pains to explain what he considers to be the well intentioned, even compassionate origins of the apartheid ideal. "I accept that some people thought this was an evil policy and he was an evil man," he concedes. "The fact is it was the opposite: it was very highly moral to do justice not only to the whites, but to the blacks. The policy of 'separate development' would enable each group to go its own way and achieve its maximum amount of control over its own destiny. We Afrikaners have striven for independence from other nations all along, and we felt this was part of our heritage that we didn't want to sacrifice. In the past our struggle was with the English, so the next threat to our national survival was from indigenous blacks.

"It's very easy now to say that these were discriminatory laws," he says of the apartheid regulations. His hands shake noticeably as he raises them to emphasize his point. "There were discriminatory aspects but they were also intended for the benefit of these black people. He had a lot of support among the blacks. It's only these ANC types who are now in power who were trying not only to take a piece of cake but the whole cake. They of course didn't support him but the more traditional people who attached value to their chiefs and customs—they found him to be the best minister that they'd ever had."

He insists that his father devoted considerable resources to black development. "It was actually a very positive period," he muses. "Everybody was convinced that this was the only way to safeguard the future."

The professor is right about the mood of optimism that prevailed under his father—among Afrikaners, not blacks. The sixties heralded an era of unprecedented economic growth in South Africa. Verwoerd and the NP had made good on their promise to uplift the Boers, unashamedly using state largesse as the vehicle for advancement. Throughout the fifties, the NP instituted a massive "jobs for the boys" program, as state employment grew faster than ever before (6 percent per year). Between 1946 and 1966, the civil service grew three times as fast as the white population.[22] State employment became an entitlement of whiteness, and virtually all semi-skilled and supervisory jobs were reserved for whites. The result was a bloated bureaucracy loaded with inept and unqualified Afrikaner functionaries. By 1997, an astonishing two million of the country's five million whites were public employees.[23]

The transfer of wealth into Afrikaner hands was equally impressive. English capital was owned by South Africa. The National Party attempted to reset the scales by directing government contracts to Afrikaner businesses. Likewise, the secretive Afrikaner Broederbond (brotherhood) encouraged businessmen to invest in Afrikaner-owned firms, ranging from insurance companies to banks to publishing houses. The Broederbond, founded in 1918, was an elite secret society that played a crucial role in securing

Afrikaner control of key sectors of the economy, culture, and government. The resulting shift of wealth was dramatic: in 1946 the average Afrikaner's income was 47 percent of what an English-speaking South African earned; by 1976 it had risen to 71 percent, and continued to rise.[24]

In May 1959, Verwoerd unveiled his plans for what was later dubbed Grand Apartheid. Eight Bantustans, later expanded to ten, were established for various black tribes. It didn't matter that many urban blacks had little or no connection with their rural roots—tribalism was the basis of African culture because the great ethnologist Verwoerd said it was. Each Bantustan would be given limited self-government and, eventually, independence. The premise was breathtakingly simple: there were no longer any black citizens of South Africa, only visitors from these black puppet states.

In reality the Bantustans served as a pool of near slave labor for farmers and industry. While the South African economy grew faster than any other capitalist economy besides Japan during the fifties and sixties, African industrial wages dropped. By 1969 the real wages of African gold miners were below the level of 1896.[25] Afrikaners celebrated their good fortune as black South Africans sank deeper into despair and unprecedented poverty.

Verwoerd became increasingly possessed with race as the 1960s began, and he looked for even more aggressive ways to subjugate the black majority. In February 1960 British Prime Minister Harold Macmillan warned an indignant South African Parliament that it must heed the "winds of change" blowing across the African continent. Verwoerd replied by announcing that he would hold a referendum calling for South Africa to become a republic and end its symbolic connection with the British crown. Verwoerd was nothing if not consistent: he was always right, and if the rest of the world disagreed, then the world be damned.

Verwoerd's relentless assault on African rights placed him on a collision course with the growing anti-apartheid movement. On March 21, 1960, anger boiled over in the township of Sharpeville, not far from Johannesburg. The Pan Africanist Congress (PAC) had called for a peaceful protest against the pass laws. Panicky white policemen opened fire on unarmed demonstrators, raking the crowd with machine gun fire. When the shooting stopped, sixty-nine people lay dead and 180 were wounded, most of them shot in the back.[26] More demonstrators were killed that day in the Cape Town townships of Nyanga and Langa.

In the wake of Sharpeville, African protest mounted. In Cape Town, fifty thousand demonstrators marched on parliament and many publicly burned their passes. International condemnation poured in on South Africa, and foreign capital poured out (by August, the Reserve Bank reported a £68 million "reversal in the balance of payments" which it blamed on "the riots").[27]

Many Afrikaner leaders were shaken by the upheaval. They called upon Verwoerd to address African concerns and relax suffocating apartheid restrictions. *Die Rots* (The Rock), as Verwoerd came to be known, would brook none of this timidity. The uprising wasn't due to apartheid, he declared on the afternoon of the Sharpeville massacre, it was a result of anti-government propaganda that "necessarily had an inciting effect on the Bantu." He reassured his nervous white flock that this was merely a routine disturbance "which came in cycles," with the deaths resulting because the usually docile Bantu were "now more bold than before."[28]

It was a chilling performance. The parliamentary reporter for the *Cape Times* wrote: "The Prime Minister looked out over the body-strewn locations of yesterday in his mind's eye, and took a detached, almost academic, view of the tragedy. It had all happened before, he implied—these things come in waves. The main thing was to have a firm police force."[29]

There were two sides to Verwoerd's personality: the smiling father figure and the brick wall. The latter was evident when he imposed a national state of emergency on March 30, 1960. On April 8, he outlawed the ANC and PAC. The next day, an event occurred that was to solidify Verwoerd's stature as a divine savior of Afrikanerdom. As Verwoerd was speaking at an agricultural fair, a deranged white farmer named David Pratt approached the stage. "Verwoerd!" he called out. When the prime minister looked over, loud pops rang out and Verwoerd fell backwards, blood streaming from two bullet wounds in his forehead.

Miraculously, the bullets entered Verwoerd's head but missed his brain. (Pratt was sentenced to a mental institution, where he committed suicide a year later.) After a brief hospitalization and seven weeks of bed-rest, the prime minister returned to give his first radio address to the nation. Verwoerd anointed himself "one of the martyrs of the Afrikaner people,"[30] and even doubters had to concede that this was a mythic figure.

With renewed energy and a God-given mandate, Verwoerd resumed his destructive march. In October 1960, whites endorsed his approach by voting to sever the symbolic relationship with the hated British crown. The following May, Verwoerd realized a long-held Afrikaner nationalist dream when he officially consecrated the Republic of South Africa.

International observers were horrified by South Africa's aggressive march backwards. In 1960, South Africa was banned from participating in the Olympic Games. At the UN in April 1961, the United Kingdom, the United States, and Australia for the first time voted for a resolution calling for action against apartheid. And in October 1961 South Africa was forced to withdraw from the Commonwealth of Nations under pressure from member countries.

Verwoerd's response was to retreat into the famous Afrikaner laager and declare his isolation a victory. "If South Africa has to choose between being poor and white or rich and multiracial," he coldly informed a group of jittery businessmen, "then it must rather choose to be white."[31]

Despite the fact that South Africa was embattled, Verwoerd was a hero to his white followers. But the glorious march of this nationalist ideologue came to a swift and shocking end one day in 1966.

On September 5, 1966, Verwoerd spent the day with his family, including his son Wilhelm. He was looking characteristically energetic, remarkable for his sixty-four years. The following day he flew to Cape Town with his wife, Betsy, where he was to address parliament about the budget. He entered the ornate wood-paneled chambers at 2:15 P.M. looking buoyant and sat down in the prime minister's seat just to the right of the Speaker. Members were filing in and taking their seats. No one noticed a uniformed parliamentary messenger enter and walk briskly to the front of the hall. His name was Demetrio Tsafendas, the Mozambican-born illegitimate son of a Greek father and a Portuguese-African mother. He had entered South Africa the previous year when a minor official failed to notice that he was on a list of "prohibited entrants."

Tsafendas turned to the right and walked toward the opposition benches. Apparently not seeing who he was looking for, he turned around and walked quickly toward Verwoerd. He stepped into the aisle next to the prime minister, then swiftly pulled out a knife and lunged for the unsuspecting leader. Verwoerd smiled momentarily, thinking the messenger had accidentally stumbled against him. Then he saw the blood on his chest, and his face turned a ghostly white. Verwoerd yanked the lapels of his jacket together in a reflexive act of self-defense. He then let out a sigh and slumped down in his seat.[32]

Members of parliament by this time had thrown themselves on Tsafendas, who fought back strenuously, slashing with his knife. The minister of tourism, forestry, and sport, a former national team rugby player, joined in the fray and took down the assailant in a tackle, pulling him backwards over a desk and pinning him to the floor. Verwoerd's bodyguards finally arrived, and as they dragged him out Tsafendas screamed, "Where's that bastard? I'll get that bastard!"[33]

Pandemonium reigned on the floor of the House. Several MPs who were physicians tried in vain to revive Verwoerd. They discovered he had been stabbed four times in the neck and heart. As blood pooled on the floor, Betsy Verwoerd came down from the gallery, knelt down, and kissed her fallen husband on the forehead before being escorted out. Defense Minister P. W. Botha screamed in Afrikaans at liberal MP Helen Suzman, a longtime Verwoerd foe, "It's you who did this! It's all you liberals. Now we will get you!"[34]

Tsafendas turned out to be psychotic and later blamed his actions on a tapeworm in his body which was tormenting him. However, journalist David Beresford recently shed new light on the killer's motives. Beresford spoke with Tsafendas in 1997, the first interview that the assassin granted in thirty years. Beresford suggests that Tsafendas was also driven to kill by the racial persecution he endured in South Africa, where the dark-skinned man was nicknamed "Blackie" at school. He told his lawyer after the attack that "history will prove whether I am right or wrong." Tsafendas may have been a madman, but he was also a man on a mission.[35] As of 1998, Tsafendas remains incarcerated in a mental hospital near Johannesburg.

Ironically, Tsafendas had gotten the job as a parliamentary messenger thanks to Verwoerd's color bar, which permitted only whites to work inside parliament (Tsafendas was actually mixed race, but he was sufficiently fair-skinned that his employer didn't know). There was a staff shortage, and the eccentric Tsafendas was reluctantly hired.

Wilhelm Verwoerd was in his office at the geological survey in Pretoria when his mother called to inform him that his father had been attacked. "Is it serious?" asked the prime minister's eldest son.

"Yes, it's very serious," replied his mother. Wilhelm and his wife, Elize, flew down to Cape Town immediately, arriving the next day at Groote Schuur, the premier's residence in Cape Town. "In the back of my mind we had probably [known] that it was a dangerous job he has," he muses sadly. Wilhelm wanted a small family funeral, but government ministers explained that a state funeral was required.

H. F. Verwoerd was buried on September 10, 1966, at Heroes' Acre in Pretoria. His funeral at the Union Buildings in Pretoria was attended by a quarter million people. On the prison colony at Robben Island, political prisoners rejoiced at hearing the news of his death. Tsafendas, who was briefly quartered on the island (its only white prisoner), was proclaimed "a hero" by fellow inmates.[36]

Verwoerd was succeeded as prime minister by B. J. Vorster. Vorster was a former general in the Ossewa Brandwag who spent two years in jail during World War II for his pro-Nazi activities.[37] Vorster assumed power with the promise "to walk further along the road set by Hendrik Verwoerd."[38]

My directions from a local woman to Pieter W. Botha's house in the small tourist town called the Wilderness end with "it's the house with the great big South African flag out front—you can't miss it." I drive up and down a short cul-de-sac looking for the flag, to no avail. Finally, a trim young man in jeans with a pistol tucked discreetly in his belt trots over to my slow moving car. He introduces himself as Mr. Botha's bodyguard, and tells me that Botha is expecting me.

I apologize for being late. "I was told to look for a house with a flag," I tell the guard as we walk across the manicured front lawn.

The cop looks askance at me, as if I should know better. "Mr. Botha won't fly *that* flag," he says, alluding to the brightly colored new South African banner.

I find P. W., as he is commonly known, standing outside in a statuesque pose at the top of some stairs. He is peering out to the sun setting on the horizon. Just as I reach the top step, he turns toward me and extends his hand in greeting. "Mr. Goodman? P. W. Botha," he says melodramatically. It all seems a bit overwrought, but I indulge his sense of drama.

Botha does not grant interviews, as he made clear to me on the phone. His self-imposed exile since being ousted as state president in 1989 has made him the most famous recluse in South Africa. As the apartheid strongman from 1978 to 1989, the glowering Groot Krokodil (Big Crocodile) was probably the most hated figure in Africa in the eighties. Under his reign, anti-apartheid protest rocked South Africa, and the irascible

Botha responded with an iron fist. Thirty thousand people were detained without trial during his reign, and thousands were tortured and killed by his "police."[39] Botha imposed virtual martial law from 1986 to 1989.

I hadn't planned to see Botha—if I had, he most certainly would have turned me down, as he has done to so many other journalists. By chance, my car broke down in his town.* I had just set off with my wife and daughter on a month-long road trip around the country in July 1996. We were one day into our journey when our thirteen-year-old car blew its transmission. We limped into the seaside town of George, and holed up for several days at a motel while our "gearbox" was fixed.

The only thing that I know about George is that it is the home of Botha. This was the conservative constituency that elected Botha to parliament for thirty-six years. After touring the P. W. Botha wing of the George Museum, I decide to make my unplanned detour worth my while: I call the old president and ask if I can come over.

"Mr. Botha doesn't grant interviews any longer," his secretary brusquely informs me.

Yes, I explain, I know that, but I am about ten minutes from his house. She says she will get back to me. Minutes later, Botha himself calls me. He repeats that he does not grant interviews, especially not to journalists, who have caused him nothing but trouble in his life. I reply sympathetically, and we chat for a while. I tell him I would like to hear his recollections of Verwoerd. He finally relents and invites me over the next day for "just thirty minutes, and no political discussions."

The next day, my "just thirty minutes" turns into three hours of talking politics. Botha was deposed in a palace coup in 1989 by F. W. de Klerk. He had a mild stroke that year, but his political opponents within the National Party spread the rumor that he was incapacitated, and then forced him to retire. As I discover in our meeting, that was a convenient lie: P. W. at eighty is as sharp, abrasive, and truculent as he ever was.

It feels strange to meet Botha. For years he personified apartheid. He

---

* I actually visited with Botha twice. After our first discussion in July 1996, I discovered to my dismay that my tape recorder had not worked. In March 1997, I called and asked to see him again. He agreed, and we had another long chat—on tape.

had been minister of defense when South Africa invaded Angola in 1974, and president when anti-apartheid protests and state violence peaked in the 1980s. When I was an anti-apartheid activist, his dour visage and finger-wagging threats came to symbolize the intransigence of South Africa's white rulers. On my first trip to South Africa in 1984, my wife and I were in fear of being caught by his security police as we traveled in the townships, and we met countless activists who had suffered under his boot. Even in the late 1990s he casts a long shadow as former deputies repeatedly implicate him before the Truth and Reconciliation Commission for having authorized assassinations and dirty tricks against his enemies.

And then there he is, shaking my hand and offering me tea. His salutational pleasantness is short-lived. He's polite, not charming—his reputation as a bully was deserved. As I place a tape recorder near him, he orders me to keep it off, until such time as he grants me permission. It is his way of ensuring that the conversation will take place on his terms.

Ever keen to issues of ethnicity, Botha quickly orients himself to his visitor. "All right Mr. Goodman, let me get straight with you. You're of Jewish descent, aren't you?" he says, not so much asking as telling me. Yes, I reply. He then talks proudly about what a close relationship he had with Israel, and what a good personal friend Israel's former defense minister Moshe Dayan had been. "I am an admirer of great men in Israel," he declares. He recalls how he first helped Israeli leaders by sending them a "small boatload of thousand-pound bombs."

We stroll around his library, and he pulls out books and gifts from the few world leaders who would meet him during his embattled rule. There is a gift from the president of Taiwan, one from the king of Morocco, several items from Israeli leaders, and a bevy of souvenirs from the black puppet leaders whom he propped up in South Africa's former homelands. In trying to demonstrate that he was not isolated during the apartheid years, he reinforces just how isolated he was.

He proudly pulls a book off his shelf about the American Revolution, flips it open, and tells me to read the inscription aloud: "To P. W. Botha— With appreciation and esteem, William Casey." President Ronald Reagan's CIA chief was a good friend, P. W. says proudly.

Botha is totally unrepentant for his violent reign. When I ask him his solution for what ails South Africa today, he replies with a rehash of what

Verwoerd prescribed forty years ago: a balkanized "confederation of states" consisting of white and black homelands. Our conversation then turns to Verwoerd. Botha, a protégé of one of Verwoerd's political rivals, had opposed his candidacy to be prime minister in 1958. Verwoerd overlooked the slight, and appointed the bellicose MP from the southern Cape to be his deputy minister of internal affairs, with special responsibility for colored affairs. In 1961, Botha was promoted to be minister of the combined portfolio of colored affairs, community development, and housing. In 1966, Botha replaced John Vorster as minister of defense, which quickly became the junior politician's power base and fiefdom. He succeeded Vorster as prime minister in 1978.

Botha originally told Verwoerd that he felt he was undeserving of a cabinet post since he had opposed the prime minister.

"I don't like bootlickers," Verwoerd retorted.

"Neither do I," Botha replied. They were fast allies after that.

Botha settles into a corner chair next to his desk. A small South African flag—the old one—stands on the corner. He is dressed casually in a tan jacket and hiking boots, and his shirt buttons strain against his bulging waist. Part of his face appears to droop, a legacy of the stroke, I assume.

"In my opinion," says Botha, cradling his chin in his hand, "Verwoerd was the most advanced politician we had in South Africa. He was a highly intelligent man. He was a giant among men—a *man's* man." He raises his bushy eyebrows, and still shows some of his old theatrical form as an orator. Verwoerd, he says, compares favorably to Golda Meir, Theodore Roosevelt, and Abraham Lincoln. "And I have a great respect for Lincoln," he says of the American president who abolished slavery.

Botha recalls an encounter he had with Verwoerd. "I went up to him and said we are using the wrong word for our policy—'apartheid'—because it can be exploited by people who don't know what it means." What would Botha have preferred to call the National Party racial policies? "Good neighborliness," he replies with a faint smile.

I ask Botha how he views Mandela. The two men have met three times: first when Botha was state president and Mandela was a prisoner, and twice since then, when President Mandela has visited Botha at his home. Botha likes Mandela, sort of. The men regularly exchange birthday cards. "I think Mandela is an intelligent man," offers Botha. When Mandela last visited, the Groot Krokodil told him, "You know Mr. President, when I was president, you were in jail and I offered you your freedom.* Now that you are president, you're a captive of forces around you."

Why does Mandela talk to you, I ask. "Because he says that he likes talking to me. When we disagree we tell each other. And when we agree, we say so." Botha adds, "I still believe he's a captive. And I don't think he is really the free man that he would like to be."

P. W. is equally candid about his disdain for F. W. de Klerk. "I like [Mandela] more than I like de Klerk. I think de Klerk is a little weakling. And I told him so. I told him, 'You're dishonest and you know it.' Because he broke all his promises. I told him, 'You took rewards from other sources, for letting your own people down.'" It strikes me that Botha and Mandela are similar. They are both strong-willed "Big Men" in the grand tradition of African politics. Both are men of principle, stubborn to the point of great personal sacrifice. They speak directly and bluntly, at times to a fault. Not surprisingly, both despise de Klerk, who is their antithesis: a slippery politician who stands on principle only when it suits him.

I ask Botha his opinion of the Truth Commission, which lately has been hounding him. "I am not applying for amnesty," he asserts defiantly while wagging his forefinger at me. He has called the commission a "circus," and stated he will answer only to God for his deeds. Botha prefers to remember the good times. He muses, "Paul Kruger used to say, 'take from the past that which is beautiful and build your future on that.' It's always good to look to the past to find the good. But it's never good to try and play revenge and repeat the Nuremberg experience."

The Groot Krokodil is at peace with his legacy. He concludes our meeting by noting, "I'm not despondent. I'm quite happy." He elaborates, "He who is prepared to sacrifice himself in the name of decency and honesty and for the cultural values of his people—his memory will live." I press him about how he thinks he will be remembered. He is unconcerned. "History will deal with me," he concludes.

---

* In 1985, President Botha offered to release Mandela if the ANC leader "unconditionally rejected violence as a political instrument." Mandela flatly refused the offer, declaring in a letter read by his daughter Zindzi to a stadium crowd in Soweto, "What freedom am I being offered when I may be arrested on a pass offense? . . . I cannot and will not give any undertaking at a time when I and you, the people, are not free" (Nelson Mandela, *Long Walk to Freedom* [London, 1994], 620-23).

The Truth Commission wanted to deal with him first. Following our meeting, Botha ignored three subpoenas to answer questions before the TRC, despite offers from Archbishop Tutu that he could answer questions in private. President Mandela urged Botha to testify and thereby avoid a trial, and said he would personally escort him to a closed-door hearing. Over the objections of his lawyers, the proud Botha refused to budge. He was finally hauled into court on contempt charges.

In June 1998, Botha sat uncomfortably in the dock for eight days as former subordinates accused him of ordering a wide range of apartheid-era attacks. A former cabinet minister revealed that Botha personally ordered the bombing of Khotso House in 1988. Former death squad commander Eugene de Kock testified that he was awarded the Star of Honor for blowing up a house in London owned by the ANC in 1981; the medal had to be approved by Botha. De Kock scoffed at the idea that Botha and his ministers did not know people would die when they ordered that activists be "neutralized," "eliminated," or "permanently removed from society." Such politicians "want to eat lamb but don't want to see blood and guts," insisted de Kock at the trial. "They're cowards."[40]

Botha's trial ended in a dramatic showdown with Archbishop Desmond Tutu. Concluding two days of grueling testimony, Tutu suddenly turned to Botha, who had been silent throughout the trial. "I want to appeal to him," the archbishop said, breaking with protocol, "to take this chance provided by this court to say he may not have intended the suffering to happen to people, he may not have given orders to authorize anything. But if Mr. Botha was able to say that 'I am sorry that policies of my Government caused you pain'— just that, that would be such a tremendous thing." Botha appeared agitated, but maintained his stony silence. On August 21, 1998, P. W. Botha was found guilty of contempt for repeatedly refusing to testify before the Truth Commission. He was sentenced to one year in jail, or a $1,600 fine, which he later paid. The magistrate chastised Botha for having "at no point shown any remorse."[41] He later snapped at reporters, "I have nothing more to say."

White South Africa thrived in the post-Verwoerd era. The sixties and early seventies were a period of global economic boom, and South Africa reaped its share of the benefits. It was dubbed the "golden era of apartheid."[42] The economy had been growing at an annual rate of about 6 percent since 1964. In the aftermath of the capture and imprisonment of Nelson Mandela and the other top leadership of the ANC and the Pan Africanist Congress, the anti-apartheid resistance retreated into a decade-long quiescence. Verwoerd had won . . . for the short-term.

The tide began to turn in the early seventies. In 1973, South Africa was rocked by waves of strikes by African workers demanding higher wages and the right to organize. The vaunted South Africa military then suffered a humiliating defeat in Angola in 1974. The South African Defense Force had invaded Angola in an attempt to thwart a Marxist takeover by the Popular Movement for the Liberation of Angola (MPLA), but the South Africans were forced to retreat under heavy fire from Cuban reinforcements. By early 1976 South Africa was in the grip of a full-scale economic recession.

The 1976 Soweto uprising represented an unprecedented new phase of black militancy. The protests disabused white South Africa of the illusion of apartheid's "morality." Verwoerd's divine master plan was unraveling, leaving in its wake only venality and white privilege, and the brute force necessary to sustain them. By the late seventies, the National Party was on the defensive, a posture which it would never be able to shake.[43] The Soweto uprising showed a new generation of blacks that apartheid was vulnerable. The battle lines were clearly drawn, and the apartheid state began to stumble from crisis to crisis. With the Verwoerdian vision shattered, apartheid leaders were cast into a stormy sea without a moral compass. They had become victims of their own *baasskap* propaganda, and they were now battered by forces they were utterly unable to comprehend.

In spite of having had arguably the greatest impact of any Afrikaner political leader, H. F. Verwoerd is today a forgotten man. It is, in fact, astonishing how quickly he vanished from the political screen. "He imposed an intellectual straitjacket on the Afrikaners which most accepted with extreme docility . . . The recollection of such spinelessness must be unpleasant today," wrote Henry Kenney, author of one of the few Verwoerd biographies published in English.[44] Indeed, Verwoerd was roundly hated by many of his political colleagues for his uncompromising posture and his penchant for carrying grudges.

For all that can rightly be said about the monstrousness of the Verwoerdian dream, brutal forms of white supremacy were hardly unique in the annals of twentieth-century colonialism. Indeed, Verwoerd was tame compared to other white minority rulers: Belgium's King Leopold II was responsible for the wholesale slaughter of thousands in the former Belgian Congo at the turn of the century. Had Verwoerd implemented apartheid forty years earlier, his racist cant would have barely merited notice from other European leaders.

South Africa simply got on the bandwagon at the wrong time. As the world was busy decolonizing—twenty-eight African countries went from white rule to black rule between 1956 and 1966[45] —South Africa went backwards, imposing *baasskap* just as it was going out of vogue. While white rule succumbed to the "winds of change" throughout the sixties, South Africa was an anachronism as it sailed defiantly into the gale.

Stellenbosch is a bucolic town nestled at the foot of the precipitous and craggy Jonkershoek Mountains. Miles of vineyards, some dating back over three hundred years, unfold in every direction. The town is a show-case of Cape Dutch architecture. The Dutch Reformed church towers im-periously at one end, its illuminated steeple showing the way at all hours of the night. Historic whitewashed buildings with thatched roofs dot the tree-lined streets. Sitting prominently in the center of this is Stellenbosch University, with its eclectic mix of small turn-of-the-century houses and more contemporary box-shaped buildings separated by neatly trimmed lawns. This is South Africa's most charming face, an idyllic respite from the grittier realities of crime, violence, and poverty that lie just a short dis-tance away in the teeming townships around Cape Town.

I turn into an orderly development called Uniepark—named in honor of the Union of South Africa. Each street is named for one of the original South African republics. I drive up Transvalia Street to reach the home of Wilhelm Verwoerd Sr.

The white-haired professor appears relaxed in a short-sleeved shirt and gray slacks. His face is tanned from the time he has recently spent at his fa-ther's former holiday home in Betty's Bay, on the Cape coast. He ushers me inside, walking stiffly, bent forward at the waist. This was the home where he raised his four children. Inside is a spacious living room punctuated with plaid sofas and stuffed chairs. Verwoerd points proudly to a portrait of his father. It was a gift to the prime minister from the Italian community of Pretoria. The late leader is shown standing in a statuesque pose. His skin tone is rendered pale and waxy, as if he were half human, half monument.

The world around Wilhelm Verwoerd Sr. has changed radically, much to his disapproval. By the mid-eighties, P. W. Botha's tepid reforms such as the tricameral parliament proved too much for the unreconstructed apartheid stalwart. Verwoerd quit his father's beloved National Party and threw in his lot with the Conservative Party, which was unabashedly devoted to the original Verwoerdian apartheid dream.

In 1990, F. W. de Klerk set about dismantling the apartheid edifice that H. F. Verwoerd had painstakingly built. Seemingly overnight, de Klerk—whose father was in Verwoerd's cabinet—was freeing "terrorists" like Nelson Mandela and repealing the Group Areas Act and the Immorality Act. Verwoerdian apartheid was ignominiously crashing in ruins.

The prophetic "winds of change" ultimately began to blow against the shuttered windows of Verwoerd's own home. Wilhelm Verwoerd Sr. watched with growing alarm as his namesake and third son, Wilhelm Jr., spouted increasingly liberal ideas in the late eighties. The drift had begun when his son accepted a Rhodes Scholarship to study theology at Oxford. The older Verwoerd had misgivings about his son accepting a scholarship named for the hated British colonialist; now all of the Afrikaner's old fears about creeping anglicization and liberalism seemed to be materializing within his own family.

Wilhelm Verwoerd Sr. drove to the local 7-Eleven to pick up the *Sunday Times*. It was an unusual errand for him—the *Times* is an English paper, a forum that Verwoerd pointedly ignores. But his son Wilhelm had called to alert him that there was going to be an article about him and his wife, Melanie. Specifically, it was about the fact that the young couple had joined the African National Congress.

The elder Verwoerd read the story with consternation, then anger. He called his son and asked him to come over to talk—immediately. Wilhelm and Melanie came by that evening. The elder Verwoerd greeted them coolly. He and his son retreated to another room to speak directly before joining their wives.

"This is definitely going to make a difference in our relationship," bellowed father to son. By the time the two men reemerged in the living room, they looked tense and drawn.

Wilhelm Sr. addressed his son and daughter-in-law. "You are dishonoring the name of your grandfather and the family. By joining an organ-

ization intent on destroying the Afrikaner nation, you have become a traitor to your own people." His voice quivered as he pronounced sentence
for this transgression.

"If you do this then you are saying that you are distancing yourself from
the family. So I am going to take the most serious step that an Afrikaner
can: I have no choice but to disinherit you. You are no longer my son."

A heated discussion followed. Elize Verwoerd wept as she pleaded with
her husband, "Please don't do this."

But this was a sacred principle to the old man. He was the eldest son
of Hendrik Verwoerd and as such bore responsibility for upholding the
family name. Like his father had done so often before him, Wilhelm Verwoerd Sr. simply refused to bend, even when it meant destroying his own
family. It was unthinkable to have the grandson of H. F. Verwoerd be a
member of a liberal multiracial political party. So Wilhelm Verwoerd Jr.
was no longer a son, or a grandson. It was that simple.

This was a display of that long forgotten Verwoerdian character flaw:
people didn't matter. Family didn't matter. What mattered was the ideal.
If reality didn't fit the ideal, then reality must give way.

"And that was that," says Wilhelm Verwoerd Sr., sounding remarkably unsentimental in his recap of his split with his son. "For the moment, I've
lost interest in what he does or doesn't do. I'm not particularly interested
in hearing details of what he's doing or not doing." He looks down as he
speaks, fiddling with his glasses. He seems uncomfortable—no, ashamed
about the whole affair. I ask him if that is the case. "It was more than just
an embarrassment. I felt that he had let down his parents and family, and
all Afrikaners."

So affronted does the elder Verwoerd feel that he has gone out of his way
to make public his contempt for his son. He has written letters to the
newspaper condemning his son as a traitor. He pointedly put down his son
at his retirement speech at Stellenbosch University, where Wilhelm Jr. also
teaches. The only concession he has made to keep a thread of family life
intact is to maintain his relationship with his two grandchildren, who visit
periodically—but not in the company of their parents.

I tell him candidly that I am amazed by the effort he has made to express
his disapproval. Does the split pain you? "Yes, of course," he says flatly, looking more pained by the probing personal questions than by the subject. "I

just hope he comes to his senses some day. In terms of the family, that he returns to his fellow Afrikaners." When I ask about the possibility of separating family from politics and healing the rift, the old man becomes annoyed. "Are you trying to facilitate a reconciliation?" I assure him that's not my motive. He then concludes dispassionately, "I would say that if he continues supporting the ANC, I see no prospect of a reconciliation."

There is a long history of Afrikaners turning out their dissenters. Theologian Beyers Naude was the son of a founder of the Afrikaner Broederbond. After Naude began criticizing apartheid in the early sixties, the rebellious cleric was banned from speaking publicly or meeting with people, and his home and institute were bombed. Bram Fischer, son of a prominent Afrikaner judge and the grandson of a prime minister of the Orange River Colony, was one of Nelson Mandela's lawyers in 1963. He was arrested a year later for being a member of the South African Communist Party. He was imprisoned until 1974, when he was released to die of cancer at his brother's home.[46]

Melanie Verwoerd, the professor's daughter-in-law (he characterizes her as an "upstart" and "violently feministic"), explains to me, "As long as you stay in the laager you can face a few ways, you can be a bit out of step—they will bear with you . . . But then when you step out of the laager and actually do something which is not in line, then the laager closes and you are out of it. It's a well-known thing with Afrikaners. It's been like that since the Boer War, with people who sided with the English." Calling an Afrikaner a "renegade," she notes, "is a vicious thing to say to somebody."

Wilhelm Verwoerd Sr. observes that his son may have inherited a "liberal streak" that runs in the family. Hendrik Verwoerd's eldest brother, who also was a professor at Stellenbosch, supported Gen. Jan Smuts's decision to join the Allies in World War II. Hendrik was "utterly against it" and thus would have nothing to do with his brother. As a result, the two men did not speak to one another for twelve years.

"So I'm philosophical about what happened in South Africa and what happened to my children. I think it was preordained," says the patriarch. "I don't blame myself about what I could have done . . . I think genetic makeup had more to do with it."

Wilhelm Verwoerd Sr. pauses and peers out the large picture window in his living room. There is a breathtaking view of the Simonsberg, the rocky peak that dominates the Stellenbosch Valley. From the cloistered safety of his home, the world is a beautiful and simple place that conforms neatly to his notions. But as the world around him changes with remarkable speed, Verwoerd is left muddling through a morass of contradictions. Black power—which Afrikaner nationalists claimed would be the end of civilization—has come, and the world still goes on. He is left lurching between old ideals and failing to grasp new realities. The tension between the past and present has left him alternately bitter about his loss and philosophical about the future.

Verwoerd grudgingly acknowledges that whites may bear some responsibility for the downfall of apartheid. "I don't want to deny that the Afrikaners also had some part of the blame, because we became complacent and didn't want to make enough sacrifices to make the policy succeed . . . We tried to keep a lot for ourselves . . . If my father had lived he certainly would have continued the policy with much more success than his successors. And who knows what would have happened?"

The solution for the vanquished Afrikaners, as Verwoerd sees it, is a white homeland. He now supports the efforts of the Freedom Front, a party headed by former South African Defense Force general Constand Viljoen, which is campaigning for a *volkstaat,* or white homeland. In the pre-election negotiations, Mandela agreed to study the idea as a way to get Gen. Viljoen to participate in the 1994 elections and thereby steal the thunder of the right wing. (Viljoen has since revealed that he was plotting a violent right-wing coup in March 1994. He aborted the plan at the eleventh hour after Mandela persuaded him to participate in the elections.) The Volkstaat Council meets perennially, but few people take seriously the idea that the new South Africa would resurrect any type of homeland.

Verwoerd is today resigned but deeply resentful about his people's plight. "We Afrikaner are by world standards a fairly small nation. We had a beautiful country in which we were able to rule over others. And this is something that couldn't have lasted. I think we all realized that the time has passed where a small minority can rule over a large majority. But the mistake we made during negotiations was [that white leaders] didn't negotiate about the division of the country. They only negotiated about the handing over of the country to the opposition. We still had physical power in those days in the security forces. So why F. W. de Klerk didn't use that to gain something for the Afrikaner, even if a small homeland, I just can't fathom it. The whole thing was a sellout," he concludes with disgust.

Nelson Mandela made racial reconciliation his preeminent mission as president of the new South Africa. To dramatize his commitment, Mandela traveled in the early days of his presidency to the white enclave of Orania, a town in the empty Northern Cape that Afrikaners hope will one day be the center of their whites-only *volkstaat*. He came to take tea with ninety-four-year-old Betsy Verwoerd. As she served him tea and *koeksisters*, the widow of H. F. Verwoerd read haltingly—with Mandela prompting her politely in Afrikaans—from a two-page letter she had prepared. She asked him to "dispose of the fate of the Afrikaners with wisdom." The image of the tall black statesman looking down gently on the frail smiling lady was broadcast around the world as a potent symbol of how South Africa had come full circle.

Wilhelm Verwoerd Sr. was unmoved by the spectacle. "It was just one of the gimmicks to appease the Afrikaner. She felt it was her duty to put our point of view to him, and I think that was a bit unfair at her age. She shouldn't have been subjected to that sort of test."

Wilhelm Verwoerd Sr. is convinced of the inevitability of conflict between the races. He can't conceive of peaceful coexistence, even intermingling. "I've got sympathy with my son. I just hope he will one day realize things will change. I don't think the ANC will be in power forever, and he may have difficulty explaining what he's doing at the moment. The winds may turn again . . . He's left his natural home and he's thrown in his lot with a different nation, with people with different ideas of morality. So there will be conflict, I'm sure. And I just hope that he'll come to his senses one day or another. I'm not being hardheaded, but I'm not so optimistic that it'll happen soon."

Verwoerd believes firmly that the Afrikaner nation will rise again. With that in mind, he tries to convince talented young Boers to remain in South Africa. It seems like a contradiction, given his grim forecast for the future of the country. But, as Verwoerd correctly observes, "It is the only place in the world where the Afrikaner can survive as a nation. As soon as you leave, you become an American, an Australian, whatever. Rather, make some sacrifices, and do whatever one can to build up this country."

Verwoerd's commitment to remain in South Africa despite whatever hardships he thinks may befall white people is telling. Even in defeat, the Afrikaners remain committed to the land of their forefathers. While white English-speaking South Africans would frequently tell me they were considering emigrating from the post-apartheid South Africa—the emigration rate rose 27 percent during 1995 and early 1996, but has been dropping steadily since that time[47]—most Boers don't have the luxury. Ironically, the hope for racial reconciliation may find its greatest promise in the mutual connection that Africans and Afrikaners feel for their native soil.

For the Afrikaner generation of Wilhelm Verwoerd Sr., hope lies in the dream that the Boers will rise once more. "The tides will turn again," Verwoerd promises, sounding more wistful than combative. "It may take a generation. But we'll get our country back, I'm sure. We've lost our country. We are in a similar position to what our forefathers were in 1902. But they were then knocked out by war, and we are not. But we are just as politically powerless."

Verwoerd is old enough to have seen the world around him change more than once. It has left him with a sense that nothing is permanent. "I've seen the young Turks become the reactionaries," he muses, recalling how his father's "radical" views were dubbed too conservative by some right-wingers when he was prime minister.

"So now Wilhelm and his mates think they are the young Turks and think they've achieved something—black rule, which is what they wanted. Sooner or later, they will become the reactionaries trying to protect the privileges which the black rulers are claiming for themselves. There will be a new black generation that will challenge them. After Mandela, there could well be a large dissatisfied body of blacks who could be further impoverished by inflation. Things could become a lot worse if the Communist Party takes up that cause. We could very well have a dictatorship following this period that we have now."

Verwoerd is bitter that people who once lauded what his father stood for are now backpedaling. "You can hardly call yourself an Afrikaner nationalist these days, because people say, 'Oh you're a racist.' So you can't take these terms at face value. Like 'apartheid'—I don't have any revulsion when I hear that.

"Nobody has the courage to say they supported apartheid now. Like in Germany, no one will admit they ever supported Nazism. The same psychology also applies here, but I think it is wrong. I am very against these confessions going on now before the so-called Truth and Reconciliation Commission. It's utterly contemptible.

"One doesn't change easily at this age," he concedes. "But I've come to accept a lot of things that I couldn't accept ten years ago. All of us have been forced to accept things. It's the sort of thing if you are put in jail or if your country is occupied by a foreign country: you either adapt or you die. So you must always make certain allowances. I think we are busy doing that. All of us. Without losing our basic faith, our basic loyalties."

I ask him if he foresees the day when he could ever look back on the past with his son and laugh together about it. He ponders it for a moment— like his father, he is not a man who forgives and forgets easily.

"It could happen, either because he changes, or because the conditions change," he finally says. He turns his gaze to his idyllic window on the world. "Maybe it will have gone much better than I prophesize. We may have our *volkstaat* by then. We may have a white president again. A lot of things can happen."

# LEAVING THE LAAGER

WILHELM VERWOERD JR.:
GRANDSON OF H. F. VERWOERD, ANC MEMBER

Wilhelm Verwoerd Jr.
at his home in Cape
Town, 1997.

Wilhelm Verwoerd Jr.
at his office at the
Truth and Reconcili-
ation Commission,
Cape Town, 1997.

The Verwoerd family
(clockwise): Wilhelm,
Melanie, Wian (4),
and Wilme (6), 1997.

**A VOLATILE BREW SIMMERS** in the night air that swirls about the Parow Civic Center near Cape Town. On one side of the street, supporters of the African National Congress chant and dance the provocative *toyi-toyi*. Across the busy road, barrel-chested members of the ultra-right Afrikaner Resistance Movement (AWB) mill about in faux-Nazi uniforms emblazoned with their trademark three-legged swastikas. In between them stand nervous peace monitors and riot police.

It is May 13, 1993, and ANC supporters are celebrating the imminent coming out of a high-profile new member. The grizzled AWB men are here to make known their displeasure with this traitor to the *volk,* whose hallowed surname is synonymous with their beloved apartheid. Emotions are at fever pitch because of the assassination just a week earlier of Chris Hani, the immensely popular ANC leader and guerrilla hero who was gunned down by right-wing zealots.

A convoy of cars flanked by police whisks up to the rear entrance of the civic center. A small entourage steps inside and takes up seats on a stage decorated in the green, gold, and black of the ANC. The spirited audience, which fills the hall to capacity, breaks into a chorus of chants.

"One president!" shouts an ecstatic young ANC supporter. "One Mandela!" comes the quick refrain.

"Viva ANC—Veee-vaaa!"

"Viva Verwoerd—VEEE-vaaaa!!!"

Viva Verwoerd? The name that meant misery to so many is now a struggle chant for the *black* masses? Has South Africa been turned on its head?

The pale, wiry figure with a striking resemblance to apartheid's most infamous icon weakly nods his acknowledgment from the stage, and a roar of approval ushers forth from the crowd. Wilhelm Verwoerd Jr., a bookish twenty-nine-year-old philosophy lecturer who is more accustomed to addressing bright-eyed Afrikaner university students than a multicolored mob of campaigners, is momentarily speechless. He is overwhelmed by the poignancy of the moment. It is Wilhelm's turn to explain why he is throwing in his lot—and the potent symbolism of his name—behind the organization that his grandfather, the notorious former South African prime minister H. F. Verwoerd, had condemned as a group of "terrorists" intent on destroying white civilization.

The nervous Verwoerd looks startled and a bit frightened by the scene. He struggles to get his first words out. Finally he croaks, "Ladies and gentlemen, friends, opponents, and . . . comrades!" It is that last word, so charged to the ears of his Afrikaner brethren, that sticks in his craw. After forcing himself to utter it, he continues with some generalities about his hopes for eradicating apartheid. But it is that one pregnant word that he returns to at the end.

"I still find it awkward to say 'comrade,'" he acknowledges. "I am still getting used to *toyi-toyi.* I still have much to unlearn and much to learn. But the bottom line is: it is exciting and liberating to join in the camaraderie of, let's call it our Comrades Marathon towards a new South Africa free from oppression in our homes, in our factories and mines, in our politics!"

Alluding to South Africa's most famous running race, he concludes, "I had wondered whether I should end with a 'Viva ANC!' But for the time being I will end with this invitation to especially the more timid, paler ones of us here tonight: Come, run with us!"[1]

The metaphor is corny, the delivery stiff, and the demeanor painfully self-conscious. Nobody will accuse him of being charismatic. But the audience forgives him his sins—and maybe even those of his ancestors. Verwoerd may have traveled farther than anyone in the room to get here. He has had to peel back decades of Afrikaner nationalist indoctrination, abandon his beloved Dutch Reformed Church, emerge from the long shadow cast by his grandfather, and defy the harsh public disapproval expressed by his own father.

H. F. Verwoerd is Wilhelm Verwoerd Jr.'s cross to bear. The young Verwoerd did not choose this fate; it chose him. He has become variously a revisionist historian of his grandfather, an anti-apartheid crusader, and an unauthorized family emissary bearing apologies for what happened in his name. Throughout 1996 and 1997, he worked as a staff researcher for the

Truth and Reconciliation Commission chronicling the legacy of his grand-father's policies (he continued to help write and edit the TRC final report during 1998); in January 1998, he resumed his former job teaching political philosophy and applied ethics at Stellenbosch University, where his father and grandfather once taught. His wife, Melanie, has even returned the Verwoerd name to the hallowed halls of government: she is now a member of parliament—for the ANC.

Wilhelm Verwoerd Jr., like his grandfather before him, is a man on a mission: to pay penance for his family's sins. He has transformed the bitter legacy of his forebears into an extraordinary family saga of crime and punishment spanning three generations. But unlike the movies, there is no happy ending to this story. His father has disowned him, the pressures of public life have strained his marriage, and the prospect for reconciliation—in his family and in the country—feel maddeningly remote. It has sobered the idealistic and penitent young Verwoerd about the prospects for change in his lifetime.

"This easy talk about a 'rainbow nation,' reconciliation, and nation-building—I think one must be very realistic about it," he cautions. "Given the inequalities, it's a lifelong process of trying to get a situation where we can live peacefully together—not necessarily be big friends—but somehow not use violence as a way of dealing with our conflicts."

He muses, "Perhaps that's what reconciliation is about at a national level—peaceful coexistence. And at an individual level I still have hope that, with my father and with other people, we will be able to work through the issues. But I have quite a strong sense also that it will take time and it will be difficult and it might not be possible. Perhaps that's the price you've got to pay when making certain commitments."

Wilhelm Verwoerd Jr. is sitting in his ninth-floor office in the Truth and Reconciliation Commission headquarters in downtown Cape Town. The nondescript corporate digs are wedged between a gift shop and a yuppie bistro. His job here, which he began in early 1996, is to document in chilling detail the fallout from his grandfather's policies. His research, together with the findings from TRC hearings, forms part of the TRC's final report to the nation. The report amounts to an official history of one of the darkest chapters in the postwar era, the reign of racist terror known as apartheid. Most important, the commission made recommendations to safeguard against the possibility of such abuses ever happening again.

Wilhelm works out of a spartan office, a mute symbol of the austere nature of his task. A poster of a black man bending prison bars with the inscription NEVER AGAIN hangs on the wall facing him. Wilhelm's skin is a pale white, and flecks of gray are already evident in his thirty-three-year-old temples. When he stands up, his narrow hips barely hold up his drab olive pants. Wilhelm's mother blames his wife for not "fattening up" her son, the job of a dutiful Afrikaner wife. Melanie laughs at this charmingly antiquated notion. "I don't even cook!" she exclaims.

Wilhelm Jr. looks the part of the rumpled, pensive scholar. He tends at times to take himself and his task a bit too seriously. Yet for all his weighty baggage, he comes across as earnest, not morose. He is quick to smile, and has not lost his sense of humor.

"He is very funny and very bright," TRC chairman Archbishop Desmond Tutu replies when I ask him about Wilhelm. Tutu recounts with a chuckle how Wilhelm has jokingly accused him of "blaming my grandfather" for all that ails South Africa.

"We do have the advantage of some of those insights that we would not have had [without him]," says Tutu. "I mean, this is someone speaking as it were from the belly of the beast. He knows the animal from the *inside.*"

Irony. It underlies all that Wilhelm Verwoerd Jr. does on the Truth Commission. There is first the obvious connection to Hendrik Verwoerd, a central figure behind the crimes being investigated. Much as he tries to shake Verwoerd's ghost, the parallels are unavoidable.

"His grandson is similar to him in many ways," Allister Sparks tells me. The veteran South African journalist has seen both Verwoerds in action. Wilhelm Jr. "is also a thoughtful intellectual, and he's quiet. He even looks like his grandfather, though a bit thinner. But," he adds the all-important caveat, Wilhelm "is compassionate, a humanist. His grandfather was not."

Then there is the issue of reconciliation, something that has eluded Wilhelm in his own family. The struggle to reconcile "sometimes makes me feel quite despairing about what we as a commission can achieve given the scale and complexity of the whole process. And even though you might take a step or two forward, then suddenly something happens, and somebody says something again or emotional dynamics or the potential for estrangement is in the air. You fall back on racial stereotypes."

Wilhelm has observed the well-intentioned but faltering effort that Melanie and others in the new government are making toward rebuilding the country. The inability of the government to redress long-standing grievances has made him keenly aware that real change in South Africa is a long way off.

"To build a kind of relationship across those divides is not just a political process," he reflects as we sit at a noisy sidewalk café in downtown Cape Town one afternoon. "It's a deep sort of personal and emotional and psychological process entwined with socioeconomic issues which makes it extremely difficult . . . We're talking about a lifelong commitment . . . If you expect suddenly that everybody's living happily ever after, there's no way that that will happen."

The die was cast at an early age for a young man with the surname Verwoerd. The third son of Wilhelm Verwoerd Sr. was born on February 21, 1964. Observing strict Afrikaner tradition, the third son was named after his father (by the same custom, the oldest son was named for his grandfather Hendrik, and the second son was named for his maternal grandfather Dirk).

When I toured the home where Wilhelm Verwoerd Jr. grew up, his father pulled out a dog-eared album of old family photos. There is Wilhelm as an infant dressed in a yellow suit sitting on the knee of the late prime minister, with his doting grandfather feeding him his bottle. This photo is one of the very few images that Wilhelm Jr. has seen of himself with his grandfather; the former prime minister was assassinated when Wilhelm was only two, so he has no memory of his brief time with him.

After his death, Hendrik Verwoerd grew to be larger than life in both the family and the national mythology. Statues and monuments to the fallen leader sprang up around the country. South Africa's largest dam was named after him, as was an airport, a tunnel, a town, numerous schools, buildings, and countless streets in myriad towns and cities. When Wilhelm Jr. attended Stellenbosch University, he attended social science classes in the H. F. Verwoerd Building. At family gatherings with his grandmother Betsy Verwoerd, there were often warm reminiscences about the private side of the public figure. His grandfather was an avid fisherman and a "gentleman farmer" with a small herd of cattle. As anti-apartheid forces attempted to tear down H. F. Verwoerd's reputation, his family took pains with the children "to show us the other side and that it's actually not true that he was such a bad person," he recalls.

Young Wilhelm was reminded early on that he was descended from greatness. "I had a positive sense [that I was] special [because he was] this great leader. It was often the way people would respond at school, but also where you go in the Afrikaans world, especially rural areas."

Even when introducing himself to strangers, he would frequently be asked if he was related to the late prime minister. Older people would then muse sadly about "'what a great pity that he is no longer with us' and 'he was the greatest leader.' Or they would start talking about the day he was assassinated with great sadness."

Wilhelm Jr. grew up in the insular world of Stellenbosch, which he freely admits "was unreal." African culture is invisible in the leafy suburb. Even Kaya Mandi, the ramshackle Stellenbosch township that lies only minutes from the town center, was out of sight and mind of the Stellenbosch gentry. Interaction with blacks, as in most of white South Africa, was confined to brief exchanges with the "garden boy" and maids who are a fixture of every middle-class white home. Yet his parents cared enough to insist that the children always show the black servants respect. It is telling that Wilhelm remembers no substantive conversations or relationships with nonwhites from the first two-thirds of his life.

Wilhelm Jr. had a typical upper-middle-class white childhood. He attended Stellenbosch Primary School, where he and his classmates participated in "cadets" each week. Someone from the police or military would come to school to speak with students about the *swart gevaar* (black peril) or the threat from communists and terrorists. Then the students, dressed in military-style khaki, would march and drill in the schoolyard. The cadets would periodically take overnight field trips under the supervision of army troops. None of this seemed unusual to South Africans. It was perfectly consistent with the Afrikaner nationalist worldview that saw itself fighting against a "total onslaught" of communist black terror from within an embattled laager. The overt militarism that infused white South African education served also as preparation for another rite of passage: the two-year national military service that all boys undertook after high school.

At age thirteen, Wilhelm became very active in the Voortrekkers, the Afrikaans equivalent of the Boy Scouts. Every week he and other boys would divide into teams and take on different projects. Often it was just outdoor play, but quasi-military maneuvers were also part of the routine. Wilhelm excelled in the group, and went on to earn the President's Medal, the highest honor a Voortrekker can achieve.

One theme ran seamlessly through school and the Voortrekkers: the on-going quest by Afrikaners to fight for and preserve their cultural identity. Anti-English sentiment figured prominently in the history that Wilhelm learned. The Afrikaner conquest of the South Africa interior was de-scribed as largely uncontested, save for occasional and heroic skirmishes with Bantu warriors and English colonialists. The history of South Africa was white history; Africans hardly figured at all.

Wilhelm was a star student, but his real passion was for the church. He and his family were members of the Dutch Reformed Church (known by its Afrikaans initials NGK). The NGK—dubbed by critics as "the Na-tional Party at prayer"—played a crucial role in providing the theological and moral underpinnings of Afrikaner nationalism. Apartheid was the civil religion of South Africa, a God-given cudgel used by Afrikaners to uphold their status as "chosen people."

Wilhelm Verwoerd Jr. took to religion with zeal. He was "born again" at the tender age of thirteen, and was a leader of the Christian Students' Union at school. As teenagers he and some friends dubbed themselves the "Soldiers for Jesus" and spent their free time holding prayer meetings and giving Bibles to "colored people, Bantoes and whites." A devastating sports injury that prevented him from entering the army only deepened his commitment to his religious work. Wilhelm prepared to pursue a de-gree in theology at Stellenbosch with the eventual aim of becoming a NGK minister. His father was concerned by what he felt was his son's "fa-natical interest in Christianity," but the elder Verwoerd concluded, "If he wants to become a minister of the church, then that's important." By the age of eighteen the "Soldier for Jesus" was making plans to devote his life to the war to uphold Christian Afrikaner values.

Wilhelm Verwoerd Jr. entered Stellenbosch University in February 1982, following in the tradition of his grandfather and father. He planned to get a B.A. in theology and then enroll in the famous Stellenbosch Seminary of the Dutch Reformed Church—known locally as the "angel factory."

Despite the rising tide of violence and political activism around the country, Stellenbosch remained pleasantly insulated from the harsh realities of the outside world. Wilhelm dabbled briefly in party politics by attending a National Party Youth Branch camp in his first year. But he shared the commonly held view of many religious students that politics was a "dirty" alternative to doing God's work.

During his first year, Wilhelm's achievements in the Voortrekkers earned him an invitation to join the secretive Ruiterwag ("mounted guard"). The exclusive Afrikaner nationalist youth group was known as the "Junior Broederbond" for its similarities with the secretive society of Afrikaner elite. He began attending regular meetings at which leading lights from the government, military, and the business world would address the young men in private. At one point when the student group perceived a liberal tilt in the Stellenbosch University newspaper, Wilhelm was dispatched to join the paper and correct this drift. He did as he was instructed, but the newspaper promptly assigned him a beat as a sports writer. After a futile stint penning blow-by-blows of college sports games, he quit the paper.

In the questioning atmosphere of the university, Wilhelm was beginning to drift ever so slightly from the conservative clutches of his upbringing. Like many of the elite white students in the 1980s, he considered himself vaguely "anti-apartheid." "'Separate development' as a policy could not work in practice," he declared. But he remained steadfastly opposed to the multiracial anti-apartheid groups that were mounting a direct challenge to government policies, and he certainly couldn't fathom supporting a "terrorist" group like the ANC. His liberal flirtation was fashionable and eminently safe.

In 1986, Wilhelm received exciting news: he had won two scholarships to study abroad. The first was a study grant from the Netherlands South African Association which would take him to Utrecht, Holland, to work on his master's thesis on "Humor and Suffering." The second was even more exciting: he had won a coveted Rhodes Scholarship to study for three years at Oxford.

Wilhelm's father greeted the news with restraint. Cecil Rhodes, the legendary British colonialist and capitalist, was a singularly despised figure to Afrikaners. The elder Verwoerd recalled how his own father, Hendrik, had turned down another Oxford scholarship rather than risk being influenced by the hated British intellectuals. Wilhelm Sr. expressed disapproval of the South Africans who went abroad and returned as critics of their mother country. He blamed these defections on "foreign propaganda" that was hostile to the Afrikaner nation. But in the end, father deferred to son.

"He had to take his own decisions," says the elder Verwoerd. "I didn't interfere. [The Rhodes Scholarship] bothered me a little, but I rationalized that it was long after Rhodes, the British Empire was no longer something to fear, and he grew up in a conservative household so he would have the character to resist whatever influences might come to him."

Wilhelm Verwoerd Jr., the Afrikaner nationalist and Christian warrior, was leaving the laager. Little could he know that he would never return.

The door opened in the group house in the Dutch college town of Utrecht on July 3, 1986, to reveal a bright-eyed young Christian scholar comically overburdened with baggage. Wilhelm Verwoerd Jr. was greeted by a young South African couple, Johan and Amor Bouwer. They were also in Holland on scholarships from South Africa and were both studying for doctorates: Johan in theology and Amor in sociology. Wilhelm was shown to his room in the three-story house and introduced to several other South African housemates. There was Rudolf Serfontein, a piano teacher, and Steward van Wyk, a so-called colored student from Swellendam, a small town in the Cape.

That evening, Wilhelm and the others sat around the television to watch the news. There was an item about the three-week-old state of emergency in South Africa and how one hundred people had died since it began. Wilhelm wondered aloud whether the news was "slanted."

Later, Wilhelm encountered Amor in the kitchen. He made small talk, but she would have none of it. "So what are you doing to stop the racists from murdering black people back home?" she challenged him.

Wilhelm giggled nervously; he had never been asked such a question before. "I am going to spread the word of Jesus. I believe his message of love can solve many of our problems," he replied, fiddling with his teaspoon.

Amor turned on him. "You're part of the problem. Black people are dying and you want to work in a white racist church that is perpetuating the system. You're just as complicit as the police who are shooting the protesters."

"That's not fair!" protested Wilhelm. "I don't support violence . . ."

"The only solution is to bring down the apartheid system and have majority rule. Anything short of that is a cop-out," Amor shot back. It was day one, and Wilhelm was on notice that his whole worldview would be on the firing line during his stay. He expected criticism from "communists" and unsympathetic Europeans, but these were fellow Afrikaners, albeit a deeply disillusioned bunch.

The next day, Rudolf nonchalantly mentioned to Wilhelm that his gay lover would be staying overnight. The priggish Wilhelm was shocked, but said nothing. He had never met a homosexual before, and he had been taught that homosexuality was a sin. Rudolf explained that he left the Dutch Reformed Church because he no longer felt at home there. That was equally troubling for this aspiring minister.

Wilhelm returned to his room, his head spinning. He decided to write a letter to his new girlfriend back in Stellenbosch about what he was learning. Melanie Fourie was three years his junior. They met when she was a student in a theology class that he was teaching at Stellenbosch. A liberal Afrikaner, she had demanded to know his political bent when she met him in 1985 and learned he was one of *the* Verwoerds.

"To the left of the National Party," he had answered. She accepted the reply, and their courtship began.

A week after arriving in Holland, Wilhelm wrote to her:

> Hello my angel!
> Amor and Johan started telling me about all the information they have picked up from banned publications, magazines and from discussions with exiles, ANC supporters. It is simply SHOCKING! It deals with the diabolical role of the Security Police . . . They also talked about visiting a woman in the Netherlands. She is an ANC member as well as a devoted Catholic and opposes violence. This woman told and showed them how the Security Police tortured her . . .
>
> Amor and Johan say . . . they have lost all their naiveté about the NP government and all its claims about good intentions. According to reliable information the Security Police even have their own "hit squad" who are paid to liquidate opponents of the NP . . . If you take all these things seriously you will go mad or paranoid . . .

Wilhelm's conversations with Amor were ongoing. They fought constantly. He mentioned the beauty of the snow on the mountains above Stellenbosch. She retorted, "I wonder if the squatters at Crossroads with no warm clothes in their tin shacks find it beautiful."

But it was the withering avalanche of information about human rights abuses in South Africa that unsettled Wilhelm the most. He read *Biko,* the book by exiled journalist Donald Woods about the life and death of the black consciousness leader. Wilhelm wondered aloud in another letter to Melanie:

> The tragedy of innocent people being tortured in the most gruesome fashion by the Security Police remains. Do the people in top government, Gerrit Viljoen or Dawie de Villiers [Stellenbosch neighbors and NP cabinet ministers], know about it?
>
> What about many people of conservative political views, who are committed Christians, such as my Uncle Carel Boshoff, my mother, Granny Smith? Did my grandfather not know about all these things? According to my father he was a well-loved Minister of Native Affairs. Or is my and their image of him the result of one-sided indoctrination? Does each of us (all the whites) bear a collective responsibility for everything the Security Police have done or are doing? Then surely we are guilty of all the wrongs done by everyone.

Just as shocking as the political revelations for Wilhelm were the sexual ones. Living with a gay man, and later with lesbians, he exclaimed in a letter to Melanie that "my prissy little soul freaks out."

The exposure to so many new people and ideas was eating away at his innocence and naiveté. He wrote in another letter, "It is as if the shackles of prejudice are dropping off. I know that these changes will make an unbelievably big difference to my life (wherever and however it proceeds), that they will create more problems and hardship and conflict (especially in South Africa) but that there is so much certainty that this is the right direction."

Wilhelm made painfully slow progress on his theology thesis that summer. By the time he left Holland just three months later, he supported economic sanctions against apartheid, endorsed the idea of majority rule in South Africa, and even expressed cautious sympathy for why the ANC was waging an armed struggle. When he reached Oxford, he abandoned his theology major altogether and instead signed up for a master's program in African politics and economics. The charmingly naive student who just a few months earlier aspired to enter the Stellenbosch "angel factory" had crash-landed on earth.

In spite of how far Wilhelm Verwoerd had traveled, he had still avoided meeting "the enemy." He came close in 1985 when he was part of a student study group that received government permission to meet with anti-apartheid activists in South Africa, including representatives of the UDF; he was not particularly swayed by the encounter. But by 1987, the first delegation of Afrikaans-speaking students went to Dakar, Senegal, to meet with the ANC, provoking the ire of P. W. Botha. Wilhelm got his chance the following year when some Stellenbosch students and lecturers arranged a study trip to Zambia, where the ANC was headquartered. They were not officially scheduled to meet ANC officials (they risked having their passports revoked for doing so), but it was common knowledge among the attendees that a meeting would take place.

The plane arrived in Lusaka and was welcomed by Steve Tshwete (minister of sport under President Mandela), a large African man with thick glasses who greeted the scrubbed-clean Afrikaner students warmly in Afrikaans, *"Goeie more!"* (Good morning!). He pumped the visitors about news of the latest rugby results, which quickly broke the ice with the sports-mad Afrikaners.

As it turned out, the entire ANC leadership was in town for a conference and they all came to meet with the visitors. Wilhelm and his fellow travelers holed up in a hotel room for two days of intense discussions with the leading lights of the struggle, including ANC spokesman Thabo Mbeki. Wilhelm's ambivalence about these meetings peaked when he met Joe Slovo, a communist and the former head of the ANC armed wing, Umkhonto we Sizwe ("Spear of the Nation," known for short as "MK"). White South Africans harbored particular hatred for this traitor to his race; the fact that Slovo was a Jewish-born atheist did not help his popularity among the devout Afrikaners.

"I feel like a traitor," wrote Wilhelm in his diary. "Here I am shaking the hands of an MK leader and a Communist when a few months ago my brother risked his life to go and fight somewhere in Angola."

Wilhelm was struck by a question posed to the group by a minister of the Reformed Church of Zambia: "Why do you Afrikaners try so hard to separate yourselves from us Africans?" It caused Wilhelm to reflect on the "irony of my *volk* and my language: We are called Afrikaners, which means we are of Africa . . . yet we have so little understanding/love for Africa and its people."

Wilhelm thought back to a story told by the late Afrikaner renegade Bram Fischer. Fischer wrote:

One night while I was driving an old ANC leader to his house far out to the west of Johannesburg, I propounded to him the well-known theory that if you separate races, you diminish the point at which friction between them may occur and hence ensure good relations. His answer was the essence of simplicity: if you place the races of one country in two camps, said he, and cut off contact between them, those in each camp begin to forget that those in the other are ordinary human beings . . . that each experiences joy or sorrow, pride or humiliation for the same reason. Thereby each becomes suspicious of the other and each eventually fears the other, which is the basis of all racialism.[2]

Many long-held stereotypes fell away on that trip as erstwhile "terrorists" became mere mortals—some even likable ones at that. But for liberal whites, the sticking point was always the issue of violence. "It was difficult to see how one can reconcile what we were trying to do and the armed struggle," Wilhelm observed. "It wasn't easy to see where we as so-called progressive white people fit into this struggle between the people and The System."

Wilhelm was thankful to be able to sidestep the cauldron of race politics by escaping back into the genteel world of academia. He returned to Oxford with Melanie, whom he married in December 1987. But the political turmoil of the outside world inevitably intruded into his academic work. In 1989, he was asked to write a magazine article about meeting the ANC, which then evolved into a thesis about his grandfather's politics. It was Wilhelm's most direct attempt yet to wrestle with his demons, to take the monkey off his back and look it in the eye. Exactly who *was* H. F. Verwoerd?

"Dr. H. F. Verwoerd: Principled Pragmatist?" is an arcane, soft-hitting attempt to humanize a political monster.[3] Wilhelm grappled with the question of whether his grandfather was an "impractical fanatic" or a shrewdly pragmatic political operator. This intellectual quest was more interesting for what it said about the author than the subject. Wilhelm used other scholars as his guide to explore the world from which his grandfather sprang. Personal reflections are submerged beneath academic jargon.

Wilhelm concluded his study of his grandfather by asserting that "it is difficult to believe that [his political views] were 'the pathological product of a satanic mind.'" He ends with a quiet call for South Africa's white leaders to end their insistence on maintaining "group rights," and he refers obliquely to the need for a "redistribution of land and wealth."

"Otherwise," he warns, "Verwoerd's ghost will continue to haunt South Africa on her difficult road to shared freedom."

But Wilhelm still had far to go before that same ghost ceased haunting him.

Wilhelm Verwoerd Jr. was quietly dipping a biscuit in his tea at the back of the small wood-paneled classroom at Oxford. It was 1989, and he had been enjoying the intellectual life during his English sojourn. Wilhelm had just enrolled in a summer school course at the Oxford Centre for African Studies and was milling around after the first lecture. An African-American professor had given a talk about W. E. B. Du Bois; it was the first time Wilhelm had been in a class with a black lecturer. As he was finishing his tea, a large, bearded African-American academic came over to him.

"Tell me, are you related to Hendrik Verwoerd?" came the query.

"Yes, he was my grandfather," replied Wilhelm, a bit put off by the intrusion.

The questioner leaned forward and stared directly at Wilhelm. "Was your grandfather a Nazi?" he demanded.

Wilhelm had just been investigating this question for his thesis. He replied that his research indicated that H. F. Verwoerd wasn't *quite* that evil but . . .

This tepid rejoinder confirmed the professor's suspicions about the white South African sitting in the back of the class. The man abruptly walked away.

The next day, a group of students and professors from the United States approached Wilhelm. They let him know he was not welcome in the class. Faced with a boycott of the African studies program, the head of the center then politely asked Wilhelm to leave. He said he would have to check Wilhelm's bona fides, just as he did with other black South African students.

A call was then made to Dr. Frene Ginwala at the ANC office in London, and also to Dr. Blade Nzimande, an ANC member who was one of the course leaders.[4] They quickly defused the situation, saying they had heard that Wilhelm was somewhat liberal, and that he had met with ANC leaders in Lusaka. They said that they were not willing to discriminate against him simply because he was white. The Americans still objected to having a Verwoerd in their midst. But the South Africans insisted on nonracialism, a fundamental ANC principle. Wilhelm was deeply impressed, and grateful, that his compatriots defended him. As for the course, he was so intimidated by the effort to oust him that he never mustered the courage to open his mouth again.

A black South African attending the course came up to Wilhelm one day after class. He told Wilhelm that he distrusted, even hated him when he learned who he was. But, he added, "Now I see that you are not like your grandfather . . . I feel different . . . you have helped me to break down the wall between us." Wilhelm was touched by the encounter. At the end of the course, he was inspired to write a poem to the South African students in attendance (but he did not have the nerve to give it to them). The poem concluded:

> My Afrikaner nationalist history amidst the seductive beauty
> of Stellenbosch feels indeed like
> a world apart from your cries for freedom.
> Still, I want to thank you for accepting me as you did,
> despite all your associations with Verwoerdian Apartheid.
> I cannot ask you to forgive—
> the struggle is not over, your suffering is too great . . .
> I cannot take responsibility for all my people had done,
> are doing
> But in humility, as a fellow "Afrika-ner"
> I can only ask you to accept my sincere apology . . .
> I can assure you of my commitment to a new South Africa
> Of my constant prayer that God will indeed
> bless (South) Africa!

Wilhelm and (a now pregnant) Melanie sat around the television with friends at Oxford on February 11, 1990, a bottle of champagne at the ready. The occasion was the imminent release of a man whom his grandfather had jailed more than twenty-seven years before. Their food and their patience grew cold as the day wore on. Finally, the silver-haired eminence of Nelson Mandela emerged from behind the prison gates, his fist thrust triumphantly in the air. Wilhelm and Melanie cheered from across the ocean, two of many celebrants around the world. For Wilhelm, who was writing his thesis about H. F. Verwoerd at that moment, it was a bittersweet moment.

"I had a deep sense of the tragedy of the whole thing, about how it could have been different," he tells me as we sit in his office at the Truth and Reconciliation Commission. It was a moment, like the assassination of Verwoerd, that South Africans have marked in their memory. Wilhelm still looks pained by the recollection of it. "I had this very intense conflict between the academic exercise of trying to make sense of [my grandfather's work] and at the same time a very strong emotional moral condemnation of that period through the life of this man walking free . . . That was a difficult, weird sort of contradiction."

Wilhelm was alternately euphoric at the dawning of a new era in South Africa and depressed by the enormous guilt he felt. He began having dreams in which he asked Nelson Mandela's forgiveness for what his grandfather did. Finally, he decided to write a heartfelt letter to the ANC leader.

*18 March 1990*

Dear Mr. Mandela,

This is a personal letter that I have not only wanted to write for a long time, but feel compelled to write. For ages I have wanted to express my thankfulness to you for your inspiring example as a true statesman, and I want to underline my support for your dearly bought ideal of a nonracial democracy in South Africa. In a sense that is the easy part of this letter.

Since your release the difficult part has become even more difficult. The more I see and read of you, the more I study our country's tragic history, the deeper my realization of how different everything could have been, of my own people's guilt. And the more painfully I feel the responsibility and guilt of "the one man who would be remembered as the author of our calamity" [quoting ANC leader and Nobel Peace laureate Chief Albert Luthuli], namely Dr. H. F. Verwoerd.

Naturally history—a long, unjust twenty-seven-year-long incarceration and the part my grandfather played in that—can't be changed with a few words. But as an Afrikaner who benefited from apartheid at the expense of other South Africans, as the grandson of the Architect of "separate development"—the man who above all others was responsible for your suffering and the suffering of so many other people—I want to say to you: I am very, very sorry about what happened.

I can't ask for forgiveness on his behalf. In any case, such a request would easily sound meaningless because I understand so little of what you endured during the past few decades. What I can do is to assure you that my wife and I want to spend our lives trying to convert words of apology into deeds. To make South Africa a country of shared, humane freedoms, in place of Verwoerdian "separate freedoms" (for some). I sincerely hope that I will have the opportunity to talk to you personally about this. In the meantime I pray for God's blessing on you, your family and Africa.

Events of the present were rapidly eclipsing Wilhelm's journey into the past. Wilhelm and Melanie felt a sense of urgency to return to South Africa. They talked of joining the ANC, of finding some way to contribute to the changes in the country.

But a few months after the couple returned, with their newborn daughter Wilme in tow, the soothing unreality of Stellenbosch threatened to once again push them to the sidelines where middle-class white society watched the dramatic goings-on like spectators at a cricket match. Wilhelm took a position as a lecturer in philosophy at Stellenbosch University, teaching his classes on the sixth floor of the B. J. Vorster Building. He marveled from afar as once-reviled speakers paraded through campus, including Thabo Mbeki and Rev. Beyers Naude. But he also took breaks at his grandfather's beach cottage at Betty's Bay. He decided he wasn't quite ready to join the ANC. As South Africa catapulted toward historic change and as violence rocked the country, Wilhelm invoked the luxury of a white liberal to "think things through" and "not do anything in haste."

The sound of clinking crystal and the twitter of high society echoed up into the cathedral ceilings of the sprawling Stellenbosch Cape Dutch–style home. A who's who of the Stellenbosch white establishment was assembled here this evening of September 28, 1991. Between nibbles of caviar and sips from the private stock of the local vineyards, the revelers bantered about the pros and cons of allowing blacks to rule their fair country. The discussion was inspired by the presence of a tall man with a regal air and a fringe of silver hair who was hobnobbing with guests in the center of the room. Nelson Mandela had come to meet the *volk* and allay their fears about the *swart gevaar*.

Wilhelm Verwoerd Jr. stood meekly off to the side. He had long wanted to meet Mandela, but when the moment arrived, the timid academic with the weighty historical baggage was barely able to speak up. He introduced himself, but Mandela did not hear him. The ANC leader dispatched him with a perfunctory handshake, a smile, and a "very nice to meet you."

Wilhelm shrank back into the crowd of his neighbors. The anticlimactic meeting left him despondent. Fortunately, the host of the party, liberal Afrikaner (and currently an ANC MP) Jannie Momberg, returned a little later. "I don't want to let this historic opportunity go by," he told Wilhelm. The shy scholar followed him back to where Mandela was chatting, and Momberg then properly—and audibly—introduced "the grandson of Hendrik Verwoerd."

Mandela smiled and shook Wilhelm's hand warmly, and then surprised the young man with a question. "How is your grandmother?" he inquires. "When you see her again, if she won't mind, would you please convey my best wishes to her?" Wilhelm assured him that he would relay the greeting.

"Did you receive the letter that I sent you?" Wilhelm asked. Mandela had not seen it. Wilhelm then repeated its contents. "I want to just say that as somebody who has a direct link to the person who was responsible for putting you in prison, I feel a strong sense of the injustice of the whole event and how tragic that you were in prison for that period. Even though I cannot take responsibility for what my grandfather did, we can take responsibility and try to make things right in the future. I am deeply sorry for what happened to you."

Mandela leaned over and listened intently. Finally, he politely interrupted. "Don't worry about the past," he said with grandfatherly tact. "Let us work together for a better future." It was classic Mandela, the great conciliator. Then the elder statesman stared Wilhelm in the eye. "As a Verwoerd, you have a great advantage. When you speak, the people will listen."

Wilhelm was deeply moved by the encounter. Mandela's counsel was driven home when he received a visit the next day from a young man from a prominent Afrikaner family who was at the party. "I want to thank you," said the visitor. "I have been wrestling with my role and responsibility in the past and future of this country. Seeing you shake Mandela's hand and what you said to him really meant a lot to me."

Wilhelm still resonated with the heady glow of the experience when his mother, Elize Verwoerd, arrived for a visit the following day. The white-haired woman cooed over her grandchild, but quickly cut to business. She had read in the Afrikaans newspaper *Die Burger* about his meeting with Mandela. "I beg you not to join the ANC," she said, tears welling in her eyes. "Your father is extremely upset, and this could cause a major rift. Please, for the sake of the family, find some other way to express your views."

Not long after, his father echoed his mother's worst fears. "If you are thinking of joining the ANC, which is a terrorist organization that will destroy our people, our relationship can never be the same," warned the perturbed patriarch.

This parental lobbying succeeded in encouraging Wilhelm to do what he did so well—mull things a bit longer. Numerous other liberal Afrikaners had by now thrown in their lot with the ANC. But not Wilhelm Verwoerd Jr. Six years after his re-education in Holland, Wilhelm Jr. was still making up his mind about which side he was on.

For Melanie Verwoerd, precious time was being wasted. "I'm sick and tired of that 'them and us' feeling," she declared to Wilhelm after meeting Mandela. She promptly joined the Stellenbosch chapter of the ANC and was just as quickly appointed to the executive committee.

After reading some more, thinking some more, and endless talking, a deeply ambivalent Wilhelm Verwoerd Jr. finally filled out an ANC membership form one Saturday in May 1992. He couldn't get himself to mail it, so Melanie did. Three months later, the media relieved the couple of their comfortable obscurity with the headline in the *Sunday Times* that announced "Verwoerds Join ANC."

The fallout with Wilhelm's father was swift and unexpectedly furious. Wilhelm expected his father to disapprove, but he was stunned by the climactic meeting in which his father disowned him. Several months later, he and his father had a final confrontation. Melanie and Wilhelm had dropped off their two children to visit their grandparents, then gone to meet some journalists. When they returned to retrieve their kids, his father was irate.

"We are not going to look after the children so that you can go and do your ANC business," declared his father.

The normally quiet and pensive son exploded. "What are you trying to achieve? Why can't you just accept that I have made different choices than you, and then we can live with our disagreements?" Wilhelm Jr. shouted.

"Who are you to talk to me like this?" bellowed his father, his hands shaking with rage. "You will respect your father in this house. I will not tolerate being spoken to disrespectfully."

"I'm not a child anymore," shot back Wilhelm Jr. He had never in his life addressed his father in this way. But his anger and frustration at the burdens that he bore—of his grandfather, his father, his *volk*—had pushed him to the breaking point. "We've got to deal with this, to accept this as adults."

The young Verwoerd continued, "I cannot stop doing what I believe is right as a precondition for reconciliation. It won't be reconciliation—it will be some kind of emotional compromise for the sake of peace within the family. But it would be superficial and dishonest." Following the shouting match, a distraught Wilhelm lost his voice for several days.

His pleas fell on deaf ears. His father had made a decision, and the legendary Verwoerdian self-righteousness and stubbornness had solidified it. Wilhelm Jr. had stepped outside the laager, only to find that it had slammed closed behind him.

Wilhelm Jr. next called his grandmother. Betsy Verwoerd was ninety-one. He had spoken to her recently and explained that his political views were different than hers. But now he had to inform her of his decision.

"I wanted to tell you myself that Melanie and I have joined the African National Congress," he explained to the family matriarch. "Please understand that this is not a rejection of you or the family, it's really my sincere belief that this is what I should do. I do not want to hurt you."

Betsy Verwoerd was quiet for a moment. The poignancy of this announcement was not lost on her. Then she answered thoughtfully, "If you are doing this out of your convictions, I can respect you." The widow of South Africa's most renowned ideologue understood the import of political principle to a Verwoerd—and the futility of trying to change it. Wilhelm breathed a sigh of relief. At least one door to his family was still left ajar.

Wilhelm and Melanie's political affiliation became the subject of irate letters to newspapers. They even received the occasional threatening phone call. Older Afrikaners, for whom the memory of H. F. Verwoerd was particularly warm, were especially offended by their defection.

The sacrifice has been profoundly painful to Wilhelm. He sees his parents periodically, but only to drop off his kids for a visit with their grandparents. When Wilhelm or Melanie enters the house, Wilhelm Sr. either pointedly ignores them, or walks into his study and closes the door. Wilhelm's mother is pleased to see them, but she is caught between her angry husband and her unrepentant son.

"What I'm doing is the right thing, but . . . I miss my father," says Wilhelm one evening as we are sitting and having coffee in Cape Town. With his wide forehead, narrow jaw, and intense gaze, he bears a striking resemblance to both his father and grandfather. "The relationship with grandchildren is very important, and he's getting older. There's this deep sense of the tragedy that he might be dead soon and then he might go into the grave without us making peace." Describing the trauma that has divided his family, Wilhelm cites an Afrikaans saying: "It's like walking around with a stone in your stomach." He reflects, "There is a real sense of loss and I think I went through a period of grieving. We have to face it, but it doesn't take away the sense of loss."

Life for the young Verwoerds was frenetic. From late 1992 to the election in April 1994, Melanie or Wilhelm spoke constantly at election rallies and community meetings. Time and again, the importance of being a Verwoerd was made clear to them.

One time Wilhelm shared a platform with Rev. Beyers Naude at a large black church. People listened politely as Naude spoke about ethics. When Wilhelm stood up to speak there was a commotion in the crowd. People demanded a Xhosa translator—they wanted to be sure they understood the descendant of Verwoerd.

"It was just because of my name," he shrugs as he recounts the story. "I am nothing . . . but because these people knew who Verwoerd was and perhaps had suffered as a result of him, they wanted to hear what I had to say. Afterward people came up and hugged me and asked me for my autograph. It was quite moving for me, particularly in black culture where ancestor worship is so honored. It had great meaning to them to hear me and come to grips with my grandfather's legacy."

As the elections approached, both Melanie and Wilhelm were nominated to be on the ANC national list for parliament (ANC nominees were assigned rankings, and most of the top 250 people became MPs). But as the demands of public life became evident, they realized that their two small children would be orphaned if both parents became politicians. So Wilhelm dropped out, opting to return to teaching. Melanie would continue as the "public" Verwoerd.

I find Melanie Verwoerd in a small cluttered office on the fourth floor of parliament in Cape Town. Her desk is stacked high with papers, and her bookshelf is crammed with everything from parliamentary records to feminist tracts by Rosa Luxembourg, Mother Jones, and Mary Daly. Stick figure drawings by her kids are stuck willy-nilly on the walls. She offers exasperated apologies for everything: the mess, and her cellular and desk phones, both of which ring constantly. She fetches some tea, expressing irritation that everyone, even the tea servers, are away on their summer holiday. It's just as well, she confides, so she can serve us in "proper teacups." ("They don't want to serve us on china anymore because they complain that MPs are stealing the cups," she says with a roll of her eyes.)

Melanie is wearing a rumpled plaid sleeveless dress with a simple gold chain. With her freckled face and round tortoise-shell glasses, she looks younger than her twenty-nine years, but her confident air makes her seem older. Her gaze is intense but warm. She speaks flippantly, as if she is tired of such interrogations, but still indulges me.

Melanie Verwoerd, at age twenty-seven, was the youngest woman ever to be sworn in to the South African Parliament. She is blonde and petite, feisty, and surprisingly candid. As an MP, she often works eighteen-hour days and travels frequently, all of which has taken a toll on the young mother of a six-year-old daughter, Wilme, and a four-year-old son, Wian. "The hardest thing about being an MP has been the personal price," she concedes. "I think women do women a great disfavor by pretending that it's easy when it's not. I don't think it's easy for anybody, especially not for women with small children."

Melanie sits erect in her chair as she speaks, looking poised, even formal. She talks about her insecurities, but doesn't show them. It is a sign of her "proper" upbringing, as South Africans would say. And yet she has broken the mold of traditional Afrikaner women—especially mothers—who usually do not work outside the house. Her role model is her own mother, a remarried divorcée who worked as a computer scientist at Stellenbosch University. But even for the rebel Verwoerds, all of these breaks with their cherished Afrikaner roles have been difficult to assimilate. She hints obliquely that politics has taken a toll on her marriage. I press her for details.

"You're becoming very personal!" she protests, suddenly blushing. She then concedes about her marriage, "The first year in parliament was very difficult and it came very close to not working anymore. But then the commitment was there." She credits her marital survival to "lots of therapy at some stage, which was necessary—and also weird in South Africa. People don't do that."

Luring her forward through the personal tumult has been the remarkable experience of being a member of South Africa's first democratic parliament. "If there were ever a time to be in politics, it's now," Melanie asserts enthusiastically. "Everything is under discussion, everything is up for change. There's an openness to do so many things which I don't think is there once it's an established age-old political system." She has immersed herself in women's issues and in rebuilding local government out of the ashes of the old apartheid structures. She revels in the nitty-gritty of reinventing South Africa from the ground up.

But power is fraught with temptation, and Melanie is concerned about the direction that politics is taking. She is sensitive to the charge that she and her colleagues have boarded the gravy train and are losing touch with the grass roots. "I'm worried that we in the ANC will become an ordinary political party . . . I think the ANC was different . . . [ANC members] didn't come here like other politicians around the world . . . for power or money. The majority of them might have been killed for joining the ANC, so they didn't join it because it would be fun or be a good career choice. But obviously that is changing in the movement, and once people are there, power is very seductive. So is money."

Will the ANC be able to keep its ambitious 1994 campaign promises? "Some of them yes, some of them not in the time span that they believed they could. And I think one has to be honest about that." She cites the promise to build one million houses by 1999. "I doubt whether we'll deliver the million," she says flatly. She has already mastered the politician's talent of sounding sure, even when she is not. She says the ANC can deliver "a better life for all" as it promised, but quickly concedes "that's very pie in the sky." It all depends "on whether people will use the opportunities that are created."

Melanie Verwoerd is refreshingly candid in her assessment of the new government. Even such tame self-criticism is becoming increasingly rare among the new politicians. The ANC had campaigned on promises of an ambitious Reconstruction and Development Program. Among the pledges were to build one million houses by 1999, redistribute 30 percent of the land to blacks, provide clean water, sanitation, and electricity to all people, and create jobs through a massive public works program. By early 1998, less than two hundred thousand homes had been built under the new government program.[5] Land reform is proceeding at an even slower pace. On a more hopeful note, the government has provided basic water supply to 1.3 million people in its first four years, and the state-owned electric utility is on schedule to electrify 2.5 million households by the year 2000.[6] In addition, 550 primary health care clinics have been built, and more than 1,500 schools have been renovated.[7]

"We didn't realize the enormous constraints that we would face once we were in government," she says. But she adds quickly, "I'm absolutely convinced that the people in the ANC are as committed as always to deliver, to the point that they actually get frantic about it. It's no easy task—the job's just too big and the resources are too scarce."

Melanie smiles as she recalls a trip she took to a remote town in the Northern Cape province. She was trying to explain to a township audience why the new government hasn't accomplished as much as they thought they would. An elderly man rose and addressed the young legislator. "You know, I've waited for fifty years of my life, and it's the first time that I've seen a member of parliament. Just the fact that you came here will make me wait for five more years."

Melanie pauses and stares intently at me. "That haunts me at night, old men like that. Because I don't want him to wait another five years," she says, thumping her hand on her desk. "I would like him to have his house by tomorrow."

The wine country town of Paarl—Afrikaans for "pearl"—is the picturesque idyll of apartheid fantasy. Rambling whitewashed Cape Dutch homes bob on an ocean of orderly green grapevines. Black laborers in bright coveralls dot the landscape as they comb the vines for their riches. The town population is about 110,000, of whom about one-fifth are white, and the rest are largely so-called colored. But as I look around I am hard-pressed to spot land occupied by anything other than white farmers or grapes.

I have come to Paarl to attend three days of hearings of the Truth and Reconciliation Commission. The TRC will hear cases of abuse that took place in the surrounding communities, including nearby Stellenbosch. I drive past the colonnades and imperious white churches looking for where the truth is spilling forth about the cost of privilege in the bucolic winelands. Truth is easy to spot here: it is in the building guarded by two armored personnel carriers, a razor wire fence, and flak-jacketed soldiers toting machine guns. The ironic counterweight to this firepower is a small black and green banner on the lawn bearing the TRC slogan: "Truth. The Road to Reconciliation."

Inside the hall on this day in October 1996, Archbishop Desmond Tutu is in hellfire preaching mode. Clad in his ecclesiastical magenta frock and skullcap, he is sitting on stage with four other truth commissioners. He is a short man with gray hair and long bony fingers that he uses to great effect as he points, waves, and stabs the air for emphasis. His presence lends a pious tone to the proceedings, as if this animated preacher was standing in for God himself.

Tutu opens the convocation with a prayer and then turns immediately to address the whites. He is eager to take on the skeptics here in the Afrikaner heartland. He dismisses the often heard charge from whites that the TRC—dubbed the "ANC Commission" in Afrikaans newspaper editorials—is engaged in a witch hunt against Afrikaners. He notes that the TRC has waited ten months before using its subpoena powers to force anyone to testify. "What kind of a witch hunt is that?" he declares, his voice rising to soprano.

He assures "my sisters and brothers in the Afrikaner community" that their contribution "is crucial to what is going to happen in this country." Then his voice turns from sweet to stern.

"If this country wanted revenge, it would make Rwanda look like a Sunday school picnic," he admonishes. "I want to say to the white community: you don't know how lucky you are that people are willing to forgive. All these people want is—not to put you in jail—but for people to come forward and say, 'We are *sorry* for what we did.'" Heads nod their agreement and a murmur of acknowledgment rises from the blacks in the audience. But Tutu is preaching to the choir. This is the last place the *volk* of Paarl want to be today.

That afternoon the scenery inside the hall changes. A busload of young, mostly white, theology students arrives from Stellenbosch. They have come to hear the leaders of the six Stellenbosch Dutch Reformed churches—"the nursery of a great deal of Afrikaner leadership," Tutu tells me—publicly apologize before the TRC. Also in attendance to hear this confession is Wilhelm Verwoerd Jr., who grew up in this three-hundred-year-old synod of the church.

Three white men—ranging in age from Frederick Marais in his mid-thirties, to the middle-aged Dr. Hannes Koornhof, to the elderly Dr. Bethel Müller—step up to the podium. They sit opposite Archbishop Tutu, a man whom their church once considered a heretic and a terrorist sympathizer.

Speaking as if he were in a church confessional, Dr. Koornhof intones that the Stellenbosch churches "either failed wholesale or made only the most timid of efforts" to speak out against abuses. He acknowledges that "apartheid radically impaired the human dignity of people all around us and resulted in gross violations of human rights." He concedes that the church "suppressed or ignored" protest both within and outside its ranks. Other dissenters "suffered defamation or found themselves being given bad names. Some were even subjected to personal injustices. At the very times when we should have continued to speak out clearly for the truth and against injustice," he says, flanked by his solemn-looking colleagues, "we grew tired and gave up protesting."

When they finish answering questions from the commissioners, Archbishop Tutu steps down from the stage and warmly embraces each of the three men. The elder Afrikaner church leader clings to the archbishop just a bit longer than the others. It is clearly a poignant moment for all of them.

I see Wilhelm at the tea break. He is in the lobby, staring at some large display panels under the banner, "From Conflict to Reconciliation: Paarl's History under Apartheid." It is part of an exhibit at the local museum that has been mounted in honor of the TRC hearings. It includes profiles of local activists, photos and news clippings of major protests, and events of the last five decades. Groups of people are huddled around the panels. Blacks point in excited recognition at incidents that they recall. Whites stare numbly at a history of their community that most of them chose to ignore.

I ask Wilhelm his reaction to seeing these men, all of whom he knows, apologize for his church's role in supporting apartheid. "I have mixed feelings," he says, looking subdued. "I was sort of sitting there feeling quite touched and moved by what they were saying. I do think it is not something that is easy for them to do."

Wilhelm Jr. is one of the casualties of his church's silence. These days, the one-time "Soldier for Jesus" is "very alienated from the church and very disappointed." From preparing to spend his life as a missionary, he and his family are no longer members of any church and only occasionally attend services. He and Melanie were strongly criticized by their church when they joined the ANC.

There is a hint of bitterness in his reaction. "I'm more prepared to forgive them in the sense that they betrayed me, they lied to me. Why did they teach me theology for three, four years? Why did I go to church two times on a Sunday? I was very involved in the church but I was never exposed to the realities of apartheid, so I had a strong sense that I was betrayed by the leaders in the church and by the professors and by people like that."

I return to Paarl the next day for a continuation of the hearings. The audience, as usual, is once again mostly black. But after the customary tea break, I notice two white men sitting in the back row. I approach them and learn that they are ministers in the local Dutch Reformed church. The men, Rev. Hans Steyn and Rev. Gawie van Broekhuizen, look distinctly uncomfortable, speaking to each other and avoiding eye contact with other community members. They tell me that they have just dropped by on their lunch hour. I ask if what they are hearing here is news to them.

"In our community, it wasn't that serious, the [apartheid] crimes," says Steyn, evidently oblivious to what was described in the hours of testimony that have just passed. "We have normal relations with the people here. We weren't *fighting* them," he says primly, as if shocked by the notion. As for the little testimony he's heard, he says dismissively, "This is all uncorroborated testimony, so what is happening here is subjective."

Rev. Broekhuizen, a short man dressed conservatively in a gray jacket and tie, offers, "My impression of Paarl is that it's a normal society, rather peaceful. I would say it's more normal than other parts of the country." He smiles blandly. It is a refrain I have heard often from whites: apartheid never happened *here*. It was *those* people in *that* town who did it. Indeed, whites who supported apartheid are a rarity now. It is heartwarming, I joke to friends, to return to a nation where everyone, white and black, was against apartheid.

I return to my seat to listen to Andile Ndinsa, now twenty-seven, recount how he was shot seven times by police, then abducted from the hospital by the same cops and interrogated. His injuries forced him to drop out of school, and he remains unable to hold a job. He is now attempting to complete his high school education. His mother sits beside him, wiping tears from her eyes as her son speaks of opportunities lost.

I turn around to see the response of the clergymen. But they have already left.

South African whites still, by and large, refuse to accept responsibility for apartheid. Their response to the TRC ranges from avoidance to facile rationalizations. And yet the truth process has made one crucial dent: South African whites with whom I spoke with now acknowledge that apartheid happened, and with it some excesses—even if they were "over there." There has been a subtle paradigm shift in white attitudes. Whites will still deny the details when I speak to them, but many now concede that apartheid went too far. "It was unnecessary," many people now tell me. It's a small but critical change. There is now rough consensus about what happened in the past. Without that, what hope there is for reconciliation would be dashed entirely.

Wilhelm and I drive through the gates of the Bishop's School, Cape Town's most exclusive private academy. He has been asked to speak about the Truth Commission to an elite group of the school's best students. We pass between symmetrical rows of massive ancient oak trees, the stately old school staring austerely at us from across several rugby fields. It is all ivy-covered white walls and red-tiled roofs, with manicured rose bushes framing the entrance. Were it not for the South African flag flapping overhead, one could mistake this opulence for the home of royalty perched somewhere in the moors of England. Wilhelm's face is pressed against the windshield. He is awed by the place. "I think this is one of the *most* expensive schools in the country!" he exclaims.

Wilhelm is greeted by a tall, freshly scrubbed young man in a navy blue blazer. "Hello Mr. Verwoerd, I'm pleased to meet you." He is blond, blue eyed, and well mannered—the very model of a bright young up-and-comer. He ushers us inside to a wood-paneled room where we are greeted by twelve clones: all white, all but two blond, all smartly packaged in their navy blazers with the Bishop's School insignia embroidered on their breast pockets.

The dark cloistered room reeks of tradition. The flags of the four former South African provinces hang from the rafters overhead, as if to emphasize that the school predates mere politics. Dusty old books with leather spines line the walls, interspersed with pictures of Bishop's School war heroes. School trophies are showcased behind glass. For an Afrikaner like Wilhelm, this is treading in the lion's den of English culture; a young Verwoerd would not have been caught dead here. Later, over Coke and cookies, he inquires whether his alma mater, Paul Roos Gymnasium in Stellenbosch, is still a traditional rugby rival. "Oh yes!" the prim boys exclaim in a rare display of emotion. "The whole school comes to see *that* match."

We are seated at a long wooden table. Wilhelm begins by asking the boys their impression of the TRC. "It's like a scab," says one young man of the effect of the daily testimonials of apartheid atrocities. "If you scratch it and scratch it, it just bleeds."

"Is that what *you* think?" asks Wilhelm.

The young scholar looks sheepish. "I don't really have an opinion. It's just what I heard."

Wilhelm embarks on his mission. "One big problem in our country is we don't have a generally accepted view of our history. One of the Truth Commission's main functions is to construct a history for the sake of the present and future. For me, just being exposed to ordinary people telling their stories, it broke through a lot of prejudice and fears that I have. It moved me." Wilhelm becomes animated, like the preacher that he once hoped to become. "The challenge I would pose is to let this touch you."

The students look on obediently. Some appear bored, staring over his shoulder into space. Others fidget nervously as loaded words fly about the room and echo overhead in the dark wood rafters. "Guilt." "Shame." "Responsibility."

"We are trying to construct an identity out of this painful history. Recognizing the painful part of our past," he continues, "I find that quite liberating."

The students are not so sure about this. One perturbed looking student insists, "I feel anger and embarrassment for the situation our forefathers put us in. Now white people are going to suffer because of affirmative action, and it's because of those who've gone before us."

Wilhelm assumes the role of group therapist, drawing out pain and offering it back to the wounded in a constructive form.

"The success of the TRC will be in the hands of your generation. That's exciting," he asserts, "the idea that we can make a contribution and build bridges."

Rising to the confessional spirit, one student offers, "This is an English-speaking school, and you see discrimination coming out against the Afrikaans speakers because we feel it's *their* problem."

"Really?" says Wilhelm, pained by this revelation. "I haven't heard that kind of thing before. That is very interesting."

Wilhelm's challenge is heady stuff for these teenagers, who are more concerned with rugby results than with how to alleviate poverty on the Cape Flats. Poverty seems like part of the natural order to these young men, like trees and mountains. "Apartheid" is something they learn about in history class; *they* would never have agreed with such an abhorrent policy.

But as Wilhelm points out, these young men are beneficiaries of apartheid. Their school is 85 percent white, the same ratio as it has been for years. Blacks have no greater access to this elite, privileged world than they have ever had. In fact, as the school's development director informs me later, liberal "guilt money" for scholarships has dried up, making it even harder for lower-income students to get in.

Wilhelm concludes, "I have a feeling that for the rest of our lives we will deal with the past."

Archbishop Desmond Tutu looks uncharacteristically relaxed in a rumpled cotton shirt and slacks. It is mid-1997, and we are sitting in the ninth-floor offices of the South African Consulate in New York.

Life has rudely interrupted Tutu's calling as father confessor to the South African people. A ripple of alarm coursed through South Africa in February 1997 when he was diagnosed with prostate cancer. His frenetic pace slowed noticeably after that, and he dropped out of sight entirely for three months when he underwent cancer treatment at the Sloane-Kettering Institute in New York. His absence temporarily left the TRC without its moral rudder in the roiling waters of post-apartheid South African politics.

The Arch, as he's known, greets me warmly in his nondescript office. He begins our conversation with a prayer. He proceeds to swiftly dismiss my profession of concern for his health. "I'm feeling fine, just fine," he reassures me. Indeed, he looks surprisingly vigorous.

Tutu has impressed me as a sharp, quick-thinking political operator in his role as TRC chair. In debates about the truth process in South Africa he is an able adversary for every comer, from smug academics to apartheid generals. In June 1997, he had a highly publicized spat with former National Party leader F. W. de Klerk. When de Klerk reiterated his oft-stated insistence that he knew nothing about police abuses during his reign, Tutu accused him of not telling the truth. A petulant de Klerk responded by withdrawing the cooperation of the National Party from the truth process, and filing a lawsuit demanding an apology from Tutu and the resignation of his deputy, Alex Boraine (Marthinus van Schalkwyk, who became NP leader after de Klerk's retirement in September 1997, agreed to drop the lawsuit after Tutu and Boraine apologized). For de Klerk, whose party may be fatally wounded by the TRC's avalanche of revelations, it was a last-ditch move to stave off political suicide.

Is F. W. de Klerk a liar? The loquacious archbishop emeritus (he retired from his church post in 1996) is suddenly struck dumb. He peers glumly up at the ceiling, down at the floor, and finally back at me. His silence speaks volumes. He appears to be wrestling with what he should say rather than what he wants to say—a bit of diplomacy he's never fancied. Reluctantly, he finally says of his fellow Nobel Peace Prize recipient, "The trouble with the position that he takes where he says he didn't know this, he didn't know the other is that someone could say you either knew—which puts you in a heck of a mess—or you didn't know, which makes you highly incompetent." The archbishop then changes tack. "It is actually irrelevant whether he knew. What is important is that their policy made these things possible."

Our conversation inevitably turns to the question of justice, or lack of it, in the truth process. Tutu is adamant in his defense of the TRC's approach. "When people speak about justice, almost always they are thinking of retributive justice—the modern equivalent of really 'an eye for an eye.' Not quite, but they are saying when you have committed a crime there must be a commensurate punishment. And that is true."

The archbishop hunches his shoulders expressively, his eyes grow wide, and he stretches his long fingers toward me as he speaks. "But we are saying that there is another kind of justice—restorative justice . . . Because if justice is the last word in our situation, we have *had it,* man. How do you break the cycle? It can't happen through the process of justice. You have to inject a new factor. And the new factor is: you've got to *forgive.*"

I question whether this Christian notion of forgiveness is sufficient to teach future generations the requisite moral lesson that crime carries heavy consequences. Tutu bounces up in his chair, shaking his head in vigorous disagreement. "You see forgiveness is no nebulous spiritual thing that is practiced by those who are crazy and idealistic and totally unpragmatic. Forgiveness is a pragmatic absolute necessity. Without forgiveness there is no *future*. And that is not a religious statement—it is thoroughly political. It is *realpolitik*."

After two years of confronting the darkest side of his country, Tutu is unremittingly hopeful. "Who could ever have thought that South Africa could be held up as a paradigm, as a model for anything except the most ghastly things?" he says in wonderment, with a high-pitched chuckle. "God said . . . I am going to use you. South Africa has something here that was a nightmare. It's ended. And I want Bosnia, Rwanda, Somalia—I mean, name it—Northern Ireland, the Middle East: you have nightmares . . . Your nightmare can end, *will* end, too."

Wilhelm Verwoerd Jr. has, in the end, fulfilled his childhood dream of becoming a missionary after all. His mission now is to somehow transform the detritus of the past into something constructive to build the future. It is an uplifting proposition, and a daunting one. His inability to achieve reconciliation even within his own family has humbled him about the realities of what he, or his country, can achieve.

Reconciliation, he now says, may just be a state of "conflictual togetherness," or "peaceful coexistence," or just "solving our differences and conflicts in a nonviolent way. That's the best we can hope for. If we can manage to achieve that, then I think we're talking about a realistic sense of reconciliation."

The most powerful message that Verwoerd brings—and the burden that he bears—is knowing that thoughtful, even well-meaning human beings were behind the depraved genius of apartheid. "It is difficult to just write off these people and say that apartheid was a crime against humanity—which it was—but that all these people were a bunch of evil Nazis. I think it makes me more humble to see how ordinary people and often people with good intentions can become involved in these evil things.

"The line between good and bad is not between white and black," he reflects. "We all have this potential to become evil. And people who are now in positions of power [must learn] how easy it is to become corrupted through this process."

All of which causes Wilhelm to look upon current events, even from his adopted political home in the ANC, with a jaundiced eye. He speaks of the need for "eternal vigilance." "What does it mean to build a culture of human rights? There might come a point, and it will be difficult, when we will have to be very critical of what ANC politicians and other politicians are doing."

Wilhelm Verwoerd Jr. does not look on the past and see monsters. His journey has shown him that when he peers over the edge into the abyss, he finds a mirror. "One shouldn't think that under similar circumstances that many people might not have done many of the things that [H. F. Verwoerd and his colleagues] have done. I have the uncomfortable recognition that I'm not necessarily better than they were. Under certain circumstances, I might have done the same."

PART THREE | **POOR WOMAN, RICH WOMAN**

# "THE BOOK OF APARTHEID IS STILL OPEN"

ADELAIDE BUSO:
SQUATTER, DOMESTIC WORKER, CITY COUNCILOR

Adelaide Buso in
her shack in Westlake
Informal Settlement,
1997.

Councilor Adelaide
Buso speaking at a city
council meeting, 1997.

**THE CITY COUNCIL MEETING** looks curiously anachronistic. I enter the crisp white room with deep mahogany accents expecting to see a bevy of newly elected councilors who reflect the demographics of the community: mostly black, with a scattering of white and colored officials. But half of the thirty councilors here are white; they sit in the front rows. The white men and the half-dozen white women are conspicuous in their designer clothes and jewelry. In the back is a row of colored councilors, who say little during the meeting.

A lone African woman is seated in the middle of the room. Her name is Adelaide Buso, and she is neatly dressed in a striped black and royal blue dress. She sits mute, nodding her head in agreement at points made by her fellow councilors. At one point her colleague, a white-haired trade unionist named Hennie van Eyck, stands up to lambaste the council.

"The National Party is trying to railroad proposals through here. It's still hanging on to *baasskap!*" he declares defiantly. The meeting erupts in indignant shouts from the accused white councilors. Adelaide roars with laughter.

Adelaide Nontsikelelo Buso—her African middle name means "blessed one"—comes from a different world than her fellow councilors. She is employed as a domestic worker in the wealthy white homes located not far from the meeting hall. In 1995 she was elected to be a councilor in the South Peninsula Municipality, which covers the communities that lie south of Cape Town. Her constituents include residents of some of the richest neighborhoods in South Africa, and some of the poorest. Now Buso is among those who determine which families will get permits to build new Jacuzzis and renovate their kitchens. Then she returns to cleaning toilets and washing laundry in those same homes. Her own home is a stark contrast to those in which she works: she occupies a metal shack in a squatter camp precariously wedged into a middle-class white suburb.

Buso represents one of those striking contradictions of the new South Africa. She now occupies the long-coveted seat of government. But she is far indeed from exercising power. Her impotence has two immediate causes. First, she is one of only four ANC councilors on a council dominated by the National Party—the same people who ran the city council in the past. Second, she is at times befuddled by the complexities of municipal governance, despite her earnest attempts to learn on the job. Political power thus defaults to where it has always resided: with white bureaucrats of the old regime.

"The book of apartheid is still open," insists Adelaide as we sit in her shanty. Rain raps loudly on the corrugated metal roof and drips onto the dirt floor beneath us. She nonchalantly moves a bucket to catch the leak. Across the road we look out onto the greens of a manicured eighteen-hole golf course.

"We going to bury the whole book of apartheid and we going to make a big funeral," she says over the din of the squall that threatens to swamp us. Only then, she declares firmly, will South Africa truly be "the rainbow nation."

The Westlake squatter camp—aka the Westlake Informal Settlement, in the new parlance—stands out like a tramp at a formal ball. The small pie-shaped swatch of "bush" that is home to some two thousand people is wedged in between the mansions of Constantia and Tokai to the north, a championship golf course to the south, an upscale shopping mall to the east, and Pollsmoor Prison (one of Nelson Mandela's former homes) next door. Look up, and you take in the majestic views of craggy Silvermine Mountain. Look down, and you see squalor and shacks.

Like many informal settlements, Westlake is almost invisible until you are right on top of it. But its presence can be inferred from the numerous African and colored people pushing shopping carts along the nearby highway. Some are returning from food shopping at a mall, a mile away. Others travel back and forth to the middle-class neighborhoods, surviving by rummaging through trash and salvaging small knickknacks or recyclable refuse that they sell for a pittance.

To reach Adelaide Buso's shack, I park near an overflowing trash dumpster (the lone municipal bin is supposed to serve the entire settlement) and wander down sandy, rubbish-strewn pathways. A drunken colored woman sees me and begs to tell me her hard-luck story. Something about being sick, and nobody cares, and she wants to commit suicide. She tugs at my sleeve and insists I come see her children. In a small, fenced-in patch of dirt, I meet three doe-eyed, shoeless kids. Their bellies are large and round, a telltale sign of malnutrition. Several adults are sitting around listening to music and drinking beer. It is only 9 A.M., and they are drunk.

Adelaide Buso's shack is a relatively solid structure built from sheets of corrugated metal. It is painted a pleasant cream color, and even has a small flower garden out front. Her home has latticed windows, a creaking wooden door, and a bench on which to sit outside. In short, all the trappings of suburban life are here, albeit in a "shantytown kitsch" rendition.

Adelaide greets me warmly inside her home. Like most shacks I have been in, hers is meticulously kept. A wood hutch showcases her best dishes and mugs. Ceramic animals—a ubiquitous adornment of South African homes—sit along the top shelf. A cast-off kitchen table sits in the middle of the room, and a hodgepodge of furniture—an old stuffed chair, a plastic swivel seat, and a wood bench—complete the homegrown dining room set. In one corner is a neatly stacked and lovingly shined set of aluminum pots sitting on a kerosene stove. In the opposite corner is a television wired to a car battery. The dirt floor is covered in a mishmash of linoleum remnants.

During the apartheid years, squatter camps that I visited were often bound together by their opposition to a common enemy: the police, who would routinely raze the shacks and leave hundreds of families homeless. These informal settlements were also havens for corrupt warlords who staked out turf, extorted "protection" money from residents, and wreaked havoc on interlopers. Some of the older informal settlements, such as KTC and Crossroads outside Cape Town, are tight-knit and mature communities with neighborhood committees and recognized community leaders that lend a redeeming sense of normality to the squalor.

Westlake is just plain depressing. When I first visit, I am struck by the complete disunity of the place. No one knows where anyone else lives, and there is no apparent order to where people settle. The camp is unusual in that it has a mixture of Africans, coloreds, and even some white squatters— something I had never before seen. It is a fractured, squalid place united only by the fact that everyone I meet there hates it.

We are sitting in Adelaide's kitchen area and she is making some tea on her kerosene stove. The thumping beat of dance music is in the air, wafting out from a nearby *shebeen* in a neighbor's home. Adelaide is dressed neatly in a pretty homemade red and white Sotho sundress. She looks slightly younger than her forty-six years and has an expressive round face which frames her large deep-set eyes. She speaks of hardship, but she smiles easily in conversation.

"I feel strong for you to see how we . . . live in a place like this," she tells me. "We are using candles, paraffin [kerosene] and gas stove to cook our food and to warm the water. You cannot read and you cannot write easily at night because the candle doesn't show the light. Even the children they must study during the day." She sums up, "The basic living conditions are very unhealthy."

Adelaide worries about the children. "They are victims of the child abuse during the day when their parents are not at home. There are also starving children." She says children from the nearby colored and white communities "have got respect, they've got everything, they've got food, they've got lights. But here we haven't got any crèche and the children are lying around, walking around day and night with empty stomachs."

As a single woman, Adelaide fears for her safety. The weekends are the worst times. "The women are not staying because the violence against the women is especially bad on Fridays, you know, because of the alcohol. The mans are hurting the womens with knives at night." With no phone, she is helpless to call the police or an ambulance. "I am also not safe . . . The people can just come and kill me if they like, anytime day and night. I'm really also a victim. I've got no voice to say 'no.'"

For many of South Africa's approximately seven million urban squatters, life has only gotten worse since the 1994 elections. Tens of thousands of rural South Africans responded to their new freedoms by flocking to the cities to claim their place in the sun. Their expectations were high: Nelson Mandela had promised them jobs and houses. They had come to collect.

The rapid influx of rural poor swelled the already jammed urban informal settlements. The Third World met the First World in grand relief. The results can be seen around the "Mother City" of Cape Town. The N2, a slick modern highway where the BMWs and Mercedes roar into the city at 100 miles per hour, is lined by miles of slatted concrete fencing. The fence is a futile attempt to dam the ever-growing ocean of squatters who reside some fifteen miles from Cape Town's downtown skyscrapers. The highway itself is a thoroughfare for an incongruous assortment of conveyances. Luxury cars race past horse-drawn carts, cows graze on the side of the road, women balance firewood on their heads as they dart across the highway, and township joggers train in the breakdown lane.

The scale of the squalor defies comprehension. A high-speed passerby peers out on what appears to be a monolithic sea of poverty. Who lives there? Where did they all come from? A visitor discovers that the vast ghetto is indeed populated by individuals, each with a unique story. Adelaide's saga is illustrative.

Adelaide Buso was born in 1950 in the rural town of Matatiele, on the border of the tiny landlocked nation of Lesotho. She had three sisters and three brothers. Her father died in 1966, and her mother passed away in 1988. She was married in the sixties to a man who worked on a chicken farm in Durban. They had three sons: Douglas, now twenty-seven; Moses, twenty-four; and Eric, twenty-two. The boys lived with their mother in Matatiele while their father lived and worked about a seven-hour drive away.

The economic backbone of apartheid was the system of contract migrant labor. Blacks would work on an eleven-month contract in the mines or at other jobs, only visiting family in December. The nuclear family became a casualty of this system: men, who typically lived in single-sex hostels, would frequently develop a relationship with a "city woman." In the early seventies, Adelaide's husband simply stopped visiting. Like many men, he opted to keep his city girlfriend and dump his wife and kids.

Adelaide's mother took pity on her. "Adelaide, you will have to stay here at my home," her mother told her. "I haven't got money but you are my daughter. I am suffering as well. But if you are facing this difficulty I have to take you back and I have to keep your children. I have to make you go to work because the boys haven't got money. They are still young."

Adelaide and her sons moved in with her mother in Matatiele in the mid-seventies. Within a year, Adelaide was forced to move in order to find work that would support her family. Her sisters were living over seven hundred miles away in Cape Town, so that is where she gravitated. The city was a big, alienating place. Adelaide had never seen such large buildings, fast traffic, or crowded living spaces. The young mother from the country felt utterly lost. She missed the life in her village, and most of all, she missed her children.

One day in 1977, twenty-six-year-old Adelaide Buso stepped off a bus after a thirty-hour ride from Matatiele to Cape Town and entered the world of big-city apartheid. She was weary from the journey and disoriented by the strange surroundings. But there was no time to waste. Other passengers on the bus warned her to keep an eye out for the inspectors. "You must run away when you see the Boo-ahs," they tutored her. "Unless your *dompas* [pass book] says you can be here, the inspectors will grab you and put you in jail."

Adelaide walked through the crowded bus station and saw the white policemen confront one of her fellow passengers. She heard a commotion, and then saw them hustle the woman into the back of the yellow police *bakkie*. She quickened her pace and followed the crowds, not knowing where she was going. She was finally directed to a bus that took her to Langa, the sprawling "legal" black township on the outskirts of Cape Town. Langa was established on the periphery of Cape Town in 1927 to accommodate African workers who were being forced further and further from the city center by restrictive land laws.[1]

In Langa Adelaide saw an urban version of African village life. The dirt alleyways teemed with people, and a goat was being slaughtered on a table in the middle. Her nose filled with the scent of wood and coal fires, which were burning both outside and inside the charmless cement hostels. She found one of her sisters living in a cramped room among six other people. Miraculously, there was always room for one more, and Adelaide made herself at home.

The next day, Adelaide took a bus to Mowbray, the main crossroads where township residents dispersed to various Cape Town destinations. She began wandering down the streets of the Bohemian white suburb, stopping in at shops and inquiring whether they needed help.

"We employ coloreds, not Africans," she was told. It was a brand of discrimination unique to the Cape, which was the only province where mixed-race people constituted the majority.

After several days of fruitless searching she was starting to despair. On her third day in the city, police raided the bus she was riding. All unemployed Africans were arrested. The young policemen seemed to take delight in manhandling the people. Adelaide was thrown face down into the back of a pickup truck.

"Trespass," another woman told her with a shrug of resignation. Adelaide still didn't understand. "Group Areas Act," the woman elaborated. "Blacks aren't allowed here unless they have a job. No job, no right to be here." Hours later, the hapless bus passengers were processed at the police station, told their court date, and dumped at a bus stop to return to the township.

The Group Areas Act of 1950 was aimed at "unscrambling the multiracial omelet" of residential living areas in South Africa.[2] It was the most ambitious attempt yet to force Africans, coloreds, and Indians into their respective ghettoes. This law, combined with various "influx control" measures and pass laws, regulated the movement of nonwhite citizens to an unprecedented degree. The result was that blacks inevitably ran afoul of the law merely for walking down a street.

The most visible consequence of the white government's attempt to force blacks into proscribed areas was the explosion in illegal squatting. Adelaide, like other blacks, would periodically be "deported" from the city to an impoverished homeland, only to return as a squatter and once again hope to find work. By the 1980s, police were battling squatters on a regular basis. I witnessed the squatters of Crossroads, the largest informal settlement in the Cape, rebuild their shacks out of plastic tarps as police repeatedly bulldozed the community in 1984.

After Adelaide's first arrest, job hunting became a game of cat and mouse. Adelaide walked the streets looking intently for work, constantly peering over her shoulder to avoid the police. She eventually switched her tactics from inquiring at shops to going door-to-door in the fashionable white suburbs. After several weeks, she finally landed a job as a live-in maid for a white family.

Life for a South African domestic worker is precarious, as Adelaide Buso quickly discovered. She began working as a "char," or maid, for a woman in Zwaanswyk, a more rural Cape Town suburb. Adelaide lived in a spartan backyard apartment with no electricity or running water. Domestics were like indentured servants: if they left their job for any reason, they would lose their home and be at the mercy of the police. So Adelaide took her lumps and didn't complain.

The "backyard servants" were easy prey for the police. Many employers refused to provide their domestics with proper paperwork, preferring to keep the relationship as informal as possible. That way they could hire and fire people at will and not be responsible for fringe benefits such as health care or food.

One night, Adelaide awoke to the sound of a pickup truck outside and voices in front of a neighbor's flat. She knew immediately who it was. Without thinking, she bolted out of her flat and began running up a steep hill. Survival instinct guided her. Neglecting to even pull on clothes, she stumbled frantically through thick undergrowth in the cold winter air. She could hear other backyard dwellers, including some children, crashing through the brush nearby.

Like a victim that senses a predator closing in, Adelaide ran, tripped, and stumbled in an effort to escape. As she dodged the searchlights that the police were training on the bush, she ran into a barbed wire fence. She screamed in pain as the barbs tore into her flesh and she slammed into the earth. Blood oozed from her wounds. Within seconds a large cop was glowering over her, shouting in Afrikaans for her to get up. She protested that she was hurt, but this only earned her a sharp whack from a police baton. The young cop, disgusted at the sight of a half-dressed black woman, ordered her back to her apartment to fetch her clothes. Adelaide was afraid to disturb her employer, so she tiptoed into her boss's house to retrieve her dress. She was then shoved into the back of the police wagon and hauled away.

In the darkness of the police vehicle Adelaide could make out the voices of several people she knew. "*Sisi* [sister] is with child," a woman declared urgently. Adelaide could hear the strained breathing of a woman in labor next to her. The men and women tried to make room around the young woman who was gasping in pain from labor contractions. The prisoners shouted for the police to go to a hospital, but the cops in front just guffawed.

Adelaide helped calm the expecting mother while other women positioned themselves between her legs to catch the baby. It was not easy: the occupants were thrown back and forth as the police van swerved fast around corners and over rutted roads. By the time the vehicle stopped at the Milnerton police station, the police opened the back to find blood everywhere. An infant cried out while an exhausted mother lay slumped against another woman's chest. Adelaide stroked her forehead, mopping the sweat from her brow.

The cops flew into a confused rage. "Why didn't you tell us she was pregnant?" said a red-faced officer, swearing at the group of people trying to help the woman and her newborn child.

"How can we tell you anything? You're just pushing us here, treating us like animals," retorted Adelaide, her round face contorted in anger.

The policeman would not have a black woman insult him. He glared at Adelaide, and barked that the new prisoners would have to stay up all night and wash out the police van until it was spotless. The cold sea air sliced through Adelaide's meager clothes as she worked on her hands and knees, polishing the yellow vehicle through the night.

In the morning, Adelaide and her neighbors were taken to Pollsmoor Prison, south of Cape Town. For over a week she languished in a cold, crowded cell. When she was finally brought before a magistrate, she faced a R 300 ($345) fine for being in the area without a pass. She returned to her backyard flat exhausted by her ordeal and penniless. All the money that she had saved in the last few months to send to her sons was gone. Then she braced herself in preparation for the same treatment all over again. And again.

Domestic workers have by necessity straddled the yawning racial fault line in South Africa. For as much as apartheid dictated that the races must be separated, black servants were needed to provide the comforts to which whites were accustomed. While whites fought to keep the black masses out of sight and mind, black domestic workers inhabited the womb of their very homes. Black domestics typically had responsibility for raising a white family's children. The resulting contradiction always made me do double takes: a black nanny carrying a white baby in an African-style papoose on her back, lounging about in a park designated "for whites only." This adult woman's right to be here was conveyed solely by the presence of the helpless white infant in tow. The police would eagerly arrest her for trespassing were this woman to rest her feet in this same park on her day off.

White employers have long been intensely ambivalent about their servants, despite the central role domestic workers play in white home life. Nowhere is this made clearer than in the compensation that a domestic receives: according to the South African Domestic Workers Union (SADWU), the average salary in 1997 for a full-time live-in servant working six days per week was R 250 per month—about $55.

After years of working as a part-time domestic for several different employers, Adelaide was relieved when she landed a steady job as a live-in domestic in 1985 for a woman named Susan. Adelaide was to work two days for pay, and a third day in lieu of rent for her backyard flat. For this, she was paid R 80 ($40) per month. The best part was that Susan's home was gated, so the police would not indiscriminately raid the servants' quarters.

Adelaide's enthusiasm for her new employer quickly dampened as the rules of the house were made clear. She was not allowed to eat anything in the refrigerator. Even when Susan's two children returned from school complaining they were hungry, they refused to open the refrigerator in front of Adelaide; evidently, their mother feared it would encourage Adelaide to eat, too. Adelaide was allowed to use their tea, but not their milk or bread at her meal times. When the occasional visitor came to see Adelaide at her flat, Susan informed her that she didn't want "your friends" coming around. Susan would regularly say, "Excuse me, I just want to have something to eat." That was polite code for Adelaide to leave and work elsewhere in the house.

"They were treating me like a slave," Adelaide declares bitterly. Actually, she was just being treated like a typical domestic worker. And that made Adelaide angry. In 1987, Adelaide joined SADWU, which was part of South Africa's increasingly militant trade union movement. Black trade unions were legalized in 1979 in response to years of wildcat strikes. The government had hoped that the new black unions would make it easier for companies to control workers. It was a fateful miscalculation. By the mid-eighties, the trade unions had become active on a wide range of social and political issues. As the states of emergency in the mid-eighties hamstrung political organizations such as the United Democratic Front, the trade unions stepped in to fill the void. Led by the Congress of South African Trade Unions (COSATU), the unions demonstrated their power throughout the eighties and early nineties by calling for national stayaways to protest police violence and government repression. In 1987 alone, there were an unprecedented 1,148 strikes, including a three-week-long strike by the half-million strong National Union of Mineworkers.[3] The actions brought businesses around the country to a halt, and established the unions as a major force for social change.

Adelaide Buso was captivated by the idea that workers could join together and improve their lot. The unions gave her a sense of power and dignity in a world where she otherwise had none. She soon began visiting other domestic workers in their backyard flats and preaching the gospel of black empowerment, higher pay, and improved working conditions. It was easy to tell others, but quite another thing to do herself: Adelaide never peeped a word of protest in her own job.

A turning point came in 1990. It was February 11, the day Nelson Mandela walked out of prison. South Africans everywhere were glued to televisions as they waited anxiously to see the figure who, during nearly three decades in prison, had become more myth than man.

Susan's husband, Michael, came home from work early that day. Adelaide had little interaction with him; Susan usually asked her to leave when he was home. He was uncomfortable around "the help."

Adelaide was surprised to see Michael enter the room and sit down near where she was working. "Yes, Mandela is out today and we will see what it's going to do for you," he said with a smirk as he turned on the TV. The news was filled with images of jubilant crowds thronging downtown Cape Town, where Mandela was speaking.

After years of compliant silence, Adelaide suddenly found her voice. She looked squarely at her boss and shot back, "Michael, I'm not working for Mandela—I'm working for you. I want to see what are *you* going to do for me."

Michael was struck speechless—it was as if a plant had talked back to him. He abruptly stood up and left the room. Adelaide roars with laughter at the memory of the exchange.

In the months following Mandela's release, Susan and her family began taunting Adelaide with their observations about current events. "What a waste: instead of building houses for the poor people, Mandela is wasting lots of money on [his daughter] Zindzi's wedding," snipped Susan one morning.

Again, Adelaide was quick to come back at her. "I've got nothing to do about the wedding of Zindzi because I'm not working for Mandela." Like her husband, Susan didn't know how to reply and retreated quickly. Her help had never spoken back to her before.

"If I say something they always have to run away from me and go somewhere else," explains a grinning Adelaide. "They don't want to face what I'm saying."

Unbeknownst to her employer, Adelaide had become deeply involved in the trade unions and with the ANC even before it was unbanned. She would leave her day job and spend her evenings debating and plotting for when South Africa would be free. Mandela's release was more than just one man walking out of jail. For this once-mute domestic worker, it was the release of her pent-up aspirations. Finally, Adelaide Buso could taste life beyond apartheid.

We turn off the paved road and bounce slowly along the deeply rutted sand track until we can drive no further. In my car are Adelaide Buso and Hennie van Eyck. As councilors on the South Peninsula Municipality, they represent the communities that lie south of Cape Town. Most people associate this area with the sandy beaches of Muizenberg or the sprawling wine estates of Constantia. It is an area of fabulous wealth and beauty, a world-renowned tourist destination. But Adelaide and Hennie represent a different constituency: the thousands of poor people who are shoehorned between the beaches and mansions, the workers who sustain the wealthy lifestyles.

Rising up out of the bush before us like a hidden pirate's den is a ragtag sea of shacks. There is a rusty metal one held together by strands of barbed wire; a pleasantly painted one with pretensions to suburbia; a shack with a lovingly manicured flower and vegetable garden out front and livestock in the back. Unlike Westlake, this community has a semblance of order and permanence. This is Vrygrond—"free ground"—the oldest and, with ten thousand people, the largest informal settlement south of Cape Town.

As we walk through this shanty city, notions of the "new South Africa" fade abruptly. The only change in this community since Nelson Mandela became president has been change for the worse. A large billboard at the entrance suggests a reason why: NO NEW HOME CONSTRUCTION ALLOWED, BY ORDER OF COUNCIL. It is a futile attempt to staunch the rapid influx of people into these urban enclaves.

Adelaide and Hennie are visiting today in their official capacity as councilors. For Adelaide, the job has been reward for the diligent grassroots work she waged as a union activist. In the aftermath of Mandela's release from prison, Adelaide traveled among the shacks and spoke to any women who would listen about workers' rights. She explained that the unions were fighting for a minimum wage, health benefits, overtime pay, and safe working conditions for domestics. For women grateful for any job, it sounded like a pipe dream that they desperately longed for. Even if the goals were beyond reach, Adelaide gave them hope and a sense of dignity.

So when the local ANC chapter looked for a woman to represent the interests of the poorest people on the newly created South Peninsula Council, the squatter communities pushed strongly for the quiet, tenacious woman who had worked among them: Adelaide Buso.

Hennie van Eyck, a short, bow-legged, white-haired man, also sharpened his skills in the trade union movement. "Oom (Uncle) Hennie" is well known in the working-class colored communities as an outspoken activist. The months he spent in detention during the 1980s only heightened his determination to speak his mind. Now in his sixties, he is a member of the South African Communist Party (SACP), and is an insightful analyst of grassroots politics.

Adelaide, Hennie, and I make our way to the home of Danger Khumalo, Vrygrond's representative to the South African National Civics Organization (SANCO). SANCO has been a voice for the grass roots, the local civics that were beachheads for the anti-apartheid struggle in the townships. Together with the SACP and COSATU, they formed part of the ANC alliance that won the 1994 elections.

Danger Khumalo ushers us into his four-room shack and motions for us to sit on a threadbare couch. Opposite us is the family finery: a shiny coffee maker, and an old hutch with plates and ceramic cats and elephants standing watch. The ever-present winds known as the Cape Doctor swirl fine white sand around outside. Danger's house is distinguished by the elaborate flower garden that he maintains outside. He has even rigged a hose from one of the few communal taps so that he can water it daily.

"All these shacks," says Danger, an older man whose face is framed by salt-and-pepper hair, "there is still nothing. Water is terrible. We got twenty-one taps for ten thousand people. Here in the Western Cape Province," he adds, "we are still living in the apartheid system. We are still in the struggle."

Adelaide is more emphatic. "People think it's a new South Africa, that everything is fixed. But it's not."

Adelaide and Danger are reacting to the fact that the white minority regime is alive and well in the Western Cape Province. The National Party still reigns supreme here, an odd testament to the effectiveness of its apartheid policies in this area and the short memory of its residents.

The NP has long had a guilt-driven weakness for the colored community. After all, this population group began as the bastard offspring of forbidden relations between the first white settlers in South Africa and their black servants. Even as they implemented apartheid with religious zeal, Afrikaners were deeply ambivalent about how to deal with their colored brethren. Boers and "Cape coloreds" share Afrikaans as their mother tongue and have the same ancestors. The very existence of coloreds threatened the entire fragile construct of the Boers as "chosen people." After all, wouldn't the offspring of the master race also be divinely endowed?

So the architects of apartheid compromised by making coloreds a class of "privileged oppressed." The Cape region, where the colored population is largest, became a "labor preference area" for colored workers. Colored schools were a little less deprived than African schools, and colored townships a little less squalid. The divide-and-rule tactics worked: many coloreds viewed blacks as inferior—or at least as a threat to their jobs. Blacks reciprocated by branding coloreds as sellouts, "black Boers." This preferential treatment engendered ambivalence and political apathy among the colored community. "So long as we get a few more scraps off the white man's table," the thinking went, "we might as well digest the spoils and shut up."

The intensifying state repression in the eighties dashed the faint sense of privilege that coloreds enjoyed. Suddenly colored youth were shot just as wantonly as other blacks, and vibrant colored communities such as Cape Town's fabled District Six—a multicultural hotbed of jazz, street gangs, and radical politics—were bulldozed into piles of rubble. Pushed to the wall, the colored community finally threw in its lot with the black resistance. Coloreds fought, were arrested, and died in the name of *the struggle*.

And then came democracy. In the run-up to the 1994 elections, the NP, or Nats, correctly identified the colored vote as the key to its survival. Fifty-five percent of Western Cape voters were classified colored in 1994, compared to 19 percent African and 25 percent white. So the Boers returned to their colored brethren—not with guns this time, but with generous public works projects that employed colored workers. Colored construction crews were given the job of erecting miles of concrete fencing around black squatter camps, much to the ire of the squatters. And the Nats revived the time-tested image of the *swart gevaar*—the "black peril." The apartheid politicians preached hysterically that affirmative action for

Africans would become official policy and that coloreds would lose their jobs in droves.

Educated colored voters saw through the racist appeals, but the masses of working-class colored voters swallowed the bait. When the votes were tallied, colored voters helped deliver 53 percent of the Cape vote to the National Party, compared to just 33 percent for the ANC; the Nats won twenty-three of the forty-two seats in the provincial legislature.[4] It was a startling victory for the former apartheid leaders. The Western Cape became the only province led by a white person, former minister of law and order Hernus Kriel. This outcome was reinforced in the 1995 by-elections, when the Nats once again resoundingly defeated the ANC in the contest for municipal councils.

I was continually struck—horrified, actually—by the deepening schism between coloreds and Africans. The attitude was typified in an exchange I had with some hitchhikers. I was traveling across the Cape when I picked up first a white couple, then a colored man, Ricky. The white couple were down on their luck and desperately hunting for jobs. Ricky, a young man who had just quit his job as a bricklayer, opened the conversation with the time-tested apartheid refrain, "Man, I'm not a racist but . . . "

Then he launched into a monologue that could have been lifted from a right-wing Afrikaner pub a decade earlier. "I tell you, the *bleks* are *lazy*. This whole country is going to *kak* [shit] under Mandela. He's giving this whole country to the kaffirs. This place will go the same way as the rest of Africa, with blacks killing each other. I'm not a racist, man, but I think it was better before." He then echoed a theme that captures the dilemma that many coloreds perceive themselves in: "Under apartheid, we weren't white enough. Under the ANC, we aren't black enough."

Even the white couple, eager to blame affirmative action for their woes, blanched at his enthusiastic vitriol. Where a decade ago I could always count on Boers to offer the most racist commentary, in post-apartheid South Africa, the ugliest racists I encountered were invariably coloreds.

"It is a slave mentality," lamented municipal councilor Philip Bam, who is active in colored politics. "They still identify with their old master."

The Cape winds continue to scour the shacks of Vrygrond. A thin wall of steel protects us from the elements as we huddle inside Danger Khumalo's home. A few more stragglers wander in. They are eager to talk, to discuss what happened to the revolution they fought for and were promised. But the revolution never happened. Or if it did, it missed Vrygrond.

Solomon Benn is angry. "The people on the ground, they've got no hope anymore. They've been promised many things, but nothing is delivered." Benn is a member of the local SANCO executive committee. A tall, thin young man, he was one of the Young Lions, the youth that fought against the system on the front lines. He has gone from fighting the freedom struggle to . . . waiting. "We have a long way to go," he says, shaking his head in disgust.

The grassroots constituency that swept the ANC into power now finds itself unable to access that power. When the restive members of SANCO and COSATU complain about government inaction or object to government policy, they suddenly find themselves persona non grata in official circles. This puts these former anti-apartheid stalwarts in a quandary, as Danger Khumalo explains. "Before 1994 SANCO and COSATU agreed to lift up the ANC. Now that the ANC has got the power, they forgot us. But if we pull out [of the ANC alliance], the ANC will be flat down."

Who will speak for the poorest people? The new government has been furiously backpedaling on its promises of social upliftment. In 1996 the ANC government released its guiding economic policy with much fanfare. Dubbed the GEAR strategy—Growth, Employment, and Redistribution—it was a masterstroke of doublespeak. The policy advocated a reduction in the budget deficit from 6 percent to 3 percent, called on labor to be more "flexible," and committed the government to a major program of privatization. Major redistributive policies and large-scale social spending were passed over in favor of making South Africa more "globally competitive." Initially ordained as "nonnegotiable" by Minister of Finance Trevor Manuel, GEAR was hailed by the World Bank, the International Monetary Fund, and the European powers as a model of fiscal restraint. Indeed, it appeared to be designed expressly to appease foreign investors. The labor movement and civic groups denounced it as "Thatcherite" and a war on the poor.

Hennie van Eyck, who has been trying to mollify Danger Khumalo's concerns during this conversation, concedes that the growing tensions may destroy the tripartite alliance—ANC, labor, and the Communist Party—that originally came to power.

"It seems there was a commitment to keep the alliance together through the 1999 elections. But we must find new ways to put pressure on the government to make sure delivery happens." As we sit around sipping tea that Danger has made for us on his kerosene stove, Hennie muses, "How long can quiet acceptance remain? Maybe five to ten years. Then down the road you will see new thinking, like opposition politics on the left."

Soon we are back in the car heading to the Red Hill squatter camp. This is a tour of the poorest communities in the southern Cape peninsula and it is Adelaide's first visit to some of her constituencies. We drive a steep winding road up the side of a mountain and mistakenly pass the squatter camp several times before finally spotting the discreet entrance. I am always amazed at how invisible many of these communities are. It is a legacy of a time when people had to stay here covertly. Red Hill is a small community of shacks tucked beneath a towering forest of pine trees. We meet Polly Poni Mzlea, a local resident. Adelaide is acting more politic now, pumping him for information.

"Who looks after the children here?" she asks. She is standing in a resplendent African dress holding her black pocketbook. From appearances she could be any well-appointed politician making an obligatory courtesy call on a constituent—which she is. But like them, she also lives in a shack.

"*Sisi* looks after them in the crèche," he says, motioning to a converted truck trailer where some children are playing.

"Do people bring food here for the children?" she continues. "Do they have breakfast and lunch?"

"Yes, some companies bring the food."

Adelaide is clearly impressed: it occurs to her that these folks are better off than she is. She then adopts a pastoral tone. "I see you are still struggling here," she offers consolingly. "But I see your community is something different than my community. You have electricity, a phone, and a crèche. We don't have that."

"We are your councilors from the ANC," Adelaide explains. "The other twenty-six councilors are from the NP." The man chuckles at the irony. "We are voices for you, the disadvantaged people. The white people live in comfortable houses. I live with no tap, no toilet or phone. We are going to start in January in council to make changes."

The bearded man stares back blankly from deep-set eyes. After a respectful moment of silence he says softly, "They told us in 1990 they would make changes. But nothing has happened. One shack burned down and a boy died inside this year."

Adelaide shakes her head in sad, silent acknowledgment. She wants to tell him that his life will improve because there's a new government and because there are squatters like her on the municipal council. But she knows it's not true. So she says nothing, and leaves.

Not far from Adelaide Buso's home in the Westlake Informal Settlement are some of South Africa's most famous slums. The name Crossroads is synonymous with the anti-apartheid struggle. When I first visited Crossroads in 1984, it was a grim battlefront. A biting winter wind cut across the rubble-strewn lots. A group of women were stretching black plastic over a frail frame of bowed sticks. What happened here, I asked.

"The police bulldozed our shacks," explained a squat, determined looking matron. "And we are rebuilding them.

A small group of women sat on the ground nearby. One of them was smoking a pipe, and stared directly at me. "This is the third time they bulldozed my home this year," she said flatly. "But we will just keep on building them up each time. We are staying here, no matter how many times they come."

The squatters of Crossroads, most of them women, fought a long, hard battle against apartheid authorities throughout the eighties. They were determined to live with their husbands and keep their families together; the white regime was equally determined to show that it could control every aspect of black society at will. And so the small black plastic shacks rose and fell like phoenixes on the rocky veld.

The steady influx of squatters finally overwhelmed the authorities. By the mid-nineties, Crossroads had evolved into an interlinked city of communities with names like KTC, Tambo Square, Mkhonto Square, Samora Machel, and Browns Farm. About a half-million people now live in the greater Crossroads area. The new government has made a priority of redeveloping the area and providing homes and economic opportunity for some forty thousand families. It is part of a national housing scheme in which poor people—individuals or households earning less than R 3,500 ($700) per month—are eligible for a subsidy of up to R 17,500 ($3,500). This subsidy must suffice to purchase a plot of land, build a house, and provide basic services such as water and electricity to the site.

Weltevreden Valley is one of the newly developed areas where Crossroads residents are relocating into permanent homes. It offers the long-awaited alternative to the dire conditions found in the squatter camps. As I approach it, I see that it is abuzz with activity, with bulldozers plowing to and fro over its vast sandy plots. The new government is trying to do all the right things here. Small local builders are being given the construction jobs. Residents are given a range of housing styles to choose from. And consultants are there to show families the basics of capitalism, such as how to buy their first homes. (I later learn how these things backfire: many new local builders went bankrupt; some of the housing styles were made with substandard materials and quickly fell apart; and a few of the consultants were accused of swindling and misleading the new home buyers.)

I arrive at Weltevreden Valley on the day that the first of the families are moving in. It is heartwarming and shocking at the same time. A smiling family stands outside their proud new acquisition: a tiny, whitewashed cinder-block room with a roof. No sooner are they moving in than they are building a ramshackle addition.

"I feel wonderful—we are so happy to have a new home!" declares a petite African woman with her three children standing beside her. "But I am disappointed that it is so small." Ten feet away, her husband and another woman are busy nailing up another room made of wooden pallets and corrugated steel. Rather than concede that this "shackification" is a sign of the woeful inadequacy of its housing program, the government has tried to embrace it. "People's housing" is the new name given to what used to be called shacks.

But Orwellian monikers can't hide the reality of the redevelopment. The homes at Weltevreden Valley are the start of South Africa's new generation of slums. These are admittedly nicer slums—they have water and lights. But they are bleak and overcrowded, just like the shacks they replace. For the battle-weary residents of Crossroads, the new South Africa will look a lot like the old.

The last stop on our tour of the South Peninsula Municipality is a squatter camp known only by its old bureaucratic designation, Site Five. I am surprised to find a wide paved road leading down the center of the sprawling squatter camp, a welcome relief from the usual rutted sand thoroughfares. The road is lined with outdoor stalls where people sell goats, building supplies, and staple foods. About six thousand people live at Site Five. One of them, Winnie Tsotso, explains how she got here.

"I stayed in Noordhoek and was evicted to Khayelitsha in the 1980s because of the Group Areas Act," the large matron recounts. Noordhoek is a pastoral Cape Town suburb with sprawling white beaches on the Atlantic Ocean and a thriving subculture of artists. Winnie Tsotso's shack was demolished in the eighties but she, like many others, returned and took up residence in the bush. The former government realized it could only disperse the squatters, not eliminate them. So the town opted to consolidate the scattered squatters by erecting a "toilet town," a monotonous plot of sand interrupted by orderly rows of latrines. This became Site Five, and it has been growing steadily since its beginnings in the mid-eighties.

I ask Winnie Tsotso what has changed since the 1994 elections. We are standing in front of a community hall, one of the few formal structures in the sea of shacks. She pauses for a moment to think. "Although we've participated in the elections," she says, a flock of kids tugging at her dress as she speaks, "nothing has drastically changed. Promises were made, but nothing has materialized."

Councilor and activist Hennie van Eyck listens impatiently. He is determined to soften the sting of the critics, which he does only half-heartedly. I understand his ambivalence: he fought on the front lines for much of his life. He desperately wants to believe that the revolution delivered. But it's hard even for him to put up a spirited defense of the new government as we stand in the middle of miles of shacks. The short, energetic van Eyck finally interjects, "The legacy of apartheid is great. Anyone who says it can be done in less than five years is not on."

"In Cape Town," he continues, "unemployment is 40 percent. The problem is broad and a financial burden on this country. But the administration is still in the hands of the old order. The army, police, and, here in the Cape, the local government are still in the hands of apartheid bureaucrats—about 80 percent of the public service is Afrikaner. So we can't blame the government that's been in power for only two years."

How long will it take to unmake apartheid, I query. "About 150 to 200 years," he asserts.

But the squatters I meet, including Adelaide, can't wait that long. The two councilors joust in front of their constituents. "The [election] slogan was 'a better life for all.' We want to have that feeling," declares Adelaide. She wags her finger as her pent-up anger bubbles up. "I feel the suffering of the people because I also don't have a house." This is a spontaneous exchange between the two councilors. It is a raw venting of feelings about what is happening, and what is not.

We proceed to walk through the squatter camp to where the local municipality has approved a housing development. Residents have been asked to move their shacks so that sites with water and electricity can be built. The National Party–dominated council is using the national housing subsidy of R 17,000 per family (the housing subsidy in the Cape—$3,500— is slightly higher than the national allowance due to higher regional housing costs) to fund this upgrade. This subsidy is supposed to pay for the serviced site as well as the actual house. But the local government has determined that in Site Five, the cost of servicing the site alone will consume nearly the entire subsidy. The "new dispensation" here will consist of people simply rebuilding their shacks on their old sites.

We arrive to find a fleet of bulldozers busily moving earth and laying pipe and electricity cable where shacks once sat. A lone overflowing trash dumpster which is supposed to serve two thousand people sits off to the side, reeking. The normally serene Adelaide can't restrain herself. Walking with the community leaders across the sandlot, she sputters, "This is a waste of money. They are really just plowing that money into the ground."

Hennie tries to mollify her by presenting the party line. "We need to find a balance of how white ratepayers will pay for it," he says. He is mindful that some rich white communities are boycotting paying their local taxes because of large tax increases that are earmarked for social programs. "There is also a problem of dependency," he adds. "People want everything from the central government, which cannot afford it. You can't build a house for R 17,000. So the housing subsidy is going into the ground just to service the land."

We continue to walk through the dusty, trash-strewn area accompanied by the roar of heavy equipment behind us. We are joined by Jeffrey Ndobongwana, a rotund man and member of the Site Five ANC executive committee. He offers a frank assessment. "This is not a good plan," he says, motioning to the bulldozers and the relocated shacks. "We need proper houses. And it is the ANC's responsibility to build proper houses.

If they don't, then people won't vote ANC in the next elections. The National Party is promising to build proper houses."

I look at him in astonishment: does he think the functionaries of the old regime would do a better job than the ANC? He just shrugs, "We need proper houses, not toilets. We expected housing after the elections . . . More important," he adds, "we need jobs. Because it will be difficult to pay rent and buy a house. So I think people must have work first, then a house."

Ndobongwana's blunt rebuke of his government's efforts is a warning: political parties, even much-mythologized former liberation movements, cannot assume allegiance from their followers. They must earn it. The view from the bottom of the socioeconomic pyramid is particularly harsh in this way. Governments are measured by what they deliver. To the poor, even former rogues can seem like liberators if the would-be savior falls off his horse.

A verdant U-shaped valley engulfs me as I drive slowly over the deeply rutted sand roads. Round huts, or rondavels, dot the gently rolling hillside. The valley is bathed in the gold light of evening, accentuating the warm earth tones of the fields and thatched roofs.

This is Hebron, the small village where Adelaide Buso was born. I have traveled for several days with my wife and daughter through the former black homeland of Transkei to get here. The Transkei is literally another world within South Africa: it is "le vrai Afrique" as Francophone Africans say—the true Africa. It is a place of mud huts, primitive roads, lazy rivers, kids running and playing, and a slower pace. The hard edge of cities such as Johannesburg and Cape Town seems like a distant universe here. The beauty around us is tempered by the endemic poverty.

We pull up alongside a hut and village kids crowd around us. A young woman offers to show us to Adelaide's place and jumps in the car. She stares quizzically at this carload containing me, my wife, Sue, and our four-year-old daughter, Ariel; she has never met whites who wanted to stay in her village before. We bounce through the grass and arrive at a pretty green rondavel. Sue and Ariel bound out and find Adelaide on all fours on the floor of the hut, her hands covered in a thick mud paste.

"I can't *be-leeeve* it!" she squeals. "You have come so *far* to see me!"

The sight of a grown woman playing in mud captivates Ariel. She instinctively yanks off her clothes and plunges her hands into the moist ooze, and commences mudding the floor alongside Adelaide. Adelaide can't stop giggling at this sight as the two of them spread the mud around in wide circular motions.

"We are working so hard when we come back here," she says, as she waits for the floor to dry before moving her furniture back. The strong smell of earth lingers inside. Adelaide rinses her hands and takes us on a tour of her property. Adjacent to her rondavel is a rectangular home where she keeps her best plates, a used dining room set (it was being discarded by one of her employers in Cape Town so she transported it back to Hebron atop a bus), a pair of footlockers for storing her possessions, and two beds. She insists that we take over this house during our stay.

As we walk around under the hot sun, she points to the chores that she and her eldest son, Douglas, who has accompanied her here, are attending to. She is rethatching her roof, mending a barbed wire fence to keep livestock out, painting both houses, replacing a wooden door, and fastening "burglar bars" on the windows, among other projects.

Adelaide, like many villagers, is perpetually busy. This is her only trip back home this year, and she may not return for another year. This routine is a vestige of South Africa's migrant labor system, in which workers only returned to their villages at Christmastime. Indeed, South African industry shuts down from mid-December to early January as much of the black workforce piles into frighteningly overloaded buses and heads for greener hills. Adelaide's village life is condensed into less than three weeks—hence the frantic pace of her work.

No matter where else she lives for the other fifty weeks of the year, Adelaide calls Hebron home. "The village is very important in my life because it's where we used to do our own traditional things," she says as a soft breeze dries the sweat on her brow. The afternoon sun makes her dark skin glisten. "In Cape Town, there's no background of the traditionals or the cultural things."

Adelaide's houses were her mother's before her. Even in death, her mother figures prominently in her world. "Next to the mountain is my mother's grave," she says, pointing to a spot about a half-mile away across the green veld. She visits the grave daily to clean around it, a customary show of respect for her ancestors.

The village is like a mother. No matter how far people wander from her, there is only one mother, and she always awaits the return of her children. She exerts an inexplicable, inevitable pull on her family to return.

Village life revolves around elemental things. Douglas and I take two wheelbarrows loaded with large plastic drums to fetch water in the morning. We walk to a large pump in the center of the village. It is a social place, where people hang out, catch up with one another, and young people pump water for older folks. Just as workmates gather around the watercooler in high-rise offices, so too does thirst unite the residents of Hebron. Old women carry off one bucket of water at a time, while we heft a full day's supply in our wheelbarrow.

The water pump is one of the tangible benefits of the new government. In the past, residents had to walk a kilometer uphill to reach a spring that trickled with suspect water. "The water was unhealthy," insists Douglas, who frequently made the arduous trip. This hand pump, which serves Hebron's two thousand people, is part of a national rural water supply scheme. Water is one of the success stories of the new government's Reconstruction and Development Program. The government is on track to provide taps to 90 percent of those without water by 2004. Hebron received several water taps, but the windmill that powers the other taps doesn't work. The lone new hand pump has nevertheless significantly improved the quality of life for these villagers.

Other changes are in store for Hebron. The village is due to get electricity within the month—another RDP program. Adelaide is already making plans to buy electric appliances for her house. In fact, she claims she will build a major addition. "I'm planning to save money so I can buy the bricks to extend the house because I really need to make a four room, because we are a big family," she says excitedly. She also plans to buy an electric refrigerator. I am astonished by her grand plans. She has often bemoaned her impoverishment to me, and I point out that fridges and the electricity to run them are expensive. "Is it?" she replies with surprise. The world of utility payments is alien to her. But she is undeterred by such minutia. She aspires to middle-class comfort just like everyone else. Practical details will not obscure her dreams.

I ask whether she has similar plans for her house in Cape Town, the home she occupies most of the year. She dismisses the notion. "In Cape Town I can have just a rental house or whatever . . . Cape Town is not my homeland. It's where I work."

Douglas effuses about how he would like to see "many many [electricity] poles here." "Our life will be *better* then," he insists. Again I question this: won't the electricity be unaffordable for most villagers, burdening them with debt?

Douglas has a pained smile on his face and an unmistakable "you just don't get it" look. "The students cannot do their studies at night," he tutors me patiently. "We must read by the light of a candle or a paraffin lamp. So the students perform poorly in school, they fail their matric [high school final exam], and they are stuck being poor." It is a simple, stark synopsis of the cycle of poverty and the way it perpetuates itself in each generation. To those who take such comforts for granted, the connections are invisible.

The village is a place of both solace and hardship. The simple beauty of life here is a blessing and a curse. "They are really suffering here," says Adelaide one night as we sit around her kitchen table. The yellow light of a kerosene lantern casts large shadows on the earthen walls of the hut. "The unemployment is very high here in the villages. They haven't got anything and there's no factories here where they can go and look for the jobs or stand by the road and wash the cars."

Rural areas, which are home to 45 percent of South Africa's population, are indeed the most economically disadvantaged parts of the country. The countryside suffered from neglect and overcrowding during the apartheid years, and rural residents continue to struggle with the absence of any job opportunities. A recent government report states that "over 70 percent of rural African households live in conditions which are inadequate or intolerable in terms of their access to shelter, energy, water and sanitation. Rural women are a particularly vulnerable group."[5]

And so the children drift away from the maternal nest out of sheer necessity. About half the population of the Hebron valley—including nearly all the able-bodied men—leave to work in the cities for most of the year. Those who remain are women, children, and the elderly, all of whom subsist on small farming and on the money remitted from their faraway relatives. Such is the symbiosis between urban and rural Africa: the city provides the economic lifeline, the village provides the spiritual sustenance.

The distant jobs that villagers go in search of, such as work in the gold mines around Johannesburg, are often hard and dangerous. But there are few alternatives. The roots of poverty are many: "Bantu education" starved most blacks of employable skills and still casts a long shadow. One of the most difficult obstacles to breaking out of poverty is simply that "you need money to make money." As Rev. Frank Chikane points out, cash and credit are the lifeblood of the small businessman. The people of Hebron have neither.

Yet Adelaide longs to return permanently to her "homeland." "As soon as I've got enough money and as soon as I uplift my skills, I'd prefer to come and work here, at home. Then I can afford to start any business or any community project." She hopes she can utilize her skills as a political activist to help her rural community. She thinks that after the 1999 election, she can return. "I'm preparing to get ready to come back home and stay at home and working very close to my house. I also prefer to make the community project, such as the crèche and the old age home and the play park for the children . . ." Adelaide hopes to market the "cultural skills" of her people, finding them jobs making traditional clothing and crafts. She also dreams of an adult education project for the elderly villagers.

I take in the pastoral landscape. A small rocky hilltop cradles Hebron in a womb-like embrace. Off in the distance the jagged peaks of the Drakensberg Mountains—the "dragon mountains"—rise up to ten thousand feet. Beyond them lies the mountain kingdom of Lesotho, a curious colonial anomaly: a landlocked nation surrounded by South Africa. The presence of a foreign border nearby adds to the "end of the earth" feel about this place. Hebron is a paradisiacal spread of greens, golds, blues, and browns. Life seems in balance here, a stunning contrast to the harsh realities of urban squatter life that await Adelaide and Douglas on their return to Cape Town. And yet the picture is bittersweet: Hebron is a mother so loved by her children that they have to leave, in order that someday they might return.

It is New Year's Day in Hebron. Adelaide informs Sue, Ariel, and me that we have been invited to lunch at the home of the village chief. Adelaide looks radiant in an orange skirt and jacket that she made out of ornate African fabric. Douglas is wearing a shirt and tie, freshly pressed with an iron that he heated over the fire.

We arrive at the chief's kraal, which sits atop a small rocky knoll overlooking the valley. The kraal consists of a large, old stone rondavel, and several large stone houses. We find the women—the chief's daughter, sister, and wife—decked out in their finest clothes. The daughter is sporting conventional city wear, pants and a sleeveless shirt. The chief's wife displays a traditional loose-fitting African dress with an embroidered collar. They usher us into the dining room where we find a long table with a huge multicourse meal laid on. We have arrived three hours late (Adelaide was busy with chores), but no one seems to mind. We are on "Africa time" here.

Our arrival is the cue for some two dozen relatives to file into the room. The chief's wife takes a seat next to us. Her face is smeared in white mud, a Xhosa beauty treatment. Everyone quiets down and she gives thanks for us coming to be with them. She then lets out a loud high-pitched ululation, which the other women join, much to Ariel's delight. Sue and I also offer our sincere thanks to them for having us. Then the feasting begins: carrot salads, beets, green salads, freshly killed mutton, sweet squash, then four desserts, soda, just-baked cookies, and beer and hard cider to wash it all down.

Just as we are finishing our last leisurely course, we hear a loud clap of thunder outside. The heavens suddenly open up with a fury unlike anything I have seen. Rain comes down as if shot out of a fire hose. Dousing, pounding sheets of water. Sue and I exchange concerned glances: we are supposed to leave the next day, and the torrent can easily wipe out the rutted village roads and render them impassable.

As the crescendo of noise on the metal roof increases, the chief's daughter goes over to a stereo in the corner. Like all appliances in the village, it runs off car batteries. She turns up some African music, and starts to dance. The hypnotic *mbaqanga* sound—a unique South African blend of African and western dance rhythms and melodies—pulls all of us up onto our feet. Moments after we start dancing, tables are pushed aside, the volume is turned up, and everyone joins in. A group of small girls gravitates to Ariel and they form a small circle around her, linking hands. Ariel whirls around, and the girls nod and ululate their approval. One by one, each of them takes her hand and dances with her, then blends back into the circle.

As the roar of the rain continues outside, the pulse of the music carries on inside. Adelaide dances to and fro, and several teenage boys mime a spontaneous choreography of cops and robbers. Portraits on the wall bearing the stern visages of five generations of chiefs stare down upon this gathering.

This is one of Africa's great gifts: despite the hardships, despite the fact that Hebron's roads are getting washed toward the sea at that moment, despite the poverty, Africans have the ability to cast aside their troubles and celebrate. A joyous, transcendent, existential dance of life.

"HAPPYYYY!" is the periodic shout from the dance floor, in recognition of the new year.

About an hour into our dancefest, one of the chief's sons comes up to me. "The chief would like to talk to you," he says earnestly. I follow him into the next house, where I find the elderly grandmother, and Chief Sibi. Contrary to my image of an all-powerful leader, Chief Sibi appears frail. The fortyish man is hunched over in a chair, one side of him paralyzed by a recent stroke. He speaks softly, and I sit next to him and listen intently to make out his words.

"Your coming here is something very special for us," he says in a voice barely louder than a whisper. "It means this will be a good year in Hebron."

I arrived in Hebron as the bearer of good news, carrying a copy of the local newspaper, the *Daily Dispatch*. Inside was page after page of names of students who had just passed their matric, the final high school exam. This is the highest academic accomplishment that most villagers ever attain. Adelaide had worried for weeks about how her boys, Eric and Moses, had fared. I handed the newspaper to Douglas, who promptly laid it out flat on the dirt floor and pored through it looking for his brothers' names. After fifteen minutes he and a neighbor let out a yelp.

"Here they are!" he said, beaming proudly and pointing to the newspaper. And there, in tiny type, were the names of Eric Buso and Moses Buso among the thousands who successfully completed this rite of passage.

It has been a long road for the Buso boys. That road began when their mother left home in 1977. Suddenly, the three boys were left in the care of their elderly grandmother. Adelaide had decided that the only way she could save and support her family was to nearly abandon them. She hoped that her earnings would enable her children back in Hebron to have a better life than her.

I ask Douglas how it felt to lose his mother. "It made us sad. But then we just surrendered," he says with a shrug.

For Adelaide, the decision to leave was all the more painful because her job as a domestic included raising children—someone else's. The love that she showered on her charges was a daily reminder of her own loss. "The employers want us to love their children but at the same time they don't love our children. They don't care about our children. Because they don't want our children to come and be part of their families."

"My children were growing up without my love for nineteen years," she says as we sit in her rondavel late one night. The night air is punctuated by the ubiquitous village sound of children playing. "I always come once a year to give my children love, you know. But the rest of my life I spend it into the employer's house because I want money to feed my children, to educate my children. But it's not easy to be away from your family . . . The children that are growing up without you, they think that you don't love them."

Douglas, twenty-seven, is the oldest son. He is a slim, quiet young man with close-cropped hair and a spray of facial hair. At first meeting, he seems obsequious. He jumps up deferentially as I enter, nods and smiles reflexively as we talk, and stands with hands clasped prayerfully in front of him. But as I spend more time with him, he starts to relax. He is completely unaccustomed to chatting casually with an *umlungu,* a white man; I am the first. He warms quickly to the new role, and I discover that behind the courteous facade is an intensely thoughtful young man with a wry sense of humor.

He recalls how he and his two brothers managed in their mother's absence. "Our mother was working in Cape Town for R 25 ($12) per day. We had no money. Our grandmother took care of us, but she was too old." Douglas was eighteen when she died in 1988. After that, "We did everything ourselves."

In 1991, Douglas passed his matric exam. But he didn't stop there. He was determined to pursue a trade so that he could get a decent job and help lift his mother and family out of poverty. He left Hebron and joined his mother in Cape Town, where he enrolled at a technical college to get trained as an electrician. But the family was desperate for money and couldn't spare Douglas. In 1993 he was forced to take a job as a driller at Western Deep Levels near Johannesburg, reputedly the deepest gold mine in the world. "It was hard work," he says of the notoriously dangerous job. Nights blended into days underground in the mines. When not working, he lived in the violent, overcrowded miners' hostels, rounding out a hellish existence.

Despite the arduousness of the job, Douglas was ambitious. He was earning R 700 to R 1,000 ($315) each month and was eager to rise up through the ranks. But his application to become a skilled apprentice was denied. "They wanted to just keep me as a laborer," he asserts indignantly. "I thought I could make more as a garden boy."

With no prospect of advancement, Douglas quit mining in 1995 and returned to Cape Town to live with his mother. He took a job as a laborer at the golf course opposite the Westlake squatter camp. When he was laid off after eleven months, he began working as a "garden boy" at the home of some white people.

"The life for me in Cape Town is very hard," Douglas says. "I am living in a shack and have little income to give my family—I make R 50 ($11) per day as a garden boy two days per week." He and his mother work "hand in glove: when I get money, we put it in an account together. Then we bought clothes and building supplies together."

Life on the mines took a toll on Douglas, and he began to drink heavily. But then he discovered God. He was "born again" into the Zion Christian Church, an evangelical, charismatic church with a following of some five million Africans, most of them poor. He was recently ordained as a pastor, and he has a small congregation that meets in a shack in KTC, the large Cape Town squatter camp.

When I see Douglas again in Cape Town after returning from Hebron, he has enrolled in a three-month bricklaying course. He has invested a precious R 1,200 ($260) in the training, and he is hopeful that he will be rewarded with new job opportunities. But for a poor person, finding a job leads to a series of catch-22s. He must call prospective employers from a pay phone, so there is no place where they can return his call. He is then reduced to walking around the city inquiring at construction sites whether they need help. It is an expensive, time consuming, and usually fruitless process. When I last saw him, he was poorer for his course, newly certified as a bricklayer, and still unemployed.

"The white government is like a glass of milk," he muses to me. "The whites took all the cream and left 2 percent with us. And now that there is the ANC government, they don't want to eat that 2 percent with us. We've still got that hope that the new government will bring us things," he concludes. "But the basic facilities are still not delivered. Without money we may commit crime."

I follow Adelaide into the conference room in the Alphen Centre, a freshly whitewashed Cape Dutch building which houses the offices of the South Peninsula Municipality. Seven men sit around, two coloreds and the rest white. Adelaide has called this meeting with council bureaucrats in order to initiate a cleanup of Westlake Informal Settlement, something she is eminently qualified to speak to. "I am really going to tell those people what I think because I live there and I know they doing *nothing*," she forewarns me en route to the meeting. Her biggest grievance is that the municipality provides inadequate sanitation and trash removal.

But once inside, she barely speaks.

The meeting is delayed by the absence of Neville Riley, a National Party councilor who, together with Adelaide, represents the area that includes Westlake. He is forty-five minutes late. The municipal officials are understandably impatient. They repeatedly ask "Councilor Buso" if she wouldn't mind starting without Riley. But she declines, even at the risk of scuttling the meeting. I am puzzled by her insistence, but she whispers to me that if the white councilor from her district isn't there, they will run circles around her. She points to one official and whispers conspiratorially, "He's with CROW [a competing political faction in the squatter camp], so he will just try to stop me no matter what I do." Indeed, Adelaide's internecine squabbles with CROW have lately consumed much of her political energy and left her feeling somewhat paranoid.

Finally Riley shows up. He is a caricature of a country club pol. He sports a blue and white safari shirt, crisp white pants, and a yellow ascot that bulges from his neck. His large belly hangs over his belt. He tells me he was the city planner for Cape Town for seven years, and before that he was the deputy surveyor general "in Northern Rhodesia, later Zambia."

One of the officials asks him on his arrival, "Isn't today your sailing day, Neville?"

"No," he replies jovially, "that's Friday."

Riley then launches right in, demanding to know why Westlake hasn't been cleaned, what the scope of the problem is, what it will take to fix it. "Who's the moneybags?" he barks repeatedly. The officials have a ready list of excuses for why they can't clean the squatter camp. The big problem seems to be that Westlake is not on any of the all-important "lists" for cleanup. Once again, it appears that Adelaide, despite being a councilor, is last in line for services.

At one point, Adelaide expresses fervently and in her characteristic slow drawl her concern that children are getting sick from the filth that permeates the squatter camp. But her plea falls on deaf ears. The officials make it appear dizzyingly complex just to get an extra "skip" (dumpster) to the site. The municipal functionaries are adept at throwing up a seemingly impenetrable array of bureaucratic chaff. There's the question of which one of four funding sources this should come from. Then, under the guise of having the cleanup be "sustainable," one fellow proposes that they postpone the cleanup until a committee can be established to draw up detailed plans. It is a disheartening display of the tyranny of bureaucracy.

In striking contrast to Adelaide's impotence, Riley works the officials masterfully. A veteran bureaucrat himself, he deftly disarms the obstructionists by agreeing with them. He then sets about laying down deadlines for how the cleanup will happen. "Jack, you'll report to me on how many rubbish lorries we'll need. Bill, you hire the temporary workers for this. John, you organize the money. And everyone reports back on what they've done by Monday. I want Westlake cleaned within ten days." The officials wag their heads obediently, and leave with nary a whimper of protest.

Adelaide understands this dynamic perfectly. She refuses to talk on her own, knowing she would get steamrolled. So she makes the system work in the best way she knows how: by allying with an old apartheid bureaucrat to get the job done.

It is a brilliant summer afternoon in February when I find Adelaide in her shack at Westlake. My daughter is with me, and we are reduced to constant blinking as sand whirls around us and into our eyes. These are the infamous "snowstorms" of the barren Cape Flats.

Adelaide is happy to see us, but her round face is long. "David, I must leave here. I can't take it anymore," she sighs. A well-thumbed copy of the classified ads from the *Cape Times* lies folded on her table. As I step into the room my foot lands in a divot beneath the linoleum floor covering. The sand pours through the hole, a reminder of the thin veneer that lies between the shack dwellers and the elements around them.

"It is not safe here. The *shebeens* play loud music all night, and I can't even sleep. People are drunk, and they can just kill you.

"At the council meetings this week, they said that nothing will happen here until next year. They are going to upgrade Vrygrond first." I suggest that it is only fair: Vrygrond is the largest squatter community in the area. "Yes, I know," she says with resignation. "It will take all year for them to upgrade there. They won't even start in Westlake until next year sometime." She grows quiet, and a bit morose. Her large eyes droop downward. She fiddles with the newspaper, and says quietly, "I can't wait anymore.

"I am looking for a flat somewhere for me and the boys. I have inquired in Fish Hoek [a predominantly white suburb popular with retirees]. Maybe we can get a two-bedroom flat." I ask her what she could afford. "If Douglas can get a job, we can pay R 600 ($130) per month. But I haven't found anything yet."

I listen sympathetically, but I know the odds are against her. Even the simplest version of the life that Adelaide longs for—a basic home, television, phone, stove—is staggeringly expensive for her. Fees for rent, electricity, and water—none of which she presently pays for—would quickly overwhelm her. Even Douglas concedes, "A phone would be out of the question." Douglas also notes that despite holding various jobs since 1991, he and his mother "haven't been able to save R 5." They can barely afford being squatters; how could they possibly manage as tenants?

Adelaide gets an allowance of R 2,000 ($400) per month as a councilor, a dramatic improvement over the R 600 ($175 in 1995) monthly salary she earned as a domestic. But her earnings haven't been sufficient to support her three sons, all of whom have now moved in with her in Westlake. She is trying to send her two youngest sons, Moses and Eric, to technical college so they will have a trade; she hopes ultimately to get them into university. So Adelaide has picked up a couple of days' work as a domestic to supplement her council income. Douglas hopes to make R 80 ($16) per day as a bricklayer—if he can find work. Eric got a job selling life insurance door-to-door in Newlands, a wealthy white neighborhood. He claims he already has four clients, but I doubt it. He probably never got past the rottweilers and razor wire in those moneyed suburbs.

Adelaide's return to domestic work confirmed to her that nothing has changed in the relations between the social classes in the new South Africa. She recently began working in the home of a judge in Cape Town. When she arrived, the judge's wife put out three thick pieces of bread. "These are for your breakfast and lunch," declared the matron of the house. Adelaide then watched in astonishment as the woman took half of her bread and fed it to her pet cat. Adelaide seethed with anger and humiliation. She politely but firmly informed the woman that the new Labor Relations Act required her to provide breakfast and lunch, and to pay a minimum of R 6 ($1.30) per hour.

"He is a judge, and he is actually undermining the constitution!" she says with obvious outrage. "They fed my food to their cat right in front of me!" Her new employers responded to her pique in predictable fashion: Adelaide was fired within a month.

Adelaide recalls her puzzlement when she heard F. W. de Klerk declare in 1990, "It's a new South Africa now. The book of apartheid is closed."

"Where is this book closed? Because there's still thousands like me," she says. "The workers are not satisfied. They've got very low wages, and they living in bad conditions although they working for the rich people. They haven't got subsidies for the houses. The employer doesn't care where she lives, they just want to see you in the morning, smiling by the front door . . . You must smile on the outside when you are crying inside. The book of apartheid is still open," she reflects in frustration.

Adelaide is stuck in poverty with no obvious way out. Perhaps if one family member lands a job with a steady income they can pull their standard of living a half-step up. But their new wages will quickly get siphoned off into paying for middle-class amenities, basic as they may be. This is the dilemma of the poor: you must earn enough to pick up everyone around you, not just yourself. It is clearly an unfair burden for someone struggling to break free. But family and community jealousies are an unavoidable reality that often threaten to drag down those who are determined to make good.

Adelaide is losing hope that her savior will appear anytime soon. Her disillusionment is poignant: even as a politician she is unable to deliver "the new dispensation." She has little political clout, and her old nemeses—National Party politicians and bureaucrats—still thwart her. Though long anticipated in Westlake, even the ballyhooed Reconstruction and Development Program, she realizes, is just a leaky lifeboat: the RDP offers only the basics of water, electricity, and a well-nailed roof. The new government doesn't offer a way out of poverty, just a more comfortable version of it.

The new South Africa has succeeded in one respect: Adelaide has higher expectations now, and as a result she can no longer tolerate her life in a crime-ridden shantytown. A slum with electricity and running water is still a slum: there will still be the *shebeens,* the drunks, and the crime. She has seen through the false promise of redemption. Apartheid may be over, but it still permeates everything that replaces it.

On the last night that I see the Busos, I drop Adelaide and her sons back at Westlake. It is about 10 P.M., and the squatter camp is uncharacteristically quiet. Adelaide says the *shebeens* don't really get going until about 11 P.M., and then they continue all night. The night is a deep inky black, and there are no lights to illuminate it here. Adelaide, Moses, Eric, and Douglas bid me a heartfelt farewell, and vanish into their dark world.

# APARTHEID JUJITSU ARTIST

TUMI MODISE: PRESIDENT AND OWNER,
AVANT-GARDE CLEANING SERVICES

Tumi Modise in her
office at Avant-Garde
Cleaning Services,
Johannesburg, 1997.

Tumi Modise giving
her cleaning women
instructions before
sending them off to
a client, 1997.

> Jujitsu: A method . . . of defending oneself without the use
> of weapons by using the strength and weight of an adversary
> to disable him.
>
> *Random House Dictionary of the English Language*

**TUMI MODISE WHEELS HER ROYAL BLUE** Mercedes-Benz 230E hard around the turn and eases into a parking bay. She hefts her large frame out of the car and bounds across the neatly kept lawn. "I gotta go fight about toilet paper," she announces.

We are at Megawatt Park, Johannesburg headquarters of the national electric utility Eskom, a sprawling hive of four thousand workers. A chorus of "Hi Tumi" follows her as she charges down the seemingly endless corridor. She is a sight to behold: parting the ocean of cell phone–toting yuppies is a squat woman wearing pumps, loud baggy shorts, and a shimmering lime green blouse. Gaudy gold horn-rimmed glasses accent her round face; her long fingernails are painted pink. She seems oblivious to the power ties flashing around her, instead honing in on the ubiquitous, nameless workers clad in gray smocks that say "Avant-Garde Cleaning" on the back. Even the workers who don't see her seem to know she's here; they turn at the last minute to nod their acknowledgment.

Tumi Modise is the founder, owner, and president of Avant-Garde Cleaning Services. The business began in 1991 with Tumi on her hands and knees cleaning toilets in small businesses. Today, Avant-Garde employs over three hundred full-time workers and more than one thousand part-time people to clean office buildings. Modise is part of the small but growing clique of "buppies"—black yuppies—clamoring for a piece of the capitalist dream that was denied them for so long. In Tumi's case, success comes with a distinctive township flavor.

"Hi cooks!" she croons to a white lady with big hair. "Do you have a cigarette for me?" she asks, barely stopping long enough to light up and take a long drag before resuming her charge. I ask who the woman was. "She manages my contract for Eskom," she chirps. "I employ her sister." I look at Tumi with a surprised half-smile. Isn't that sort of a conflict of interest?

"Hallelujah—that's right," she shoots back as she blows through a set of tinted glass doors.

Tumi Modise is big, brazen, outrageous, and lately, rich. She is a Soweto street fighter–cum-businesswoman who has applied the tactics of township survival to the business world to great effect. Where others see insurmountable obstacles—such as the notion of a black woman succeeding in a white man's business world—she sees opportunities. She has learned quickly how to play the game. Pity those who get in her way. Like the Afrikaner man she's about to meet to resolve the toilet paper squabble.

"This company thinks I should pay R 7,000 ($1,520) a week for their toilet rolls. That is *not* part of the contract," she declares with a rising tone of indignation.

And if they don't agree with you? Tumi looks askance at me, as if I don't get it. "I'm not here to *ask* 'em what I want. I'm here to *tell* 'em."

Tumi strides into the steel and glass office flushed and sweaty from the long walk over here. She yanks off her blazer to reveal a blouse and thick lumberjack-style red suspenders, which keep popping off. "They keep m'pants up!" she declares to the flummoxed executives. She sits down at a large, round, wood table with Bart Viljoen, a silver-haired contracts manager with Eskom, and a thirtyish, honey-tongued black man named Themba, who is a "facilitator." Themba is there to help emerging—read "black"—firms work more effectively with Eskom. It is all part of the affirmative action efforts that are the rage now in South Africa. Viljoen looks nervously over at photographer Paul Weinberg and me. Before he can finish asking who we are, Tumi announces emphatically, "They work for me. They're preparing my annual report."

Viljoen does the talking, but Tumi is in charge. "We don't have R 7,000 for toilet rolls in our budget to just add on," Viljoen bleats with a weak smile.

To everything Viljoen says, Tumi replies, "I agree with you completely Mista Bart." Viljoen looks perplexed; he's the boss, but he senses he is losing. Viljoen looks plaintively to Themba for help, but none is forthcoming. It is obvious that the tables have deftly but decisively been turned. The Bart Viljoens of South Africa are being swept aside. It is Tumi Modise's turn now. She walks out of the meeting with the deal she wanted: Eskom pays for the toilet paper.

At age thirty-seven, Tumi Modise is a poster child for the new South

Africa. She is a true-believing free marketeer with her sights on greater glory. She exploits white guilt to her advantage, fires black workers who she thinks are lazy, and slaps down the unions when they get in her way. She came from poverty and can speak the lingo of the oppressed, but doesn't flinch at blaming blacks for not striving hard enough. "Stop whining—just do it" sums up her philosophy. Her in-your-face political incorrectness makes me squirm, and I frequently challenge her. But she counters every objection with a blunt reminder that she has fought her way out of the trenches and doesn't need my advice, thank you. She replies to charges that she uses racist stereotypes to get ahead—a broadside that freezes white liberals in their tracks—with a dismissive laugh or a steely glare.

"Now you listen to me honey," she comes back. "Apartheid is a reality. And I'm *not* gonna let it hold me back."

Funny how things turn out: South Africa's post-apartheid icon of success is not a grizzled guerrilla carrying the torch of the liberation struggle. She's a Republican-sounding capitalist behind the wheel of a Mercedes.

"Black economic empowerment" is the new mantra of South Africa's aspiring elite. In simple terms, it means that getting rich is patriotic. Black millionaires—so recently branded "bloodsuckers" and "apartheid profiteers"—are the new revolutionary vanguard.

Black South Africans are now taking a page from the Boers' book. Large black economic empowerment deals have been making daily headlines in South Africa. A small number of black investors have been aggressively acquiring stakes in the South African economy. In the four years following Nelson Mandela's election, blacks gained control of twenty-eight companies worth a total of more than $13 billion.[1] The charge is being led by former liberation leaders and trade unionists, who have moved from the shop floor to the trading floor of the Johannesburg Stock Exchange. Notable among these is ex-ANC boss Cyril Ramaphosa, who lost a fight to become Mandela's heir apparent (the crown went to Thabo Mbeki, although Ramaphosa remains on the ANC National Executive Committee) and was reincarnated as the millionaire head of New Africa Investments Limited (NAIL).

Seemingly overnight, a black aristocracy has ascended to power in South Africa. They are hailed in new glossy magazines that celebrate the lifestyle and material aspirations of "buppies." Critics charge that a black elite is rushing in to replace a white elite with little concern for redistributing the wealth. The poor, as they always are, are left begging at the gates.

Tumi Modise and I are sitting on her patio on a sultry summer night. She lives in a comfortable rambling home in Randburg, a formerly all-white upper-middle-class Johannesburg suburb. When I arrive, Tumi is deep in conversation with a white investor and his wife who are enticing her to go in with them on an investment venture. Her eight-year-old daughter is watching a large-screen TV in the living room. The decor drips with nouveau riche accents: a stuffed white leather couch, a glass dining room table, and faux marble floors speak of her success. The white investor leaves with an "I look forward to hearing from you, Tumi" and I take his place on the stuffed patio chairs.

After some chitchat, I get to what's on my mind: is "black empowerment" merely black enrichment for the few? Tumi's eyes narrow as she rivets her gaze on me. She drills back a quick response. "Black people also wanna be rich. That's normal. They're not allergic to money," she asserts. She is holding a Coke in one hand and a cigarette in the other. She sits cross-legged and confident and speaks in a rapid-fire cadence. "I think it's about time that people who work hard actually make real money. If you a black person and you make money, you are automatically expected to be Mother Teresa and carrying the world on your shoulders," she complains. "I think that's too much. I've found you can't please everybody. And it's about time black people learn it is not criminal to make money." She adds acerbically, "I think it's part of black culture to feel for people who are losers, rather than winners."

For Tumi Modise these are observations born of experience. Growing up poor in Soweto, she knows the wrath of those she has left behind. She is matter-of-fact in her descriptions of it all; little bitterness or anger creeps into her voice. That is her secret: she refuses to be bitter—doesn't have time for it. Tumi Modise is focused on the future, not the past. She's impatient: "Let's get on with it," she says frequently. These days, she cares less about what apartheid did to her people and more about how she can use apartheid to her advantage. "You have to," she says. "Otherwise just go and die, or emigrate."

I ask Tumi how a township girl like her has managed to succeed in the rough-and-tumble world of big business. A broad smile spreads across her face, and she leans back and hooks her thumbs behind her suspenders.

"Growing up in Soweto, you learn to do two things," she says. "You learn to sing, and you learn to *donder* [fight]. And I do both very well."

Tumi Modise grew up during the worst years of apartheid repression. But she somehow managed to stay a few steps back from the front lines, where the bullets were flying. She was born in Soweto in 1959 in Orlando West, not far from Nelson and Winnie Mandela's house. Her parents were divorced when she was eight years old, and her mother moved her and her three brothers to a township near Kimberley, the diamond boomtown on the edge of the arid Karoo Desert. She enrolled in an Anglican mission school, one of the few places a black child could get a decent education. Numerous black leaders trace their roots to South African mission schools, among them ANC leaders Mandela and Oliver Tambo, and Zimbabwean president Robert Mugabe.

Good education was one key to Tumi's success. The other was having experienced a bit of life beyond apartheid. Tumi's mother, Rose, was a claims adjuster for a South African insurance company. From a family of fourteen children, Rose Modise nevertheless was well educated, and managed to land a good job.

At South African Claims, Rose Modise did what the white adjusters would not do: investigate claims in black areas. So Rose traveled around southern Africa in her car for months at a time with her children in tow. She spent stints of up to six months in the neighboring nations of Lesotho and Mozambique, during which time Tumi was enrolled in local mission schools. In the Mozambican capital of Laurenco Marques (now Maputo), she was one of four blacks in a predominantly white school. These were crucial formative experiences: unlike other South African blacks, she grew up thinking that whites were just regular people like her. Apartheid was not a central part of her worldview.

Young Tumi admired her mother's strength raising her children as a single working woman. "I think my mum is the brightest woman on Earth," she would boast to her friends. She was proud that her mother had a good job and her own car—a black woman driver was a rarity. Tumi was also aware that her family was more fortunate than many others in Soweto. The Modises lived in Meadowlands, a middle-class Soweto neighborhood. Just before moving there, Tumi pleaded with her mother for a house with a bathroom. Her mother obliged, and the Modises had the only bathroom in the area.

Tumi received most of her schooling around Kimberley in the English-speaking mission school. When she turned sixteen in 1976, her mother thought it was important for her to learn Afrikaans, the language of commerce in many parts of South Africa. She sent Tumi to attend school in Soweto in January 1976 to learn the language of the Boers. In hindsight, the move was comically mistimed. Tumi came to settle down just as Soweto students were on the verge of revolt.

Sixteen-year-old Tumi Modise woke up on June 16, 1976, to the sound of children chanting and singing outside her family's modest Soweto home. She dressed quickly in the standard uniform of black dress and white shirt and ran outside to join the other schoolchildren. She saw several of her friends, and they motioned giddily to her to join in.

"No school today?" she asked her girlfriend.

"No, today is for protesting!" she replied excitedly. A young man standing nearby explained that they were protesting against having to learn "the language of the oppressor."

"You mean Afrikaans?" replied a mystified Tumi, recalling the reason for her move to Soweto.

"Ja! The Boers want us to learn it so we can be their slaves. We say no!" Tumi shrugged. She was happy to join in the action, and especially glad to have the day off from school. Before long, she was dancing the *toyi-toyi* and chanting, "Down with Afrikaans! No more Bantu education!"

The noise of the protest hid the low rumbling sound in the distance. The sound grew progressively louder, like an avalanche picking up speed. All of a sudden, a giant Casspir thundered around a bend and came charging toward the children. The students started screaming. The Casspir stopped, idling and belching menacingly in front of them. A boy in the front picked up a stone and heaved it at the vehicle. It hit the side of the troop carrier with a tinny metallic clank. Soon Tumi was searching the dirt for a weapon, finding it in a jagged rock. She picked it up and, flush with the excitement of battle, launched it toward the Casspir.

Suddenly the back doors flew open and camouflage-clad policemen poured out. They crouched and brought their rifles to their shoulders. "Oooooooohhh," came the shocked response from the schoolkids. They didn't believe the police would do anything, but they couldn't be sure. Tumi's eyes were wide. Tumi and her classmates soon broke into a sprint to get away. A loud "pop pop pop" cut the air, and clouds of tear gas enveloped the group of kids. Tumi gasped and coughed, tears streaming down her face. "Get down! Cover your mouth!" yelled one of the leaders. She did as she was told, but still gagged. She saw through her tears that the police were running toward her and whipping her classmates with *sjamboks*. The crowd splintered. Tumi and a group of children ran down a long alley and finally reached the house of a neighbor. They ducked inside, panting hard and hacking from the suffocating gas. The students laughed nervously at their narrow escape.

That night Tumi went with her friends to an emergency meeting called by Soweto's student leaders. Tumi still wasn't really sure what they were fighting about. She was caught up in the excitement of the chase, and filled with the sense of power that she and her classmates seemed to wield. A young man stood up at the meeting. He was a tall thin boy; Tumi had seen him around school and knew him as a popular athlete, but she had never seem him speak as passionately as he was doing now.

"If you don't do anything about this system—your education, the way our parents are being treated—you will live your whole life as a slave to the white man!" he declared, his high-pitched voice ringing through the community hall. Tumi was awestruck: "This boy is clever," she thought to herself. Much cleverer than she was.

"How much do you pay in rent?" he demanded, stabbing the air with his finger. "How much are you paying for bread? In ten years, the cost of bread will double, but we black people will be making the same money as now. So we will just get poorer and poorer. We must put an end to apartheid and Bantu education and throw out the Boo-ahs! *Amaaand-laaa* [power]!" he shouted.

"*Ngweee-thuu* [to the people]!" came the thunderous reply. Tumi added her voice to the chorus. She was amazed by the fervor of the crowd, and ready to take her place in the struggle.

The next morning the protest resumed. A crowd of students formed once again, with Tumi milling in the middle. Like the day before, police Casspirs soon thundered down the township roads trailing a wake of dust. This time, the cops dropped their restraint. Loud cracks and pops cut the morning air. Tumi heard simultaneous "thuds" as metal hit flesh.

A friend standing next to her abruptly fell to the ground writhing. Tumi looked at him in horror as he clutched his stomach. Blood soaked through his shredded white school shirt. She blinked back tears, unsure if she was crying or reacting to the tear gas.

"You're okay—it's only birdshot," yelled one of the older students. "Get up! Run!" The students ran willy-nilly. Tumi rounded corners and sprinted for her life. Finally, she and some friends reached safety. They spat the acrid tasting tear gas from their mouths and wiped their watery eyes. Their lungs burned from the irritating gas.

The game was over. Tumi was deeply shaken by the blood, by the brief thought that her friend might die. "This is too serious," she told her girl-friend through her sobs. "I don't wanna die from suffocation. I don't wanna get shot. I don't like all this politics," she wailed.

Tumi's stint as a soldier in the revolution was short-lived. "I couldn't cope with the responsibility that came with the passion that the people were feeling at that time," she confesses now. "I felt exactly the way they did. But where they were so taken up with this thing and so angry about it, it sort of exceeded the way that I could get angry."

The Soweto uprising changed Tumi, as it changed everyone who experienced it. It introduced her, at age sixteen, to the harsh realities of apartheid. "I wasn't even aware that there was apartheid," she says, her voice rising in amazement at her own naiveté. The riots "opened my eyes that as a black person you will never become anything . . . You will struggle."

But Rose Modise was not going to let her daughter be consumed by the angry fires of the anti-apartheid struggle. In the wake of the June 1976 riots, many black schools in the country closed for the remainder of the year. Rose searched and found a secretarial school that was still operating, and promptly enrolled Tumi. She graduated a year later and went on to get her bachelor of commerce degree at a local university.

Tumi was now ready to enter the work world. But she had yet to lose her innocence about apartheid. She applied for a secretarial job that advertised a salary of R 900 ($1,035) per month. She was interviewed by a white woman and asked what she would like to earn.

"R 900," said Tumi, thinking nothing of it.

The woman scowled at her. "Have you ever seen R 900 in one place? Don't come in here with your jokes." Tumi felt utterly humiliated. In truth she never had seen that kind of money, but she assumed that's what she would be earning. Hell, she was probably better educated than the woman who interviewed her—why *shouldn't* she get paid well?

Tumi began asking black people what they earned. She was amazed by what she learned. Other black professionals revealed to her that they were earning R 250 to R 300 per month. "Nooooooo, but I don't want *that* kind of money," she declared proudly. Nevertheless, she decided reluctantly to lower her asking price to R 500.

Her next interview was for a job as an invoice clerk with Alfa Romeo. From the moment she walked in, Tumi was awed by the sparkling glass facade, the shiny silver, the plush carpets, and the mahogany tables. She felt as if she were in a fantasy world. "I've never *seen* such a beautiful place," she thought to herself.

As she sat in the interviewer's office, Tumi spotted another black secretary working at lightning speed. She was so intimidated by this secretary that when it came time for the standard typing test, she flubbed it. She was just about to head out in defeat when the interviewer came back and said, "We'll make you an offer."

Tumi was ecstatic—until she heard the details. "We're willing to pay you R 287 ($330) per month," said the lady, "plus some lovely benefits."

Tumi's jaw dropped. "Excuse me?" she stuttered. The white lady repeated herself. Tumi just stared at her, dumbfounded. Finally, she spoke up.

"Please, I don't want to look ungrateful," she began, "but you look so nice, you look so clean. If I'm here with R 287, I mean, I can't even talk about transport to work. And there is no way I can wash, let alone smell better." She smiled weakly, trying to be sweet and pushy at once.

"Listen, that's it. That's all we can pay you," snapped the lady.

"Okay, I'm sorry, I can't take the job," said Tumi, and promptly excused herself.

Tumi was proud of holding her ground. She came home and informed her mother what happened. "Are they *mad*?" she asked her mother.

Her mother scowled from across the room. "You think R 287 is not nice? Who gives you R 287 for sitting at home?" Tumi couldn't believe her ears—even her mother was deserting her. She protested, but couldn't help concluding that she had made an irreparable mistake.

Three days later Alfa Romeo called back. They would raise their offer to R 300. "I'll take it," blurted Tumi. Her career had begun.

Tumi Modise was a woman possessed. Never before had the other secretaries at Alfa Romeo seen someone take to the job with such zeal. Tumi identified the other black secretary—"Speedy Gonzales," she dubbed her—as the standard to beat. She promptly vanquished her. Within two months, she was typing more invoices per hour than any secretary in the office. Her appetite for work seemed insatiable, and her bosses took note. One day, Mr. Feldman, the head of the department, called her into his office.

"You have potential, Tumi," he informed her succinctly. She understood this corporate code. They would never tell her she was good, just that she had the chance to do even better. He asked if she would like to move into credit control.

"Yessssss!" blurted the excited new hire. "Say when." Tumi was soon preparing accounting reports and even visiting clients. When the opportunity arose to learn how to use new technologies such as a computer, telex, and fax, she was first to get trained. Her competence and productiveness earned her a promotion to be the most senior black secretary at Alfa Romeo. Along with the promotion came raises: she was now earning R 500 per month.

"Five hundred bucks!" she shouted exuberantly to her mother when she received the news. A year earlier it seemed paltry; now it was exalted.

"I've always had an enthusiasm for anything that I do," she explained to anyone who queried her success. "If I like something, I *like* it."

Apartheid always shadowed the fringes of her success. Once, in the mid-eighties, a television crew wanted to come and film her on the job after her selection as secretary of the year. Her boss agreed, but two days before the film shoot the top brass vetoed it. "It's company policy: no cameras on the premises," she was informed without further discussion. The TV crew never came.

Tumi had a bad habit of beating whites at their own games. There was, for example, her fiercely competitive table tennis talent. One colleague, an Italian man, frequently challenged her to play Ping-Pong on her lunch break. She delighted in trouncing him, much to his annoyance. Soon she had the whole department coming to view the spectacle of an African woman beating a white man at the Ping-Pong table. He would become furious, stomping about the office in a rage, and occasionally trying to humiliate her.

"You went to college?" he asked repeatedly, ignoring her previous responses.

"Ja, I got my B.Comm. through UNISA [the University of South Africa offered correspondence courses to blacks]," Tumi replied proudly.

"And you were registered? You completed the degree?" he would ask patronizingly.

"They cannot believe I took it upon myself to get educated," she complained to her friends. "I don't know what they think I sprang from."

Tumi's black friends and colleagues were also critical of her, for different reasons. They resented her meteoric rise through the ranks. "What is wrong with you?" asked another black secretary at lunch one day. "You are letting everybody send you all over the place—why? You're doing everybody's job, and you have become everybody's fool."

Despite her success—she was earning R 800 per month after three years—the memory of growing up perpetually broke was always fresh in her mind. Tumi could never earn quite enough to feel secure. So she would wake up at 4 A.M. and make two large cooler bags full of "professional sandwiches," which she would sell at the entrance to Alfa Romeo before heading into her office. She used the money she was accumulating to treat herself to a flashy Nissan sports car.

"That was like—it!" she bubbles. "I had the best car, I had the best things."

Tumi loved her job at Alfa Romeo, but she wasn't advancing fast enough. After three years, the company gave her a R 130 raise—and then insisted they made a mistake. When her boss told her they only meant to give her half that amount, Tumi flew into a rage. "Oh no. You didn't make a mistake. And if you did, I quit," she told him. Then she did just that.

Modise's next move was over to South African Breweries (SAB), the largest producer of beer in the country. She bowled them over in her job interview, then lied when they asked what her salary at Alfa Romeo had been. Tumi got the job at SAB and doubled her old salary overnight.

The pleasant clink of glasses signaled it was teatime. This is a peculiarly British colonial ritual: no matter how fast-paced or modern the business, "tea at three" is sacred in South Africa.

Tumi Modise looked up from her new desk at South African Breweries to see one of the other secretaries coming over with a tray of teacups and biscuits.

"This is your cup," the woman said pointedly, a fake smile spread tautly across her jaw.

"That's fine—you can put it right there," said Tumi, motioning non-chalantly to a spot on her desk.

"No, *this* is your cup," she repeated more emphatically, still with a smile. She was trying to make a point: we white secretaries use these cups, but this one is just for you. Tumi continued to ignore the slight, until she couldn't any longer.

An hour later, the same secretary came over to explain the rules to Tumi. "This is your chair. Don't move it here, don't sit over there. And this is my desk—don't touch my pens." She waved her finger at Tumi as she spoke, like a schoolmarm wagging her finger at an unruly pupil.

Tumi was bristling. She finally stared her new colleague in the eye and shot back, "I don't have a problem with your chair or your desk or your pencils. Just make sure your finger doesn't touch my eye, that's all. And make sure that you don't use my things either." The white lady recoiled in shock. She had never had a black person talk back to her.

A few weeks later, Tumi returned to her desk after lunch to find another one of the white secretaries sitting in her chair talking with the lady who had lectured her.

"Move your arse. NOW!" snapped Tumi, pulling her occupied chair back from the desk.

The two women looked at Tumi in horror, one of them sputtering, "We don't speak that way around here." But Tumi wasn't concerned with what they thought of her behavior. She was making a statement: push me, and I'll push back. It was the beginning of Tumi's education in the finer points of dealing with South Africa's racial caste system.

SAB had a reputation as a modern and reasonably progressive company. The salaries were good, even for black employees. SAB executives considered themselves among the trendsetting business elite, and SAB jobs were prestigious. When Tumi first walked through the automatic doors into the sleek offices, she thought to herself, "This is too cool for words—like NASA!" But no matter how modern the corporate trappings, the mentality was rooted in old-fashioned racism.

Tumi took stock of what she saw around her at SAB. She was a bursary administrator for SAB's scholarship program for gifted students. But she quickly assessed that "all black people never became anything. They all had 'potential.' They all got training—of the seven-year type. On a junior job, you go for seven years with the same qualification as anybody else.

This was downright unbelievable. People pretended that they want the best for you. But you had to know who you are: You're a black person, finished and *klaar* (complete), so don't get ambitious now, hey! It was as if we were all queuing up to be whites. In the meantime you just wanna earn a living, like everybody else."

Fighting the system was not easy, even for a "cheeky black" like Tumi Modise. "If you're on the wrong side of a white person who happens to be South African, you in deep shit," she says, peering at me over the top of her designer glasses. "A white person, [even] one that's below you, with less qualification or even less in class, can make or break you . . . If one of them says you're not good, you never get a job. You're dead meat. So you had to watch your words, you had to control yourself, you had to behave like they do.

"Me, if I'm upset, I speak loud, I throw my hands all over the place," she declares in her typically animated style. Lowering her voice to a passive-aggressive monotone, she continues, "I had to start learning to say, 'You know, I'm very upset,' instead of showing that I'm upset." Tumi breaks into a giggle at the absurdity of it. SAB "was like university. I learnt [the realities of racism] full-time. I learnt it from people who can push you off, physically. People who can put you down completely in front of others. People who will take a side, even though they are wrong."

There were countless incidents intended to put Tumi in her place. There was the secretary who took food out of her hands and threw it in the trash without a word. Then there was an office in which Tumi got the silent treatment, despite the fact that she was supposed to get trained by her stony colleagues. In another case, a temp who replaced her during maternity leave burst into tears for no reason when Tumi returned. It was a setup, says Tumi, which allowed her boss to reprimand her. "Who the hell do you think you are coming in here and bulldozing people like that?" he bellowed.

"Those were the things that were humiliating to me," she recounts.

No shrinking violet, Tumi did her share of fighting back. When the boss took the rest of her department to lunch without her, Tumi confronted him. "Excuse me, I'm sure you work here like I do," she said, standing directly in front of him as he and the other secretaries returned from their meal. "I also want to eat."

Then there was the time that Tumi was sent to a satellite office on the

West Rand outside Johannesburg to help out for a few months. It was a community where "people openly called blacks 'kaffirs,'" she recalls. She began getting into fights with colleagues her first week there. Finally, she declared she'd had enough, abruptly packed her bag, and returned to her office in Johannesburg. Her old colleagues were waiting to confront her.

She was hauled into a meeting of managers, where she was told that she had been "bossy and difficult." After she patiently presented her side of what happened, her boss cut her off and asserted, "Do you realize that whatever you say doesn't matter, because you have ruined your reputation?"

This was too much, and Tumi exploded. "In all my life, I've never experienced apartheid like I have here. And guess what? I promise you now in front of all these people," she said pointing right at him, her voice rising, "I will not tolerate it." The group of managers tried to silence her, but she wasn't finished with them. She was tired of politely responding to abuse.

"Don't tell me about *kak* reputation, that you people decide whether it's good or bad. I don't care what reputation you think I've got. As soon as somebody applies their behavior that they've learnt from their great-great-grandfather on me, I will fight it head on." She didn't wait to hear their response. She charged out of the meeting and went back to her desk. And then she waited for them to fire her.

But they didn't. She was frequently told "you're different," a backhanded compliment that implied that other blacks didn't have the courage or the intelligence to speak out. In fact, for most of her white colleagues, Tumi Modise was the first black person whom they ambivalently considered their equal. Much as Tumi credits SAB with educating her about apartheid, she also changed the attitudes of many of her colleagues about the capabilities of a black woman. The bottom line was that Tumi was too good to fire: both Tumi and her bosses knew that she couldn't be easily replaced.

This did not mean that Tumi would be promoted. After five years of working first as a bursary administrator and then in the personnel department, Tumi was passed over for a promotion to personnel manager in 1990. Instead, the job went to a newly hired young white woman from Zimbabwe. Rather than get mad, Tumi decided to get even.

One morning she phoned a senior personnel official with a seemingly innocent question about an SAB policy. "Listen, tell me, if somebody wants to resign, what happens, how does a retrenchment package work?" She suggested that he use her as an example and fax the details. Her boss duly filled out a sample form with her name, salary, and seniority on it, then faxed her the sample letter. The next day, Tumi marched up to his office with the same letter and announced, "I'm leaving, I want my retrenchment package—*this* package," she said, pointing to the letter. He protested and said she couldn't go. "Tumi, you have set an example," he said, trying to flatter her.

"Oh well," she replied, "This is an example too: I won."

Tumi left SAB and landed on her feet. She had an unusual relationship with two other women at SAB: a white woman named Janine, and Joan, a Chinese woman. The unlikely threesome—such casual interracial friendships were an anomaly under apartheid—had become fast friends, taking vacations together, sharing the ups and downs of their love lives with each other, and ultimately all leaving SAB around 1990. In fact, Janine helped lure Tumi away. She was working as a human resources consultant—better known as a headhunter—and boasted to her old friend that she was making R 20,000 per month. That sounded good to Tumi, especially since she hadn't banked much money and had nothing to cushion her while she was unemployed.

Tumi plunged into the new job with characteristic zeal. It was a good time to be a black woman in the headhunting business: Nelson Mandela had just been released from prison, and many large companies were eager to employ blacks in preparation for the political changes that they anticipated. Tumi was having little problem in finding work for her clients. The problem was getting paid: the high-flying consulting firm was months behind on what it owed her. The last straw came when the owner of the company insulted an elderly friend of Tumi's mother who had stopped by the office. After upbraiding the owner, Tumi announced that she was quitting.

After five years at SAB and eight months as a consultant, Tumi Modise was on her own. But this time was more complicated. She had signed a restraint of trade agreement with the consultancy owner that prohibited her from working in the same field for several years after leaving the firm. When Tumi tried to take her clients with her, the owner's lawyer came knocking. Tumi was beside herself. Even worse, she was broke.

Tumi had by now fashioned a comfortable middle-class life for herself. She had a nice car, a townhouse in a safe Johannesburg suburb, and was sending her daughter to a respected private Jewish school. But it was a hand-to-mouth existence, and the well had just run dry. Within a month of leaving her job, she was kicked out of her house and landed on her mother's living room floor. She was so destitute that she couldn't even afford to pay a moving company to move her possessions. She ended up hiring her daughter's father, from whom she was estranged, and compensated him by simply giving him all her furniture. All she saved was clothing for her and her daughter.

Tumi's abrupt fall from grace shocked her. "When you used to earning big money, it's amazing what you take for granted," she mused. "You earn R 15,000 to R 20,000 a month on commissions. On a good day you make R 7,000. You don't save, you spend and spend. So I didn't count on being this broke."

Rose Modise was shocked to have her daughter arrive back on her doorstep in such dire straits. "Why don't you wanna work?" asked the bewildered matriarch.

"Don't worry ma, I'll sort it out," Tumi replied. Firms called to offer Tumi a job, but she didn't want to work for someone else again. She was through with being patronized and exploited by white bosses. She had tasted real money and knew she had the moxie to succeed in business. What she didn't have was the seed money to go out on her own. She approached a bank to ask for a R 700 loan. The bank manager turned her down, but not before giving her a condescending lecture. Though she might have been broke, Tumi did not lack for self-respect.

"I'm gonna be a millionaire one day," the down-and-out businesswoman warned the bank manager. "And ya know what I'm gonna do? I'm gonna come in here at 9 A.M. and put in the money, and at 10 A.M. I'll come and take it out." The Afrikaner manager just snickered. He had seen dreamers come and go, but a black woman millionaire? It was preposterous.

The idea of an office-cleaning business began as a lark. A friend said she didn't think Tumi could make it as a cleaner, to which Tumi replied that she could get the business by making five phone calls. Tumi made the calls, and landed cleaning jobs at three different offices. There was just one problem: she had neither the equipment nor the expertise to follow through. Then a friend mentioned that her son cleaned carpets. So Tumi called him, and offered to give him the jobs and 50 percent of the job fee. Not knowing what to charge, she set rates that were about five times too high. But the clients agreed, and this business "joke" suddenly blossomed. Friends heard Tumi was in the cleaning business, and soon began passing her the phone numbers of potential clients.

Tumi was soon cleaning toilets on her own in small offices. Word spread, and she hired four domestic workers to help her after they finished their jobs cleaning suburban homes. Her big break came when a friend recommended her to a company that managed a large office building. When she called, she was informed that the job involved 894 toilets. Had she cleaned on such a large scale before?

"Of course. And I have references," she replied without hesitation.

How long would the job take her? "Five days," she shot back.

Tumi got off the phone and called three friends, all of whom worked in offices with one toilet. "Listen," she told them, "I gave your name as a reference on a big cleaning job. You must tell these people that you have twenty-four toilets and that I do an excellent job cleaning them each week." Tumi landed the R 15,000 cleaning contract within the week. "I've never seen that much money in my life!" she giddily told her mother.

Tumi rounded up eight domestic workers and promised them R 60 ($21) per day for five days—double what most of them earned as chars. "They all got sick where they worked [as domestics]," she recounted with a mischievous grin. "I had no uniforms, so I got T-shirts, and they were at my house at 6 A.M. ready to go. I was *organized,* my brutha!

"The building was bloody intimidating: it was 175,000 square meters. We were on the move, nine of us. By 11 A.M., everybody knew there was a black-owned company cleaning the toilets, and they were saying, 'The toilets smell very nice! They're clean!' I can't tell you how I felt. We *hammered* the toilets!" She is beaming as she tells the tale. She roars as she describes how she "looked like a criminal—my hair stood on end for days!"

Her hard efforts paid off. The owners of the large office building awarded her a contract to clean their toilets every three months. By 1994, she had 157 full-time employees working for her. Her mother, who spoke some French, said the name for the new business should sound "sophisticated." Avant-Garde Cleaning was born.

The office is ugly, but functional. Avant-Garde Cleaning Services is shoehorned into an office complex that houses a variety of small businesses.

The Avant-Garde storefront, such as it is, faces out onto an indoor parking garage devoid of natural light. The small office building is located in an industrial section of downtown Johannesburg. Since 1994, this whole area has been hastily vacated by white businesses out of fear of skyrocketing crime. As I walk the streets I find myself doing the "Jo'burg Shuffle": looking with paranoia over both shoulders, walking briskly, avoiding eye contact, and trying to shut out thoughts of impending doom.

It is 8 A.M., and inside the glass doors of Avant-Garde sits a small quiet group of women. The waiting room is spare: the cream-colored walls are graced only by a clock, a map of South Africa, and a faded flower painting. Dog-eared magazines lie helter-skelter on the tables. Even the bathrooms are just for business: the urinal is packed tight with bottles of extra cleaning supplies.

The one concession to vanity is the glass display case filled with awards that Tumi has received; her mother has carefully organized it and placed it behind the front desk. There is a plaque she won from the Afrikaner insurance company SANLAM for 1996 Entrepreneur of the Year, the cover story on her that appeared in the black business magazine *Enterprise,* the 1996 Woman in Business Award, and several Entrepreneur of the Month awards from the *Sowetan* newspaper. A framed letter from an official at the Johannesburg Stock Exchange reads, "Keep it up! I hope black young women are going to look up to you as their role model."

I sit next to Magdalene Martins and ask what brought her here. She is a shy, forty-four-year-old colored woman neatly dressed in a plain summer frock. "There is no work," she says softly. "If you are a mother of kids, you must lift yourself. You must do it for food." She cleans offices for Tumi now. "I think I will be doing this the rest of my life. I'm old now."

Martins and four other women are ushered into Tumi's office. Her desk is a cluttered mess, plaques adorn her walls, and her phone never stops ringing. Yet through the chaos and distractions, Tumi somehow conveys a bit of compassion for these ladies. She holds no air of being above them; she is one of them. With the four women standing quietly around her desk, Tumi proceeds to give them a talk that is part instructional, part inspirational, and laced with straight-shooting advice.

"This contract is with a company called CCMA. The people are the problem. Don't drink their tea. They complained the [previous] people are not clean, so I suggest your hair is neat. They are not your friends, but you treat them friendly. Do not get into long conversations with them. They are secretaries, you are cleaners, and they think you are nothing. *You* know you are not nothing, you are important people. But they want to see that you know your place."

With that, the women don their gray smocks and head out the door to begin their cleaning day.

"I don't get caught up with how white people treat me," asserts Tumi as we hustle to her next appointment. She is usually on the road all day, cruising from one job site to the next. "If they push me in the toilet, I push them back, or go to another toilet."

Tumi then launches into a story about how an Afrikaner boss wanted her to fire a Chinese employee because the man's English was so bad. Tumi gleefully recounts her chat with the Boer. "I said to him, 'I speak seven languages. And my English is better than yours. How many do you speak?'" She pointed to the Chinese man before the Afrikaner could answer. "He stays," she snapped.

We are on our way to a weekly meeting at Eskom between union shop stewards and Avant-Garde supervisors. As Tumi breezes past the company executive offices, a white woman who manages one of Avant-Garde's contracts asks to keep a particularly good temporary worker. "She's so good, if I sat still in my office she'd give *me* a bath," the manager declares.

Tumi keeps stride as she fires back, "If she's so good, how come you turned down my tender?"

"Oh, that was a joke," says the sheepish contracts manager, who suddenly looks crestfallen.

Tumi smiles. She enjoys this game, and plays it well. "You'll get your lady back," she assures her.

Tumi barges into the meeting and parks herself at the head of the room. She opens by explaining to the eight supervisors present that she is starting a training school to upgrade her employees' skills and self-esteem. "People say if you a char, you nothing. That's *not* true. You are a qualified person. You have training and you have a certificate . . . It's not an easy job." In the ensuing discussion, she switches between speaking in Afrikaans to a colored woman, in Xhosa and Zulu to two African men, and in English for the others.

As we leave the meeting, I ask Samuel, one of the supervisors, how he finds working for Tumi. "Well, it can be hard," he says, lowering his voice. "She doesn't let you get away with anything. If you like the job, and you proud of it, it goes fine."

As we reach the parking lot, one of the supervisors asks, "Tumi aren't you gonna buy us lunch? We're hungry!"

Tumi yanks open the door of her Mercedes and calls back, "Noooo, I'm just a small business. I can't afford it." As she locks her door, she turns to me and says, "They'll take you for a ride every chance they get. You can *never* give in."

Tumi Modise is like a jujitsu master. Rather than complain about apartheid attitudes, she uses them to get ahead. She coldly assesses the current geography of apartheid, from white guilt to black defeatism, and converts liabilities to assets. In the spirit of the ancient martial art, she has used the energy of the enemy to defeat it.

"The English [-speaking South Africans] are the worst racists in the world," asserts Tumi as we wheel around Johannesburg. "But that's where I make money." There is not a trace of resentment in her voice, because she doesn't feel any. The best revenge is simply to take their money. "English people in this country are the most patronizing people. They are not very supportive. They would say [to me] as a black person that you are not good for anything else. So I say if I'm good for cleaning toilets, pay me for it. I'll do it . . . You've got a job, I've got a service, you will pay for it. That's all, hallelujah, everybody's happy."

Tumi then tosses off nonchalantly, "I would like to get the cleaning contract for Heathrow Airport. I understand it's huge."

Tumi continues spinning her hardheaded business strategy. "The Afrikaner feels *guilty* about racism and what they did to us," she continues. "So I take advantage of their guilt, without making them feel guilty. They say, 'Ja, I think we should give you a chance.' Then they give you a chance."

It is a sentiment that I hear repeated often: how blacks and Boers have a great deal in common, and are often able to bridge the apartheid divide more easily than English-speaking South Africans. After all, it wasn't that long ago that blacks and Afrikaners worked the land together and occupied the same social class—the bottom. With the National Party victory in 1948, the Afrikaners set about changing their socioeconomic status from lower class to ruling class. Apartheid was first and foremost an economic strategy. Afrikaner self-advancement was the primary motive behind apartheid; notions of racial purity came second.

Now it is the blacks' turn to reverse their fortunes. And Tumi has found that many Boers are aware of their debt and willing to give her a chance. "They implemented the same systems themselves—they empowered one another. So they are experienced in this."

Some of Tumi's harshest criticism is reserved for her black brothers and sisters. "A black person thinks you have been given a job, so they can just not show up tomorrow, like they're my sis-ta." She adds acidly, "I'm an only daughter—I don't know how I got so many sis-tas."

Tumi insists that many blacks are lazy, and she won't tolerate it. "The culture of work has to be put in our brains . . . I'm not saying everybody is like this, but the black woman works like a dog. The black man—maybe he was oppressed more than we were oppressed as black women. I dunno. But there isn't any ethic to work! Our old great-grandparents, *they* knew what work was all about." Tumi even fired her own brother for not working up to her standards. She still employs her mom, two other brothers, and her ex-husband. "They're good workers," she states. The brother whom she fired now "parks cars in the street," she says flatly.

As we walk around the sprawling Eskom grounds, Tumi brings me into a drab, smoke-filled office to meet one of the supervisors who works for her. Julie Potgeiter is an older Afrikaner woman. I am surprised: I would have thought Tumi would put blacks in positions of authority. After all, isn't that what black empowerment is all about?

Black workers will take orders better from a white manager, she tells me. I look at her in disbelief—that's apartheid! "But it's the truth!" she fires back. "That's why I've got all white managers." She corrects herself—she's got a few black managers.

Is it fair to promote a white manager when you have a black worker who has been there longer? "It's not fair, but it's practical," says Tumi. She is not the least bit ruffled by the grilling. To her, these truths are self-evident.

"A white person doesn't give me grief, he gets on with the job, and if he doesn't do that I rap 'em on the knuckles. Then he changes and things work nicely." She pauses and turns to Julie. "Can I have a light sweets?" she coos, leaning over to fire up another cigarette.

"And another thing," she continues, "whites also put emphasis on work. They understand that when you get into an environment that requires you to work, you work. You don't care what car your boss drives. You *work!*"

When Tumi leaves the room, I ask Julie Potgeiter how the workers view their boss. The Afrikaner woman is dressed plainly in slacks and a faded sweater; an ashtray full of cigarette butts is the lone adornment on her steel desk. She recounts the workers' comments: "They say, 'What is Tumi? She's nothing. She's just got a black skin like we've got . . . ' They say 'We not scared of Tumi.' So they must be scared of her."

One drawback of having white managers, says Tumi, is that they are easily guilt-tripped. "When my white manager meets with the union, he gets pushed around because he's afraid he'll get accused of racism," she says. She calls the union stewards "shit stirrers," and recalls an incident where a steward reduced Julie Potgeiter to tears in front of the staff.

Tumi declares, "Picture this: there's a white lady working for a black woman, and Mandela is president and you a black union president. You feel powerful, so you take it out on this lady, because you know she's not used to being treated like that. So I told them off." She wrote an angry letter to the union, demanding, "You will not make my supervisor cry or humiliate her."

Tumi then shifts gears and returns to one of her themes: how blacks have undermined each other in the business world. "Blacks don't like seeing another black person succeed. Every time a person gains prominence, he gets cut short. His skeletons from the closet get out, and [other blacks] break him down business-wise. With us blacks, it's 'How come my boss is doing this? He's wearing an Armani or Calvin Klein.' . . . When you put black people in a job, you get blocked by the same black people."

Tumi is kicking back and holding forth in her dingy corner office. She props her large frame in the small chair, and fiddles with her red suspenders. As we are talking, workers in gray Avant-Garde smocks wander in and out. They all know her. "Hi Tooo-meee!" they say. She greets them all, hands out the odd cigarette, and switches effortlessly between Afrikaans, Xhosa, Zulu, and English, depending on whom she is addressing.

Tumi insists that the black unions have fanned the jealousies. "The union told my workers: 'Do you know what car she drives? Where she stays? Where her kid goes to school? You making her rich. She lives a better life than you.' They don't see it as, 'She's creating jobs for us, she's paying school fees for our kids and putting food on our tables.' They see it in terms of what I have, and what they don't have."

And there's the rub. In the new South Africa, race is no longer the central organizing force of society. "If I stayed in Katlehong in a shack, I would be a star and a half," quips Tumi, breaking for a second to take another drag on her cigarette. "Race is not the issue anymore. It's class."

The union organizer from the National Union of Metalworkers of South Africa (NUMSA) was on a roll. He was at Eskom headquarters, and had a group of Avant-Garde workers as a captive audience. Moketsi was a wiry, excitable man whose voice rose to emphasize every insult and epithet.

"That bitch you work for thinks she's better than you. She is living high, while you struggle to feed your families. She is whitey's ass-licker!" he railed.

Tumi Modise is a hands-on boss. She treats the office buildings that she cleans as if they were her offices. She takes pride in the work she does, and frequently drops by to see how things are going. So her workers were not surprised to see her squat figure ambling up behind the NUMSA organizer. Their eyes grew wide as they shifted from her, then to the organizer, whose back was to Tumi.

"Maybe that black bitch thinks she's white, and she wants to return things to the way they were. When you join our union, you can tell her to fuck off!"

Tumi felt a knot tightening inside her stomach. She stood grimly for a moment; her workers were shrinking back from the impending conflict. Tumi decided to act coolly in front of them. She calmly tapped the organizer on the shoulder. He wheeled around and glared at her.

"What you want?" he snarled.

Tumi struggled to keep her cool. "Why don't we sort this out in your office," she said tersely. She turned around and began walking down the hall.

"You're nuthin' but an Uncle Tom!" he yelled after her. "Why don't you show these workers how you lick the *baas's* arse?" He followed her down the hall spraying obscenities in her wake, even after she'd turned a corner and he couldn't see her anymore. He pivoted around the corner to his office. That's where Tumi Modise was waiting for him.

Moketsi turned the blind corner right into Tumi's brawny fist. "You piece of *rrrrubbish!*" she yelled as she grabbed his tie and began battering his head like a floppy punching bag. "I'm gonna fuck you up!"

This was Township Tumi in her finest form, settling scores fast and definitively. Her feet were planted solidly on the ground as she waled on the startled man. She felt better with each blow. Moketsi yelped for help as she buried her knuckles in his jaw, on his nose, in his eye. Finally, he broke away and stumbled across to the office of several executive secretaries, screaming in fright. But Tumi was not finished with him.

"Don't you *ever* insult me in front of my employees!" she roared at him. Tumi picked up a trash bin and heaved it at the fleeing organizer. She grabbed his collar and yanked backwards, ripping the buttons right off his shirt. As he wheeled around to defend himself, she hit him again in the ribs. Finally, he lurched sideways and sprinted through the doors, past the stunned Avant-Garde workers who only moments before watched him abuse their boss. When it was all over, Tumi returned to her office and smoked a half-pack of cigarettes to calm down.

"Dammit!" she sputtered to one of her managers, who was soothing her like a boxing coach huddling over his prizefighter. "Now we gonna lose this contract."

Ten days later, Tumi was called into a meeting with Eskom managers and representatives from NUMSA. She knew what they would discuss. That morning she spent a little extra time putting on her makeup, donned pumps, and a tight skirt. She looked like she was about to go out on a date, not attend a business meeting. But she knew exactly what she was doing. She wanted to look as dainty as possible.

"Hello gentlemen," she cooed coyly as she entered the room. "How are you today?" The Eskom executives smiled their reply; the NUMSA reps scowled morosely.

The meeting began with some routine business. And then it was time for item number eight on the agenda: "Assault of NUMSA organizer."

Tumi was intrigued by how the union reps would handle this. She knew that there were few greater humiliations for an African man than being put in his place by a "sis-ta." Would they really admit that she had pummeled one of their boys?

The union rep stared down at his report and read in a monotone. "Ms. Tumi Modise assaulted a NUMSA organizer who was performing his regular duties on the job site." He then itemized the eight blows delivered: "one blow to the nose, a second blow to the head, a third to the ribs . . . "

Tumi listened with a look of shock on her face, as if this were the first time she'd heard about the incident. When the NUMSA rep was finished, a white-haired Eskom manager asked for her response. She paused for a moment, thinking to herself, "What would the union say if they were in my shoes?" Then she sat up in her chair and gave her reply.

"Sir," she said with a tone of deep concern, "I never laid a finger on him."

The union officials kept their eyes glued to the desk and their mouths shut. "Next item on the agenda please," said the Eskom executive.

Tumi Modise thinks overcoming apartheid was the easy part. Dealing with the unions is now her biggest problem.

"The funny thing is, I was doing well before we got independent [in South Africa] . . . Because then the union was focused. They knew who the enemy was. Now all of sudden I'm an employer, and you get hammered the same way. They've lost focus. Before they used to go sabotage a particular person's business because of problems. But they haven't grown out of it. They haven't changed with the times.

"I used to think unions were a white man's problem," bemoans Tumi. "That's why I did so well then. But as soon as South Africa got independent, I got the largest contract that a black person has ever had, and I had a strike. Now what was that all about? I was black and a sis-ta!"

She quickly provides the rejoinder to her own question. "It's all about the haves and the have-nots. If you don't have, you a good person. You deserve a chance, you deserve help, you deserve assistance, you deserve support. If you *have,* forget it. You're a bad one."

The upshot of this is that Tumi has become gun-shy about giving people entry-level jobs. "If someone comes in and they have a sorry story and I see they really need the job, I will do anything to give them a job," she asserts. She says that she pays all her workers "the legislated wage," which for full-time employees starts at around R 800 ($175) per month. But then she claims that the union convinces that person that they're being "exploited."

"I found when I was helping people in that way I was knocked from here to Israel. The union was on my back and fought everything I was doing.

"The union is black and I'm black. That doesn't give me the right to take advantage of black people because I'm black. But the union gives me grief. Our small business is struggling to make ends meet." Now, she says, her reputation with the union is that she's *hardegat* (hard-assed) and so must be dealt with roughly.

For the unions, dealing with Tumi Modise has also been an education.

Where playing on white guilt has won them points in other situations, it goes nowhere with Tumi. She is unrepentant about firing incompetent workers and putting organizers in their place. She has fought them—literally—to a draw. Just ask the NUMSA organizers who have tangled with her.

Moketsi, the organizer whom she pummeled, was promptly shipped off "to the bush," according to Tumi. He was replaced by another shop steward who was intent on teaching Tumi a lesson. A short time after he arrived at Eskom, the new guy went for Tumi.

"You think you're tough?" said the new steward. "I'll put you out of business!" With that, he lunged for her neck. Tumi stood her ground coldly, while other workers restrained the man. Then she stared back at him like an indignant mother and began to dress him down in Zulu while other workers looked on.

"What kind of zoo do you come from?" she taunted him "If you so strong, you should use your energies elsewhere, like in the farms or plowing the fields." Infuriated, the man lunged at her again, only to be restrained once more. Tumi knew that it was an unbearable insult to a Zulu man to be publicly insulted by a woman.

Later, Eskom executives informed Tumi that they would have the man fired; she need only lay charges against him. But the street fighter in her knew better. "They wanted to use me to get rid of him. Tough luck—I was *not* gonna be used in a plot like that. Because the poor white man has no clue that we are living in war. Black people go through the worst of things. I would get shot by unknown people in the streets and die. For nothing. People in South Africa kill for 2 cents. For R 1,700, they'd kill my whole family. I live in Beirut, so I know how to deal with these guys," she says. What she did was . . . nothing.

When the new shop steward learned that Tumi refused to bring charges against him, "he came to me and apologized profusely and even kissed me for saving his job. I said, 'You guys should know better. If I go out and create jobs for people, I don't really want 'em out of those jobs.'"

She and the unionist became fast allies. And her labor disputes, for a while at least, vanished.

Enoch Godongwana has been on the hot seat lately. As general secretary of NUMSA,[2] he has openly criticized the new ANC government for not doing enough for the poor and working class. Now he is getting slammed by businesspeople like Tumi Modise who say that unions are holding back aspiring black entrepreneurs.

To step into the NUMSA headquarters in Johannesburg is to suddenly return to South Africa's heady days of struggle. Posters adorn the walls. WE DEMAND: CLOSE THE APARTHEID WAGE GAP! THE STRUGGLE IS NOT OVER—*A LUTA CONTINUA!* VIVA NUMSA!

Somehow these slogans sound more like nervous pleas than potent threats these days. Trade unions, which so recently spearheaded the anti-apartheid struggle, now find themselves in the crosshairs of their former allies. When they are not being denounced by business, there is the problem of having Nelson Mandela, South Africa's patron saint, imploring workers to temper their wage demands for the sake of "nation-building." Labor is caught between defending the hard-won gains of their members and challenging a new government which appears less and less sympathetic to labor's priorities. The desertion of former allies, among them stalwart trade unionists, has left labor momentarily confused and aimless.

I ask Godongwana what is labor's biggest challenge in a democratic South Africa. The compact man dressed in a NUMSA T-shirt breaks into a wide grin. "It's a million-dollar question!" he replies. He notes that in the eighties, "our preoccupation was the destruction of apartheid and the creation of a democratic social order . . . Our support base was the working class and the poor." Under an ANC government, "how do you make sure the labor movement remains independent and vibrant and doesn't become a transmission belt of an ANC government? And that we continue to champion the poor and working class? It's a delicate balance."

Godongwana has been one of the more vocal critics of the ANC's post-apartheid economic policy. The Growth, Employment, and Redistribution (GEAR) strategy is "a nice document whose fundamental pillars reveal it to be a self-imposed structural adjustment program," he says, comparing it to the disruptive austerity programs prescribed by the World Bank and the International Monetary Fund (IMF). "In Africa, a number of countries followed these principles . . . and experienced nothing but poverty and destruction of jobs." The new ANC government, he complains, "wants to spend less on basic necessities and more to pay off apartheid bureaucrats," a reference to the generous retirement packages being given to thousands of white civil servants.

"If GEAR is adhered to rigidly we'll witness a decline in jobs in manufacturing. If that continues to happen, it will create problems with the balance of payments. I think we'll slide slowly into an economic crisis." He says the resulting social unrest would make current protest "look like a Sunday picnic."

Then there is black economic empowerment: should labor cut the emerging entrepreneurs some slack? I describe Tumi Modise to Godongwana, including the stories about how she has thrashed his organizers. Godongwana, who does not know her, guffaws at the tale. "I would like that lady to work for me!" he declares.

The unionist dismisses the kind of black "empowerment" under way in South Africa. "Black economic empowerment for her is empowering herself," he snips. "The way I understand black economic empowerment is that it is a process by which you transform ownership in the economy in such a way that income differentials are not as wide . . . You mustn't do it in a way that undermines the rights of people." But Godongwana concedes that new businesspeople "might need breathing space. The unions wouldn't oppose that."

Godongwana insists that unions have become the convenient whipping boys of struggling businesses. "Some companies produce shit, so they can't compete."

I take my questions across town to the brass and mahogany suite occupied by Tommy Oliphant. Oliphant was a trade unionist for some twenty-five years, serving as general secretary of the Metal and Electrical Workers Union of South Africa until 1995. Soon after the South African elections, Oliphant was invited to an annual conference in Spain sponsored by the World Bank and IMF. A South African stockbroker paid for his plane ticket, and while he was there he was invited to a bullfight with the chairman of Fedsure, a major Johannesburg-based insurance company.

"What are your plans, Tommy?" the insurance tycoon asked the trade unionist. Oliphant was just then seeing his former union colleagues snap up plum jobs in government and business. He decided that capitalism might not be so bad after all.

"I want to move," replied the labor activist.

Tommy Oliphant now manages about fifty union pension funds for Fedsure. He is also deputy chair of the National Empowerment Consortium (NEC), a coalition of thirty black business groups and four trade unions. In September 1996, NEC ponied up $52 million to become the biggest shareholder of Johnnic, a major industrial holding company that was owned by Anglo-American, South Africa's largest corporation.[3]

Oliphant is upbeat and unapologetic about the emergence of a new breed of black capitalists. The goal of black economic empowerment "is to ensure that blacks get into the mainstream of business. In the past, blacks only ran small township businesses like cafés or coal merchants. All big business was owned by white conglomerates." He says the black empowerment deals will "assist black people to gain experience and develop skill in how a business is run and create opportunities." He notes that unions have gained leverage by buying their way onto corporate boards.

Despite the frenzy of black empowerment deals, blacks controlled only 6 percent of the capitalization on the Johannesburg Stock Exchange as of mid-1998.[4] This toehold is nevertheless impressive: it took Afrikaners over three decades after coming to power to acquire the same stake in the corporate economy that blacks have claimed in less than five years.[5]

The transfer of large amounts of capital from white to black hands in recent years has yet to deliver a tangible payoff for the average township dweller. The large corporations continue to fight with their unions over wages and working conditions. And the highly leveraged black takeovers are heavily indebted to white capital. Complicating matters further, some of the new black-owned businesses have faltered badly, while others have been exposed as fronts for opportunistic white investors. Indeed, many of the high-stakes deals are characterized by what Jimmy Manye, head of the Black Management Forum, calls "'the Irish Coffee problem': blacks on the bottom, whites on top, with a sprinkling of black faces like cinnamon on the foam to lend respectability."[6] It will be a long time—Oliphant says five years, while Wendy Luhabe of Women's Investment Portfolio says it will be closer to a decade—before blacks actually own any of the businesses they are acquiring.

Oliphant is acutely conscious that black capitalists have a larger social mission. He says the black empowerers "should be able to assist common people in the communities in development projects and ensure that we add value to the man in the street, and in the townships, and schools."

And how does the rise of a new clique of black millionaires fit into this mission? Oliphant smiles wryly and quotes Dr. Nthato Motlana, formerly Mandela's physician and now a successful businessman. "If someone has worked hard and becomes successful and it yields profits and he benefits, I don't have a problem with that. I have a problem," says the born-again capitalist, "with some people who sit back and complain."

How do you break out of poverty?

For Tumi Modise, psychological freedom has translated into financial success. She is cheeky, combative, and tenacious in pursuit of her goals. Her confrontational attitude has its roots in her worldly education and in having glimpsed egalitarian race relations as a child. "What apartheid has done . . . " her voice trails off and she shakes her head in frustration. "The black man has such low self-esteem. They think white people shit diamonds in the toilet."

Tumi believes that poverty has become an accepted part of the African worldview. "People are actually used to poverty to such an extent that they don't even know the difference," she insists. "For me, I don't know whether it was because of my upbringing . . . but I knew I wanted the best things for myself." She saw the middle-class Soweto residents—the black doctors, nurses, and teachers—and aspired to what they had. And like many prosperous Sowetans, she has now abandoned the township for the wealthier suburbs. In the future, young Sowetans will have to look elsewhere for their role models.

"I was in Soweto like everybody else," asserts Tumi. "You start from where you are to do something about the situation. If you can't handle where you are, then make a change. Take the risk."

I ask Rose Modise, now sixty-seven, the secret of Tumi's success. Rose still occupies a central place in her daughter's life—I find the heavy-set woman staffing the cluttered front desk at Avant-Garde Cleaning. "Hard work," she replies succinctly. "And she is allergic to poverty."

I describe Adelaide Buso to Tumi: a hard-working woman determined to pull herself up, but seemingly caught in an unending cycle of poverty. How can she break out? "If she's in a shack, unless she can feel the hunger herself, she won't get out of it," says the typically unsentimental Tumi. "Me, I didn't get successful because I had such a great idea, a great mind, and some money. Uh uh. I wanted to achieve so *bad,* I wanted to get out of the situation. And if it took cleaning people's houses, I will do it. If it took cleaning the streets, I will do it."

Tumi's sights have always been focused ahead, not back. "I was given the situation as it revealed itself to me. It's an apartheid system. For you to get a better job you have to work harder. For you to achieve anything you have to push, you have to strive for it. It was not going to be easy . . . But I wasn't going to let that become a barrier.

"There's a saying in my language: 'If an animal is looking for help, you will help the cow that's trying to stand up.' Those who try from the shacks, help them up a little bit. Then they'll get out and get on with it. But the poor people in the shacks must want to get out of the shacks first. They must want better things. They must know they deserve better."

Tumi tries to offer a bit of what she's learned to the women who work for her. "I always preach to my workers. I say please make sure you educate your kids. Because your kids deserve to have it better than you, to be part of a new South Africa, to share the wealth. This time," she implores her workers about their problems, "we don't want to blame Mandela and say it's his fault."

Tumi preaches self-help because that is how she has succeeded: no one has given her handouts—not before Mandela, or since. In fact, she notes with dismay, "I don't have a single government contract. But how many statements have you read that we have black empowerment and want to promote black women, black this and black that?" She claims that nepotism and corruption are to blame for why her contract bids have been passed over by government agencies. She insists the fact that she's not "an arse licker" and that her family doesn't have political connections have also cost her government jobs.

She says "of course" she voted for the ANC in 1994 "because they were going to take out the whites. That's it. I just wanted change. And I think we deserved a chance." She concedes that the black government has helped improve her confidence and the self-image of other black people. But she's not sure if she will vote for the ANC again.

"I don't think they've done well so far. The ANC government hasn't done a thing for me. I haven't got any government jobs, people aren't getting the houses they were promised, and there isn't any employment available. Things are just the same, if not worse.

"I don't see anything different of significance," concludes Tumi. "That a few black people stay in the suburbs is not a reflection of what's going on around them. It shouldn't only be me that's successful."

It would be easy for me to dismiss Tumi Modise's prescriptions for breaking out of poverty. Her impatience with those who blame apartheid for all their problems is refreshing. But she can sound pat and smug. At times, she seems to blame the victims for their own poverty. Her rants against organized labor aren't particularly novel; she sounds like many bosses frustrated that they can't have their way with workers.

But I am given pause by a simple fact: Tumi Modise has beaten the odds. She has overcome a double hurdle in the South African business world—being black and being female. Of the few black women achievers in South African business, some have ridden to success on political connections and a few have had the benefit of a famous spouse. Tumi Modise has had neither. Her success can be chalked up to a good education and a street fighter's tenacity. She has literally brawled her way out of the ghetto into the middle class. If for no other reason, this extraordinary accomplishment makes Tumi Modise worth listening to.

Tumi Modise is no revolutionary. She pays only the minimum wage. She is less concerned with advancing black interests than in advancing her own. And she doesn't pretend that getting rich is part of some revolutionary movement by the underclass, as other black capitalists are in the habit of doing lately.

But Tumi Modise does dream of making a difference. She'll start, as she likes to say, where she is: among the domestic workers and maintenance men. "I want to be the largest employer of black people in this country in the next ten years," she tells me. "I want to employ thousands of people, and have good policies in place . . . I want to indoctrinate the culture of work."

Tumi has been preaching her gospel of hard work at a small school she has started for her domestic workers that mixes lessons on how to clean an office with Dale Carnegie–style motivational talks. "We help each other become a success," she declares. "Because when I become a success, many people benefit from it. That's why I have my school: because I want people to know that success is achievable. It's something you can actually do.

"Before I used to think I just wanna make money," she concedes. "But once you can get your basic things, you don't have worries of money. Then you have other targets—your goals change. But I know one thing: you can't do anything without money. That's for sure. *Puh-lease*—without money you can shut up and die and go away.

"I would like to have enough money to make changes, to be able to influence decisions. That will be the role of the money that I make in the future. But first, I would like to ensure that people do work. Because you can never negotiate with a very hungry man. He's listening to his stomach. He won't make sense. But if you give people the opportunity to utilize what they have, to better their lives, the better they become. They have time to listen.

"If I can play that part, affect ten thousand or twenty thousand people in the future, I will be able to make such a change for their kids. They will get educated, become better human beings in the future—that's what I would like to see."

Tumi Modise peers out through her gold-rimmed glasses and takes another drag on her cigarette. This is pie-in-the-sky talk for a small businesswoman from Soweto. It may simply be the guilty musings of the black nouveau riche. Tumi is no philanthropic saint, and she is far indeed from employing armies of workers or influencing social policy. I would be tempted to dismiss this as so much idle talk. But this jujitsu master has always aimed high. And then turned her dreams into reality.

PART FOUR | **ON THE LAND**

# TENSE PEACE IN THE *PLATTELAND*

## LIEB AND NANETTE NIEMAND: AFRIKANER FARMERS

Lieb Niemand
on his land, 1997.

Nanette Niemand on
her dairy farm, 1997.

Lieb Niemand's
farmworkers clearing
stones from a field,
1997.

Lieb and Nanette
Niemand on their
farm, 1997.

**A PAIR OF CEMENT EAGLES PEERS** down threateningly from high atop two faux Roman columns. An ornate arch curves delicately overhead, with the names "Nanette and Lieb Niemand" etched into the concrete. It's a bit much—this is, after all, just a driveway entrance. But out here in the heartland surrounded by miles of golden cornfields, white farmers have always staked their claim boldly. Call it "*platteland* kitsch"—it is Lieb Niemand's stamp on his world.

I follow the winding drive until it reaches a sprawling house. A brilliant flower-lined walkway ushers me toward the enclosed veranda. Nanette Niemand, bedecked in tight polyester pants, Gucci glasses, and dripping with gold chains, greets me at the door. I am somehow expecting something more, well, country. I'm in the wrong place for that. Nanette Niemand, fifty-six, a farmer's wife and lately a farmer in her own right, is proud to wear her riches on her sleeve. She is part of the Afrikaner nouveau riche, and she is clearly queen of her domain.

Life has been very, very good for the Niemands. Nanette escorts me on a tour of her spacious home. Paintings of flowers are interspersed with real flowers. A large, colorful bird called an African Grey cackles incessantly. We walk through a breezy den into a spacious game room with an Olympic-size snooker table. Trophy heads—including one of a massive kudu cow that Nanette shot—peer down at us.

We step outside onto a meticulously kept lawn and flower garden. A sparkling pool with a thatched *lapha* (gazebo) sits empty. The grounds are maintained by four "garden boys" she explains. "A good boy . . . is very, very scarce," she says, insisting that most are "not honest." She and her husband also have two maids who cook and clean the house. "We can't go without them," she admits.

A call over a two-way radio produces her husband Lieb (short for Gottlieb). He is a squat man with a prominent gut that strains against his blue coveralls. His energetic pace belies his sixty years. His most prominent feature is his wide, mottled pug nose, a legacy of his days as an amateur boxer. The former pugilist has retained his old form, as I quickly discover.

Lieb extends a firm handshake but withholds the smile. He is deeply suspicious of my motives. He feels foreigners, especially journalists, have been unfairly critical of right-wing Afrikaners such as himself. When I pose a question in English, he replies brusquely.

"When you are a guest in *my* house, I speak *my* language," he snaps. I shrug my consent. Language is a sensitive issue for Afrikaners, especially now as Afrikaans is swiftly receding from its former status as the language of commerce to its present state as a minor tongue. Many Afrikaners are deeply insecure about their facility in English, even when they are quite fluent. Nanette, who was born into an English-speaking family, offers to translate. She begins the cumbersome task of repeating what he has just said. He cuts her off in the first sentence.

"No no no, what I said was . . . ," he interjects with annoyance. He continues our conversation in perfect English without further comment.

The Niemands live in the small town of Ventersdorp, about one hundred miles due west of Johannesburg. On the approach to town, two features are prominent. The first is the sprawling gold, green, and brown patchwork of cultivated earth that rolls out in all directions. Farmworkers appear like colorful ants combing the fields. The second landmark is the rank of grain silos that tower over the town. Both speak of the lifeblood of this area—farming. This is the *platteland* ("flat land"), the breadbasket of South Africa and the heartland of the *Boer*, which literally means "farmer."

Ventersdorp has also been fertile ground of a different sort: it gained notoriety in the last decade as South Africa's most right-wing town. It was the home and headquarters of Eugene Terre'Blanche, the charismatic leader of the neo-Nazi Afrikaner Weerstandsbeweging (AWB), or Afrikaner Resistance Movement. By the early 1990s, Terre'Blanche had fashioned himself the torchbearer of Afrikaner survival. Those were heady and tense times, when rural *volk* would strut around town with pistols strapped to their hips to show that they were True Believers.

Ventersdorp has mellowed since the end of apartheid. The AWB is ostensibly defunct, and the pugnacious Terre'Blanche has been in and out of court on a variety of petty assault charges. These days, he is only heard from when a reporter needs an inflammatory sound bite to spice up a dull news day. The town council is now dominated by blacks. But the white farmers of the area still live extremely well, thank you.

I first visited Ventersdorp in 1990 to see how it was getting along with one of its neighbors, the black farming community of Mogopa. The farmers of Mogopa, who were forcibly removed from their lands in 1984, began "illegally" returning in 1989, and are now struggling to farm on their ancestral land.

A tense peace now prevails in the heartland. The Mogopa farmers are deeply ambivalent about their white neighbors, including Lieb Niemand, who they say profited from their misery. As for the right-wing white farmers, their bellicose pre-election threats in the early nineties have been replaced by a self-pitying insecurity.

"I don't think there's any future for us or for our white children in this country," says Lieb. "Definitely not."

It is 5 A.M. and still dark outside, but Lieb Niemand's day is beginning. The maids have already prepared a breakfast of eggs and sausage for him and Nanette, and the two of them sit quietly in their kitchen, a spacious room with avocado Formica decor that is reminiscent of the sixties. Tall, straight-backed chairs lined up around the table give the place the feel of an empty castle.

After breakfast, Lieb heads out in his pickup truck to check on his workers. He cultivates mealie (maize) and sunflower on thousands of acres spread over eight different farms; he owns four of the farms, and rents the rest. As we bounce along in his truck, he tells me about the life of a farmer.

"You know, me and my wife, sometimes we plan, ach, two or three times a year to . . . go to Sun City [a famous casino resort] or to go and eat out or something like that. You get dressed up and by 4 o'clock you want to go. Then somebody phones you from one of the farms, or one of your blacks coming in and calls you and says there's a cow that can't calf. Then you just have to undress, and you get the vet sometimes if you can't get the calf out yourself. Now what time do you get finished there? Nine o'clock on a Saturday night. Then you just cancel everything, because you're a white farmer and you've got responsibility."

White farmers don't actually farm in the hands-on sense. They are supervisors, overseeing black workers who do virtually all the manual labor. We drive about fifteen minutes from his house and pull off onto a dirt road that leads into a 240-acre field. It is a treeless expanse where the wind blows steadily. Gold winter grass carpets the surrounding hillsides and waves softly in the breeze. Two dozen black workers are spread out in a haphazard line, bent over in the barren field. Most of them are boys and girls, and some appear too young to be legally employed. They are picking up stones and tossing them into milk containers, clearing the field in preparation for planting. When they see Lieb, they begin working in earnest. Some of them giggle nervously.

Lieb struts over to talk to them. He wears a gray felt top hat ingrained with red dust, and he seems at ease out here. He is a gruff, aggressive, loud man, but he prides himself on being a regular guy, somebody with whom the workers feel some kinship. He barks orders, waves and points animatedly. It is a one-way communication; they respond hesitantly, looking down as he talks. Suddenly a few of them burst out laughing. He turns to me with a big smile. "I says to them, 'You people must kill all the *boere* [farmers] and then you can have the tractors and everything to yourself!'

"You see they laughing and they playing and they kidding around and there's no hard feelings between me or them," he tells me, trying a bit too hard to demonstrate his rapport with his workers. He says that the previous day it was so cold that he told them not to work.

Lieb is sensitive about the bad reputation that white farmers have for mistreating their workers. He insists that proposed legislation that will limit the hours of farmworkers is unrealistic. "If anybody in any country can run a farm eight hours a day, five days a week, I would like to go and stay in that country and I would like to be a worker there . . . You can never ever do that, not on a farm, never." During planting or harvest season, his workers must rise at 5 A.M. and work until dark, six days per week.

He attempts to justify providing housing for his workers that lacks basic amenities. "I would like to build some beautiful houses for my blacks. I would like to give them electricity. But where must I get the money from? You know this is a very very difficult country to farm in and the subsidies we're getting from . . . the white governments before were very very poor."

In fact, South Africa's white farmers were lavishly subsidized during the days of National Party rule. "It's fair to say that South Africa was among the most heavily subsidized agricultural sectors in the world," asserts Professor Nick Vink, chair of the agricultural economics department at Stellenbosch University. He estimates that by the early eighties, about half of a white farmer's net income was from government subsidies (by comparison, American farmers received a subsidy of 30 percent in the mid-eighties).[1]

"It was a form of political patronage," explains Vink. Rural votes were more heavily weighted under the old South African constitution, so farmers had disproportionate political clout within the NP; agricultural subsidies were the price of those votes. When rural voters began to flee the NP in the 1980s in favor of the right-wing Conservative Party, farm subsidies started to drop. Under the ANC government, the subsidy level is under 15 percent, which is comparable to what American farmers receive in the late 1990s.

Lieb Niemand fears that the loss of white privilege is a sign that he and other farmers are being victimized. "This, this black people, this black government, basically is gonna force our whites into a corner by laws . . . [with] this unions, taxes, ach—there's a lot of things."

Lieb Niemand hails from a long line of farmers. His great-great-grandfather arrived in South Africa from Germany in the early 1800s. He married a French woman, and they took part in the Great Trek in 1838. Niemand's grandfather was among the first whites to arrive in Ventersdorp in 1880. He quickly established himself as a small-scale farmer and occasionally sold his goods to local Indian merchants.

Lieb's father farmed part-time in a nearby town. He also owned some drilling machines, which was his main business until he resumed farming full-time in the fifties. Like most Afrikaner farmers before him, Lieb's father had a subsistence farming operation with a few head of cattle and sheep, and a small plot of maize and vegetables. It was a hardscrabble existence.

Lieb Niemand was born in 1937, the sixth of eight children. He vividly remembers the poverty of his childhood. "We were living more or less like these blacks, like they living now . . . We had to eat coffee and black porridge every day. We didn't even have jam, because there wasn't sugar. Even if there was sugar in the shops, we couldn't afford to buy it. You just had to go without it. You know if I tell this to my kids today, they laugh at me. They say *'Nee'* [no]. But those were difficult days."

When the Carnegie Commission studied South Africa's "poor white problem" in the 1930s, it defined its typical subject as "a person who had become dependent to such an extent . . . that he is unfit, without help from others, to find proper means of livelihood." This depiction was captured by the plight of the Afrikaner *bywoner,* or tenant farmer, who roamed the countryside with a few head of cattle, settling down to eke out a meager living by farming someone else's land. In spite of their destitution, *bywoners* were loath to remedy their condition by working as farm laborers. Even as a pauper, the white man fancied himself a *baas;* he would never do "kaffir work."[2]

The Carnegie report stressed that the plight of poor Afrikaners was not due to "laziness" or their high birthrate (the white population more than doubled between 1904 and 1936), as many affluent whites charged. Carnegie researchers found that "poverty was in itself a demoralizing influence which often caused a loss of self-respect and a feeling of inferiority."[3]

Part of the problem was that Boers were subsistence farmers, growing only enough to feed their families. They failed to adopt commercial surplus farming techniques and consequently were eclipsed by African farmers at the turn of the century. A Pretoria merchant declared that "Kaffirs take away £47,000 from the local market for every £26,000 taken away by Boers." Ironically, black farmers had dramatically increased their maize production in response to high taxation, which had been levied in an attempt to give white farmers a competitive advantage.[4]

The South African government tried to hamstring black workers by promulgating a series of laws that favored white labor. Widely disparate race-based minimum wages were established. An unskilled Afrikaner overseer would be paid £10 per week, while his African counterpart would get only 12 shillings. These labor preference laws, combined with the Land Acts of 1913 and 1936, which prohibited blacks from purchasing land, steadily eroded the position of black farmers.

For the Niemands, the move out of poverty was slow. "We worked hard and we saved up," recalls Lieb. "Instead of going on holiday I bought myself two or three cows. After nine months or a year they had calves there. That's how we got on."

Lieb got his first job at age nineteen in the gold mines in Johannesburg. But he was a country boy and longed to be back on the land again. "The love I have for the soil, for the ground, for farming—that's what made me come out here. I thought I could make a better living, more healthier, as a farmer," he recounts.

In 1959, at the age of twenty-two, Lieb Niemand began his life on the farm. "I had about nothing, *nothing*," he says of his beginnings. He started by sharecropping, renting land from a successful local farmer, Oom (Uncle) Tiennie Fourie. He would give Fourie one-fourth of his crops as payment for the land. Niemand lived with his first wife and two children in a small farmhouse with no water or electricity. He owned a van, but couldn't afford to put gasoline in it. A local Indian merchant gave him a stove and a bicycle on credit, which he paid for after his first harvest. "It was very hard, very hard in those days."

Lieb bought his first sizeable farm—nearly seven hundred acres—in 1963. In the early seventies, after having four children, he and his wife were divorced. He met and married Nanette in 1974, after which he finally moved into a house with electricity. Such amenities were extravagant for a struggling farmer. As his mentor, Oom Tiennie, told him, "Putting electricity in a place is just a waste of money. You could rather buy yourself a few cows."

Lieb credits his survival to the fact that he diversified his business. In 1980, after his sons Jannie and Paul completed their training as engineers, Lieb bought a few trucks and began building up a small trucking business. Today, he has fifteen trucks and handles everything from delivering construction supplies in the local black township to long-haul moves. He has continually plowed profits from the trucking business back into his debt-saddled farm operation.

The Niemands now boast of two farmers in their family. In 1991, Nanette started a dairy farm. Today, she employs five black "girls" for milking and seven "boys" to work the fields around her dairy. Strolling around pens of mooing cattle and women hunched over swollen cow udders, this lady in gold jewelry, frosted hair, and fancy clothes looks incongruous. Even she admits to being out of place here.

"I was a city girl," she concedes. She grew up in the Johannesburg suburb of Florida as the offspring of an Afrikaans grandmother and an English grandfather (Ventersdorp locals still say she speaks Afrikaans with an accent). She had one son by a former marriage and was divorced in the early seventies. She and her son came to live with her father, who was a traffic policeman in Ventersdorp. After she and Lieb were married, the farm became her life. "And I wouldn't change it for anything . . . I'm not a person who associates with a lot of people, you know. I stay to myself . . . My friends is my animals."

Lieb shows up at Nanette's dairy farm in the late afternoon. "Hi cookie," he says, strutting over and planting a kiss on her cheek. The tenderness seems out of character for the gruff *baas*. They stroll around the farm hand in hand, joking and smiling like teenage sweethearts. They are clearly very much in love after a quarter-century of marriage.

The Niemands are today viewed as one of the most successful farm families in Ventersdorp. Lieb dismisses the compliment. "All of us farmers are struggling." He cites droughts that have plagued the country throughout the eighties, high interest rates—South Africans pay around 22 percent interest on loans—and the cost of farm "inputs" (such as seed, fertilizer, and equipment) which rose about 17 percent in the mid-nineties.[5] In addition, farm subsidies from the government have largely dried up.

As Professor Vink observes, "the irony is that the subsidization led to gross inefficiency" in the white farming sector. Farmers were up to ten times less efficient than their counterparts in Europe or the United States.[6] Vink insists the new austerity has a bright side: "The withdrawal of subsidies has proved that the farmers can actually look after themselves. The sector is actually a lot more efficient now than what it was."

With the loss of their hefty political and economic patronage, many white farmers must either improve their profitability or go under. By 1997, 70 percent of agricultural loans were in arrears or in default. Hennie du Plessis Sr., a Ventersdorp farmer who is on the board of directors of the Central West Cooperative, the largest farm co-op in South Africa, told me in 1990 that there was a direct link between the woes of farmers and the rise of ultraright politics. "Ninety-nine percent of the farmers who are failing are the very conservative ones," he said then.

One result of these increasing pressures is that white farmers are now getting their hands dirty. "White farmers are doing much more work themselves now," observes du Plessis today. "We now have some white farmers who don't employ any laborers," he says, chuckling at the novelty. "In the past that was unheard of."

When I arrived in Ventersdorp in September 1990, it appeared to be a typical South African *dorp* (village). A pretty tree-lined boulevard was the main thoroughfare through town. Large church steeples dominated the downtown skyline. The most prominent feature on the village green was a replica of an original Voortrekker covered wagon, which sat beneath a thatched *lapha*. A cement walkway had the eternally preserved tracks of another ox-wagon that passed through here in 1988, during the 150th anniversary of the Great Trek. Like every *platteland* town, the streets all bore the names of Afrikaner pioneers. There was Van Riebeeck Street, Voortrekker Road, and so on. The town strove to be a shrine to Afrikaner nationalism.

I turned off Van Riebeeck Street that September day and found a small storefront on a side road. It was nondescript save for the three-legged swastika hanging in the window. I had come to pay a visit to the high priest of the neo-Nazi movement, Eugene Terre'Blanche. With their goose-stepping, straight-armed salutes, and swastikas, he and his Afrikaner Resistance Movement (AWB) were magnets for the international media. The cameras devoured the made-for-TV theatrics, and Terre'Blanche reveled in the attention. He conferred on Ventersdorp the dubious distinction of the cradle of modern South African fascism.

Terre'Blanche was a struggling pig farmer and a former actor who initially only dabbled in politics. He was intent on managing every aspect of his public persona, and when situations got out of his control, he would get punchy. He and his followers seemed to take particular pleasure in beating up journalists; several colleagues who suffered his wrath had warned me about him before this visit.

The histrionics began the moment I entered his office, the national headquarters of the AWB. A brown-shirted AWB "commando" greeted me with a "Heil Hitler" salute. As I waited, I helped myself to a sampling of neo-Nazi literature from around the world. A blonde-haired Afrikaner secretary brought me tea.

The AWB was formed in 1973 as a paramilitary offshoot of a far-right party known as the Herstigte (Reconstituted) Nasionale Party. Terre'Blanche, a former bodyguard of Prime Minister B. J. Vorster, had run as an HNP candidate in the 1971 elections. After his defeat, he dismissed electoral politics as a "British-Jewish invention designed to weaken Afrikanerdom."[7] Terre'Blanche then formed the AWB, and it existed as a fringe group for many years. But as the National Party began to dilute its brand of nationalism in the 1980s, the AWB came to be a haven for disillusioned elements of the Afrikaner working class, including farmers. Its public appearances were always dramatic but its following was small. The AWB made a far-fetched claim of fifty thousand to one hundred thousand members; more realistic estimates put its 1993 membership at around eighteen thousand.[8]

The AWB first gained national attention in November 1988 when one of its members, Barend Strydom, then twenty-three, walked around downtown Pretoria indiscriminately shooting black people. He killed seven people and wounded sixteen before being disarmed by a black bystander. (Strydom was released from jail in 1992 along with a number of other political prisoners, most of whom were from the ANC.)

Photographer Paul Weinberg and I were finally escorted into Terre'Blanche's office. His styled hair lay impeccably on his head; he had heard that we would photograph him. He sat framed by flags of the original Boer republics on one side and the AWB swastika on the other.

Terre'Blanche spoke in a deep, rich voice. He recounted how his forefathers "discovered" this land and "shed their Afrikaner blood" to defend it. He warned that he and his followers were prepared to do the same.

Our conversation turned to economics, and Terre'Blanche proudly declared himself a free market capitalist. I pointed out that capitalists do business with anyone who has money, be they black or white. Did he support that notion, too? The bearded self-styled military leader suddenly turned dour. He wagged his finger at me accusingly. "This interview is over!" he roared.

"Commandant!" he shouted as his face turned beet red. He began barking orders in Afrikaans to men in the other room. Paul bolted to his feet and yanked on my arm as he moved for the door. "Time to go!" Paul announced. We smiled weakly at several beer-bellied brownshirts who suddenly appeared to "help" us out; they seemed quite familiar with this routine. Terre'Blanche followed us, yelling. The secretary looked slightly embarrassed at this spectacle of grown Afrikaner men playing soldier and browbeating a pair of *uitlanders* (foreigners), but she said nothing. She had evidently seen this all before. We beat a hasty retreat to our car and jumped inside—only to discover that it wouldn't start. Terre'Blanche and his cronies continued shouting at us as I got out and frantically pushed the ailing car while Paul popped the clutch. We escaped unscathed, save for our bruised egos.

The AWB garnered considerable attention between 1990 and the 1994 elections, when Terre'Blanche was daily threatening to mount an armed insurrection. It was widely known that the AWB had many sympathizers in the security forces, which explained why the state rarely took action against the fanatical group. But the "Battle of Ventersdorp" on August 9, 1991, forever changed the nature of the relationship between the white government and the far right.

President F. W. de Klerk was taking his message of reform into the heart of AWB country: he planned to speak at a rally in Ventersdorp that day. In response, two thousand armed AWB members lined the streets of the town in an attempt to stop the de Klerk rally. De Klerk and his wife arrived by helicopter and left in an armored police vehicle. Unable to confront the traitor to the *volk,* the AWB took out its wrath on several minibus taxis filled with black commuters. They began pulling out passengers and beating them. Police opened fire and when it was over, three AWB members lay dead. Today, a small black marble obelisk with the AWB swastika stands on the Ventersdorp town common to commemorate the men who died.

The AWB's best-known action came on June 25, 1993, when Terre'Blanche and two hundred other uniformed rightists crashed a military truck into the glass lobby of the World Trade Centre near Johannesburg. Inside, negotiations were taking place between the ANC, NP, and twenty-four other parties. ANC members stormed the hall, beat up anyone they could find, and caused over $200,000 in damage. They denounced the elections and called for an Afrikaner *volkstaat.*[9]

Terre'Blanche's delusions of grandeur finally came crashing down on March 11, 1994. One month before the elections, the AWB staged an "invasion" of the black homeland of Bophuthatswana. Terre'Blanche claimed they were invited in to defend the homeland, which was one of the last of the ten Bantustans to resist reintegration into South Africa and was on the verge of collapse. It was a bizarre sight: Afrikaner men drove through the streets of the homeland capital of Mmabatho in their Mercedes sedans and pickup trucks, shooting randomly at black passers-by and killing several of them. The vigilantes didn't count on resistance from the Bophuthatswana Defense Force. In a chilling spectacle, a soldier executed three AWB men in front of international television cameras. The remaining "commandos" retreated in humiliation to the comfort of their farms.

Lieb Niemand is proud of being a right-winger, but he winces at the mention of his neighbor, Eugene Terre'Blanche.

"Everybody's laughing at him because he's a *dronklap* [drunkard]," he says. I am sitting with Lieb and Nanette in their living room after a day's work. Lieb has changed into khaki shorts with knee socks pulled high. His maids come in and serve us tea. Nanette explains that Lieb hates Terre'Blanche personally, and consequently never allied with him.

"I would have never ever thought of planting a bomb in Johannesburg or shooting anybody. But I thought there was going to be a war," says Lieb—and he claims he was prepared to fight. "If we had the right leaders in this country I would have fight to the bitter end and even if I had to die . . . I wouldn't worry. All I wanted was a certainty that my kids and their kids would have had a place where they could make a living if they were prepared to work."

What did whites fear? "Deep inside they fear the day that the blacks are gonna start killing each other and the whites will come between them. Like this Inkatha and ANC," he says, referring to the deadly battles that have occurred between the rival political groups.

Lieb remains unrepentant about the apartheid dream. "I think [apartheid] was definitely unfairly criticized, definitely. Because until today, most people they don't want to mix . . . I felt like Dr. Verwoerd said: give [blacks] the homelands and let them rule themselves, like their culture say to them."

Nanette adds that the mixing between blacks and whites is "breaking the country . . . Now you take our schools: our schools had a high standard. You know they, they dropping our school standard down to the level of the blacks." It's a refrain that I hear often in the new South Africa: talk of declining "standards" is polite code for complaining about integration and affirmative action. But Nanette Niemand isn't particularly concerned with being polite.

"You get a lot of people says you could bring them out of the bush, but you can't take the bush out of them," she says with a giggle.

"I think their culture is very different," she continues. "That's why . . . the blacks will never be able to farm like the whites. They haven't got much responsibility." As evidence of this theory, Nanette points to what she claims is the high birthrate among blacks. "We feed, they breed," she quips with a coy smile. This explains how blacks became the majority in South Africa, she insists. Ironically, this same put-down was leveled against poor Boers like Lieb's father just a half-century ago.

Lieb Niemand's greatest anger about the end of white supremacy is reserved for the Afrikaners who negotiated it away. "I'm thinking much more [highly] of Mandela than what I think about de Klerk. Because Mandela is fighting for his people, for the blacks that look like him and think like him, that's got the same culture like him. But this de Klerk and P. W. Botha, all of them, they just give the county away to other people . . . They're *skelms* [rascals]. I always said I wouldn't mind if black people are ruling the country, but please for God's sake, then they must do it fairly . . . As long as we can make money, as long as we can make a good living and people doesn't hate each other and kill each other and things like that."

To hear Lieb tell it, South Africa is on its final downward spiral. "I think it's getting worse every day. If you look to this affirmative action for instance, taking people out of jobs, giving them [severance] packages just to leave and to put blacks in there that doesn't know a thing about it . . . It's getting worse every day.

"Most of the whites in this country, since they realized that a black government was definitely going to take over—they were down. They were out. They just feel that there was nothing left for them in this country. We just carrying on from day to day, just waiting for what's going to happen tomorrow and the day after tomorrow."

The *swart gevaar* always took the form of a two-headed bogeyman in the conservative white worldview. The first threat was black power—the fear that blacks would kill whites if they gained power. That never happened. But to Lieb, the second threat remains: communism.

"If this government tomorrow comes and says: 'Listen, I want this farm of yours and I'm gonna take it for this and that and that reason.' What can you do? . . . Because there's a lot of communists in this government and we know what communists are."

Which leads Lieb to his grim conclusion: "I really think that whether we like it or not we whites will have to stand together in time to come, whether it's two or three or five or ten years' time, and we will have to fight to the bitter end, whatever will happen there. That's what I really think."

It has become common fashion among white South Africans to specu-
late on where in the world the grass is greener. Australia, New Zealand,
and the United States are frequently mentioned as idyllic escape routes, as
if these places were free from the crime and other social ills that have be-
set the new South Africa. Some Afrikaner farmers have quietly begun another Great Trek further into Africa. Boers have established farms in Zambia and Mozambique, where they hope to start over again just as their
ancestors did in South Africa.

Lieb scoffs at all this talk of a white exodus. "Where can we go to?" he
asks, the frustration evident in his voice. It is the point that Afrikaners have
long made: they are white Africans, people of the soil of South Africa. Unlike English-speaking South Africans who often hold a British passport,
there is no back door for the Boers. No other country is waiting to welcome them home.

"I'm not going to let kaffirs chase me away . . . We must stay here and
we must carry on. We've got our belongings here and I saved and part of
this belongs to me. I was born here. My forefathers, my father, they were
born here. So where must I go to today? I don't think all the whites can
just leave the country and go elsewhere and go make a better living there,
isn't it? . . . All of us just can't run away."

One might assume from Lieb Niemand's despondent ruminations that
his lifestyle and business have taken catastrophic turns since the end of
white rule. But nothing of the sort has happened. When I ask him later
whether life has changed much since blacks came to power, he admits,
"No, it hasn't changed really. I think we just carry on like we did before."

Indeed. And that is precisely what has galled so many blacks. Life looks
much as it always has in the *platteland.* The whites are the *baas,* the blacks
are the workers, and barring massive land expropriations—which the
ANC government has emphatically ruled out—the balance of power
won't change anytime soon. Whites still enjoy a standard of living unmatched anywhere else in the world for their income levels. The Niemands' life—with their palatial home and staff of six workers—is the life
reserved for the rich and famous in any other western country. But in
South Africa, it is a white farmer's birthright.

I nevertheless feel a guilty sympathy for Lieb Niemand. Deep insecurity has long been a hallmark of Afrikaner culture, and it has found new
expression in the uncertainty he feels about the future. As well he should:

the Boers have everything to lose. Their language is on the decline, their social privilege is eroding, and the economic prospect for the next generation of Afrikaners is in doubt. The only solace they can take is in the present, where they remain rulers of their rural kingdom.

Later, Lieb and I walk around on his lands. "We right-wingers should have done our thing before the '94 election," he laments. "We could have settled this in a month's time. But instead we got de Klerk who said 'negotiate.' Now the blacks control the military and it's too late." He says of the onetime plans for a preemptive right-wing coup, "All the plans these right-wingers tried to make, they failed terribly. But *jerrrr,*" he says with a roll of his tongue, "they were stupid. They were terribly stupid."

I ask him what will happen when he retires. "I dunno," he shrugs. "I don't think I ever will retire." His sons are not farmers, I point out. So who will take the farms?

Lieb looks at me and cracks a wry smile. "Maybe Mr. Mandela."

It is payday on Lieb Niemand's farm. I enter his office, which is tucked in behind a large garage that houses his trucking operation. A group of white men sit in an adjoining room smoking cigarettes, drinking beer, and watching the South African cricket team play Australia on TV. The smoke-filled room with metal furniture and bare walls has the feel of a seedy bar.

A fellow with gray hair and ill-fitting pants informs me that Lieb can't see me today; I must come back some other time. I look over through a window to see Lieb grim-faced, hunched over a stack of colorful South African rand notes. He is flanked by his thirty-eight-year-old son, Jannie, and his strapping foreman, Hansie. He glances at me, but does not acknowledge my presence.

I decide to wander over and chat with some of the workers. The living quarters sit opposite the garage. They are austere affairs: the rooms are constructed of bare cinder block and topped by thin metal roofs. A long coil of razor wire runs along the top of the building. Electrical wires stretch across the parking area to the office and truck repair shop just fifty feet away. But the workers' quarters have no running water or electricity.

I step inside a small square room and find thirty-three-year-old William. He informs me that he earns the equivalent of $70 per month operating a bucket loader. I ask him how he likes working here.

"These guys are no good," he says, shaking his head. "The old owner,

Lieb, is too dangerous. He hits people. If there is a small problem—not even a big problem—then he hits them, punches them."

He senses my surprise. "Where does he hit you?" I ask.

"In the face!" he declares. I ask him why he stays.

"There's no job outside," he says. In the new South Africa, "nothing has changed for me. The whole South Africa must change and they must give us good money."

I meet another fellow in greasy blue coveralls. He is a truck mechanic here and has just collected his $40 monthly salary. He sometimes works from 6 A.M. to 6 P.M., and on Saturdays until noon or 1 P.M. He says, "If you make a mistake, sometimes they *donder* [beat] you." I ask him whether it is any better since 1994. "*Nee,* there's no difference here. If I can get another job, I'll go. Maybe you can help us."

I am shocked by these revelations, although I know I shouldn't be. In my visits with Lieb I had come to understand him and empathize with him. I had crossed the line and seen the world through different eyes. I understood some of his fears, and saw that behind his blustery talk was a warm and sincere man simply concerned about his family's future, and determined not to slip back into the poverty from which he came.

These epiphanies fade quickly as his workers fill in another side of Lieb Niemand. I had thought this kind of abuse ended with the darker days of apartheid. But as I am rudely learning, the past is the present here on the farms.

Lieb's farmworkers arrive on a flatbed truck that has been collecting them during the afternoon. He employs about twenty men on his farms, and more in his trucking business. I step inside Lieb's office and talk briefly to him. He explains that his workers get between $60 and $100 per month. He adds that they "get everything for nothing": an allotment of mealie, occasional meat, milk, medical care, and free lodging for the men and their families. He boasts that two men have been working for him since 1957.

Another Ventersdorp farmer, sixty-nine-year-old Hennie du Plessis, confirms to me that Lieb has "got a very good relation with his blacks. His blacks are probably the best off in the district in terms of housing, subsidy, and bonuses. In fact, he's probably one of the leaders as far as his black workers are concerned . . . He's very hard with them, but he's very fair with them . . . He's got his own system of handling them. I don't think one of his laborers belongs to a trade union, because they quite happy to be with him."

The men gather around Lieb and Hansie. Their dress varies from torn coveralls to threadbare trousers. One wears worn-out moccasins, another is in Top-Siders with no laces. They remove their hats when they greet Lieb. He announces that he is postponing their twelve-day vacation for a month because the mealie fields need weeding. He turns to me, "You see, they've got no problem with that. They're happy!" The men remain silent.

The pay ritual then begins. Each man comes in one at a time. They extend two hands toward Lieb in a pose that resembles either begging or praying. Peter, a farmworker for three years, stands erect as Lieb peels off his month's salary and hands it to him: $47. I can see that Lieb is feeling self-conscious as I watch what he pays each man. He finally turns to me and says, "There's no place in the world where everyone is rich and has water and electricity. Isn't it?" he queries, a bit flustered. "There must be workers and there must be *baases*. And on my farm, I am the *baas*."

*Baasskap* is still the norm out on the farms. Farmers have a deeply paternalistic relationship with their workers. Nanette captures it when she tells me later over dinner, "They call us their mother and father. We got to help them. If their child gets burnt, they run to the white person. We got to take them to the doctor."

I wander back outside and speak with the men. They are huddled quietly, watching Jannie and Hansie fawn over a gleaming new motorcycle that Jannie just bought for $850. Nearby, a group of workers is busy with a daily ritual—washing the private cars of the white bosses. I ask Peter, a tractor driver on the farm, how the work is. "That money is not okay," he says, pointing to the $47 he's just received.

The government has just tabled legislation that will establish a minimum monthly wage of $145. Lieb scoffs at the idea. "I'm sure they'll send black inspectors and give me hell. I refuse to do that."

Later, I tell Lieb that a worker claims he hits them. I ask him if it's true. His mouth pulls back in a tight smile, and he shakes his head. "He's a liar. Maybe years ago—but nowadays I don't touch them."

The men mill around waiting for a ride into town so they can buy provisions with their money. Lieb sputters, "They'll just spend it all on booze. They'll be drunk 'til Tuesday."

I turn down Van Riebeeck Street, pass the Voortrekker ox-wagon and the imperious steeple of the Dutch Reformed church. My destination is the black township of Tshing, the dusty flats on the outskirts of town that are crammed with small homes and shacks. I quickly get lost in the serpentine dirt roads and ask the driver of a beer delivery truck where "Mayor Meshak" lives. He waves for me to follow him, and soon deposits me in front of a well-kept green shack on a tiny dirt plot. A young man sporting a T-shirt and backward baseball cap emerges from the shack and extends his hand. This is twenty-seven-year-old Meshack Mbambalala: squatter, former student activist, and the new mayor of Ventersdorp.

During high school in the mid-eighties, Mbambalala was a member of the Azanian People's Organization, which was considered more radical than the ANC. He switched his allegiance to the ANC in 1990, attended university in Soweto, and returned to Ventersdorp to work as a community organizer. "I used to think every white people was an enemy of me," he recalls. He was elected to the Ventersdorp town council in November 1995, and his fellow councilors elected him mayor that same month. The council now consists of five members from the ANC and four from the Conservative Party (CP). I ask him how the councilors get along with each other.

"It's *marvelous*," says the soft-spoken, earnest young man. "At the beginning I thought there will be a fight. But there is a lot of friendship amongst ourselves. You would not say these guys are with different political ideologies."

We sit inside his one-room shack. There is a double bed and a wooden vanity, all meticulously neat. Two posters of Bob Marley grace the corrugated metal wall. His mother lives in the neighboring shack. "Outside the chamber we are different people, but inside we are one council," he asserts. The CP councilors consist of two farmers, a retired cop, and a local electrician. "Even if someone don't agree with something, it is based on facts and constructive arguments. It is never arguments that are based on political things since I took over." He says he smoothed the transition to black leadership by monopolizing discussion in the early meetings so that arguments wouldn't start. "From there, maybe a miracle happened."

I express my surprise at this picture of political tranquility, noting that CP supporters whom I meet are typically unyielding and tough. "Sure, most of them they are that way. But maybe we are tough also. That's why we making a team with them. We are getting full cooperation from them."

Mbambalala says that his harshest critics are not the whites—it's his Tshing neighbors. "I get more respect from the white people than the black people," he concedes. "Our people . . . say we are slow. There is always criticism on us. Criticism is a good thing, but sometimes it is overdone. But when you get into town, you get all the necessary respect that a mayor can get with the whites. I guess they know what our duties are compared to our people."

Mbambalala acknowledges that there is good cause for criticism: very little has changed in Ventersdorp for the poorest people. "The needs that we are having are bigger than the resources that we are having," he says. He notes that of the forty paid municipal officials, only three are black. He attributes that to the "sunset clauses" that allowed white civil servants to keep their jobs, and to the fact that there are few blacks presently qualified for these jobs.

Sixty percent of the Ventersdorp town budget is now earmarked for upgrading Tshing and the nearby colored township of Toevlug. The council works together to address these issues. "There's always consensus. There's nothing that went through just because of a [majority] vote."

It's not all this rosy around town, of course. I stop in one night at the Ventersdorp Pub. There are no "whites only" signs anymore, but there may as well be. Posted on the wall is the drink menu: I can order "Nelson's Blood," an "ANC," or a "Multi-Racial." A haggard looking white lady with pancake makeup tends bar. I ask her what is in an ANC. "I wouldn't know," she snaps and walks away.

I pull up next to an older white farmer. He says he's a liberal, then tells me a "joke." "I'd rather shoot a kaffir than a baboon any day," says the rotund man with the bloodshot eyes and ruddy face. "A kaffir doesn't scream as much as a baboon."

I ask Mbambalala if the AWB has given him any problems. "Definitely not," he says eagerly. He notes that Terre'Blanche recently refused to appear on a television interview with him and spread a rumor that the new mayor was a criminal. But Mbambalala is unfazed. "As long as [AWB supporters] get the services they want from the council and they are not causing problems for our people, I don't have a problem with them."

The ANC and CP councilors are in complete agreement on one issue: they both detest the National Party. Mbambalala recounts what one of the CP councilors told him while they were having tea: "I hate the NP. These guys taught us to hate blacks. And they gave us all the bad ideas about what the ANC is. They told us it's a terrorist organization, [it would] take their cows and their wives if it was allowed in the country."

It all sounds a bit improbable: have there been *any* conflicts on the new council? Mbambalala stops to think for a moment. "Oh yes," he suddenly recalls, "in August. When there was a conflict between two CP guys, not with ourselves."

And so a hotbed of hatred has been transformed into a model of change. "I think there is a lot that people from outside can learn from Venters-dorp," says Mbambalala."That [having] differing political ideologies doesn't mean you can't work together, live together. There is a lot of po-litical tolerance here."

Mayor Mbambalala is upbeat about black-white relations. "I think fu-ture relations are going to be good," he predicts. "As long as we can start practicing now, especially among the younger generation. Because we don't expect a person who lived sixty years under National Party rule to suddenly understand what is taking place now. So one has to work hard among the younger generations to improve race relations. But there's a bright future."

Mogopa. It looms on the horizon of Ventersdorp, a silent, perpetual re-minder of the cruel ways that neighbors can turn on one another. Ven-tersdorp's progress will always be measured against progress made in the rolling hills of Mogopa. In 1984, this prosperous seventy-two-year-old black farming community which held title to its land was forcibly evicted and its residents dumped into a barren Bantustan. Their self-sufficient lifestyle as farmers came to an abrupt end, and they were reduced to ab-ject poverty. They have now returned to start over, but the road to recov-ery is slow and painful.

Lieb Niemand, along with many other Ventersdorp farmers, was in-volved in the Mogopa removal. It wasn't his initiative—forced removals were the policy of successive National Party governments that Niemand supported—but Ventersdorp farmers were silent as their black farming neighbors were uprooted, village by village. And Lieb, like many white farmers, participated in the plunder. In Mogopa, Lieb provided the trucks to cart away people's goods, charging them $75 per trip. He showed up when families were leaving and bought their cattle at a fraction of their market value. When they were gone, he harvested their mealie in their ab-sence and kept the profit. During the years of exile, he grazed his cattle amid the ruins of his black neighbors.

Lieb doesn't like to talk about Mogopa. It's a bit awkward. Perhaps shameful. After all, the things that he says he fears most—losing his land and livelihood, having no opportunity for his children, being unable to make a living despite his willingness to work—are the very things that were done to the farmers of Mogopa. He's afraid, in short, that they will treat him just as he treated them. It won't happen like that, of course—he's rich, they're poor, and money talks. But it haunts him all the same.

And so Lieb, like many white South Africans, cloaks his memory in a shroud of denial. In his version of events, he has been a friend to Mogopa all along. Now it is white farmers like him who are the real victims.

"This [Derek] Hanekom, the minister of land affairs and the minister of agriculture, he's busy taking white farmers' farms away from them, giving it to the blacks. This Doornkop, Goedgevonden, Tsetse, and Mogopa—that's altogether twenty-one thousand hectares. Now who lives there? It's only a lot of squatters." The communities he mentions were all declared "black spots" in "white areas" and forcibly removed beginning in the mid-1970s. Their homes and schools were all demolished. Starting in 1989, they have all slowly returned to their former lands.

Lieb, who owns farms next to Mogopa, asserts, "I know these people for years and years and years. Since I started in 1961–62 to farm here, I know them all . . . You can go in there—all those places—and you ask them who is Lieb Niemand and everybody will know who we are."

When Mogopa was uprooted in 1984, Lieb, like any good neighbor, "helped them to [move] there" to the Bantustan.

"The older ones, they're very nice people," he says of Mogopa. "Y'know they live in their places and they come to us for help and we go there and I hire some grazing for my cattle from them there. But we get along with them very very very well. But it's the youngsters, you know, that '76 generation. . . . ,' that grew up from that time. They're about twenty, twenty-one, twenty-two years old now. Most of them they don't want to see the whites."

Nanette interjects, "They're lazy too. They don't want to work."

"They just sit around there smoking *dagga* [marijuana] and drinking beer," Lieb continues. "They do nothing. They just sit there. They live from the pensions that the older ones get."

I ask him if Mogopa was a viable farm community before it was removed. "No, no," he says dismissively. "They just go to the big cities, they work there where the electricity is, where the *dagga* is, and where everything that's nice is. Then all the children that's born there, they bring it [to Mogopa] to the grandma and the grandpa that lives here and the [grandparents] must bring the little ones up. Then they go back and they have another one and they bring them here."

Lieb notes that there are a couple of black farmers in the area who farm "like we the whites." He says he goes out of his way to help them, lending them money and equipment. "I thought if you can establish a black farmer on those places then it would be fine because then . . . you've got a friend there next to you.

"I did help them planting [in Mogopa], I helped them plowing some of those lands, and I gave them some sunflower seeds, and I sent one of my tractors with a planter there. And I tried to help them." It didn't work, he says. "They put squatter camps there," he says, referring to the shacks of the resettled communities. "They just sit there," he continues in disgust, "and at night they steal. They stealing cattle here. You can't believe it." He softens a bit and adds sympathetically, "When you're hungry I think then you must steal, you must do something to eat and to get clothes and things like that."

As I sit and drink tea in their living room, Nanette offers her assessment of events. "Now if Mr. Mandela wanted to really make something of this country . . . they won't mention apartheid. That's the past, it's buried, it's gone, it's forgotten . . . Bury the past and start new again.

"If you wanna start a new country, start it with new things, new ideas— shaking hands on TV and showing little white doves flying there. It doesn't mean to say now everyone's loving each other—that's a lot of nonsense. Apartheid is always there . . . It's past, but not past for them [blacks]. They mention it whenever they want to. So soon as they stop [saying] 'apartheid' and . . . telling [about] the white people doing bad things to the blacks, the sooner our country will start going somewhere."

# RISING FROM THE RUINS

MATTHEW MPSHE: FARMER, VICTIM OF FORCED REMOVALS

Archbishop Desmond
Tutu at a vigil pro-
testing the threatened
forced removal of
Mogopa, 1984.

Meeting of Mogopa
villagers to plan
resistance to forced
removal, 1983.

Women of Mogopa
walking to a com-
munity meeting, 1984.

Matthew Mpshe
working the land,
1994.

Minister of Lands
and Agriculture Derek
Hanekom driving the
tractor for Mogopa's first
plowing since the return
of their land, 1995.

Matthew Mpshe in the
Mogopa mealie fields,
1996.

Mogopa farmers'
committee meeting
(Matthew Mpshe on
right), 1996.

Matthew Mpshe in the
Mogopa mealie fields,
1996.

**A LOUD BANGING NOISE** on his front door awakens Matthew Mpshe. He stumbles toward the noise, disoriented and frightened. It is 2 A.M. on February 14, 1984. Flashlights shine through the window into his home. The light falls on the neatly presented dinnerware that Matthew's wife had laid out in a corner cabinet. In the center of the room stands a handsome wooden dining room table, its surface burnished to a smooth finish by years of use. The house is a sturdy stone structure built by Mpshe's father when he settled the rural farming community of Mogopa seventy years earlier. Mpshe takes great pride in this home.

"Open up—police!" the men shout impatiently as they shine their lights through each window.

Mpshe obliges, and suddenly steps outside into a nightmare. The African farmer flinches at the bright lights glaring overhead. He sees his Mogopa neighbors looking similarly bewildered. Police dogs bark and lunge, barely restrained by their leashes. Children cry.

"We are the South African Police. We are here to defend you," comes the voice over the loudspeaker. It is a curious claim, since Mogopa has no enemies. "Everybody must move out of their houses—now!" barks the cop.

Mpshe, a tall, thin, bald-headed man of forty-four, stands by numbly as government laborers march into his neighbor's house, carry out its belongings, and unceremoniously heave them onto a flatbed truck. A parade of these trucks, which belong to local white farmer Lieb Niemand, stand in a long line belching fumes as they wait to cart away the villagers' possessions.

Mpshe walks briskly to join other village leaders to plot strategy, but he slows when he sees several policemen approach. Without saying a word, the cops lash into the small group with *sjamboks,* which can rip a man's skin. Police dogs snarl at the terrified villagers, who disperse rapidly. "They are going to kill us!" Mpshe thinks to himself in a growing state of panic.

Mpshe dashes frantically to the corral where his thirty-five head of cattle are penned. A policeman holds out his baton to stop him. "What are you doing?" demands the cop.

"I am bringing my cattle with me," replies the distraught farmer.

"No, man. Leave them here. No cattle can go. Only people and possessions," snaps the man in the light blue uniform with the gun at his side.

Mpshe cannot believe what is happening. The wealth he has carefully built up over the years, the days he has spent herding his animals, the fields he has painstakingly tilled—it is all being dashed before his eyes. Then he notices white farmers from Ventersdorp beginning to swarm, like vultures over an ailing beast. He knows these men: they are neighbors with whom he occasionally does business. They have come to do business one last time—on their terms.

Lieb Niemand strolls over to Mpshe and, scowling, scans the herd. "I'll give you R 35 ($28) for that one," he says with an air of disinterest.

"But *meneer*," Mpshe protests, motioning strenuously, "these cattle are worth R 350 each!" Niemand shrugs with annoyance and starts walking away. The sound of trucks revving their engines softens the frantic black farmer. Another white farmer, the brother of local neo-Nazi zealot Eugene Terre'Blanche, is also surveying the herd. "Ja man, I'll give you R 35 each. Take it or leave it."

The first convoy of trucks begins rumbling out. "Okay, okay," says an anxious Mpshe. He motions for Niemand to come back. He thrusts his empty hands toward the white farmers. Niemand buys one cow and Terre'Blanche's brother walks away with the rest. Mpshe hastily stuffs the R 1,225 ($980) in bills into his pocket. He can't bring himself to thank them.

It is the end of Mpshe's life as a farmer. Tears well in his eyes as he walks away. The forlorn sounds of his cattle linger behind him.

The Boers kept their promise. Mogopa was plucked from its rural tranquillity on the fields around Ventersdorp and declared a "black spot" in an area reserved for whites. Prime Minister P. W. Botha had given orders for the community to be moved to "alternative accommodations" near the arid "independent homeland" of Bophuthatswana. Preparations for this day had begun in June 1983, when government bulldozers razed Mogopa's primary school, two churches, and several houses. An ultimatum followed: the village was to be vacated by November 29, 1983.[1]

Mogopa's elders refused to go quietly. Unlike some black communities, Mogopa was a stable and modestly prosperous farming village. The Bakwena ba Mogopa tribe ("Bakwena" means crocodile, the symbol of their tribe) had purchased two fertile farms, Swartrand and Hartebeestlaagte, in 1912 and 1931, respectively. The first settlers were farm laborers from the Orange Free State who bought the farms with savings from the sale of some of their cattle. The community grew to be home to some six hundred families by the early 1980s. People lived in sturdy permanent homes made from the rust-colored stones of the surrounding veld. The village grew most of its own food and was largely self-sufficient.

The Mogopa people defied the government removal order and appealed to church leaders for help. Instead of leaving on November 29, the Mogopa people held a vigil on their land with Bishop Desmonddal Tutu, Rev. Allan Boesak, Rev. Beyers Naude, and a coterie of local and foreign journalists. The authorities declined to provide a photo opportunity that day. Instead, the government resorted to a well-honed tactic: waiting. The community mistook this reticence for victory—they were farmers, after all, not seasoned activists. They spent R 15,000 ($12,400) of their own money to rebuild the primary school in December 1983, and they replaced the water pumps that had been destroyed.

When the police and moving trucks showed up on February 14, 1984, the community was taken completely by surprise. The people of Mogopa had postponed their fate, but they couldn't avert it.

The government was careful to insist that nobody was being forced to leave; this was strictly a "voluntary removal." That explained why the cops had turned out ninety-strong and had sealed off the area to the outside world, temporarily declaring Mogopa an "operational zone." Children were thrown willy-nilly onto trucks along with furniture. The rationale was that hysterical parents would then leave the community to find their kids. "Voluntarily," of course.

One policeman was more forthright about the nature of Mogopa's voluntarism. Major A. Scheepers of the special police task force sent to oversee the eviction parroted the line about "voluntary removals." However, he added, "If they don't want to move, we'll just take them."[2]

It is late afternoon in September 1996 when I carefully maneuver my car across the rock-strewn, green veld. I am startled when a springbok sud-

denly bounds across my path. Meercats dart to and fro across the landscape. The encounters remind me of the name of this farm: Hartebeestlaagte, or "antelope plain." Off in the distance I see a small procession of
slow-moving vehicles. As I approach, I make out three large, red tractors.
Two are pulling harvesters, while the third strains to convey a large wag-
onload of people. Men and women bob up and down in the wagon on the
lurching ride. I bring up the rear of the parade.

A distinct gold line on the horizon marks our destination. An emerald
green carpet gives way to the deep brown furrows of a mealie field. Our
procession comes to a halt, and fifteen men and women climb down
from the wagon. A chilly winter breeze blows across the veld. Matthew
Mpshe is dressed in a long overcoat and a knit hat. He smiles broadly as
I approach, removing his hat and dipping his head deferentially as he extends his leathery hand. I am surprised that he remembers me from my
last visit here, six years earlier.

Matthew motions proudly to the fields. At fifty-seven, he still has an
erect gait and strong wiry limbs. He is a gentle, soft-spoken man who
breaks easily into a wide toothy smile. "We are harvesting three hundred
acres of mealies. It is our first big harvest since the removal. We will have
plenty food this year!" he beams.

The notorious uprooting of the Mogopa people in 1984 was to be the
last major forced removal in South Africa. In 1989 the Bakwena ba Mogopa "illegally" reoccupied their lands, becoming the first dispossessed
people to return. Their stubborn refusal to sacrifice their birthright became
a powerful symbol of rural resistance to apartheid. They inspired other
communities to undertake similar land seizures.

The gold light of afternoon illuminates the mealie fields as the noisy
harvesters grind their way across. Matthew cannot talk for long; he must
continue harvesting until nightfall. The farmers are eager to get their
maize to market.

I head over to the village of Mogopa, which is about a mile from the
mealie fields. The rubble of hundreds of homes remains strewn on the
ground, an enduring reminder of the cataclysm that befell the community.
In place of the beautiful old stone houses, metal shacks have now risen up
from the rubble. It is a sad juxtaposition of poverty rising from the ruins
of wealth.

As I emerge from my car, a flock of chirping schoolgirls passes by. They are dressed in their school uniforms, a black jumper and white shirt. The girls are returning home from school, a handsome structure that sits on a knoll overlooking the countryside. I stroll around and take in a boisterous soccer game that is under way. A team from Mogopa is playing against a team from Goedgevonden, another nearby settlement that was forcibly removed and has now returned.

I am moved by these scenes: it all looks breathtakingly . . . normal. The sad saga of what happened here, seared into the landscape on every smashed foundation, suddenly recedes. Mogopa, for a moment, is just another rural village teeming with life. It is just as the villagers prophesied on the day they were driven from their ancestral lands: the Bakwena ba Mogopa would return.

Land. It is easily the most emotive issue in South Africa. In rural areas, land is a lifeline. Who owns the land, who profits from it, who was there first, and who are the rightful heirs to it—these have been South Africa's most hotly contested issues since the arrival of whites in 1652.

To the farmers of Mogopa, the land is imbued with spiritual as well as economic power: "Land is bucks. Land is money and it is life," says farmer Andrew Pooe, who, with Matthew Mpshe, is a member of Mogopa's agriculture committee. "Everything comes from the land."

Land has also been a potent weapon in South Africa. African land ownership was being steadily restricted by the turn of the century. But it took the far-reaching Land Acts of 1913 and 1936 to formally dispossess blacks on an unprecedented scale. The Land Acts stripped Africans of their right to own land outside of prescribed native reserves, the forerunners of Verwoerd's Bantustans. The acts also banned sharecropping, in which African farmers could cultivate lands owned by absentee white landowners. Eighty-seven percent of the population was suddenly confined to 12 percent of South Africa's landmass. As African writer Sol Plaatje observed, "Awakening on Friday morning, 20 June, 1913, the South African native found himself, not actually a slave, but a pariah in the land of his birth."[3]

The Land Acts were intended to definitively resolve two vexing problems for white settlers: the shortage of wage labor needed to expand agriculture and industry, and the competition posed to whites by successful African farmers. In spite of the legal impediments being cast in their way, African peasants had been modestly prosperous right into the early twentieth century. Indeed, most Africans living in Transkei and Zululand did not need much money, since they were self-sufficient agriculturalists. In the 1890s, most of the Transkei was producing a food surplus.[4]

The Land Acts were a knockout blow to the African peasantry. The native reserves quickly became desperately overcrowded. By the 1920s, many of the reserves could barely support farming. Over one-fifth of African children died within their first year in the reserves. Less than a third of the children received any schooling. As Africans became increasingly destitute, they were forced to seek low-paying work on white farms and in the cities.

When the National Party came to power in 1948, it stepped up forced removals as a way to quickly realize its dream of total racial separation. Removals came to be the most notorious and destructive of all apartheid strategies. It was a program that systematically transformed wealth into poverty. "It reduced us to beggars," says Andrew Pooe of his once self-sufficient community.

About four million black South Africans have been forcibly removed from their homes since 1948—about one-fifth of the population.* The goal was to create a white republic run by Afrikaners with, as former cabinet minister Connie Mulder proclaimed, "no more black South Africans." What followed was "one of the most ambitious and widespread examples of social engineering in recent history."[5]

The pace of forced removals picked up steadily during the fifties. South African industry was growing and the demand for cheap labor intensified. Gold output doubled during the decade.[6] White agriculture, heavily subsidized by the National Party government, was also expanding rapidly. Both of these sectors desperately needed laborers; the unemployed and dispossessed victims of removals were cheap and compliant candidates.

Prime Minister H. F. Verwoerd accelerated the pace of forced removals

---

* Estimates vary as to the total number of people affected by forced removals. In 1983, the Surplus Peoples Project published a widely quoted report which estimated that 3.5 million people had been forcibly removed between 1960 and 1983. A 1986 study at Stellenbosch University determined that at least 4 million people had been forcibly removed since 1948. Unterhalter notes that "the true figure may be almost double this" (Elaine Unterhalter, *Forced Removal: The Division, Segregation and Control of the People of South Africa* [London, 1987], 3).

dramatically in the 1960s. He demarcated swatches of the country destined to be black homelands, and identified numerous "black spots" of freehold land within "white areas." The immunity enjoyed by places like Mogopa, and the Cape Town neighborhood of District Six with its multiracial population of fifty-five thousand people, suddenly became vulnerable to the whims of racist bureaucrats.

Economics remained the driving force behind forced removals. The 1960s witnessed unprecedented economic expansion: the size of the manufacturing workforce increased 63 percent during the decade.[7] Rural removals were further catalyzed by the expansion of the commercial farming sector. Political and economic imperatives coincided neatly in the drive to create a larger class of acquiescent low-wage laborers.

Matthew Mpshe's father worked as a tenant farmer in the Orange Free State and saved his meager earnings year after year. The elder Mpshe set out with other members of the Bakwena ba Mogopa tribe in 1912 to find land where the community could settle and farm independently. They found their slice of heaven in the rural western Transvaal, part of South Africa's fertile heartland. Along with other farmers, Mpshe's father sold off part of his cattle herd to fund the purchase. They took title to a four-thousand-acre farm known as Swartrand ("black land") that same year, outside the small farming community of Ventersdorp. It was a fortuitous time to buy: the Natives' Land Act would have prohibited the sale just a year later. But the tribe had obtained legal title to the land, so they were safe—for the moment.

The Bakwena ba Mogopa steadily increased their numbers at Swartrand. They continued to move from the Orange Free State twenty and thirty families at a time, and each family was given a plot of farmland by the tribal headman. By the early thirties, the community population had swelled to several hundred families. In 1931 the tribe purchased an adjoining 3,800-acre farm called Hartebeestlaagte. Now the community would have all the land it needed to sustain itself.

Like most black farmers in South Africa, the Bakwena ba Mogopa practiced subsistence farming. Each family plowed its own fields with machinery drawn by cattle. Some families only produced food for home consumption, while others harvested enough to be able to sell excess crops through the local agricultural co-op. The community consistently produced a surplus of food. The extra income it earned was used to purchase cattle, tractors, and other farm equipment. The community also invested in communal property, such as a water supply, school buildings, and a clinic.

The Mogopa school was a particular source of pride. The school served children from a number of surrounding black farm communities, and students could attend classes all the way through high school. Mogopa became an anchor for the scattered population of black farmers and laborers in the area. This was achieved without loans or subsidies from the government.[8]

The key to Mogopa's viability was its mixed economy. Families combined subsistence farming with a cash income from migrant labor. Teenage children would help cultivate the family fields, but as young adults they would often move away to take jobs in the towns and cities. The income that they would send home funded the schools, equipment, and other infrastructure. In late middle age, many of these migrant laborers would return to Mogopa to pursue full-time farming. When they were too old to farm, they would lease their fields to others who would sharecrop, thereby ensuring a supply of mealies, beans, and other staples. It was a system that both fostered and relied on tight social cohesion. Even during drought times, this mixed economy proved resilient enough to sustain the community.[9]

Interdependence was a necessity on the farms. The community was divided into *kgoros,* or clans, which would work together during labor-intensive periods such as planting or harvesting, when virtually everyone was involved in farming. Growing mealie, sunflower, and beans was combined with rearing livestock for meat and dairy products.

"There was no hunger," confirms Mpshe as we walk through Mogopa's reinvigorated mealie fields. "They had good sufficient food in that time." Corn stalks crackle underfoot as we traverse the long furrows. He periodically picks up a mealie and peels back the husk to check its color. "Unlike when we were removed from Mogopa, there was no hunger here.

"I would look after the cattle and sheeps for my father," recounts Mpshe, who was born in 1940 in Mogopa. "There was a school here, and I went to school until standard six [equivalent to the American eighth grade] in 1956." Some other boys left Mogopa to work in Johannesburg or on the mines, but as his father's only son, Matthew was needed at home. "I stayed at home here doing that small farming, plowing with cattle, growing mealies and beans. I didn't want to go somewhere else," he insists. "Because this land is very fertile for us. You can *live* on it.

"In the city," he continues, "everything you have to eat or do is *mon-ey*. Here, money is important, but it not so important like in the big city. Because here once you got food, that's the *most* important thing. You don't pay rent, you don't pay for water, and things like that."

Contact with white people was minimal in the early years of Mogopa. But as the surrounding white farms grew into commercial operations, the demand for seasonal laborers increased. A symbiotic relationship developed between the black and white farmers in the Ventersdorp area. "We used to work as tenant laborers there in the harvest," says Mpshe. "They used to come and take us to go and help them harvest, paying us that little money. So the contact was good."

Matthew eventually inherited his father's fields and became a successful farmer in his own right. Cattle are the measure of a man's success in the villages. With thirty-five head of cattle by the 1980s, Matthew was viewed as a man of some means and was respected as a community leader. Little did he suspect that his modest wealth and lifestyle were about to be wiped out by the stroke of a pen in Pretoria.

Administration in Mogopa, as in many African villages, rested with a traditional leader known as a headman or chief. These leaders come to their jobs in a variety of ways. Some inherit the title, while others are elected by the community. Under apartheid, these traditional leaders were often appointed by the white officials who were charged with administering black affairs, such as a local magistrate. The system of traditional leaders thus became vulnerable to manipulation. Headmen were often beholden to those who paid them and were easily coerced or bribed into doing the white man's bidding. By the 1980s, corruption and duplicity were rampant among traditional leaders. In the case of Mogopa, the headman was so malleable that he was persuaded to annihilate his community.

Jacob More was elected headman of Mogopa in the late seventies. Each community member contributed to tribal funds, which were to be spent on communal property such as the schools and the water supply. More was responsible for overseeing the tribe's funds and accounting for all income and expenses. He had no authority to allocate land.

Beginning in the mid-1970s, a number of black farm communities around Ventersdorp were forcibly removed. In 1980, rumors began flying that the government wanted Mogopa's land. Government officials would periodically come and threaten the community with removal, only to be swiftly dispatched by the tribe's leaders. But the community was left with a growing feeling of insecurity. Anger focused on Jacob More as the tribe began to suspect he was misusing funds. He was accused of charging residents for services that were previously free, such as processing pension applications and labor contracts. When asked to open the tribal accounting books, he refused.

In September 1981, the tribe voted to depose More. He was accused of "corruption and failing to respond to tribal discipline."[10] But it fell to a local "native commissioner" in Ventersdorp—in this case a white magistrate—to approve the community decision. The magistrate refused.

"I as a white man and magistrate of this whole area say Jacob More will rule until he dies," he declared.[11] His remark caused an uproar in Mogopa, but he was technically correct. Under apartheid, the prime minister (and later, state president) was the "Paramount Chief" of all blacks. As his agent, the magistrate was within his powers to govern local black affairs at his whim.

The Mogopa people did manage to persuade local authorities to convene a Commission of Inquiry into More's financial dealings. Hundreds of people testified over several weeks. At the end of the hearings, government officials arrived not with a verdict, but with a shocking ultimatum: the people of Mogopa would have to move. It was a "black spot" in a "white area," something that could not be tolerated. None other than their "chief," Jacob More, had already agreed to this.

In the succeeding months, officials from the Department of Cooperation and Development (the perversely named government agency in charge of black affairs in the 1980s) met secretly with a planning committee made up of the deposed headman and his cronies. Attempts to force the committee to hold open meetings were unsuccessful. These negotiations culminated in the first stage of the forced removal.

In June 1983, Matthew Mpshe and his neighbors awoke to the sound of bulldozers rumbling through their village. They watched in horror as the machines descended on their beloved village landmarks: first to go were the two stone churches, next were the primary and secondary schools, and last were some houses. The village water pumps were destroyed for good measure. What had taken years to create was destroyed in moments, done with the blessings of the "chief."

Jacob More and his "planning committee" then moved to Pachsdraai, a compound of empty white farmhouses in the nearby homeland of Bophuthatswana. More took the main farmhouse and allocated the other houses to his cohorts. The doors, window frames, and roofing material from the smashed Mogopa buildings were stored in a shed in his yard. About a dozen families moved with him. The rest of the village refused to leave.

This was the time-tested divide-and-rule tactic of the apartheid regime. A willing accomplice is identified among the populace, often through bribery or intimidation. Sham "negotiations" are then held, and a small cadre of followers is brought in to rubber-stamp the deals with the government. The community is left bitterly divided, and infighting replaces unity. The government then moves in and, with the "legitimacy" conferred on it by its collaborators, does what it likes. The ensuing denunciations are dismissed as the sniping of malcontents.

These pretenses of democracy may seem like a lot of trouble to go to when the result is going to be universally condemned anyway. But there was a warped logic to this. Prime Minister P. W. Botha had announced with great fanfare in 1983 that South Africa was on the path to "reform." A new constitution giving limited voting rights to Indians and coloreds had been enacted. Forced removals were over; communities would only be removed "voluntarily" now. The appearance of consent was thus crucial, if only to help maintain the self-delusion of the perpetrators.

It didn't quite go according to plan in Mogopa. Instead of following Jacob More, most of the community decided to remain and fight. The June 1983 attack on their village only stiffened the resolve of the people. The community rallied South African churches, press, and foreign dignitaries to its side. And so the November 1983 deadline passed without incident. But unbeknownst to the villagers, they had only won a ten-week stay of execution: February 14, 1984, was the official start of their nightmare.

As Lieb Niemand's trucks hauled away people's worldly possessions and bulldozers leveled their homes to rubble, the fragile social fabric of the seventy-two-year-old community was rent apart.

Most of the Mogopa families refused to go to Pachsdraai, where Jacob More had ensconced himself. Instead, people opted to resettle several hours away in the small town of Bethanie, where they knew the local chief. Bethanie was little more than a squatter camp of metal shacks and pit toilets. Farming was impossible on its sandy soil.

"There was no job. There was nothing. We just sitting there," recounts Mpshe. "Even the neighboring whites, you couldn't work for the lousy wages, because there was no neighbor that can hire people."

The community's losses were catastrophic. The lucky ones sold their livestock for a tenth of its value. Others failed to escape even with that, losing their entire herds in the confusion of the move. Samuel Lebethe, Mogopa's most successful farmer, left a nine-room house and seven cultivated fields behind. The value of his crops alone was worth more than $7,260, the token amount that the government compensated him for his loss. Lebethe says that Lieb Niemand helped himself to his crops in his absence. The looting and theft of Mogopa's property by local farmers was staggering.

The psychological blow of the removal was even more devastating. When I ask Mogopa farmer Andrew Pooe about the effect of the removal, he is at first unable to talk to me about it—twelve years later. Pooe is a bright, thoughtful young man, a key figure in the committee that fought for Mogopa's return. Finally, he says, "I can only describe that feeling like bringing up a child, when you have got to see the fruits of all your labors, seeing him being on his own, building his own family. And suddenly he dies, he was murdered. Your life becomes destroyed just at the wink of an eye." He snaps his fingers to emphasize the suddenness. "Then you understand what it's like. You are very helpless, frustrated at the system itself, the people at the wheel," he says, shaking his head slowly and stroking his short goatee. "It was really sad. Really bad."

The Mogopa removal caused a furor at home and abroad. In parliament, veteran liberal MP Helen Suzman accused Cabinet Minister F. W. de Klerk of lying for having reported that there were no schools in the village, and for referring to Mogopa's titleholders as "squatters." Deputy Minister of Development and Land Affairs Ben Wilkins shot back that "people who had been resettled had written to the department thanking it for the kind way in which they had been treated."[12] He accused Suzman, "The reason why they don't want to go [to Pachsdraai] is because you indoctrinate them not to go."[13] Even the Reagan administration, a sympathetic ally of the apartheid regime, was moved to summon the South

African ambassador to the State Department and file a formal protest.[14]

The Bakwena began fighting back immediately. With the help of the Transvaal Rural Action Committee and the South African Council of Churches, they filed a lawsuit charging that the removal was illegal. They won the case in September 1985 and prepared to move back. But the government was determined to crush these farmers once and for all. It expropriated their land before they could move, claiming that Pachsdraai represented fair compensation. When the tribe later protested the squalid conditions in Bethanie, the government offered to resettle them yet again, this time in Onderstepoort, a town about an hour from Mogopa. Many people agreed to the move in the vain hope that they might be able to begin farming there.

All the machinations simply confirmed to the old farmers that there was only one solution to their problems. "The very same day when we were removed, we vowed that we would return," recounts Andrew Pooe. In 1989, having exhausted all legal remedies, Mpshe, Pooe, and other community leaders hatched a plan. They sent a request to the government asking to return temporarily to Mogopa to clean the graves of their ancestors. A bureaucrat approved the request, thinking little of it.

"They fell right in the net!" exclaims Pooe, clapping his hands and laughing.

I first see the stones, the ruins. Stretching off into the horizon are orderly rust-colored mounds that form the rocky silhouettes of houses. Long dirt roads to nowhere connect these phantom homesteads. It is like entering an archaeological site of a civilization that lived centuries ago, or as if a great natural disaster transpired here, driving away all the people in a panicked flight for life. Which indeed is what happened. This is Mogopa, September 1990.

Plunked down amid the detritus are shanties made from scraps of wood and metal. The shiny sheets of steel glint in the harsh midday sun. On close examination, I can see from the foundations of the smashed houses that these homes were elaborate structures made from hand-cut stone. They took years to construct. No one I meet has the energy or the resources to re-create what was lost. But they are not deterred. Like a phoenix rising, the shacks symbolize the stubborn reclamation of their birthright.

I find Daniel Molefe, Matthew Mpshe, and Andrew Pooe sitting in the shade of one of the shanties. They are the core members of the Mogopa Community Committee, the farmers who are leading the charge to save their village. Beginning in December 1989, the community hired trucks to transport groups of people back to Mogopa, ostensibly to clean the graves of their relatives. The police in Onderstepoort insisted they had no right to return.

"We just told them we are going back home," recounts Molefe, a farmer in his late fifties. "You can't stop us."

As the trucks rolled through the surrounding towns toward Mogopa that first day in December 1989, Matthew Mpshe and his neighbors grew more excited. Finally, they turned into the familiar bumpy dirt road that led to their old homesteads. Mpshe quickly set out on a walk around his village. He was stoic as he surveyed the wreckage; other people wept from the bittersweet mix of joy at their return and anguish at the loss.

"I dreamed all my ancestors that night. Because I didn't believe that I can come back and sleep on this ground, in this village, again," says Matthew.

As we sit on chairs in the dirt, Daniel Molefe speaks for his fellow farmers. "I am not afraid of the Boers because the land belongs to me and to my grandfather who bought the land for me. The community is moving no more. You can arrest us, you can put us in jail, you can kill us. But we shall be happy we died on our own land."

Once it began, the tide of returnees couldn't be stopped. Within months of the first arrivals, some 250 families—over one thousand people—came back to their land. They started cleaning the overgrown graveyard, but that was just a ruse: they had no intention of leaving again. A month after their return, President de Klerk released Nelson Mandela from jail and began repealing the most odious apartheid laws. He declared that there would be no more removals. The Bakwen ba Mogopa called de Klerk's bluff: evicting them again would be tantamount to another forced removal.

"We tricked them!" declares Mpshe with an impish smile.

I ask what is so important about the graves. Andrew Pooe, who at age thirty is one of the younger men to return, explains. He speaks perfect English, a legacy of working as a computer operator on the gold mines in the early eighties. The mining company targeted him for his union activism and laid him off.

"There are times when you encounter some problems throughout your life. That is why sometimes someone says, 'I dreamt my grandfather or grandmother giving me some instructions.' Then it is the norm that maybe you go to his grave and pay homage. It's our culture . . . That's why people don't want to bury their dead far away. Because they want to visit the graveyard on a periodical basis."

Matthew Mpshe adds, "All my generations are buried here: my grandfather, mother, sister, my niece. My mother died in 1986 while we were in Bethanie. We came to bury her here."

I join Matthew on a walk through the village. He takes me to visit the metal-sided clinic that the returning villagers have rebuilt, and introduces me to the health care worker whose training the community has helped pay for.

Later we stroll up to the school. It was destroyed not once, but twice. The first demolition was in June 1983 at Jacob More's behest. In December 1983, Matthew supervised the construction of a new school. It was destroyed in the February 1984 removal.

Matthew runs his hands over the rough surface of the cinder-block building. The empty window frames open onto spacious views of the surrounding fields. One of the first actions the people took upon their return in early 1990 was to reconstruct this school. It was for the children, the symbol of Mogopa's future. In just seven days, the community erected everything but the roof. The government, realizing that the Bakwena were resettling, abruptly ordered them to stop. The de Klerk regime might not be willing to oust them, but they would at least try to make life difficult. The half-finished school reopened in February 1990 in a joyous celebration, the students temporarily attending classes in the open air. The discomfort was a small price to pay for the privilege of being back home.

Matthew pauses among the classrooms to reflect on the rationale for the community's removal. Their land had simply been used by local farmers for livestock grazing during their exile. "They expropriated this land for their cattle," he says softly, shaking his head incredulously. "I don't think cattle are better than people."

We walk over to where his home stood. Only the foundation of the comfortable five-room stone house remains. "Here was the kitchen, and that room is where my wife and I lived. My parents stayed there. We had a very nice view here . . . " It was bulldozed six years earlier, but he still falls silent as he contemplates the loss.

Driving into Mogopa in September 1996, I immediately notice the gleam of sunlight reflected on a shiny metal roof. I bounce along the main dirt road of the village to investigate and pass several newly constructed water tanks, which provide water to most of the residents. A sign greets me at the first house: "Bakwena Bakery Welcomes You!" The smell of fresh bread hangs in the air.

I pass the bakery and move on to admire a large, new community hall and clinic that has been erected. Beyond that is the giant equipment shed whose roof I spied from afar. Inside, a group of men, surrounded by an impressive array of farm machinery, including a large combine harvester, rolls of fencing, and three tractors, are hunched over a tractor wheel they are repairing. The farmers of Mogopa are once again plying their trade.

Small children run around on the dirt byways of the village. I walk over to the school. It is a handsome brick structure, long since completed. I peer inside and find it packed with students reciting their lessons. Two hastily erected shacks have already arisen in the schoolyard to accommodate the overflow of students.

From the haunting ghost town I saw six years earlier, the trappings of normal life have now crept in. The village landscape is still dominated by the ruins of old homes. But there are also attempts at new construction. A Mogopa resident who is a Soweto taxi driver has erected two modern ranch homes; the neatly painted houses are conspicuous among the shacks. Several families are reconstructing their stone homes. It is a painstakingly slow process. Most families satisfy themselves with shelters made of corrugated steel held together by an assortment of wood and wire.

I can't resist the smell of the bakery, so I step inside. Thirty-five-year-old Emily Hector is a large woman, one of four bakers. "Because of our removal, we are the poor," she tells me. She pauses to pull out four loaves of freshly baked brown bread. The bakery produces forty loaves per day, and 120 packets of cookies. The goods are sold in Mogopa's *spazas,* or small shops. She is lucky: she has one of the few jobs in Mogopa. But the bakery is struggling. "If not for the removal, we would be very far into the future. But now we are suffering."

After I last visited Mogopa in 1990, the community continued to battle with the National Party government over the return of its lands. The de Klerk government partly relented in 1991, giving them back Swartrand, where their village is located. But they refused to give back 3,800-acre Hartebeestlaagte, which was their productive farmland. Without the latter, they could not hope to support themselves.

On April 28, 1994, the people of Mogopa cast votes in their first national elections at a polling station in their school. On August 13, 1994, President Mandela's new land affairs minister, Derek Hanekom, stepped from his car in Mogopa to address the community. He was greeted warmly, a first for a government official here. Hanekom, a former land rights activist and a farmer, was intimately familiar with what happened at Mogopa. He declared to a joyous community the news they had fought for a decade to hear: "The land is yours!"[15] He then made a special request: he asked to be invited back to drive the tractor when Mogopa plowed its first furrow of land. The long exile of the Bakwena ba Mogopa was officially over.

Some 350 families have returned to live in Mogopa today. Minister Hanekom kept his promise and sat atop a noisy ancient tractor on the day in 1995 when the Mogopa farmers planted their first row of sunflowers. Around that same time, Mogopa and several other resettled black farm communities in the Ventersdorp area were designated a Presidential Lead Project (PLP), making it a priority development scheme for the new government. The PLP allocated $733,000 to resettle the communities. In Mogopa the money is being spent on a number of infrastructure improvements, including water taps all around the village, a new secondary school, electricity, phone service, and improvements to the village road.

Farming—the time-tested mainstay of the community—has been a notable success story in the reinvigorated village. Mogopa is nearing the end of a one-year agricultural pilot project to "kick start" its farming operation. Agricultural extension officers have worked closely with the community in advising them on cultivating 741 acres of mealies. I have arrived for Mogopa's first major harvest since its removal. By the end of the week, they will have harvested six hundred tons of mealies, enough to give every family a half-ton of ground maize—an eighteen-month supply of food.

There is even enough mealie left over to sell; the Mogopa farmers estimate they will earn about $60,000, which they will invest in next season's agricultural operation.

The meeting with government officials in September 1996 begins like countless others that have been held in Mogopa. Indeed, it seems like Mogopa has been in one long meeting for the past decade. But this one is different.

First, there is the venue itself. People are gathered in the gleaming modern community hall that sits proudly in the center of the village. It was built not with foreign aid or church donations, but with funds provided by the local municipality. Guilt money, perhaps, but it signifies another milestone of normalcy: the formerly white town is including Mogopa in its routine infrastructure expenses. Never mind that Mogopa wanted a clinic and a school more than a community hall; it is now a well-used fixture of daily life, and the community uses part of the hall as a clinic.

Then there is the dynamic between officialdom and the assembled guests. Facing the audience are two black representatives from the government's Reconstruction and Development Program (RDP), two white general contractors, and a black engineering consultant. Job creation is an RDP priority, and the group is discussing how to hire local men to dig trenches for water pipes throughout the village.

Tom Wanakwanyi, a Ugandan-born consulting engineer, explains to them, "In the past, we would just bring someone from Klerksdorp to do the job. But not now in the new South Africa. We want to give the work to local people." Manfred, a white contractor, asks the Mogopa men if they have a tape measure, picks, and shovels.

"No," says Peter, the Mogopa crew chief. He wears ripped greasy coveralls and a tattered sweater.

Tom turns to Manfred and orders, "Then you must give him." Manfred shrugs, and consents. He has no choice.

The next day, another meeting is held. This one is to assess how all the resettled black communities in the Ventersdorp area have fared after their first year of farming. The meeting is remarkable for the audience. Throughout the morning, battered old cars and minibus taxis arrive from nearby farms and disgorge the leaders of the various communities. They are veritable combat veterans of the forced removals era. There are the men from Goedgevonden, forcibly removed between 1974 and 1978, "illegally" reclaiming their lands in 1991; Doornkop and Tsetse, both removed in 1978 and formally returned in 1994; Welgevonden, removed in 1978, returned in 1993; and Mogopa, removed in 1984, "illegally" returning in 1989 and formally reinstated in 1994. They represent thousands of shattered lives that are now tenuously rebuilding.

The history of this small area is etched deeply on the faces of the twenty-seven black farmers who have gathered here. There is Mogopa elder Daniel Molefe, clad in thickly insulated coveralls and worn white sneakers. Matthew Mpshe, his shiny bald head emerging from his stained lemon yellow coveralls, listens intently with hands clasped together as if in prayer. Red earth clings to everyone's feet.

At the start of the meeting, Mpshe walks silently forward and plunks down a fistful of mealies on the table in front of the government officials. The simple action grounds the meeting in reality.

The officials are relaxed and informal. For the first time, the skin color of the government representatives and the audience is the same. They speak in Tswana, a language common to all. An air of respectfulness pervades. People rise one at a time to speak. They address one another as "brother" or "father" in the traditional African style. Periodic laughter breaks the solemnity of the meeting.

Malakia Matlhabe, resettlement program manager from the North West Province, rises to explain the results of the pilot agricultural project. In addition to receiving tractors, implements, and an equipment shed, Mogopa was granted $183,000 for crop production and a vegetable plot. "Priority number one is food security at a household level," explains Matlhabe.

Matlhabe tells me later that other communities were hamstrung by internal conflicts, but that Mogopa "was a model." "The Mogopa people wanted to do more than what we did," he says. "They feel that the government departments are holding them back. We say start with planting 420 acres; they say 'we want to plant 1,235 acres.'" (When I return in March 1997, I learn that Mogopa has planted 890 acres of crops for the next harvest.)

The group makes plans for a ceremony the next week where it will receive checks for the surplus crops that it sells. The provincial minister of agriculture will attend, and the assembled men decide they will slaughter a goat in celebration. The meeting closes with a prayer: "We are thankful for the fruitful meeting, and ask God to bless everyone here, and make their way safe wherever they go."

Mogopa is rich in poignant symbols of rebirth and recovery. But if it is a "model" of development for the post-apartheid era, it does not bode well. Despite being the focus of extraordinary government attention, development efforts have been slow, bumbling, and at times self-defeating.

At the end of the first year of the three-year Presidential Lead Project, the pace of development is agonizingly slow. Myriad officials from various government ministries visit each week, making ever grander promises about upgrading Mogopa. But by March 1997, no nonagricultural project had come to fruition.

There is, for example, the saga of the Mogopa school. The existing school building that was erected in 1990 is already hopelessly overcrowded, as evidenced by the shack classrooms that have sprung up. In 1995, the provincial department of education informed the community that funds had been approved to construct a new school. The community quickly drew up plans. Two years later, there is still no new school. Similarly, the government promised funding for new houses soon after the 1994 election. Three years later, not one government-subsidized house has been built in Mogopa. Water pipes and extra taps were installed, but the pipes leak. The government water ministry insists its job is done, and says Mogopa is responsible for fixing the defective pipes. But Mogopa has no money for the repairs. So the taps are dry.

I hear numerous explanations for the problems and delays. They range from confusion between the new government departments, hostility and inefficiency of the old civil service, to the inevitable birth pangs of start-up ventures. The excuses don't soften the consequences: with the exception of farming, little has changed in the life of the Mogopa community.

"I never expected that this bureaucracy would be the same as the National Party—it is moving *very* slowly," laments Andrew Pooe. "The people are going to lose confidence in the government. People don't want promises, they want delivery." It is a plea I hear repeatedly throughout South Africa.

The community itself also bears blame for some of its failures. The Bakwena Bakery that I visit in September 1996 is gone when I return in March 1997. I'm told that when its donor money ran out, the bakery collapsed. Andrew hints that some bakery money may have been misused by community members.

Then there is the sad and bizarre story of the community garden. The provincial agriculture department built an impressive irrigated vegetable garden in 1995 that was intended to supply much of the community's produce. But some community members insisted that the government should pay them to work there. The authorities declined to pay people for working on a self-help scheme. So the garden failed. When I saw it in early 1997, the large plot with modern irrigation was overrun with weeds and hadn't been used in a year.

I am left with two contradictory images of Mogopa. One is heartwarming: the scene of the farmers returning to their land, at long last. They have had a bumper crop of maize during my visit, and they are joyous. This is development at its best.

The other image is one of despair: promises of help that are made and not kept. A community that remains demoralized by a lack of progress. Once self-reliant villagers who have become dependent on aid handouts, to the point that they are unwilling to work for themselves. And social problems that run so deep in the community that people are often unable to lift themselves up even when given the chance.

Development in Mogopa remains a case of one step forward, one step back. For every problem solved, an equally burning problem remains unaddressed. Such is the quandary posed by trying to unmake apartheid's most enduring legacy: poverty.

Mogopa's difficulties mirror those of South Africa at large. Land reform was singled out as a priority initiative of the ANC government. Whites controlled 86 percent of cultivable land, while comprising about one-eighth of the population.[16] During the 1994 election campaign, the ANC promised to redistribute 30 percent of white farmland by 1999 (giving blacks control of only 44 percent of farmland, and thus still preserving white dominance of agriculture);[17] it also promised restitution of land to displaced communities within the same time frame.

The election promises were wildly ambitious, particularly in light of the self-imposed constraints. The new government ruled out wholesale land expropriation from white owners, even when land was unjustly taken in the first place. Instead, the ANC government committed itself to obtaining land at market value on a willing-buyer / willing-seller basis. Critics argue that white landowners are being compensated for theft. The cash-strapped government is now in the process of paying off numerous white landowners.

Another complicating factor in the land reform process is that the new constitution guarantees property rights of existing owners. A land claims court has ultimate responsibility for settling competing claims. This free market approach to land reform prompted Judith Edstrom, the World Bank's South African representative, to observe that the ANC government was less interventionist than the previous government when it came to land reform and fiscal policies.[18]

The most obvious result of the ANC's cautiousness and conservatism is that land reform has been proceeding at a glacial pace. By the end of 1996—halfway into the initial five-year land reform time frame—the government had transferred a mere .4 percent of farmland into black hands. By mid-1998, more than twenty-six thousand land claims had been filed with the Land Claims Court, but only nine claims had been settled.[19] Land Claims commissioner Joseph Seremane acknowledged that it could take up to twenty years to settle the outstanding claims.[20]

Pilot land restitution programs—in which victims of forced removals were either compensated or had their land returned—were nearly invisible. By April 1997, the provinces had only spent 6 percent of the funds allocated to the pilot restitution programs; four of the nine provinces had not spent any money at all on restitution.[21]

The government has responded to failure by trying to tamp down expectations. The RDP goal of redistributing 30 percent of farmland by the year 2000 was officially abandoned in late 1996. Instead, the government is now promising to redistribute 18.5 percent of farmland by 2007. The Ministry of Lands and Agriculture concedes that meeting this revised target would still only satisfy 56 percent of South Africa's land hunger. David Cooper, an advisor to the ministry, insists that the original goals were unrealistic. "Nowhere has land reform taken less than twenty years," he now says.[22]

For victims of forced removals, the end of apartheid was merely the beginning of a long journey to justice.

The lively beat of township jive wafts into the night from the large metal shack which serves as one of Mogopa's *shebeens*. I duck my head to enter and find myself in a dimly lit room with a round table and a tinny radio at full blast. A young girl scoots back and forth to a propane-powered refrigerator, where the stock of lukewarm pints of Lion Lagers is kept. In the next room, a group of old men are sipping beer and singing African spirituals.

Matthew Mpshe is already at the table having a glass of beer. He is joined by Andrew Pooe, and they are relaxing and joking after the long day of harvesting mealies. It is a good crop, and they are feeling upbeat.

"We fight for Mogopa for many things," declares Matthew. "Like today we have plowed, we have lands, we got food, and we can have food and more money for the future. So we can make a living next year." His voice is soft, periodically fading beneath the din of the music.

I ask Matthew about the lasting effects of their experience. The warm flicker of the yellow lantern reflects in his large brown eyes. His head has a dull shine from the sweat of the day's labor. "That removal destroyed the whole entire community's life. We been delayed by that removal," he says.

Matthew reflects that people have lost both past and future wealth. "I was having more than thirty-five cattle and I sell them [at] the peanuts price. Today I don't have any cattle, sheep, whatever. From 1984 to this time, the thirty-five cattle should have calves, and I should have nearly two hundred cattle. One cattle now goes for nearly R 2,000 ($435). So I could be a rich somebody!" We quickly calculate that his thirty-five cattle would be worth over $15,000 today. It is an unimaginable fortune to him. He shakes his head in disbelief.

Mpshe reflects on how the children of Mogopa will bear the scars of the removal for their whole lives. "Most of the schoolchildren gave their time and their future—it has been destroyed. Because our children have moved from one place to another place—two to three months, and then they move."

A feeling for the land—the fuel of the long Mogopa struggle—is not innate. It grows on a person. It comes from years of working the soil, understanding its fickle appetite, sensing what makes it thrive. The nine-man agricultural committee is the core group of farmers in the community. They are all older men. At age thirty-six, Andrew Pooe is the youngest member of the committee. The other young men who I see around the village say they are not interested in farming. So they hang out and drink themselves into a daily stupor. Unemployment is rife. Yet Andrew, who used to work on the gold mines, understands the ambivalence that many younger people feel about farming.

"I never before thought that I might be on a tractor, with all the dust on me and all that. This is something that I hated, because I felt that it is a very inferior job to do," he says, gazing intently across the rickety kitchen table that serves as a centerpiece in the *shebeen*. "But I became wiser, looking around and seeing the white farmers doing the job the right way." Andrew saw that he could support himself as a farmer. "You cannot get life out of anything, except on the land." Nevertheless, he adds, farming is not for everyone. "On the farm here, we are not all farmers. Some are plumbers, some might choose to be a teacher, or whatever he wishes."

For Andrew, the return to the land means he will have a chance in the new South Africa. "It's frustrating not knowing where you come from, not knowing where you are, and where you going. But now, there is a 90 percent likelihood that I'm going to have a life where we can have our own future, where we can function. One thing is for sure: we know we have got a future. And our kids, and the next generation, and other generations— the foundation has been laid."

The people begin gathering before dusk. They arrive in small groups, often by minibus taxi. The city folk come in their fancy threads, their high heels, and matching suits. The country folk are cloaked in overcoats, knit hats, and their carefully preserved Sunday best. They mingle in one seamless group.

The people have come to attend a funeral. A twenty-two-year-old woman, Elizabeth Rampou, was killed in a murder-suicide by an irate boyfriend a few days earlier. She was born in Mogopa, and was working as a schoolteacher in Ventersdorp at the time of her death.

Funerals are a major community event in African culture. A person's passing is marked by an all-night vigil of singing, praying, and offering testimonials to the deceased. The family has hired a large tent and set up dozens of chairs to accommodate the guests and relatives who are streaming in steadily from around the region. Some travel eight hours or more to be here. Although Elizabeth Rampou no longer lived in Mogopa, it is to her family's village that she returns in death. She must lie beside her ancestors.

As night falls, the women build a large cooking fire. Big three-legged cast-iron pots are brought out and they commence cooking a huge feast, which will be served to the entire village after the funeral the next morning. A sheep is slaughtered, bags of mealie are emptied, and the women stir the pots with large, wooden paddles. The cooking goes on all night.

Around midnight, Bethuel Rampou, the brother of the deceased, asks if I would accompany him and two other men to the graveyard. By the light of flashlights, Bethuel walks around and points out the headstones of other family members. He ponders briefly where to dig, then scratches into the dirt the outline of a plot. The two men with him then heft pick axes and begin chipping away at the hard ground. A biting wind blows across the fields and cuts through my clothes. Bethuel just stands around and watches, directing the men where to dig. Over the next hour, men appear at the cemetery in ones and twos, materializing like apparitions out of the inky black night. From the two men who began, there are soon twelve. Without asking, they take up shovels and join in the digging.

Over the sound of picks and shovels chipping away at the earth, Bethuel leans over to explain, "The relatives of the dead are not supposed to do this work. The community does it. Everybody knows their roles. That is our tradition."

Bethuel works as a policeman in the nearby town of Koster. Being a cop under apartheid "was very tough" because "we were targets of the community." He says he had to do it "because of financial problems." He hopes to make enough money to be able to quit and become a farmer in Mogopa, like his father.

Bethuel and his family live in the black township outside Ventersdorp now, where his wife works at a racetrack for $50 per month. They are sending their kids to the previously all-white school in Ventersdorp. "We were told that we've got now a new government, there's no more racism. We hope to unite [our children] with the Boers. So we decided to take our children to learn with the white children, maybe to improve their standard of education." But the local whites were not as eager for the multicultural experience: they removed their children from the public schools rather than have them mix with blacks. Only two white children remain in class with Bethuel's kids.

"Apartheid is rooted in their bodies," he says resignedly of the older whites in the area. "Their children are a little bit changing day by day. But not the old ones. They still think that they are superior to blacks." He worries about his children's future, noting that some students have been agitating to boycott school. "We are trying our hardest to let the children have patience with the new government."

How long will change take? "It can take maybe ten years. Maybe our children will live better than us. They can unite better than us."

We return to the night vigil. The casket lies in the center of the room. An all-black girls' choir from the Ventersdorp school is singing a beautiful hymn. There is the air of a New Orleans funeral about all this, as festive celebration mixes with the occasional tearful testimonial. The smell of cooking food hangs in the chill night air. By 2 A.M., I am falling asleep in my chair. Andrew Pooe and I retire to his mother's home, a neat prefab rondavel. We lay mats and blankets on the floor and collapse.

At 7:30 A.M., everyone in Mogopa begins streaming out of their shacks in a long procession to attend the funeral under the family tent. Afterward, the people walk to the cemetery and gather around the freshly dug grave, where they launch into soulful hymns and spirituals. The soaring multipart harmonies would rival a well-rehearsed Baptist choir. The casket is lowered into the ground and the men quickly shovel it under. They top off the grave by pouring cement on it. "It's to prevent grave robbers from digging it up," Bethuel whispers in my ear.

The long procession then reverses and overflows the tent back at the family's home. Neighbors and relatives line up patiently to partake in the feast of mutton, mealie, sweet potato, and cole slaw. The family provides the meal as a customary gesture of thanks for the community's support. Bethuel insists I go to the head of the line and sit with his parents. I protest the special treatment, but he insists that it is an honor for them to have me here. People drift off slowly afterward, some to their shacks, some to the far-off city. But the soul of this far-flung community—its rituals of life and death, its celebrations marking rites of passage—remains in Mogopa.

Lieb Niemand was one of the last white farmers from Ventersdorp that Matthew Mpshe saw as the trucks hauled him away from Mogopa in 1984. And Niemand was one of the first local farmers that Mpshe did business with once Mogopa began farming again in 1995. The community hired Niemand to help with their first harvest of sunflowers, and rented a mechanical planter from him. They paid him $1,000.

"He's trying to be a friend to us," says Mpshe, looking grim-faced. "But

I don't see, because he's a CP [Conservative Party]. I'm sorry to say but . . . he's not my friend."

Andrew peers stonily across the table, obviously agitated by the subject. "He's gaining from that friendship," he snaps. He can barely restrain his anger. He says he was opposed to hiring Niemand because of what he's done in Mogopa. He recounts how Niemand bought eleven cattle from his family as they were being forced out. Niemand paid R 1,100 ($890)—about one-fourth what they were worth.

"We were desperate, and those farmers took advantage of the situation," says Andrew. "And now they complain—they say that we steal their cattle. Ach," he says shaking his head in disgust at the irony. Indeed, I have heard a number of Ventersdorp farmers accuse the Mogopa people of stock theft, although those same farmers would never acknowledge their role in the theft of the Mogopa livestock ten years earlier. It is one of the many burning contradictions and tensions that linger on the land.

I ask Mpshe if any of the white farmers have apologized for what happened. "No one has come here to say sorry, no." He shakes his head from side to side, and is silent for a moment. "At the end of the day, God will deal with them. They must never say to the people of Mogopa 'you must move.' We didn't take *nothing* from [them]," he says.

Is he bitter? "Ya, very much. I'm bit-ta."

"But that does not mean we cannot live with them," Andrew suddenly pipes up. The younger man is angry but philosophical. He is also drinking himself into a reflective stupor as we down glass after glass of beer. The singing in the next room has carried on apace through it all.

"There's one problem that still remains: mistrust," says Andrew. "We are taking efforts to make them not fear . . . What they did to us in the past is not something that we are going to revenge."

Andrew's logic is simple: Mogopa lost many battles but won the war. The nation got democracy; the community won back its land. Bitterness and revenge could cost it that prize. "Some people have got to realize that times have changed. And that to reverse the wheels, it's going to take an effort. We don't want to find ourselves [like] Rwanda, Mozambique, and Angola . . . Let us just rebuild the country and keep it for the other generations. Let us live side by side."

Do you forgive them? Andrew and Matthew peer at me through the dim yellow lantern light. Matthew answers first. "We have to *forgive* that

[they] are part and parcel of that forced removal. It is part of that truth and reconciliation," he says. He is echoing his national obligation, as ordained by President Mandela.

But for Andrew, a young man whose life lies before him, the answer is more complex. "Maybe time will heal. But to forgive P. W. [Botha], and forgive the police, and all those who collaborated into this," he says, shaking his head, "we can forgive, but not forget.

"Maybe the next generations who were not there and did not see it personally will say, 'Ah, that was the past.' But the living generations . . ." Andrew falls silent for a moment and stares intently at me. "It's not easy to forgive."

Later, Matthew and I wander outside into the chilly, clear night. As we walk past a row of broken homes, he pauses to tell me about a shop that used to stand there. He quietly surveys the damage done. A brisk wind blows across the village, rattling a nearby metal shanty. Finally, he breaks the stillness. "What the Boers break, we will build," he says softly.

# CONCLUSION

UNMAKING APARTHEID

One morning in the winter of 1984, I accompanied a church field worker on a visit to Crossroads, the embattled squatter camp outside Cape Town. In the shadow of what is rightly described by travel guidebooks as "the most beautiful city in the world" lay the most desperate poverty I had ever seen. People were living in shelters made of black plastic stretched over a frame of branches. The squatters were fighting against police who were trying to uproot them and force them to move to a new, tightly controlled government-built settlement. As desperate as the conditions in Crossroads were, it was nevertheless a home where families could stay together. The struggle of these squatters seemed like the ultimate symbol of the inhumanity of apartheid.

From Crossroads, I next visited a vast sandlot. Dozens of bulldozers were busily destroying sand dunes and leveling a huge area of bush. I walked across the sand to a clump of shiny pre-fab two-room metal homes that had just been constructed. These were some of the first houses built in a place known as Khayelitsha ("new home").

Khayelitsha was yet another social engineering scheme of the white government. In response to the growth of urban squatting, the government announced that it was consolidating all Africans from Crossroads and its adjoining squatter areas into one vast camp twenty-five miles from downtown Cape Town. Khayelitsha was denounced by activists as a dumping ground that would entail the forced removal of thousands of Africans. It was hard to imagine that this barren wasteland could even support life.

On my return to South Africa in 1996 I made Khayelitsha one of my first stops. I was eager to measure progress in the "new South Africa" by a place that I identified as a symbol of oppression from the old days. I knew that housing was a top priority of the new government, and recalled an ANC election promise to build a million houses by 1999. I looked forward to seeing the results.

I turned off the highway and drove slowly into Khayelitsha. In the span of two hundred yards, I left one world and entered another. The sleek black highway vanished behind me, and I was suddenly surrounded by a teeming, vibrant scene that bore no resemblance to the comfortable suburban community that I had left just fifteen minutes before. It was Friday afternoon, and people streamed down the sides of the road (there are no sidewalks, so the dirt shoulders suffice as a promenade). Minibus taxis crammed with people returning from jobs in the city careened by, the loud rhythms of African music pulsing from the windows. Shacks of all kinds— some leaning like the tower of Pisa, others painted the bright colors of the South African flag—lined the main thoroughfare.

The township that I had last seen as an empty sandbox was now a slum that sprawled for as far as I could see. The original spartan metal houses were surrounded by miles and miles of squatter shacks. Estimates of Khayelitsha's current population range from 500,000 to three million. The vastness of the place defied my attempt to "get my head around it."

This is the world that South African whites fear to the depths of their soul. It is a slice of black Africa, in all its crowded, lively, squalid, jubilant glory. It is a world apart from the Bohemian neighborhoods of Cape Town. Yet the two communities are intimately bound to one another. Cape Town could not function without Khayelitsha and its workforce. But the cosmopolitan city may not be able to function *with* the burden of its impoverished progeny, either. It makes for a strange family these days: the so-called Mother City and its abandoned child, which has just returned to the family nest to claim its place in the sun.

I stopped to visit with a man named Shedrick Moreki. An infamous Cape southeaster was blowing straight off the Atlantic Ocean and raking the closely huddled ramshackle homes. Wind-driven rain blew through the flimsy roof, doors, and windows of his house. Despite its shortcomings, Shedrick was as proud as any suburban homeowner showing off his wares. He showed me his small garden, and declared, "I have the most beautiful home in Harare." The neighborhoods around him were named for African capitals, including Lusaka and Maputo.

I joined Shedrick for tea in his living room. I sat on a rummaged sofa while he stoked a small fire in a cement hearth that he built. African music played on the radio, and steam rose off his soaked clothing. He explained that "comrades" had burned down his house in 1993 because they accused him of not being an ANC supporter. He soon rebuilt, and five people now live with him in his shack. He pointed proudly to an electricity meter on the wall; his is one of the few homes in the neighborhood with power.

I asked him what had changed since Mandela. He looked at me with a puzzled expression, as if the answer should have been obvious. "I don't see any change," he said.

Perhaps I was naive. But I expected to see something—anything—that signified that a new era had dawned in Khayelitsha. Instead, I saw poverty on a scale beyond anything that I had seen here before. What was once an expression of the warped geography of apartheid is now simply the natural landscape.

That is one of my fears for South Africa: that after the initial outpouring of energy to redress the problems spawned by apartheid, poverty will begin to look normal. Like it was always there, and always will be. The black nouveau riche will become comfortable with their privilege, and grow tired of dealing with the seemingly intractable problems of the poor. Compassion fatigue will set in. What follows will be apartheid in blackface: the new South Africa will differ from the old South Africa only in the darker skin of the new elite. For the masses, little else will change.

I only worry about this on bad days. I'm not normally that pessimistic. I have more faith in the ideals of the anti-apartheid struggle than that. Or maybe it's just that I can't bear to believe that South Africans would finally reach the Promised Land, only to discover that it looked a lot like where they came from.

Unmaking apartheid is at heart a process of reconciliation. Apartheid contaminated virtually every sphere of life. South Africa's current transformation has involved exposing and unraveling apartheid in each realm. And so citizens of the new South Africa are struggling to reconcile with the old South Africa in their political life, economy, civil society, and in their personal and spiritual lives.

The results of this reconciliation process have been decidedly uneven. As I have traveled across the "new South Africa," it has been alternately thrilling and wrenching, inspiring and disappointing to take the measure of the society that is emerging from these efforts. Reconciliation has often proven to be elusive; in its place, contradictions simply linger. My journey has taken me into communities and lives that are caught somewhere between the old and new order. It is a place of great tension and possibility, where people are haunted by memories, unsettled by changes, and tantalized by potential that remains maddeningly out of reach.

In the political realm, South Africa has had a remarkable transition. The most dramatic symbol of this has been in the person of Nelson Mandela, the prisoner who emerged from more than twenty-seven years behind bars to forgive his tormentors and assume the mantle of world statesman. Another achievement is that the South African Parliament finally resembles the country it represents. As Archbishop Desmond Tutu joked to me, "It's nice to sit in the parliamentary gallery and look down on all the 'terrorists'" who are now making laws and engaging in thoughtful debate.

The dramatic political turnaround can also be seen on a local level. Town and city councils at last reflect their constituencies. They are starting to give attention to the neighbors they so recently tried to hide from view. Adelaide Buso, a shack dweller and domestic worker, now sits on the city council for one of South Africa's richest communities. She is a powerful symbol. And she is starting to make a difference.

In September 1997, a few months after my last visit with Adelaide, officials of the South Peninsula Municipality council on which she sits made a major announcement. Westlake Informal Settlement will be the centerpiece of a R 1.1 billion ($234 million) upgrade project. The plan for Adelaide's squatter camp includes building homes for seven hundred families, and creating a light industrial and commercial area nearby that will provide jobs for the residents.

These developments will take time: the project is expected to take three to five years to complete. But Adelaide has already seen other changes. Hers was one of five shacks at Westlake to get a telephone in late 1997. And she returned to her rural village of Hebron at Christmas that year to find that electricity had finally arrived.

The transformation of the Westlake squatter camp into formal housing, if completed as planned, would be a remarkable achievement. It would be a significant improvement in Adelaide's life, representing the most tangible payback that she and her family have yet received from the South African "miracle." But the reality is that the Busos will be part of a small minority of poor people who are getting services. With only one-fifth of the promised million houses built by 1998, the new government finally abandoned its highly touted pledge. Housing Minister Sankie Mthembi-Mahanyele declared in February 1998 that the million-house goal would be met "at a later date, subject to the availability of resources."[1]

The municipality's focus on addressing the needs of local squatters also suggests that Adelaide's quiet presence has made a difference to her fellow councilors. In the person of this dignified African woman, the masses of shack dwellers have suddenly been given a face, a voice, a life, a family, even a sense of humor. It is further evidence that one of the most profound contemporary changes for South Africans has simply been to breach the walls that apartheid built between neighbors.

Adelaide's son Douglas wrote to me about eight months after I left South Africa. The twenty-seven-year-old man with the gentle presence and warm smile noted that he had found casual construction work, but that "the pay is not enough." He has enrolled in a business management course so that he can earn more money. But he can't afford the fees, so he is uncertain whether he will be able to complete the course.

Douglas's dilemma captures the fundamental contradiction of South Africa's transformation. The Busos may gain the urban home they have longed for, complete with electricity and water. But they are likely to still be poor. The root of this paradox is apparent: South Africa has had a dramatic political revolution, but no parallel economic revolution. For proof of that one need only visit Khayelitsha, or spend time with Adelaide and her struggling family.

South Africans are now seeing the results of the political bargain that was brokered to end white minority rule. Whites were guaranteed their economic privilege in return for giving up political power. So apartheid's inequalities are preserved in contemporary South Africa. The richest (and overwhelmingly white) 10 percent of South African households receive 40 percent of total income, while half the population of the country scrambles to divide 11 percent of the income. Over three-fourths of households headed by African women are poor.[2] The plight of the Buso family is the human price of that fateful political deal.

The process of unmaking apartheid has moved the fault lines on the South African landscape. The South African struggle has always been one of class as well as race. Until now, race and class were inexorably linked:

the rich were always white and blacks were always poor. In the post-apartheid era that nexus is fraying. Class divisions within the black community are becoming increasingly pronounced; indeed, income inequality among Africans now mirrors the dramatic skewing found within South Africa as a whole.[3] As middle-class blacks like Tumi Modise begin to reap the benefit of new opportunities and aggressive affirmative action programs, black society is reordering itself along the lines of haves and have-nots that has until now been a hallmark of white-black relations.

Economic transformation for South Africa's poor does not appear to be in the cards anytime soon. After indulging in lavish campaign promises about rebuilding the country, the new government is retreating on its commitment to redress past inequities. The cabinet-level office of the vaunted Reconstruction and Development Program, the social welfare centerpiece of the 1994 ANC campaign platform, was closed down in June 1996 and its minister reassigned. While RDP programs were supposedly taken over by other government ministries, the unmistakable impression was that the government was backing away from its commitment to an aggressive program of social uplifting.

The most dramatic and visible economic changes in South Africa have been confined to the top strata of society. A black elite is taking root under the guise of "black economic empowerment." Too often this has merely been self-enrichment dressed up in patriotic garb. The idea that driving a new BMW is an expression of revolutionary change is a bit hard to take.

The most conspicuous recipient of opportunity is the new class of black bourgeoisie who run the country. The new government bureaucrats wasted little time in rewarding themselves. Soon after the 1994 election, politicians gave themselves a raise: the president would earn $220,943, cabinet ministers $132,394 (including benefits), and members of parliament $54,422.[4] In a country where the average annual household income for Africans is R 23,000 ($4,600), there was widespread resentment of the politicians' "gravy train."[5] Even Archbishop Tutu decried the inflated salaries. The president and his cabinet subsequently reduced their raises.

One day a black judge gave me a lift home in the gleaming Mercedes that was a perk of his new government position. I casually expressed surprise that a civil servant would be entitled to such luxurious fringe benefits. He replied brusquely that he and his family had suffered under apartheid and he had no qualms about assuming the privileges of power that his white predecessors had enjoyed. His attitude highlighted the growing rift between the new elite and the people who elected them.

As Professor Heribert Adam, a veteran political analyst and author of *Comrades in Business,* opined, "The new leaders need to be reminded that they have to 'walk the talk.'" He advocates "a Gandhian vision of austerity and lived solidarity" from the new leaders. "While white fat-cats make no excuse for reaping profits at any cost, one hopes, perhaps in vain, that the new black bourgeoisie remembers its origin."[6]

A far more telling sign of the gap between the governors and the governed is the economic policies being pursued by the new leaders. The new government has quickly dispensed with talk of revolutionary change. The rhetoric is no longer about sharing the wealth and taking back the land; now the poorest people are simply encouraged to be patient. It is an astonishing retreat by a government that campaigned on the slogan "A Better Life for All."

Rev. Frank Chikane is among those activists who would have condemned the government's rightward drift before he assumed his position in the inner circle of power. He offers some insight into this contradiction when I ask him what is the most difficult aspect of apartheid to eradicate.

"It's in the economic field," he responds quickly. We are sitting in his elegant suite in Tuynhuys, the presidential office in Cape Town. "The other things you can fix very easily." He identifies poverty reduction as a burning need. But he bemoans that government can't harness "profits gained through apartheid . . . to correct the damage." Numerous people testifying before the Truth and Reconciliation Commission spoke of the need for a "reparations tax" on big businesses to compensate black South Africans for their losses. But Chikane says with a smile, "If you talk about it, it's very sensitive, you know. It's like you are anticapitalist and want to dispossess people of their assets."

Suddenly the noble issues that the liberation struggle championed are pushed aside. We are talking numbers now. That's all that any of South Africa's new bureaucrats want to discuss. Chikane points to the debt—a huge crippling albatross that is hamstringing the new government.

The apartheid debt may be the most onerous hangover from the apartheid era. In 1989, government debt stood at R 80 billion (about $31 billion). By 1997, the debt burden of the South African government had risen to a whopping R 311 billion (approximately $68 billion), with most of the increase occurring under the de Klerk regime. In the 1997–98 national budget, one-fifth of government expenditure was dedicated to repaying the debt. Debt repayment is the second-largest government expense; only education receives more money. The main beneficiary of this debt repayment is the state pension fund, which was lavishly expanded by the outgoing minority government in its final years to ensure generous golden handshakes for white civil servants.[7]

"It's the victims who must pay the debt, you know. It's the same amnesty thing: the victimizer gets amnesty, the victim pays. It's how the system is structured," observes Chikane. He shakes his head in dismay.

"You know, I used to be one of those church leaders who said 'cancel the debt,' which some church leaders are still saying. And I sympathize with them. Because then you discover that debt in South Africa is not like the debt in Tanzania or Malawi or Mozambique . . . This debt is not an external debt. We are owing our own insurance companies and banks here. Only about 4 to 6 percent of our debt is external; the rest is internal. If you stop [paying] it, you are stopping . . . the business in South Africa, and if you did that you risk destroying the economy . . . Because of that you have to pay the debt and it cost us last year up to R 34 billion ($8 billion) to service the debt. Now, that 34 billion you could be using to alleviate the poverty. It's a *helluva* lot of money, but you can't [spend it on poverty reduction]. And so you begin to realize—gosh, the world is really rough! . . . The international systems naturally work against the poor for the rich and against the powerless for the powerful."

Chikane clearly grasps the cold calculus of international aid and finance. But he and his colleagues have done nothing to challenge this system. Many hoped Nelson Mandela might use his bully pulpit as a revered global statesman to establish South Africa as a model for how to aggressively redress the crippling legacy of poverty in an emerging democracy. But in just a few years, the policies coming out of Pretoria echo the priorities of Washington and London: cutting back social welfare spending, living foreign investment at any cost, trimming government, and tempering the power of trade unions. While ANC politicians talk of redistributing the wealth, the reality is that progressive economic thinking has been decisively routed in the new South Africa in favor of policies that do little to close the wealth gap.

Minister of Trade and Industry Alec Erwin offers a case in point. Writing in the *African Communist* in mid-1992, Erwin asserted that the key challenge facing South Africa was to "lay the basis for a future socialist society." Erwin advocated a radical redistribution of wealth and "a redistribution of the access to economic power."[8]

By 1996, Minister Erwin was preaching the gospel of privatization to foreign investors, extolling the virtues of South Africa homeland casino magnate Sol Kerzner ("he invested money and employed people," insisted Erwin), and promising to continue the policies of his National Party predecessor.

Erwin's about-face moved veteran South Africa analyst R. W. Johnson to conclude wryly, "Perhaps there should be a touch more embarrassment, an acknowledgment of past errors, or some sort of explanation . . . Erwin, who has gone from Communism to casino capitalism in just four years, deserves praise for his flexibility."[9]

The World Bank has issued its stamp of approval for South Africa's rightward economic drift. In May 1997, the World Bank approved a $46-million loan to South Africa to support programs to increase the international competitiveness of South African businesses. It was the World Bank's first major transaction in South Africa in over three decades.[10] Many activists opposed the bank loan, arguing that South Africa was fortunate to have little foreign debt and should maintain its distance from World Bank policies. But the die had long since been cast.

When I question the logic of laying off teachers, underfunding housing subsidies, and scaling back development projects, I am told by government ministers that South Africa is competing for foreign capital in a global marketplace. If it is not profitable for a company to operate here, they will simply relocate somewhere else. So the government keeps its spending in check by requiring the poorest people to pay for land and housing which, in many cases, were stolen from them.

The new government's embrace of market-driven solutions to South Africa's problems has been so ardent that its alliance partners—the trade unions, civic organizations, and the Communist Party—are denouncing the about-face of their erstwhile comrades. With strains growing steadily, the "tripartite alliance" of progressive activists that swept to power in 1994 is unlikely to last.

It has fallen to the Congress of South African Trade Unions, the most powerful remaining nongovernmental political force, to insist on a different blueprint for change. COSATU has put forth an alternative economic scenario for South Africa. It has called for significantly increased social spending, and an expansion of the public sector to provide jobs. Ironically, this is not unlike the policy advanced by the National Party in the 1940s to uplift poor Afrikaners.

COSATU argues that the centerpiece of post-apartheid economics must include redistributing wealth. "The extreme contrast of wealth and poverty in South Africa makes redistribution a necessary condition for economic growth," declared the COSATU September Commission in late 1997. "The contrast between the blatant wealth of a minority and the desperate poverty of the majority will continue to tear apart the fabric of society, generating crime and social instability. This is hardly going to improve investor confidence." COSATU identifies the state, the largest employer and consumer in the economy, as "a critical agent for the redistribution of income and wealth."[11] By contrast, the ANC is downsizing the government and privatizing major state assets including telecommunications and transportation.

Frank Chikane is aware that conventional economic prescriptions will force the poor to wait even longer for salvation. He responds to criticism by offering a swift, brutal scenario of the excruciating position that the new South African government finds itself in. "If you went overboard and pushed lots of resources into social expenditures to uplift the lives of people, you just widen the debt, and the debt servicing becomes higher, and you go tumbling down on your own. And then five years, ten years down the line, the World Bank and IMF will be here, you know, and come and tell you how you can cause more pain to the victims in order to correct the economy."

Chikane is stung by critics who accuse the new government of selling out. "I always ask them if you were given a chance and the world could allow you to do what you want—what would you have done? And all that they tell me equals a military takeover, and dispossession and forcefully equalizing. And that's really it. Short of that you're not going to do it overnight."

How do you achieve economic justice? "The expectation of waking up and equalizing with whites in this country, which all of us did expect, is a grand one. But you need to say in economic policy terms, what must you do to achieve that? The only way to do it would be to redispossess and re-distribute," he asserts matter-of-factly. "Any other way will not achieve that equation over many years. And the government has opted not to go that route because we know the consequences."

But South Africa's conservative economic choices may also have dire consequences. University of Ottawa economist Michel Chossudovsky, author of *The Globalization of Poverty*, describes South Africa's misnamed Growth, Employment, and Redistribution (GEAR) strategy—its guiding macroeconomic policy under Mandela—as a "photocopy" of World Bank structural adjustment programs (SAP). The basic SAP blueprint includes cutting government spending, privatizing state enterprises, and the dereg-ulation of trade—all of which are well under way in South Africa. Chos-sudovsky, who has consulted on development projects for the UN and other agencies in over a hundred countries, notes that such policies can act as "shock therapy" that "can destroy and destabilize an economy in a mat-ter of a few months."[12] He points out that both Rwanda and Yugoslavia implemented a World Bank/IMF SAP shortly before their respective geno-cides. He links the fallout from the SAP—including slashed crop prices, re-duced wages, and higher interest—to the social disintegration that followed in these countries. Chossudovsky is especially perturbed by the new gov-ernment's commitment to paying its debt. "Apartheid debt was borrowed to oppress and kill people. Now those same people are being asked to sacrifice to pay it back."[13] Indeed, South Africa has already witnessed one by-product of its fiscal conservatism: as President Mandela warned in his annual address to parliament in February 1998, the economy "continues to shed too many jobs."

South Africa's next leaders will not have the honeymoon that Mandela enjoyed. Even Thabo Mbeki, who is expected to become South Africa's next president in April 1999, warned in late 1997 of the potential for race riots in three to five years unless whites voluntarily agree to redistribute their own wealth.[14] But absent a strong hand from the government, whites have shown no appetite for willingly doling out the spoils of the apartheid plunder. And despite Mbeki's bluster, the ANC government has done little to rebalance the skewed scales of wealth in South Africa.

Reverend Frank Chikane has already felt the sting of South Africans who are growing dissatisfied with the slow pace of change. In late 1997, Chikane was resoundingly defeated in a race to become premier of Gauteng Province when grassroots ANC activists abandoned him in favor of a populist candidate, Mathole Motshekga. Chikane, a hero of the liberation struggle, is now closely identified with Mbeki and his establishment policies. His defeat was seen as a warning to the ANC leadership that the loyalty of restive rank-and-file supporters cannot be taken for granted.

Far from being a "miracle," South Africa's economic recovery has been quite ordinary. Indeed, the struggle for economic justice in South Africa is a rather depressing story of idealism that fell flat just when it was most needed. South Africa now takes a place alongside other developing countries, where the rich get richer, and the poor get a little social welfare, and a lot of excuses.

Nelson Mandela elevated racial reconciliation to be the new civil religion of South Africa. His single-minded zeal made political sense: peace was what everyone thought would be impossible in South Africa. Thanks largely to Mandela's lead, the skeptics were proven wrong. The "miracle" that is rightly applauded in South Africa is the peace that prevailed both during and after the 1994 election. The glaring exception is in Kwa-Zulu/Natal where political and ethnic conflict have continued at a slow but steady burn.

Some of the most moving scenes that I witnessed during my South Africa travels took place at the hearings of the Truth and Reconciliation Commission. The TRC spearheaded a remarkable process of national introspection. Every day in towns across the country, ordinary people rose to speak about the extraordinary hardships they had endured under apartheid. Over seven thousand people applied for amnesty, and more than twenty-one thousand victims' testimonies were taken.[15] Each day on the news and radio, the nation heard these stories. The truth gleaned from this experience is a milestone for postauthoritarian societies.

The South African TRC has been more successful than most of the world's truth commissions or tribunals at ferreting out the truth. In Argentina and Chile, the truth commissions deliberated in secret, only going public with a final report. Neither of these commissions cracked the veil of secrecy around the police and military.

If international experience in places like Rwanda and Yugoslavia is any guide, the choice facing South Africa was not really amnesty versus justice, as critics often insisted. It was a choice between getting some truth or getting nothing at all—the latter being what most inquests, truth commissions, and courts end up delivering. Indeed, South Africa's successful formula for prying out the truth was cited by the *New York Times* in mid-1997 when it called for a TRC-style amnesty-for-truth deal to resolve the long-simmering mysteries that surround the assassinations of John F. Kennedy and Martin Luther King. Coretta Scott King has also endorsed this approach.

Truth has been a potent antidote to revenge in South Africa. A good example came with the testimony of police torturer Jeffrey Benzien in November 1997. Benzien, who is still a cop, testified to how he tortured political activists with a "wet bag." He would place the bag over his victim's head and then tighten it until the person was on the verge of suffocation. He also confessed to raping victims with a broomstick, using electric shocks, and brutally assaulting activists for hours on end. He was by all accounts a feared and sadistic interrogator who could break even the most hardened activist.

Benzien was grilled by truth commissioners and confronted by many former victims. He broke down in tears and confessed that he has asked a psychiatrist "what type of person am I" that is capable of such depravity.

One of his victims, Peter Jacobs, was asked whether he thought Benzien should go to jail. Jacobs, now a policeman himself, dismissed the idea. "He came out and we exposed him. What's it really going to serve now, not to give him amnesty? What strategic value would be served? I can't see it."[16]

Does all this truth-telling translate into national reconciliation among South Africans? I think not. "Reconciliation" implies a sense of reciprocity and mutual recognition of wrongdoing between former antagonists that does not exist in South Africa. Whites such as Lieb Niemand and Wilhelm Verwoerd Sr. are still in denial. And the impoverished farmers of Mogopa have no way to vent their displeasure with those who wronged them.

Peaceful coexistence is a more accurate description of the fragile peace that prevails in South Africa. Such coexistence cannot be taken for granted. The peace that has reigned in South Africa took place under the persistent prodding of Mandela and Archbishop Tutu, who made forgiveness a matter of patriotic duty. As these moral beacons pass from the public stage, old animosities may yet resurface, particularly in places where little change has taken place. As Truth Commissioner Mary Burton told me, "It's not good enough telling people to reconcile when they are still as poor and disadvantaged as they've been in the past." Old disparities are a daily reminder that, as Adelaide Buso insists, "the book of apartheid is still open."

Creating a new society out of the ashes of apartheid is a process, not a fait accompli. South Africa's political triumph in 1994 was just one victory; many more are required. South Africa has taught a skeptical world a lesson about how reconciliation can happen across the racial divide. Can South Africa bring a similar miracle of reconciliation to close the economic divide? That remains the central challenge facing the young democracy.

It is the Adelaide Busos—the poor who are striving to break free of poverty—who pose the acid test of South Africa's transformation. Whether she can realize her modest aspirations—including living in her own home, supporting her family, seeing her sons get decent jobs, and delivering basic services to her poorest constituents—will be the measure of the new South Africa. Will she have the opportunity to realize her dreams? Or has she fought in the struggle merely for the right to wait even longer for redemption?

It seems cruel that the afterglow of a stunning peaceful transition to democracy should fade so quickly, eclipsed by urgent development needs. It is also unfair that people expect that a system of racial and economic exploitation that took 350 years to craft could be undone in a few years.

But revolutions must yield quickly to the mundane tasks of providing basic services to those who have been neglected, and of offering economic opportunities where there have been none. The fall of apartheid was the end of a long arduous trek for South Africans. Unmaking apartheid is another difficult journey. As Nelson Mandela concludes at the end of his autobiography,

> The truth is that we are not yet free; we have merely achieved the freedom to be free, the right not to be oppressed. We have not taken the final step of our journey, but the first step on a longer and even more difficult road. For to be free is not merely to cast off one's chains, but to live in a way that respects and enhances the freedom of others. The true test of our devotion to freedom is just beginning.

. . . I have discovered the secret that after climbing a great hill, one only finds that there are many more hills to climb.[17]

It was my last week in South Africa. I was busy visiting friends and saying good-bye. At dinner one evening, my friend Adam was talking about the support work that he did in the 1980s for families of detainees. Like many acquaintances, Adam would prefer not to talk about the past, but he was indulging my questions.

Adam described how he would prepare activists and their loved ones for the experience of "going inside." He would show them a film, *Profile of a Torturer,* about a brutal Greek interrogator who worked under the Greek military junta in the early seventies.

I asked Adam how long he continued with this anti-apartheid work. He hesitated, looking pensively at his wife, as if he were embarrassed by my question. Finally he broke his silence. "It got so intense that I dropped out of political work completely. I became an auto mechanic for many years. I couldn't deal with it," he finally acknowledged. He said he had recently begun getting counseling at the Trauma Center for Victims of Violence and Torture in Cape Town. "It was the first time I was able to talk about what happened to me all those years."

Adam was one of a number of friends who confided in me about their personal difficulties in reconciling the past and present. Time and again, friends hinted obliquely at the enormous psychological toll taken by apartheid. On a personal level, it was the most striking phenomenon that I encountered in South Africa. People told me about personal problems and marital difficulties that they traced to the upheavals in the country and in their lives. Apartheid broke people on all sides of the political and racial divide.

The repression of the apartheid era required ordinary people to do extraordinary things. People were called upon to take a stand. Some, like Frank Chikane, rose to the occasion. Most could not. Many people collaborated with apartheid, sometimes even with good intentions. Maybe they gave the police one name instead of five. Or they kept quiet, turning a blind eye when a colleague was persecuted, weakly believing he had "done something wrong." Little things, stuff they'd like to forget. But they can't. Each person now lives with the consequences of those choices.

The very next night we visited with our friends Jeremy and Ntsiki.*
They are a mixed-race couple—she is black and he is white. They lived together illegally in a "white" neighborhood during the eighties.

"In the past, people would stare at us in shock when we would walk
down the street," said Ntsiki. "Now they don't seem to take much notice
of us."

Jeremy agreed. "It's the little things—like people not noticing us—
where we feel the biggest changes."

Jeremy had been active in the United Democratic Front since the early
1980s. He has three kids now and doesn't like to talk about what happened
a decade ago. He reluctantly indulged me. At one point I asked him if he
had ever considered working underground. Jeremy paused and looked uncomfortably at Ntsiki. Then he said, "I've been a member of the ANC for
many years, and was underground since the late seventies. But please
don't say anything about it—I've never told my parents or my brothers."

I was surprised—not by his revelation, which I long suspected, but by
his reticence. I asked him why the secrecy.

"Because I wasn't anything special. I was just a regular guy who did
what the times required. And I wasn't a big name or anything. Half the
time I was shit-scared, and a lot of people probably thought I was too
timid. I didn't go for the big high-profile stuff. I was too scared. And I
wasn't a member of MK [the ANC armed wing] or the [South African
Communist] Party. I didn't work on instructions. I just did my own
thing in ways that I decided were consistent with ANC strategy."

I was still puzzled: the struggle is over. Why not be open about the past?

"Because I want to get on with my life," he said, his voice tinged with
ambivalence. "That was the past, and I don't want to relive it. Those were
scary times, hard times. When you have a family to think about, it becomes very difficult to just make decisions about your actions because they
affect someone else."

On my last night, I visited with an old friend, Father Michael Lapsley.
"Father Mike" is the ANC priest who lost his hands and an eye in a
parcel bomb attack in 1990. He works as a chaplain at the Trauma Cen-

---

* I have used the pseudonyms "Adam," "Jeremy," and "Ntsiki" to protect the privacy
of the three individuals who shared these stories with me in confidence.

ter, and holds three-day workshops around the country called "Healing of the Memories."* These are forums for ordinary people, white and black, victim and perpetrator, to come to terms with what happened during apartheid.

I related the stories of Adam and Jeremy to him. He nodded knowingly as I spoke. "There are thousands of Adams and Jeremys out there," he interjected. "People who felt they didn't do enough, or couldn't take what they were doing, or just did nothing. That's what my work is now—trying to help people heal those wounds.

"Apartheid is not like a dirty shirt that you can just take off, and replace with a clean shirt," he reflected. Lapsley would know—soon after I visited with him, he had to have major brain surgery to correct a problem that occurred seven years earlier when he was bombed. The past lives on in the present.

Lapsley sat on the couch with his prosthetic arms and steel hooks crossed in his lap. The scarred cleric mused, "It'll take a hundred years to heal from the wounds of apartheid."

The South Africans who grew up with apartheid as a daily reality are part of a wounded generation. For older South Africans—such as Wilhelm Verwoerd Sr. or Lieb Niemand—it is too much to expect that they will adopt the changing values of post-apartheid society. I place my hope for South Africa's future with the young generation: the first South Africans who will grow up in something resembling a humane, multiracial, democratic society.

Despite the disappointments of a revolution that has not lived up to its ideals, I remain fundamentally, and perhaps irrationally, hopeful about South Africa. Maybe it is just that I cannot bring myself to part with the vision that I and many others have had for South Africa to be the peaceful, egalitarian, "rainbow nation" that exists nowhere on earth.

My stubborn optimism has its roots in having seen where South Africa has come from. Fifteen years ago, I disembarked from a long train voyage and plunged into the dark world of apartheid. That was South Africa's nadir. It can only get better; indeed, it already has.

---

* Lapsley left the Trauma Center in 1998 and now leads the workshops through the Institute for Healing of Memories, which he directs.

My hope for the future is inspired most by the ordinary South Africans whom I have met. Lieb Niemand, for all his crude racism, is committed to staying and making it in the new South Africa, for better or worse. So too is Adelaide Buso, who with her quiet dignity and tenacity is also determined to make her leaders deliver on their promises. Wilhelm Verwoerd Jr. has paid a painful personal price for his stubborn insistence that the future of his *volk* lies in unity, not division. Tumi Modise has set ambitious goals for herself, and is finally free to attain them. Rev. Frank Chikane has moved from jail cell to presidential suite in pursuit of his quixotic mission to bring about a just Kingdom of God in South Africa. Paul Erasmus, who has cultivated an improbable friendship with his former nemesis Winnie Madikizela-Mandela, tells me that he wants to "symbolize what the new South Africa is all about." And Matthew Mpshe continues to work his Mogopa lands in the eternal hope that the next harvest will be more bountiful.

What all these individuals have in common is a depth of conviction that inspired me during my first travels in South Africa. People of all colors feel passionately about this land. I have felt that passion in a crowd of protesters dancing the *toyi-toyi,* and in the soaring riff of a guitar in a bustling township *shebeen.* I have felt it among women squatters who are laying the bricks for their first formal homes. And I have felt it walking alongside Afrikaner farmers through the rich, brown furrows of their mealie fields. That passion—for the land, their country, their freedom—has been the force behind South Africa's salvation. It is sustenance for the long journey ahead.

# NOTES

## Introduction: Fault Lines

1. Julie Frederikse, *None but Ourselves: Masses vs. Media in the Making of Zimbabwe* (London, 1982), 326.

2. *The Constitution of the Republic of South Africa, 1996* (Pretoria, March 1997).

3. Nedcor, "Report of the Nedcor Project on Crime, Violence and Investment" (Johannesburg, 1995).

4. Office of the Executive Deputy President, "Poverty and Inequality in South Africa," Summary Report (Pretoria, 1998).

5. Personal communication, Max Coleman, former commissioner, Human Rights Commission, February 1998.

6. World Bank / Reconstruction and Development Program, *Key Indicators of Poverty in South Africa* (Cape Town, 1995); Office of the Executive Deputy President, "Poverty and Inequality in South Africa," Summary Report (Pretoria, May 1998); Suzanne Daley, "A Post-Apartheid Agony: AIDS on the March," *New York Times,* July 23, 1998.

7. Lynne Duke, "Mandela Calls Jobs Top Priority," *Washington Post,* February 7, 1998.

## Victorious Victim

1. The account of Chikane's interrogation and torture is based on personal communication with Chikane and on his autobiography, *No Life of My Own* (Johannesburg, 1988).

2. Wessel Ebersohn, "The Kingdom and the Power," *Leadership,* no. 6, 1987, 44.

3. Ibid., 51.

4. Ibid., 44.

5. Dele Olojede, "Building a Better South Africa: Freedom to Live How They Choose," *Newsday,* June 2, 1997.

6. Unless otherwise noted, the account of Chikane's early years (including direct quotations) up until his days in the United Democratic Front is drawn primarily from *No Life of My Own.*

7. As head of state of South Africa, P. W. Botha initially held the title of prime minister when he came into power in 1978. In 1983, South Africa enacted a new constitution which made him state president in 1984. I refer to him with the title that was effective on the date that I am writing about.

8. Christopher Saunders et al., eds., *Reader's Digest Illustrated History of South Africa,* 3d ed. (Cape Town and New York, 1994), 477.

9. Tom Lodge and Bill Nasson, *All, Here, and Now: Black Politics in South Africa in the 1980s* (New York and Cape Town, 1991), 51.

10. Saunders, 476.

11. Lodge and Nasson, 67.

12. Ibid., 65.

13. Chikane, 105.

14. Ibid., 120.

15. Saunders, 485.

16. Chikane, front matter.

17. Saunders, 346.

18. Charles Villa-Vicencio, *The Spirit of Hope: South African Leaders on Religion and Politics* (Berkeley, 1995), 67.

19. "Press Statement," South African Council of Churches, Johannesburg, June 1989.

20. Charles Villa-Vicencio, "Leading Country's Churches to New Society," *The Star* (Johannesburg), July 20, 1992.

21. Anton Harber and Barbara Ludman, eds., *Mail and Guardian: A to Z of South African Politics* (London, 1995), 19.

22. Villa-Vicencio, *The Spirit of Hope,* 73.

23. Throughout 1996 and 1997, Cape Town mounted a high-profile campaign to host the 2004 Olympics, becoming one of the five finalist cities to be considered. In September 1997, the International Olympic Committee voted to hold the 2004 Olympics in Athens.

24. Mayibuye Center / University of Western Cape, *Apartheid: The History of the Struggle for Freedom in South Africa* (CD-ROM) (Cape Town, 1994).

## The Vanquished Assassin

1. Gavin Cawthra, *Policing South Africa: The SAP and the Transition from Apartheid* (Cape Town, 1993), 16.

2. Allister Sparks, *The Mind of South Africa* (London, 1990), 36.

3. International Defense and Aid Fund (IDAF), *Apartheid: The Facts,* 2d ed. (London, 1991), section 3.1 in *Apartheid: The History of the Struggle for Freedom in South Africa* [CD-ROM] (Cape Town, 1994).

4. Christopher Saunders et al., eds., *Reader's Digest Illustrated History of South Africa,* 3d ed. (Cape Town and New York, 1994), 444.

5. Cited in Cawthra, 18–19.

6. Ibid., 56.

7. General Smit and Human Rights Commission statistics are cited in Cawthra, 57.

8. South African Police statistics are cited in Howard Barrell, "Conscripts to Their Age: ANC Operational Strategy, 1976–1986" (Oxford, Ph.D. dissertation, 1993), 458.

9. IDAF, *Namibia: The Facts,* 2d ed. (London, 1989), section 7.1 in *Apartheid* [CD-ROM].

10. "Prime Evil Sentenced to 212 Years," *Cape Times,* October 31, 1996.

11. IDAF, *Namibia,* section 7.1 in *Apartheid* [CD-ROM]; Gavin Cawthra, *Brutal Force: The Apartheid War Machine* (London, 1986), section 8.6 in *Apartheid* [CD-ROM].

12. Cawthra, *Brutal Force,* cited in section 7.1 in *Apartheid* [CD-ROM].

13. Accounts of Namibian interrogation are based on several sources: personal communication with Erasmus; human rights reports in IDAF, *Namibia: The Facts;* and Paul Erasmus, "Koevoet and Their Own Radio Moscow," *Mail and Guardian,* July 21, 1995.

14. Paul Erasmus, "Nocturnal Paint Bombs, Gun Toting Neighbors," *Mail and Guardian,* June 30, 1995.

15. Personal communication, Max Coleman, former commissioner, Human Rights Commission, February 1998.

16. Eddie Koch and Stefaans Brümmer, "What the Goldstone Report Revealed," *Mail and Guardian,* July 7, 1995.

17. Stefaans Brümmer, "The Secrets of Stratcomm," *Mail and Guardian,* June 23, 1995.

18. "Chikane Forgives His Tormentor," *Mail and Guardian,* June 30, 1995.

19. Tangeni Amupadhi, "Crime Could Rocket," *Mail and Guardian,* May 12, 1998.

20. *New York Times,* September 19, 1996.

21. *Mail and Guardian,* July 14, 1995.

22. *Mail and Guardian,* July 21, 1995.

23. Ibid.

24. David Beresford, "Ecstasy and the Apartheid Strangeloves," *Mail and Guardian,* June 11, 1998.

25. Michael Morris and John Yeld, "Chikane's Plea to His Poisoner," *Cape Argus,* June 10, 1998.

26. Ibid.

## Architect of Apartheid

1. Allister Sparks, *The Mind of South Africa* (London, 1990), 27–28.

2. Ibid., 33.

3. Ibid., 35.

4. Quoted in Leonard Thompson, *A History of South Africa,* rev. ed. (New Haven, 1995), 88.

5. Thompson, 88.

6. Christopher Saunders et al., eds., *Reader's Digest Illustrated History of South Africa,* 3d ed. (Cape Town and New York, 1994), 256, 266.

7. Henry Kenney, *Architect of Apartheid: H. F. Verwoerd—an Appraisal* (Johannesburg, 1980), 26.

8. Ibid.

9. C. J. Beyers, ed., *Dictionary of South African Biography,* vol. 4 (Pretoria, 1981), 731–40.

10. Saunders, 332.

11. Kenney, 29–30.

12. Dan O'Meara, *Forty Lost Years: The Apartheid State and the Politics of the National Party, 1948–1994* (Athens, Ohio, 1996), 92.

13. Kenney, 20.

14. Ibid., 62.

15. Ibid., 64.

16. Jan Botha, *Verwoerd Is Dead* (Cape Town, 1967), 10.

17. Saunders, 316.

18. O'Meara, 23.

19. Kenney, 92.

20. Ibid., 79.

21. Ibid.

22. O'Meara, 76.

23. Timothy Garton Ash, "The Curse and Blessing of South Africa," *New York Review of Books,* August 14, 1997, 10.

24. Heribert Adam and Hermann Giliomee, *Ethnic Power Mobilized: Can South Africa Change?* (New Haven and London, 1979), 174. Cited in Thompson, 188.

25. O'Meara, 81.

26. Saunders, 403; Thompson, 210.

27. O'Meara, 101.

28. Quoted in Kenney, 183.

29. Ibid.

30. Kenney, 194.

31. Quoted in Sparks, 201.

32. Kenney, 266.

33. Botha, 5.

34. O'Meara, 151.

35. David Beresford, "The Madness of Demetrio Tsafendas," *Mail and Guardian,* October 13, 1997.

36. Personal communication, former Robben Island prisoner Lionel Davis, March 1997.

37. "South Africa: The Delusions of Apartheid," *Time* (Atlantic edition), August 26, 1966, 23.

38. Kenney, 267.

39. Lynne Duke, "South Africa Delays Trial for Botha," *Washington Post,* April 17, 1998.

40. Suzanne Daley, "Ex- South African Leader Guilty of Contempt for Refusing to Testify Before Truth Panel," *New York Times,* August 22, 1998.

41. Suzanne Daley, "Tutu Asks Botha to Give an Apology, but in Vain," *New York Times,* June 6, 1998; and *New York Times,* August 22, 1998.

42. O'Meara, 170.

43. Ibid., 181.

44. Kenney, 9.

45. "South Africa," *Time,* 20.

46. Joshua Lazerson, *Against the Tide: Whites in the Struggle against Apartheid* (Boulder, 1994), section 4.4 in *Apartheid* [CD- ROM].

47. R. W. Johnson, "The Best and Worst of Times: South Africa's Government at Half-Term" (Helen Suzman Foundation), *Forum,* November 21, 1996; Central Statistical Service, "Demography: Tourism and Migration, October 1997" (Pretoria, May 1998).

## *Leaving the Laager*

1. Excerpts from Wilhelm Verwoerd Jr.'s letters and journal entries are from his memoir, *My Winds of Change* (Johannesburg, 1997) and are used with permission of Ravan Press.

2. Quoted in ibid., 67.

3. Wilhelm Verwoerd, "Dr. H. F. Verwoerd: Principled Pragmatist?" (Oxford, B.A. thesis, 1990).

4. Ginwala is currently Speaker of the South African Parliament and Nzimande is an MP for the ANC.

5. "Whatever Happened to the Dream of Low Cost Housing?" *Mail and Guardian*, February 24, 1998.

6. Office of the Executive Deputy President, "Poverty and Inequality in South Africa," Summary Report (Pretoria, May 1998).

7. Gavin Lewis, " . . . Just Slow Off the Mark," *Mail and Guardian*, May 16, 1997.

## *"The Book of Apartheid Is Still Open"*

1. Hildegarde Fast, "An Overview of African Settlement in the Cape Metropolitan Area to 1990," Working Paper No. 53, Urban Problems Research Unit, University of Cape Town (Cape Town, 1995), 5.

2. Christopher Saunders et al., eds., *Reader's Digest Illustrated History of South Africa*, 3d ed. (Cape Town and New York, 1994), 376.

3. Leonard Thompson, *A History of South Africa*, rev. ed. (New Haven, 1995), 239.

4. Andrew Reynolds, ed., *Election '94 South Africa: The Campaigns, Results and Future Prospects* (Cape Town, 1994), 200–204.

5. Office of the Executive Deputy President, "Poverty and Inequality in South Africa," Summary Report (Pretoria, May 1998).

## *Apartheid Jujitsu Artist*

1. Donald G. McNeil Jr., "Heavily Laden Black Chips," *New York Times*, April 17, 1998.

2. Enoch Godongwana left NUMSA in mid-1997 to become minister for economic affairs, environment, and tourism in the Eastern Cape Province.

3. *Cape Argus*, March 4, 1997; and *Financial Mail*, February 7, 1997.

4. Donald G. McNeil Jr., "Heavily Laden Black Chips," *New York Times*, April 17, 1998.

5. "Capitalism's Bonding Power," *Financial Mail*, February 7, 1997.

6. *New York Times*, April 17, 1998.

## *Tense Peace in the* Platteland

1. Personal communication, Nick Vink, March 1997; Organization of Economic Cooperation and Development, *Agricultural Policies, Markets, and Trade: Monitoring and Outlook 1998* (Paris, 1998), 11.

2. Christopher Saunders et al., eds., *Reader's Digest Illustrated History of South Africa*, 3d ed. (Cape Town and New York, 1994), 332.

3. Ibid.

4. Ibid., 331.

5. Personal communication, Hennie du Plessis, Central West Cooperative, Ventersdorp, September 1996.

6. Dan O'Meara, *Forty Lost Years: The Apartheid State and the Politics of the National Party, 1948–1994* (Athens, Ohio, 1996), 143.

7. Saunders, 498.

8. Anton Harber and Barbara Ludman, eds., *Mail and Guardian: A to Z of South African Politics* (London, 1994).

9. Saunders, 522.

## *Rising from the Ruins*

1. Transvaal Rural Action Committee (TRAC), *Mogopa: And Now We Have No Land* (Johannesburg, 1988), 5.

2. "Struggle Not Given Up in Mogopa," *Sowetan,* February 16, 1984.

3. Sol Plaatje, *Native Life in South Africa* (1916), quoted in David Goodman, "The Long Walk Home," *World Monitor,* September 1991, 41.

4. Christopher Saunders et al., eds., *Reader's Digest Illustrated History of South Africa,* 3d ed. (Cape Town and New York, 1994), 227.

5. Ibid., 424.

6. Elaine Unterhalter, *Forced Removal: The Division, Segregation and Control of the People of South Africa* (London, 1987), 14.

7. Ibid., 18.

8. TRAC, "The Economic Viability of Mogopa" (unpublished research document, 1991), 5.

9. Ibid., 6.

10. TRAC, *Mogopa,* 2.

11. Ibid.

12. "'Misinformed' on Mogopa," *The Star* (Johannesburg), February 17, 1984.

13. "Row Erupts as Suzman Slams Mogopa Move," *Rand Daily Mail,* February 17, 1984.

14. "US Raps South Africa on Mogopa Removals," *The Star* (Johannesburg), December 1, 1983.

15. "'The Land Is Yours,' Declares Minister," *The Star* (Johannesburg), August 15, 1984.

16. "Land Reform at a Glance," *Mail and Guardian,* November 22–28, 1996.

17. Merle Lipton, "The Politics of Rural Reform in South Africa," in *Land, Labour and Livelihoods in Rural South Africa,* vol. 1, ed. Michael Lipton, Mike de Klerk, and Merle Lipton (Durban, 1996), 422.

18. "A Relationship of Interdependence," *Business Day,* August 25, 1997.

19. Louise Cook, "Hanekom Issues Orders to Accelerate Land Restitution Process," *Business Day,* August 26, 1998.

20. "Uphill Battle for Land Reform Could Take up to 20 Years," *The Star* (Johannesburg), September 19, 1996.

21. "Land Redistribution Flops Badly," *Mail and Guardian,* August 11, 1997.

22. "Land Reform at a Glance," *Mail and Guardian,* November 22–28, 1996.

## Conclusion: Unmaking Apartheid

1. "Whatever Happened to the Dream of Low Cost Housing?" *Mail and Guardian,* February 24, 1998.

2. Office of the Executive Deputy President, "Poverty and Inequality in South Africa," Summary Report (Pretoria, May 1998); Central Statistics Service, "Earning and Spending in South Africa: Selected Findings of the 1995 Income and Expenditure Survey" (Pretoria, 1997).

3. Office of the Executive Deputy President, "Poverty and Inequality in South Africa," Summary Report (Pretoria, May 1998).

4. Leonard Thompson, *A History of South Africa,* rev. ed. (New Haven, 1995), 273.

5. Trade Union Research Project, *A User's Guide to the South African Economy* (Durban, 1994), 79.

6. Heribert Adam, "Empowerment or Self-Enrichment?" *Mail and Guardian,* October 31, 1997.

7. Brian Ashley, "Challenging Apartheid Debt," *Debate* 1, no. 3 (Johannesburg, 1997), 165–71.

8. Cited in R. W. Johnson, "On the Way to First Base," *London Review of Books,* October 17, 1996.

9. Ibid.

10. World Bank, "First World Bank Loan to Post-Apartheid South Africa," News Release No. 97/1371, May 30, 1997.

11. Congress of South African Trade Unions, *The Report of the September Commission on the Future of the Unions,* August 1997.

12. Michael Blake, "Development Expert Decries South Africa's Macroeconomic Plan," in *Poverty Profile,* Institute for Democratic Alternatives in South Africa (Cape Town, September 1996), 2.

13. Gwen Ansell, "Governments Can Say No," *Mail and Guardian,* February 14–20, 1997.

14. *SouthScan,* November 7, 1997.

15. "TRC Update," Adv. Denzel Potgeiter, commissioner, Truth and Reconciliation Commission, August 7, 1998.

16. Suzanne Daley, "Apartheid Torturer Testifies, As Evil Shows Its Banal Face," *New York Times,* November 9, 1997.

17. Nelson R. Mandela, *Long Walk to Freedom* (London, 1994), 751.

# PERSPECTIVES ON SOUTHERN AFRICA

# INDEX

Adam, Heribert, 351

affirmative action: for blacks, 224–25, 249, 298, 299, 350; for whites, 141, 146, 150, 292

AFM. *See* Apostolic Faith Mission

Africa, 232; Angola, 92, 157, 161, 184, 343; "black" vs. "white," 12; Congo/Zaire, 72, 162; Gabon, 12; Lesotho, 236, 252; Mozambique, 36, 153, 252, 300, 343; Rhodesia/Zimbabwe, 1–2, 3, 8–9, 139–40, 252; Rwanda, 343, 355, 356; Senegal, 184; Tanganyika/Tanzania, 1; Zambia, 184, 186, 300. *See also* Namibia; South Africa

Africa Nations Cup, 15

*African Communist* (Erwin), 353

African National Congress (ANC): Ball and, 109; banned, 44, 152, 161; "Better Life for All" slogan, 351; black consciousness movement and, 37; Buso, 212, 221–22, 223, 227; campaign promises (1994), 195–96, 226, 230–32, 240–41, 278, 337, 345, 348–54; Cape vote (1994), 225; Chikane and, 48–49, 355–56; Coetzee defection to, 95, 114; COSATU and, 226; Dalling, 129; Evans, 125; and farm subsidies, 291; GEAR economic strategy, 226, 274–75, 355; Ginwala, 186; Hani, 173; vs. Inkatha, 53, 56, 108, 298; Joseph, 103; and Khayelitsha, 346–47; and land distribution, 16, 195–96, 300; Lapsley, 69, 360; legalized (1990), 12, 13, 52; London office, 160, 186; Luthuli, 134, 188; Mbambalala, 304; Mbeki, 184; MK/Umkhonto we Sizwe (armed wing), 32, 89–90, 184, 360; and

Modise vote (1994), 278; Momberg, 190; Natal, 53, 108; National Executive Committee (1997), 49; and Nietverdient Ten killing, 87; nonracialism principle, 15, 37, 187; NUMSA vs., 273–75; Nzimande, 184; police vs., 89–90, 108–10, 116; Ramaphosa, 35, 250; RDP, 73, 195–96, 234, 244, 334, 338, 350; and redistribution of resources, 16, 195–96, 226, 337, 353, 354–55; SACC and, 47; SANCO and, 226; Sisulu internal leader, 13, 55; Site Five, 231; Slovo, 15–16, 32–33, 184; students meeting with (1980s), 184; Total Strategy vs., 42, 108–10; and TRC, 197; tripartite alliance (1994 election), 223, 226–27, 353–54; underground members, 360; Ventersdorp councilors, 305; Verwoerd (Melanie) and, 18, 163–64, 175, 189, 191–96, 199; Verwoerd (W., Jr.) and, 18, 134, 163–64, 165, 167, 173–74, 180, 183–93, 199, 205; Verwoerd (W., Sr.) vs., 150, 163–64, 165, 167; Vilakazi, 9; World Trade Center meeting (1993), 297; Youth League, 109. *See also* Mandela, Nelson R.

Africans, 17n. *See also* blacks

Afrikaans: Bantu education and, 84; Boers and "Cape coloreds" sharing, 224; Modise learning, 253; Nanette Niemand's, 293; receding status of, 288

Afrikaner Broederbond, 150–51, 165, 180

Afrikaner Resistance Movement (AWB), 173, 288, 295–98, 305

Afrikaners/Boers, 18, 137–39, 288, 299; AFM led by, 38; Boer Republics, 138; Boers' "people's army," 138–39; Boer

| | |
|---|---|
| DESIGNER | Nola Burger |
| COMPOSITOR | Integrated Composition Systems |
| TEXT | 11/13.75 Adobe Garamond |
| DISPLAY | Franklin Gothic ITC Book and Demi |
| PRINTER AND BINDER | Data Reproductions |